Flaubert and Madame Bovary

Francis Steegmuller

FLAUBERT

and

MADAME BOVARY

A DOUBLE PORTRAIT

Revised Edition
with new Author's Note

THE UNIVERSITY OF CHICAGO PRESS

The University of Chicago Press, Chicago 60637

© Copyright 1939, 1966, 1977 by Francis Steegmuller

All rights reserved. First published in 1939
Revised edition, 1950. Second edition with corrections, 1968
Phoenix edition 1977

81 80 79 78 77   9 8 7 6 5 4 3 2 1

ISBN: 0-226-77137-7

Contents

Author's Note

Since this book about Flaubert and his creation of *Madame Bovary* was first published in 1939, it has been reissued in a number of editions, into each of which I have incorporated new findings of Flaubert scholarship. In the present edition I have amended the Bibliography, indicating by asterisks a few recent works recommended to those whose interest in Flaubert incites them to read further.

I am responsible for the translation of passages from Flaubert's letters and travel notes, from *Souvenirs Littéraires* of Maxime DuCamp, and from all other works originally in French, quoted in my text. Passages from two or more letters have sometimes been combined, the French edition used being in most cases that published by Louis Conard (9 volumes, 1926-33). This has recently been in part superseded by the Pléiade edition of Flaubert's letters, edited by Jean Bruneau, mentioned in the Selected Bibliography. Also mentioned in the Bibliography is my translation of *Selected Letters of Gustave Flaubert* for which I used mainly the same Conard edition. I hope eventually to replace that book by one with a more lengthy selection translated largely from the Pléiade edition.

F.S.

Part One

Romanticism

The Temptation of Saint Anthony

$\mathcal{O}$NE morning in May 1845, a handsome, blond, English-looking young Frenchman was standing in the picture gallery of the Palazzo Balbi-Senarega at Genoa. Unlike most of the visitors to the gallery he was not examining the Titians, or the Rubenses, or even the famous frieze by Domenichino Zampieri. He was staring with fixed, unwavering gaze at a repulsive canvas by the elder Breughel, entitled *The Temptation of Saint Anthony*.

He was not a connoisseur, young Flaubert. Of the art of painting he knew nothing whatever. But for very definite reasons—all of them connected with quite another art—he was deeply impressed by this Breughel, far more deeply impressed than by any other picture he had ever seen. To his astonishment and delight it seemed almost to have been painted expressly for him. For at this particular moment he was in quest of a subject for a large and ambitious piece of writing that would test his powers and allow himself to see of what stuff he was made; and this picture, ignored by most visitors to the Palazzo Balbi-Senarega, suddenly offered him a subject which seemed to be suitable in every way and far more promising than the vaguely conceived "oriental tale" which up to now he had thought would be his next work.

Drama and history, both with a strongly romantic cast, were young Flaubert's favourite territories, and the subject of the temptation of Saint Anthony would allow him to indulge in a long, romantic orgy of more-than-historical drama. The subject was dramatic, especially as portrayed by Breughel: the saint's temptations were strong and varied and his struggle was great. Therefore, the dramatic form should be retained. Flaubert was confident that he could retain it, for in addition to several non-dramatic works he already had a dozen or more dramas to his credit, of varying lengths and on historical and philosophical subjects, all lying in the drawers of his desk at home. Furthermore, to be treated as it could and should be treated, the subject would require weeks of research into the lives of the fathers of the church, into the heresies and schisms, into the world of Alexandria, into the anatomy of mysticism. Nothing pleased Flaubert more than the prospect of burying himself in books and papers in the corner of a library, seeking in the colour of the past to forget the drabness of the present: at twenty-three he felt himself sadly out of key with his age, and constantly lamented that he had not been born into another and more interesting one. It was this prospect of losing himself in ancient books, of escaping into the glamour of the ancient world, that was suddenly held out to him in the gallery at Genoa; and in the painting before his eyes it was at this prospect, rather than at the colour or the line or the composition, that he kept staring with such rapture.

And there was still another reason for the startling appropriateness of the subject. Saint Anthony was a hermit, a mystic monk who lived alone in the Egyptian mountains above the Nile, his head full of dreams and visions; and young Flaubert, too, after an active childhood and adolescence, had lately been forced, for a strange, almost a supernatural reason, to lead a life of lonely inactivity. Despite his vigorous appearance, the state of his health had recently been bad, even alarming. For a year and a half, before setting out from Rouen on this Italian journey, he had been almost as complete a hermit as Saint Anthony, and on his return he expected to resume his solitude. Secluded from all, except from one of his two friends (the other was abroad), he had lived in Normandy beside the Seine much as the saint had lived in the Thebaid beside the Nile. Although he loved his parents and his sister, the spiritual companionship he derived from them was no more (now, at least, he suddenly enjoyed imagining) than that which Saint Anthony had derived from the occasional pilgrims who found their way to his cave. And the company of the one friend, a romantic young man named Alfred Le Poittevin, might be likened to Anthony's communion with God. For to Alfred he owed, or thought he

owed, his entire literary being; so that another reason for
the excellence of the subject of the temptation of Saint
Anthony was that it was certainly a subject of which
Alfred would approve.

Young Flaubert's retired life had done nothing to diminish the wildness of his imagination, which long before the
beginning of his strange illness had been fanned into a
blaze by the romantic winds sweeping over the western
world. In his life he was no dull bourgeois, in literature
he was no grubbing realist, Gustave Flaubert! Indeed he
could paint a word-picture of the old hermit which would
give the same seething, grotesque effect as the canvas by
Breughel! The fanatical, fantastic core of the story; whiffs
of the divine odour of antiquity; great slices of the burning exoticism of Egypt and of the frenzy of the early
church; the sensuality and bestiality of the temptations: it
was all perfect! He could do wonders with it! What a
success it could be on a stage! The succession of monsters,
the troops of women singing, swaying, and dancing before
the saint! And along with this a vivid, historical recon-
struction of the old hermit's state of mind and soul!

Into a notebook which he carried he jotted down a description of the canvas, and then he continued to stare at
it as fixedly as before.

As her brother stood motionless before the unattractive
picture, Caroline Hamard began to exchange uncomfortable glances with her husband. She did not want to disturb
Gustave; she knew he was happiest when he was in one of
his trances, one of his day-dreams which were so much
deeper and longer than those of other people; and yet
sometimes it was just these trances that turned into the
attacks, the fits, the sudden lapses into complete unconsciousness which were—she and everyone else supposed
—the curse of his existence, from which he awoke in
a state of weakness lasting for days and which prevented
him from leading the normal life of a young man of his
age. The attacks baffled all doctors, including his father
Dr. Flaubert. They resembled epilepsy, except that there
were no convulsions, no biting of the tongue: the boy's
unconsciousness was always immobile, death-like. He in-

variably knew, for a moment or two, what was about to happen. He always had time to hurry to a bed or a sofa or a chair, or to lie down on the floor. Even now he was still weak from an attack which had come upon him a few days before, in Nice. Fortunately, he had been in the privacy of his room in the Hôtel des Etrangers, and he seemed to be recovering his strength more quickly than usual. It was unlikely that he would have another fit so soon; during the past few months they had been coming less and less frequently.

But the longer Gustave stood in his trance before the Breughel, the more troubled Caroline became, the more eager that he should come back to reality—and back to the hotel. It was time for lunch. Madame Flaubert would cover them with reproaches were they to return later than they had promised. Finally, whispering to her husband to remain where he was, she walked over to her brother and laid her hand on his arm. He came to himself at once, and smiled at the pale girl as he would have smiled at no one else who interrupted him at any occupation; she smiled back, told him to come, and he followed her obediently.

At the hotel, they discovered that the severe eye pains from which Dr. Flaubert had been suffering ever since they had left Lyon were no better. Madame Flaubert (a tall, severe-looking woman with hollow cheeks and spectacles) was fretful and nervous, and lunch was eaten in the dreary silence that had all too frequently surrounded the party from the very beginning of this supposed pleasure-trip. The doctor's eye pains were but one of a series of difficulties which had combined, ever since the Flauberts and the Hamards had left Rouen, to make the trip an almost complete failure. Gustave's health was a continual worry to all, and besides that he was silent and moody, not the lively companion he could be; Caroline was not a strong girl and seldom felt well, particularly in trains and carriages; Madame Flaubert was a woman to invent causes for worry when none existed; there had been tactless letters from Achille, Gustave's older brother, complaining of the burden of work at the hospital, of the difficult cases which were awaiting Dr. Flaubert's return. And Caroline's

husband, Emile Hamard, was at the moment a far from
gay young man. This Italian journey was—or had started
out to be—the Hamards' honeymoon, and although Emile
was not over-exigent by nature, he would most distinctly
have preferred to be alone with his wife. But parents-in-
law who will invite themselves to participate in a honeymoon and will propose bringing along their son are difficult people to overrule. And since Caroline was more accustomed to being a daughter than a wife, and since
Gustave was quite correct in thinking Hamard mediocrity
incarnate, a person without will or character, Dr. and
Madame Flaubert had had their way.

Caroline's marriage had been a blow to Gustave. They
adored each other, the brother and sister; each had been
the other's close and dear friend until less than a year
before. But the day Caroline had told Gustave of her
engagement to the stupidest of his contemporaries at
school, a boy whom he knew to be not only empty-headed
but also debauched, almost a dipsomaniac, whom he had always found particularly contemptible when he had thought
of him at all, he had been so shocked that his only reply
had been a gasp, an "Ah . . . !" This had wounded Caroline to the quick, kept her from ever mentioning Emile to
her brother from that day on, and greatly changed their
relationship. Gustave never mentioned Hamard either,
and during the engagement, at the time of the marriage
and after it he treated his brother-in-law as though he
were the slightest of acquaintances, someone who was far
from being any connexion of his or of Caroline's either.
Dr. and Madame Flaubert also had a low opinion of their
son-in-law; Gustave had been as blundering as they in
coming along on the trip at all (the lure of Italy at any
price had been too strong for him); and so, among the
palaces and the pictures, Hamard was smarting under the
silent but unmistakable contempt of his wife's family,
which he was too weak to combat. Poor Caroline had
expected that the strain would be lessened, that here in
Genoa she and Emile would take a boat for Naples, leaving the rest of the family to continue south by land. But
she had been recently feeling strange, even less well than
usual; Madame Flaubert, tearfully suspecting the cause, had

begged Hamard not to take her only daughter from her at this moment; Caroline had felt too ill to insist, and angrily Hamard had given in. Now, half the trip cancelled (to Gustave's secret relief: he felt he could not have borne to have his first sight of Rome and Naples spoiled by his unpoetic company), the entire party was about to turn homeward. It was as gloomy a tour as one could imagine.

The next morning they set out in a diligence for Turin, which Gustave found a regular and stupid place, and then they continued to Milan, where there was much to see and where Dr. Flaubert's eyes improved. But the weeks of sight-seeing in the company of his family were beginning to wear on Gustave's nerves, and the delay between his conception of *The Temptation of Saint Anthony* and the moment when he would be able to embark upon it was beginning to make the whole project seem unreal and improbable. He would have liked to set to work at once, at the very moment of his inspiration; now it was becoming difficult to imagine setting to work at all. And at Milan— as was usual when he had something to say and no one to say it to—young Flaubert wrote a letter:

"By everything you hold most sacred, dear Alfred, never travel with anyone, with anyone at all! I wanted to see Aigues-Mortes and I have not seen it, nor Sainte-Baume, nor the grotto where Mary Magdalen wept, nor the battle-field of Marius, etc. I have seen none of those places because I have not been alone. At Nice I didn't even get to the cemetery where our old friend des Hogues is rotting away, as I had intended to. No; 'That would look queer,' I was told.

"And now I have once again left my beloved Mediterranean. I bade it farewell with a strange sinking of the heart. The morning we were to leave Genoa I left the hotel early, at six o'clock, as though to take a stroll, but instead I hired a boat and was rowed out as far as the entrance of the harbour, where I took a last look at the blue waters I so love. The sea was running high; I let myself be rocked with the boat, thinking of you, Alfred, and missing you. And then, when I began to feel that any minute I should begin to be seasick, I went back to shore and we set out. I was so depressed for the next three days that more than once I literally thought I should die. No matter how great an effort I made, I could not utter a word. I begin to disbelieve that people die of grief, since I am alive.

"The love of antiquity is in my very entrails. I am moved to the depths of my being when I think of the Roman keels that once cut the changeless, eternally undulant waves of this ever-young Mediterranean. The ocean is perhaps more beautiful, but here the absence of the tides which divide time into regular periods seems to make you forget that the past is far distant and that centuries separate you from Cleopatra. Ah! When shall you and I stretch out on the sands of Alexandria, or sleep in the shade of the plane-trees of the Hellespont?

"I long to see what you have written since I left. In four or five weeks we shall read it over together, alone, by ourselves and sufficient unto ourselves, far from the world and from the bourgeois, secluded as bears in winter. I still think about my oriental tale, and a few days ago I got an idea for a play on an episode of the Corsican war which I read about in a history of Genoa. I have seen a picture by Breughel, *The Temptation of Saint Anthony*, which made me think of arranging the subject for the theatre, but I begin to suspect that that would need a different sort of person from me. Nevertheless, I would certainly give the entire collection of the *Moniteur*—if I had it— and a hundred thousand francs besides, for that Breughel, which most people undoubtedly think bad. . . ."

At the Villa Sommariva on Lake Como, where the Flauberts and the Hamards went after Milan, Gustave lingered behind the others and printed a surreptitious kiss in the armpit of Canova's Psyche; thence they continued over the Simplon to Vevey, Lausanne, and Geneva. Switzerland, full of memories of Byron and Rousseau, enraptured Gustave. He visited the Castle of Chillon, the site of Madame de Warens's house at Clarens, and Voltaire's château at Ferney. "You tell me," he wrote to Alfred, "that you are more and more in love with nature. My own passion for it is becoming uncontrollable. At times I look on animals and trees with a tenderness that amounts to a feeling of affinity; I derive almost voluptuous sensations from the mere act of seeing." This was the only portion of the tour which he thoroughly enjoyed, and he enjoyed it too intensely: the entire party had to wait a few days until he recovered from the fatigue of a new attack. Then, on the way across France, he visited the birthplace of Victor Hugo at Besancon, where he experienced additional emotions.

On the fifteenth of June they were in Paris. The adored Alfred was there to greet them, but even his company and his approval of the subject of the temptation of Saint Anthony did not entirely dissipate the feeling of despair that settled on Gustave when he learned definitely that his sister was pregnant. Caroline, pregnant by Hamard! And Hamard's sudden defiant announcement that he and Caroline would remain in Paris, instead of settling in Rouen as they had planned—or as had been planned for them—sent Madame Flaubert into floods of tears. At the station the parting was painful to all, and Gustave was glad when the train finally deposited them in Rouen and all was over.

The trip had been the opposite of pleasant, but as a trial of his son's present state of health Dr. Flaubert considered it encouraging. In the seven or eight weeks they had been away the boy had had only the two attacks, in Nice and in Switzerland. This was far less frequent than in the past, and since the regime of quiet living appeared to be responsible for the improvement it was decided to continue it for a time.

With the docility to which his family was accustomed, Gustave entered again into his retreat. A few days after their return from Italy the three Flauberts moved out of Rouen to their country house on the banks of the Seine, and there the quiet life began once more. Without Caroline the house was silent; there were few callers. Even Alfred Le Poittevin, after paying one or two visits, left for the seashore with his parents, to be gone until fall, and as July set in Gustave took to his books. He resumed his study of Greek, reading Herodotus mornings under a huge tulip-tree on the terrace; he read Shakespeare, he studied the style of Voltaire, he discovered Stendhal. He did almost everything, in short, except what he had burned, in Genoa, with desire to do: he did absolutely nothing about *The Temptation of Saint Anthony*. That was because his health was too good and he felt himself in danger of being forced back into a life which he had already once led and hated.

2.

He had had his first attack of all on a cold January night, a year and a half before. It was during the New Year holidays of the law school of the University of Paris, and the precise spot was a cabriolet in which he and Achille were returning to Rouen from a hasty trip to Deauville, where Dr. Flaubert was planning to build a summer sea-side cottage. There was little sympathy between these two brothers. They were nine years apart in age and much further in tastes; it was only on family matters, such as the present excursion, that they ever had cause to act in unison; and, sitting side by side in the carriage which was bearing them along the black and silent country road, they were exchanging scarcely a word. Gustave held the reins, and it was as they were approaching the lights of an isolated farmhouse that he first became conscious of a distant sound which was beginning to add itself to the pounding of the hoofs of his own horse. It was, he quickly recognized, another horse and a heavy country cart, as yet invisible but coming toward them through the darkness. The sound grew louder and louder, and finally the light of the cart became visible from around a bend. The lights of the farmhouse, too, were drawing nearer, and finally, at a given moment, the lights of the cart, of the Flauberts' carriage, and of the farmhouse before which they were passing were all glowing together in the night. The dark road was momentarily illuminated, and it was in the midst of this glow that Gustave suddenly felt within himself a weird sensation which seemed to grow out of the bright-ness of the road itself, but which, instantly going a thou-

sand degrees beyond that, became something else altogether, something fantastic, incredible.

Golden lights, blazing with indescribable intensity, began
to flash before his left eye, and his whole brain seemed
simultaneously to be bursting with a million multicoloured
visions and scenes, some of which he recognized as former
dreams; he felt his life slipping away; in the midst of the
noise of the horses, the carriage, and the cart he uttered
a cry of amazement and fright; Achille quickly demanded
what was wrong; but already the mystic golden lights
were flashing before Gustave's right eye as well, he was
blinded outwardly, while inwardly seeing old dreams and
new visions in the light of a golden incandescence; and
although he did not know it, he had let the reins slip from
his slackened hands and had slumped, unconscious, to the
floor of the carriage.

Shouting out to the other driver to stop, Achille seized
the reins and pulled up the horse; the two men quickly
carried the youth into the house beside the road, where
Achille bled him profusely. His breathing was so imperceptible that for a time he seemed to have died, but
gradually it improved, and he was as though in a deep
sleep. He lay there for several hours, then woke sweating
and extremely weak; and in response to his brother's
questions he asserted that he had been conscious all the
time. Not of the place or the circumstances—he admitted
he had no remembrance of falling in his swoon, or of being
carried to the house—but he seemed eager to insist that
although unable to move or speak he had been in the constant, conscious presence of a thousand images, that there
had been no moment of blankness. But when Achille
asked him to tell just what these images had been, he could
reply only "Golden lights" and "Dreams," and sank back
into a trembling weakness and evident depression. Wrap-
ping him warmly, Achille carried him back to the carriage,
then drove on to Rouen with all speed.

There, amidst general agitation, Gustave was put to bed;
and there, despite repeated bleedings, he suffered, during
the next few days, several more attacks, identical with the
first except that now the glowing lights on the road and
the sounds of the carriage and the cart were included in

the vision itself. They began it. First the glow, the sounds; then terror, caused by the feeling of the ebbing away of his personality and the approach of annihilation; then the million thoughts, images, fantastic combinations of every kind crowding at once into his brain like blazing rockets in a flood of fireworks. He himself later described his visions as "seminal losses from the pictorial faculty of the imagination," or as combinations of "Saint Theresa, Hoffmann, and Edgar Poe." He never knew at just what point he lost consciousness of outward things, but he always knew that the attack was coming: the golden lights and the road-sounds told him so. Never, on awakening, could he describe with any definiteness what he had seen; he never had any idea of how much time had elapsed between the first warning and his awakening; and every attack was followed by the same severe reaction: intense depression, long-continued weakness, and trembling.

Madame Flaubert was constantly in tears; Dr. Flaubert was unhappy, baffled, nervous. One day, when Gustave lay unconscious and the blood did not come quickly in the bleeding, he poured what proved to be boiling water over his son's hand, burning it terribly. He begged him to try to recall something that might be identified as a cause, or at least as an anterior warning, of this series of attacks; but all Gustave could remember was that several weeks before, in Paris, he had awakened one morning invaded with the same depression and weakness which he felt these days, and with the impression that the night had been full of particularly vivid dreams, none of which he could remember. Perhaps he had suffered an attack that night in his sleep. The doctors whom Dr. Flaubert summoned to his aid—his colleagues in the Rouen hospital and from other cities—were as baffled as he. Epilepsy was the only remotely possible diagnosis, despite the atypical features which they recognized. It was, they admitted, quite possibly not epilepsy at all; but if it was not that, they did not know what it was. Partly because of their doubt, partly because of the dread that would be inspired and the gossip that would be caused by the word "epilepsy," they pronounced, vaguely and cautiously, that young Flaubert suffered from an "excess of plethora, too much physical energy." They forbade him wine, coffee, red meat, and tobacco, and ordered him to lead a perfectly quiet life and to abandon, at least for the time being, his law studies in Paris.

After two or three weeks the attacks appeared to have stopped, and Gustave insisted on going to Paris himself, his burned hand in a sling, to arrange his affairs—sell his furniture, give up his room, withdraw from his courses. But no sooner had he arrived than the attacks began again; leaving things undone, people unvisited, he hastened back to Rouen, and before the end of January he was installed, for how long no one could foretell, in the room he had occupiéd as a child. When he could, he read, or wrote letters to the people he had not been able to see in Paris, or talked with Alfred Le Poittevin; when he could not, he lay quietly in bed. "I seldom leave my room," he wrote to one young man. "I see no one except Alfred, and live alone, like a bear. My health is better on the whole, but in these damnable nervous diseases recovery is so slow as to be almost imperceptible." Recovery *was* slow. For several months he did not dare leave the house, and finally, in the early spring, when he did attempt a walk in the fields outside the city, he saw his lights and heard his sounds, and after lying prostrate in the grass until he awoke had to be assisted home. He did not try it again.

The idea of the cottage at Deauville was abandoned, and Dr. Flaubert bought, instead, a house on the Seine at Croisset, a village just beyond Rouen, where during the summer months he could be with his son. It was an old, graciously long and low white house, formerly the country house of the Benedictine monks of Rouen, and in it the Abbé Prévost was supposed to have written *Manon Lescaut.* In June, though the house was still incompletely remodelled, the family moved into it, and there they spent the summer amid carpenters and painters. The river flowed past, but it was of little benefit to Gustave. He was forbidden to swim, and even the pleasure of boating was spoiled for him by his father's order that an attendant be with him at all times on the water. During the entire summer he seldom left the shade of the tulip-tree on the terrace. Everyone marvelled at the docility with which this large and vigorous young man accepted the sad change in his existence. Except to lament that he missed his swimming and boating, he never complained; that seemed extraordinary, almost perverse, for his entire career was threatened.

But "extraordinary" and "perverse" were two words whose application to himself Gustave Flaubert would at any time have welcomed with delight, and their particular appropriateness at the present moment he would have been the first to admit—at least to himself. He was better off than he had been for some time, and he knew it. His illness was a godsend.

He was born on the twelfth of December 1821, in a wing of the Rouen municipal hospital, of which his father was head. The windows of the Flauberts' apartment looked out into one of the hospital courtyards, where in summer patients sat or strolled, wrapped in their bandages and wearing their long white gowns. Almost daily the court was crossed by porters, carrying paupers' corpses into the dissecting room or the bodies of dead patients out of the hospital. Directly across the court was the dissecting room itself, from which town dogs were constantly rushing out, bits of human debris hanging from their jaws. As they played in this grisly garden, Gustave and Caroline often did what was not encouraged but also not forbidden: climbing up the trellises against the wall, they peered in through the windows and watched their father and his assistants and students peeling and dissecting cadavers. The bodies, covered with flies, lay on their marble slabs; on the trunks and limbs of what had once been human beings the students carelessly rested their burning cigars; occasionally Dr. Flaubert would look up, frown, wave his children away. But usually he was too busy, too absorbed: medicine was his entire life, and he had little time for Gustave and Caroline. Achille, on the other hand, was with him constantly; he was to be his successor. Gustave adored this eminent, busy father, and sometimes the doctor delighted him by allowing him to come along on carriage drives into the country, where he had to diagnose or operate on some sick peasant or fisherman. As the doctor worked, the boy sat on the doorstep or beside the fire, drinking milk or cider; then they would return home, the doctor's fee in herrings or vegetables lying on the floor of the carriage. But generally Gustave saw his father only at meals; night and day he spent in the hospital, and even on Sunday afternoons, after a few restless minutes in the family circle, he would get up, say he was going "for a walk," and disappear into the wards or the dissecting room. Gustave was left in the charge of others—of his mother, who was also nervous and preoccupied; of the country girls in the kitchen, who told him the tales of their villages; of an old man across the street, an amiable monomaniac who whenever a small child came in sight began to read aloud from *Don Quixote;* and of Uncle Parain from Nogent, a gay, feather-brained little goldsmith who had married a sister of Dr. Flaubert and who, from some strange feeling of sympathy, seemed to prefer his youngest nephew to his own children and was always paying visits to Rouen, taking Gustave on delightful excursions: to the street of the prostitutes, where the goldsmith loved to linger; to the insane asylum, where a dozen wild-haired, half-naked madwomen, chained to their cells, screamed and tore at their own bleeding faces with their filthy nails, as the child of six stared, fascinated. Once, coming home, they passed a guillotine which had just been used; the pavement around it was bright with fresh blood. About this time Gustave began to be afraid of the dark.

Before he knew how to read, he was often content to sit alone for hours in an empty room, finger in mouth, brooding on nothing in particular. He was not thought very bright, and it took him a long time to master the alphabet, but once he had done so he read incessantly; with a book in his hands, he was intensely, completely absorbed, absently biting his tongue till it bled or twisting a lock of hair till it hurt; he wandered, reading, about the house, bruising himself against the furniture, falling down, cutting himself against the glass fronts of the bookcase. After his first simple books he was given Corneille— every young Rouennais is made to read the works of the most famous Rouennais of all—and he was enchanted by the dramatic form, reading speeches aloud to himself for hours at a time. Before long he was sent out to a class of boys of his own age, and in a year or two began to bring them home afternoons and give theatrical performances on his father's unused billiard table. The young company presented the plays it could lay its hands on, buying or borrowing the texts, sometimes sending to Paris for the successes of the day. They also wrote plays of their own, and Gustave was the most prolific of the authors: his *Last Hours of Marguerite of Burgundy*, his *Two Hands on One Crown*, and his *Secret of Philip the Wise* delighted his friends because of the murders and corpses with which they abounded; the greater the number of violent deaths in a play, the greater its popularity, and frequently the stage was strewn with skulls, bones, and entire skeletons borrowed from the hospital stock.

And for the further amusement of himself and his friends Gustave wrote and read aloud stories: "Matteo Falcone, or, Two Coffins for One Outlaw," "The Plague in Florence," "The Iron Hand," "A Dream of Hell"; and these too were full of corpses, graves, moonlit cemeteries. Through incessant practice on the billiard table and before his mirror he became such a vivid mimic of grotesque, macabre, and blood-thirsty characters that his services were constantly in demand and he could terrorize Caroline at will. One of his imitations, that of an epileptic beggar whom he had seen at Trouville, where the Flauberts spent their summers, was so particularly hideous, so unbearably successful, that Dr. Flaubert put a stop to it. And Gustave had other pastimes: he used to scrape the verdigris from copper coins and eat it, having heard it was poisonous; he used to lean far, far out of windows, half hoping he might lean just too far, then swing dizzily back just in time. Everyone found him decidedly bizarre, and at eleven he was sent to live at school.

It was not only the bloody sights he was constantly seeing that turned young Flaubert into such melodramatic channels. Young people all over France were being swept into them by the currents of the age: blood, melancholy, and exoticism were the mode. Gustave was only five when in 1827 a company of English actors came to Paris and acted the plays of Shakespeare to audiences which rose to their feet and cheered: young Frenchmen were thunderstruck at the difference between this glorious English madman and the accustomed pomp of Racine and Corneille, and their ears had already been somewhat prepared for the new measures by their reading of Rousseau, Bernardin de Saint-Pierre, Chateaubriand, and translations of Byron. Two years later the young Alexandre Dumas, who had been particularly inflamed by the Shakespearians, wrote a thunderous play in prose, called *Henri III et Sa Cour,* which received a welcome as wild as that accorded its models; and in 1830 all the youth of France was thrilled by Victor Hugo's *Hernani,* a romantic play by a romantic poet. At the first performance of *Hernani,* a near-riot took place in the theatre: rival literary bands, the classicists and the romanticists, the latter led by Théophile Gautier in a scarlet waistcoat, tried to scream each other down; the romanticists, being composed largely of younger men, were easy winners; romanticism had arrived in France, and a flood of the new literature began to appear. Hugo and Dumas produced a steady stream of plays, novels, and poetry; Lamartine, Gautier, Vigny, Musset, George Sand, and hundreds of others reinforced them. But though romanticism was triumphant, classicism did not cease to protest; the plays of Racine and Corneille almost disappeared from the repertoire of the Comédie Française, but there were always conservatives to whistle and groan at plays by the moderns. At an ill-timed unveiling of a statue of Corneille in Rouen, it was judged wise to have both literary schools represented, and the academic classicist of the occasion, whose name is now forgotten, gradually wound himself into a trembling, crimson-faced denunciation of the new school, whose representative of the day, Alexandre Dumas, sat smiling imperturbably beside him on the platform.

The lives of thousands of young Frenchmen were ready for this literary bath of blood and sentiment in the 1830's. Their fathers and grandfathers had had their romanticism in the raw: the drama of the French Revolution, the glamour of the Napoleonic campaigns in Europe and in Africa had filled their lives with colour; now the young people, listening with envy to reminiscence and tradition, knew they were living in a world that had become flat and dull. For the unshackling of the Revolution and the pageantry and devotion of the Empire had been succeeded by two colourless Bourbon kings, who had learned nothing from the times and were so stupid as to insist on absolutism without providing any splendour to justify it; and when their line was expelled in a minor revolution in 1830 they were replaced by their even more colourless cousin, Louis Philippe of Orleans, a constitutional monarch whose virtue was that he was more bourgeois than the bourgeois and whom the newspapers caricatured unendingly, strolling with his family past the shops he owned, carrying an umbrella under his arm. In placing him on the throne the French bourgeoisie consolidated the gains it had begun to make forty years before, and his prime minister gave the watchword of the day when he urged his fellow-citizens to make as much money as they possibly could. The French bourgeois—the revolutionaries of 1789, the conquerors of Europe under Napoleon—became rich, smug, tenacious, and fearful of change; and their children and grandchildren, the young men of Flaubert's generation, were raised in an atmosphere of careful, commercial materialism, of complete lack of interest in literature and the arts, and of complete distrust of impulse and imagination.

Unable, therefore, to express the society in which it found itself, because that society was antipathetic to literature, the very contrary of anything imaginative, literature became a denunciation of it. Young writers gave vent to their discontent either by revelling in past and more glorious times, the Middle Ages and antiquity, or by seeking escape in distant scenes, the Orient, America, and Italy, or by expressing a melancholy wilder and more desperate than Hamlet's over the atmosphere of the age. Young poets, young dramatists, and young novelists formulated the feelings of their generation, and to the consternation of their elders the young public began to act like the characters in the plays, poems, and novels which it read. The novels of George Sand were particular sources of inspiration. Students and shop-clerks took to writing feverish letters like those which George Sand's characters

wrote to one another; wives, fermenting like George Sand
wives, demanded separations because their husbands were
uncomprehending and unpoetic, or would not give them
trips to Italy or Greece. The comic journals laughed at the
pale, languishing victims of "Adriaticism," "Florencitis,"
and "Venicitis." Husbands, on the other hand, brought
separation suits against wives who had taken lovers as a
result of reading George Sand; one such woman, in fact,
had left behind her a note of farewell which, although she
did not know it (her lover had written it), was a faithful
transcription of a passage in George Sand's *Jacques*. In
1835 Vigny's tragedy *Chatterton*, the final scene of which
shows the suicide of the young English poet, brought on a
wave of suicides throughout the country; one young man
killed himself in the theatre where the play was being
given, dying happily with Chatterton; another ended his
life before an open window, at sunset, his hand resting on
a copy of the play open at the last fatal page. Lithographs
of a painting by Decamps, *The Suicide,* sold by the hundred. One young romantic, desperate in the face of a brief
separation from his mistress, found it appropriate to rush
out into the woods howling like a demon, roll on the
ground, break snapped-off branches between his teeth, and
chew at the bark of trees. Literature seethed with contempt
for the bourgeois and the commonplace; one romantic
writer, asked when he would publish his complete works,
replied: "The instant the world is rid of the last of the
bourgeois." Of all French writers, only Balzac seemed able
to write of commonplace situations and keep his popularity.

It was in the midst of this turmoil that Flaubert was sent
to school. In the French way he was entered as a boarding
pupil in the local Rouen "college," which prepared for
the university. It was a grim building, only a few blocks
from the hospital on the road to the cemetery, and he was
free to come home Thursday afternoons and Sundays.
Among his classmates were the boys who had taken part
in the billiard-table dramas, and there were others, from
smaller Norman towns. Almost all of them were passionate
romantics. Flaubert was not the only one to carry a dagger
always on his person and to sleep with it under his pillow,

or to read Victor Hugo surreptitiously during study hour or in bed by the light of smuggled candles, or to steal out at night, fighting against the terror of the dark, and prowl around the courtyards of the college in search of thrills. Even the heights of romantic despair were occasionally achieved by the collegians: at least two of Flaubert's schoolfellows committed suicide, one blowing out his brains with a stolen pistol and the other hanging himself with his necktie.

For the college was a microcosm, a little world in which the collegiate romantics found things as intolerable as the older rebels outside. The boys kept speaking and dreaming of romantic, exotic mistresses; and they slept not even in rooms of their own, but in a huge bare dormitory, in small white beds separated from each other only by white curtains. They dreamed of oriental travel; and those who had no homes to visit on Thursdays and Sundays were conducted on long cold walks through dreary parts of the city, made to keep in line, forbidden to talk. Classes were begun and ended with drum-rolls; everything was done in routine. They read and dreamed of writing romantic literature of all kinds; and they had to study the old rules of rhetoric, listen to the dronings of old-school professors.

Only occasionally was there a professor who understood: the young history professor, for example, who complimented Flaubert on a medieval Norman chronicle he had written and a play he had composed after reading, with the rest of his class, a history of the dukes of Burgundy; the young rhetoric teacher who urged his students to borrow the manuscript of a novel on Marie de Médicis written by a collegian in one of the upper classes. In general they were hostile, sneering at what they called their students' "disease," jeering at Flaubert for being absent-minded in class, making any cheap joke to gain a laugh.

And among the students, too, Flaubert gradually began to realize that all were not as awakened, as literary, as he had at first supposed. He began to divide them into true and false romantics; for many of them, it was clear, were doing nothing but following the mode. Many a false romantic could be detected by his too easy and too inclusive contempt for the classics: to jeer at Montaigne and Rabelais, Corneille and Racine, might be fashionable, but it was certainly transparent. A true romantic was romantic because some deep need of his nature drove him to it, and one by one Flaubert eliminated those whose natures all too obviously had no deep needs at all, in whom romanticism was merely a form of youthful exuberance, and who would in a few years be as smugly bourgeois as the families from which they came. One by one they failed to pass his requirements, until finally only a handful of true romantics remained—himself and one or two others. In short, Flaubert found few friends. Somewhere in the world there must be people whom he could admire, but there were none, certainly—or almost none—in Rouen.

Rouen! Accursed, dreary city of rain and bourgeois! And he railed, with his few confidants, against what was until our own day the richest medieval city in France, a romantic paradise. The market-place where Joan of Arc was burned, the archbishops' palace where she was condemned and exonerated, the cathedral with its three spires and its glass, the dozen Gothic towers, the ancient twisting streets—all these were fine, but they could not save Rouen. For Rouen was home. It was the domesticity of his family; it was his family's bourgeois friends. Against these disadvantages, nothing could prevail; to be worth while, things had to be distant. The further away, the better, but even twenty-five miles away was far enough: there was a ruined medieval castle at that distance up the valley of the Seine that Flaubert adored. Compared with the ancient masses of Rouen it was nothing, and yet he visited the rather dull young schoolmate who lived near it whenever he could, lying hours dreaming in the ruins.

As the unworthiness of almost everyone he knew became increasingly apparent he began to spend more and more time by himself. He abandoned the billiard-table theatre, and went to the real theatre when he could. Thursday afternoons, instead of going home, he wandered alone about the city, wishing he were somewhere else. Time and again he entered the street of the prostitutes, talking with them, giving them the tiny tips he could, tortured by the longing to do more but held back by something. He sat in the cathedral, listening to the organ and wishing that he might believe. He climbed church towers to conquer his fear of heights, and walked tremblingly out along the balustrades around the roofs. Gradually he began to be considered as queer at school as he had been at home. And in his white cubicle his dreams became frenzied. Chained to the earth and powerless to help her, he watched his mother drown. Bands of horrible figures, daggers held in their chattering teeth, opened the white curtains around his bed with bloody fingers; their faces, half flayed, dripped with blood that left its stain on everything; their laughter had the sound of a death rattle; they were, in fact, corpses; he realized that he had first sensed their approach by their fetid odour; he awoke, screaming. He ate a meal of human flesh: the obsession that he had actually done so haunted him for days afterwards. His fancies took a thousand forms. He longed to be an emperor, a sultan, with absolute power over thousands of slaves; he longed to be "king of the Indies," or an ancient Greek. He longed to be a woman, for the sake of the beauty which would always be with him and which he could admire when he bathed, for the sake of the long hair which he could let fall to his heels.

Summers, at Trouville with his family (every summer was spent in the midst of countless relatives of both Dr. and Madame Flaubert), he strode along the cliffs or sat alone on the beach gazing at the sea. The summer before he was fifteen, he saw a plump, pretty young woman of thirty open her dress and give her white breast to her baby: instantly he was filled with feelings so tempestuous that he could scarcely believe he was still himself; and the rest of the summer was torture. He became acquainted with the woman and her husband, and saw them every day: it was agony. Finally, the day before they were to leave, he went walking over the sands with the woman's dog, and far beyond the town, hidden behind a dune, he dropped to his knees, whispered in the ears of the beast the words he longed to breathe to its mistress, kissed its nose where she had kissed it, and burst into tears. This experience made virginity no longer possible; he had to know, and to do. Back in Rouen, one night before the reopening of the college, he stole up into the attic of the hospital and into the bed of one of his mother's maids. It was quickly over: was that all there was to it? He could scarcely believe it, and feelings of disgust were the only result.

Then he came to know Alfred Le Poittevin.

They had always known each other and always seen each other—as two boys of the wrong ages in two intimate families know each other, see each other constantly, and remain strangers: their mothers had been schoolgirls together and their fathers (each the godfather of the other's sons) were close friends, associated in civic affairs. Alfred was five years older than Gustave, and though he had sometimes come with friends of his own age to watch the billiard-table plays, he had always been a superior, sophisticated being, who treated his younger friend with the distance the circumstances demanded. But now he had finished the college, and was remaining in Rouen for a year, studying at home for his entrance examinations to the law school; his friends had dispersed, and, in search of company, he discovered that young Flaubert was a person of possibilities.

They began to see each other every Thursday and Sunday in Gustave's room in the hospital (they avoided Alfred's house because Monsieur Le Poittevin, a business man, was, according to his son, the most boring man in the world, an indefatigable interrupter of young people's conversations), and before long Gustave was completely under the spell of his new friend. At last, a romantic as a romantic should be! Alfred's appearance—his long black hair, high, pale forehead, and unhealthy, melancholy air, which Gustave infinitely preferred to his own blond healthiness—was but the outward manifestation of his soul; and his ways of thinking and speaking filled Gustave with admiration. "I am a Greek of the late empire," he announced early in their acquaintance, and immediately and thereafter Flaubert felt in his friend all the superb decadence of Alexandria. "I would give all of Horace's odes for one chapter of Apuleius," he declared; and that, too, was as it should be. He had read even more widely than Gustave, and one of his favourite modern books was George Sand's *Jacques,* out of which he liked to quote sentences which he said applied directly to himself: "How can so active a mind subsist in so indolent a body?" and "Every day I feel more inert, more indifferent, more paralysed. I am no longer conscious even of the weather." For Alfred was languor personified: his eyelids drooped over his dreamy eyes, his shoulders were bent, and his feet dragged as he walked. And he displayed not only this physical languor, the result of his interestingly weak heart and generally poor health, but also a psychological languor that Gustave found intoxicating. He was not languid mentally—in his drawling, mocking voice he skimmed over a thousand subjects, opening a thousand doors in Gustave's brain; but his attitude toward the world was one of complete passivity, utter lack of resistance. There was nothing, for example, that he found more absurd and uncongenial than the study of law, and yet he was undertaking just that because it was his father's wish. What was the use of rebelling? All human occupations and speculations were equally vain. He had read the philosophers, and nothing gave him deeper satisfaction than describing to Gustave the farcical disagreement of the greatest thinkers of the ages concerning the nature of the universe. He excepted, from his general raillery, Kant and Hegel, who said that all the world is illusion; and particularly Spinoza, who declared that man is a helpless toy in the hands of God, that resignation to God's will is the greatest of all virtues, and that far from being, in any important matter, a cause (the role in which he fancies himself), man is but an effect, the result of the divine will. This had impressed him profoundly, and from it he had learned the futility of struggle. He had had, when younger, grandiose literary ambitions, but he had not hesitated to abandon them all in response to his father's wishes, and he now spent all his time with Justinian's Institutes, contributing only an occasional poem or essay to a Rouen newspaper under a nom de plume. Of the few pleasures in life, he declared, the greatest was the realization that the frantic struggles and rivalries of one's fellow-beings are in vain. Like Goethe—to whom he had written a poem—he aspired never to be astonished at anything; and Gustave, listening admiringly, felt that he had succeeded. Unconscious and unmindful of his friend's confusions, Gustave drank in his expositions of the comedy of religion and heresy, the farce of history. Alfred read aloud his own poems; those on the Orient were as nostalgic as Hugo's *Les Orientales,* and his medieval stanzas betrayed, as they should, more the influence of *Notre-Dame de Paris* than that of daily life among the monuments of Rouen. The two boys talked of the voyages they would make together to the Orient, of the mistresses they would have—oriental mistresses, preferably, though the finest, the most subtle accomplishment of all would be to have for one's mistress some oriental beauty of the past: Cleopatra, Semiramis, the Queen of Sheba. This, they admitted, would be possible (time being what it is) only in dreams. But are not dreams a superior reality, a triumphant victory over time and space? Certainly the dream of a night with Semiramis was preferable to the reality of a night with Madame Flaubert's kitchen-maid or the whoring Alfred had recently been doing as the result of a hopeless, passionate encounter which he, too, had had by the seaside. The grotesque side of prostitution, however, was not without its merits: the very contrast between love as it should be and love as it existed in the modern world was capable of affording considerable bitter but satisfying pleasure to anyone properly attuned. At times Alfred was confined to his house, even to his bed, with palpitations or spells of coughing; then their conversations took place there, subject to boring interruptions by Alfred's dull father. These, and the general spectacles of the Rouennais, were productive of much cynical comment on the bourgeois. What the boys found particularly ludicrous in this oppressive but comical class were the ready-made opinions, the clichés, with which the bourgeois judged his world: every young girl is pure, every young man is a rascal, every pauper is a thief, every countryside delicious. Laughing, or smiling bitterly, according to their mood, Gustave and Alfred wrote down lists of these *idées reçues* for their own enjoyment; they listened eagerly for new ones to drop from the lips of their families and their families' friends; and they even invented a character, the "Garçon," who was the exaggeration of everything bourgeois, who spoke in nothing but clichés, and who had a particularly brash, bourgeois laugh, very like that of Monsieur Le Poittevin. The boys greeted each other with this laugh whenever they met, and after considerable trial and revision they evolved an axiom which they found excellent and repeated on every possible occasion: "Hatred of the bourgeois is the beginning of virtue."

Alfred laughed at a sketch of the typical petty bourgeois office clerk which Flaubert had written a year before in imitation of the prosy, detailed Balzac, and he praised him for keeping his writing secret from his family, as he had been doing ever since abandoning the billiard-table theatre. It was impossible that any family should understand or approve of its son's writings, or make any comment on them that was not ridiculous and blundering; therefore, better hide all manuscripts from them, and not allow one's self the slightest hope that when the time came to choose —or rather, to be assigned—a profession, literature would receive any consideration at all. Gustave's writings were good, Alfred said. The plays and tales had the true romantic frenzy, and lacked only two of the requirements of distinction: richness of style (to acquire this he urged Gustave to reread Chateaubriand: *René* and *Atala* were real schools of style) and an ideological base which could be obtained only through the study of philosophy. Gustave could write drama and descriptions, but he lacked general ideas: he must learn to know himself and express his thoughts. Alfred advised him to study philosophy at once, rather than wait for the college courses which would not come for a year or two. His pupil unquestioningly obeyed, burying himself in metaphysics to the further detriment of his work in class, which had already suffered considerably as the result of romantic reading, writing, and the study of English with Caroline's governess, Miss Jane. Sitting beside Gustave's fire (there was a skull on the mantel-piece), master and pupil indulged in endless metaphysical conversations. Flaubert quickly grasped— quite accurately, he was sure—the various conceptions of the universe and the implications of the contradictions between them. And in the matters of daily life he learned from Alfred to watch for the cankers in roses and for starshine in puddles. By the end of the winter he was able to write down a long collection of the new thoughts inspired in him by his study, and he dedicated the manuscript to its solitary reader:

Agonies
Thoughts of a Sceptic

To my friend
ALFRED LE POITTEVIN
these poor pages are dedicated
by the author.

Strange like his thoughts, faulty like his soul,
they are the expression
of his heart and of his brain.

You have seen them unfold, my dear Alfred: here they are gathered together on a few sheets of paper. Though the wind scatter the pages, though memory forget them, this sorry gift will bring back to you our long hours together in the year that has gone by.

Doubtless your heart will swell at the remembrance of that bland perfume of youth which embalmed so many hopeless thoughts, and if you cannot read my words, then come instead and read every day in the heart which wrote them.

I am sending them to you like a sigh, like a gesture of beckoning toward a friend whom one hopes to see again.

Perhaps you will laugh, later when you are a settled and moral married man, as you cast your eyes over the thoughts of a poor child of sixteen who loved you above all else in the world and who even at that tender age allowed his soul to be tormented by such silly matters as these.

Gve. Flaubert.

Alfred was pleased by *Agonies,* the complete scepticism of which was such a satisfactory echo of his own, and he likewise approved of *La Danse des Morts,* a long philosophical dialogue on mortuary themes, in which Gustave combined his old obsessions and his new profundity. Then he proposed another subject. Why should Gustave not write an account of his passion for the lady at Trouville, seen in the philosophic light he could now cast upon it? Certainly by now he could expose the emotions of the past summer to the rays of reason, and the result should be an amusing novel. Poor Gustave set to work, but the result was not what he and Alfred had intended. Gustave had loved the woman on the shore with all the passion of an adolescent, and as he wrote he felt his love rise up in him again; despite a few Rabelaisian and cynical touches which he managed to insert here and there, his account proved to be far more lyrical than reasonable, and far less a novel than a confession, and he apologized for his shortcomings in the title and in a dedication which Alfred accepted as evidence of good faith.

Mémoires d'un Fou

To you, dear Alfred,
      these pages are dedicated and presented.
They contain a soul entire. Is it mine? Is it another's?
I had at first thought to write an intimate novel, in which scepticism would be pushed to the furthest limits of despair; but little by little, as I wrote, personal feelings began to pierce through the fable: the soul moved the pen, and broke it.
Therefore I prefer to leave my question unanswered, and I know you will make no conjectures.
However, you will perhaps think, in many places, that the expression is forced, and the picture wantonly darkened. Remember that it is a madman who has written these pages, and if the words seem often to be too strong for the sentiments they express, it means merely that the author has staggered under the weight of his own heart.
Adieu; think of me and for me.

As spring became early summer, the scene of their conversations was transferred to the river, where they boated and swam, and at the end of the college year, when the families separated for the summer, the boys visited each other in Le Havre and Trouville. In an effort to redeem himself, Gustave produced a second philosophical dialogue, *Smarh*—not unlike Byron's *Cain,* which he had recently been reading—ridiculing the impotence of humanity. At Le Havre, he shook his head at Alfred's invitations to accompany him on certain intimate errands: his two bitter experiences with love made him shrink from trying another, and Alfred did not insist. In the autumn, their parting was sorrowful. As Alfred left for Paris and the law school, Gustave pitied him for the arid months ahead, and he pitied himself even more—for in losing Alfred he was losing part of himself, to such an extent had he taken over his friend's ways of thinking.

The boys corresponded at length. Alfred expressed his contempt for everything and everybody he saw in Paris—except for Théophile Gautier, whom he had the joy of meeting. And Flaubert wrote his meagre news. His family, finally taking pity on him for his misery in the dormitory, was allowing him to live at home and attend classes as a day student; this permitted him "to see less of the stupidities of his fellow-beings," to have more time to himself. But without Alfred he was horribly lonely and bored. He enjoyed the company of only one person: his sister Caroline, and she spent much time in bed, suffering from a weak chest. Furthermore, a not entirely unexpected cloud had appeared on the horizon. Dr. Flaubert, basing himself on some of the very *idées reçues* that Gustave and Alfred had noted down—"i.e., that one must establish one's self, that one must have a position in the world, that one is bored when idle, that one must be useful, that man is born to work"—and encouraged by Monsieur Le Poittevin, who said it was the obvious thing, had announced that Gustave would follow his friend to the law school. He would not, of course, protest. And in the meantime he continued to write, and he sent his writings to Paris, where they were invariably praised.

Two years went by in this way—"a long boredom," Gustave called them, "several winters of yawning, of desiring to have done with living"; the friends saw each other only occasionally, during vacations. Toward the end of the second year Gustave's literary output was cut

down considerably, for he saw himself faced with failure
to graduate unless he applied himself to the curriculum.
He did apply himself and, in August 1840, finally finished
the detested college. Now he would live at home for a
year, as Alfred had done, preparing for his entrance examinations to the law school, and then he would move
to Paris. For one of the years in the law school he would,
at least, have the daily company of Alfred, and he chose to
look no further ahead than that.

In celebration of his graduation Gustave was offered a
trip to the Pyrenees and Corsica with a friend of Dr.
Flaubert, a doctor from Paris, and despite the unpromising
sound of the company and the separation from Alfred he
quickly accepted. He had a glimpse of Spain, bought a
stiletto and talked with former bandits in Corsica, swam
in the Mediterranean and wrote back ecstatic letters about
the colour and the sunshine: the little journey was a gay
success. The doctor, to Gustave's surprise, proved to be an
excellent companion, and in Marseille, saying that his company was insufficient for a young man of Gustave's age,
insisted on arranging a meeting between him and an
amiable, not too vulgar young lady who was separated
from her husband and with whom despite himself Gustave
spent several charming, instructive hours, sending back,
of course, a full description to Alfred.

But this was only a brief reprieve.

Back in Rouen, the Institutes of Roman law proved so
very much more dusty even than expected that he soon
sought refuge in writing a hundred-page book—he considered it almost a novel—about those hours in Marseille.
To get the full flavour of detail he made copies of the
letters he had written to Alfred, and the whole story was
recast and set in a confessional, lyrical framework not
unlike *Mémoires d'un Fou* and ended in a glorious vision
of the Orient. He called it *Novembre*, and even before
getting Alfred's opinion he knew it was by far the best
yet. It soon joined the other manuscripts in the drawer,
and the Institutes, reopened, were if possible more repulsive than before. Furthermore, it became evident, too
late, that he had lost a great deal of time and would need
an additional year of preparation, so that he and Alfred

would not be together in Paris at all. Bitterly he gave himself up to law books entirely, and after months of cramming he was admitted to the law school a few weeks after Alfred had left it. "I don't know what fatality pursues us," Alfred wrote him, "but it would seem as though something were trying to place obstacles between us. That, of course, is like trying to divide two oceans with a wisp of straw. Why can we never be in Paris at the same time? It is as though the city refused to shelter us together, but the day will come when we will force her to receive us. Let us hope so, at least." And Gustave replied: "Do you know that the bond between you and me is a completely logical thing? Sound rises, the stars follow their courses—you and I do likewise. We are ordained by Providence to think and feel in harmony."

The success of *Novembre* and the ease and exaltation with which he had written it made it more difficult than ever for Flaubert to open a law book, and, barely registered in the school, he began another tale, even longer than *Novembre* and more complex, which he provisionally entitled *L'Education Sentimentale*. It was concerned with the gradual maturing and estrangement of two young friends, one a true romantic, the other a false. But it advanced slowly, interrupted by the studying which did, after all, have to be done, and Gustave was made restless by the sight of the manuscript lying incomplete on his table. Life in Paris was, as expected, completely detestable. In his hideous furnished room and in the students' cheap restaurants he missed the comfort of his bourgeois home, and wrote long letters of complaint to Caroline. The lectures at the law school were intolerable, and the French law books so badly written that he feared for his style. "The Institutes are written in Latin," he wrote, "and the Civil Code in something even less resembling French." The famous student bohemianism of the Latin Quarter he found tawdry and filthy, a paradise only for false romantics. He had dozens of acquaintances but here too he made almost no friends, and he began to play considerably to the gallery. He became known for his cynicism on the subject of women. "The most beautiful woman is scarcely beautiful on a table in the dissecting room, her bowels draped over her face, one of her legs peeled to the bone, and a half-extinguished cigar lying on her feet," was one of his typical remarks, and when he went with a band to a brothel he always ostentatiously chose the ugliest of the girls and made love without even removing his cigar from his mouth. Occasionally he dined with the couple from Trouville—he still felt a kind of adoration for the rather vague heroine of *Mémoires d'un Fou*, whose husband was a music publisher in Paris—and he spent long periods neither writing nor studying, simply staring out of his window or smoking cigars. At other times he strolled aimlessly in the Luxembourg, or walked all over the city at night, or paid visits to the morgue.

It was the dreariest possible winter. He seldom left the students' quarter. Occasionally he visited the studio of a sculptor to whom Alfred had introduced him, but the artistic and literary people he met there made him more discontented than ever, and he did not go too often. During one visit he was electrified to find himself suddenly face to face with Victor Hugo; he stammered a few words, the great man replied kindly, the boy took heart, and the two of them had a long conversation. After that, Gustave's feeling was not only of boredom in the law school, but of a deep inner uneasiness and discomfort: Hugo would not have put up with such a life, nor any of Hugo's heroes, nor René, nor Werther, and these were the men Gustave admired. People seeing his love of literature and his hatred of the law sometimes asked him why he didn't write; he blushed, and kept his secret; but it lay less and less quietly within him. Was he perhaps doing wrong? Had Alfred perhaps done wrong? For Alfred's letters from Rouen were certainly sadder than the letters of a man who had done right should be. He wrote cynically about beginning to practise, sent an occasional desperate-sounding poem, and wrote: "The vulgarity of the life I am leading almost frightens me" and: "The flood of my boredom, which I had expected to be able to direct, is carrying me away. The race which I had expected to win is becoming a shipwreck. . . ." Surely these were indications that something was awry! But Gustave was trapped now, and there was nothing to do but work.

He began to work hard; but he worked absurdly. Thinking he was taking notes, he copied down page after page from the Institutes and the Civil Code; but as he copied, he thought of other things; the pile of paper mounted, and when he had finished he had acquired absolutely nothing except fatigue. The act of copying, the fatigue, made him think he was really studying; and at the end of the year, in August, he was considerably offended when, unlike dozens of students whom he knew to be dolts and debauchees, he failed in his examination. The year had been not only odious, but wasted.

The only thing to do was to study all summer and all fall, hoping to pass the make-up examinations in January at the close of the New Year holidays. There was a brief holiday with the family at the seashore, a visit to Alfred, who was spending the bar recess reading Kant and the æsthetics of Hegel, and then a return to the furnished room and the books. His effort to study was pathetic; the things he read meant nothing to him at all, and meanwhile he worried over the unfinished manuscript of *L'Education Sentimentale.*

Although Gustave did not yet know it, he had a nature which accommodated itself less easily than Alfred's to endless acceptance, resignation, and concealment. Unlike Alfred, he had a will—a will which was protesting increasingly against being denied. His dreams became more troubled than ever. At Christmas he went to Rouen for the holidays. Before they were over he got into the carriage and drove to Deauville with Achille; and on the way back to Rouen he suffered the attack which solved the problem of his law career.

That is why Gustave Flaubert was so "extraordinary," so "perverse," so docile under what seemed to all the curse of his mysterious attacks, so willing to let the tongues of the Rouen bourgeois wag, gossiping that he had collapsed as the result of too many women in Paris, or of masturbation in his solitudes. He was perhaps as much in the dark as anyone else concerning the cause of his illness, but he suffered from no illusions concerning its effects. To fall unconscious in a carriage or in a meadow, to have golden visions for which one paid by days of weakness, depression, and quivering nerves, even to be forbidden swimming and solitary boating, wine, coffee, red meat, and tobacco—all these, he was well aware, were minor inconveniences when compared with the obligation to study law. He even suspected that the atrocious depression following every attack might be due to the contrast between the gloriously fulfilled dreams which he saw in his visions and the inglorious, unfulfilled life to which he returned when he awoke. And though he knew better than to say as much to the people who were in charge of his life, he did not hesitate to express his satisfaction to Alfred and to the occasional former comrade who wrote him sympathetically from Paris. "One good thing has come of my illness," he wrote, soon after his first series of attacks, "and that is that I am allowed to spend my time as I please—no small item in life. I can think of nothing in the world I enjoy more than a nice room, well heated, with the right books and plenty of leisure."

Under the tulip-tree on the terrace, he was able, as summer progressed, to take up the unfinished manuscript of *L'Education Sentimentale* between his attacks, without having to shudder at the thought of law books lying near by. He was not happy—how could a sensitive person be *happy* in a bourgeois world?—but he was less harassed. When autumn came, and the Flauberts moved back to Rouen, he was able to converse with Alfred not only Thursdays and Sundays, as when he had been at college, but almost any night they chose, after Alfred's absurd duties were done for the day. During the winter, in the privacy of his room, he finished *L'Education Sentimentale*. It was less good than *Novembre*, Gustave knew; it had suffered from being interrupted; and he put it away in the drawer. Early in the spring came Caroline's inexplicable marriage. The trip to Italy was proposed, Gustave bought Vincent's *History of Genoa* and Mérimée's *Notes of a Journey in the South of France*, and in April the Flauberts set out.

3.

The danger after the return from Italy, of course, was that in the autumn his father would declare him well enough to go back to Paris and the law, and it was the presence of this menace that prevented him from making any beginning on the subject which he had found in Genóa. All of July he was restless, and in August he was very glad to receive a visit from the one sympathetic person he knew who was also practical and with whom he could discuss possible ways and means of escaping for ever from the threat of the Institutes and the Civil Code.

This young man, Maxime Du Camp, was Flaubert's second friend—the one good thing, Flaubert was fond of saying, that he had found in Paris.

Du Camp was a dapper, dark, and clever young Parisian, romantic as Flaubert and Le Poittevin and rich enough to be able to live, at least from time to time, in a way of which they could only enviously dream. They had met one afternoon in the apartment Max shared with a law student in the Latin Quarter, and although Gustave was at first suspicious of Max's dandyish appearance and Max amused by Gustave's provincial black clothes and white gloves, each quickly felt a sympathy in the other and for a time they were together as often as Gustave's hours of study and brooding solitude allowed. One night, in a burst of confidence, Gustave made Max the second repository of his literary secrets, and followed his confession by reading aloud the entire manuscript of *Novembre.* When he had finished at dawn, Max said solemnly: "A great writer has been born to us, and I am among the first to receive the news," and Gustave felt that his confidence had not been misplaced.

Max was also the son of a doctor, a fashionable surgeon. His father died when he was small, and at eleven, like Gustave, he was sent to "college" in Paris. Also like Gustave he hated his dormitory and his classes, and one evening during his thirteenth year—at the first night of Vigny's *Chatterton* at the Comédie Francaise, with which

his mother was rewarding him after an attack of the
measles—he had a profound emotional experience. At the
end of the performance, when the entire audience was
screaming its applause and the eyes of Madame Du Camp,
among others, were red with tears, she was alarmed to see
her young son quietly faint away at her side, unable,
evidently, to bear the degree of ecstasy which the play
had generated within him. When he regained consciousness he burst at once into uncontrollable sobs and began
to shake with convulsions, and at home, where he was
finally put to sleep with difficulty, his mother held his
hand all night to aid him through the nightmares with
which he was continually assailed. After this experience,
this complete conversion to romanticism, his detestation of
college knew no bounds. Instead of his texts, he lost himself in *The Last of the Mohicans* and other works of
Cooper; he was almost expelled when Hugo's *Feuilles
d'Automne* was found in his desk; and at seventeen, after
a series of stormy scenes with his professors, he was
actually expelled for absenting himself from the college
for an entire day, which he passed with friends in a book-
shop, reading Hugo's *Lucrèce Borgia* and *Le Roi S'Amuse*
and Dumas's *Antony*.

Placed by his mother as a day student in another college,
he devoted his increased leisure to medieval and oriental
subjects. He devoured Froissart's chronicles and the same
history of the dukes of Burgundy which was inflaming
Flaubert at almost the same moment in Rouen; he wrote a
long satirical poem on human morality and a medieval
novel called *Capeluche le Bourreau, ou, l'Homme Rouge;*
and instead of imitating Hugo's *Les Orientales* like Alfred
Le Poittevin, he was stimulated by these adored poems to
read translations of the oriental poets themselves. His
mother died as he finished college, and, living with his
grandmother and drawing a liberal allowance from the
estate which he would soon inherit, he spent his time
sitting in cafés in the company of other rich young
romantics—one group, whom he found particularly smart,
called themselves "The Cousins of Isis"—railing against
the machine and the bourgeoisie and lamenting the times
of chivalry and the Crusades. Soon he was spending more

than his allowance on clothes, horses, and women, and signing notes payable from his inheritance on his twenty-first birthday.

But suddenly one day, in a revelation almost as instantaneous as his conversion at the Comédie Française, the scales fell from his eyes and he saw the inanity of the life he was leading. Making a package of his most loved books —his Plutarch and Rabelais, Montaigne, Hugo, and Musset —he fled from Paris to a farm owned by his grandmother in the Sarthe, and there he stayed alone, with only an old peasant woman for cook and housekeeper, for six months, reading, meditating, riding in the forest, and, above all, plotting in detail the itinerary of a journey to Asia Minor. On his coming of age he returned to Paris to take over his estate, and then again temporarily quitting his grandmother's apartment in the fashionable Place de la Madeleine he moved into a garret in the Latin Quarter, where he studied "the institutions of Europe," thinking it wise to know them better than he did before exploring Asia. Philology interested him particularly, and as his intimacy with Flaubert progressed the two friends talked of undertaking together a vast philological dictionary of European words, to be called *Les Transmigrations du Latin.* But after Christmas Flaubert did not return to Paris and Max left for the Orient in April as his friend lay convalescent in Rouen.

During the months that followed, an occasional letter had come from Malta, from Smyrna, from Constantinople, from the Greek Islands, or from Algiers; Max was absent almost a year, and now the two boys were seeing each other for the first time since the separation which had come just when their friendship was ripening. Sitting on the terrace at Croisset, Gustave listened enviously as Max related his adventures in the East. He described the bazaars of Smyrna, told of how he had suffered a sunstroke while riding an Arab horse across the desert, painted a vivid picture of Constantinople and the Sultan, and gave an account of his friendship with a pasha, to whom he had presented his rifle in exchange for an ancient Circassian dagger. He was enviable indeed—the one enviable person whom Gustave knew. But he was not oblivious of everything except his own good fortune, and during his three weeks' visit in Normandy he encouraged Gustave to speak at length about the fear that was besetting him.

Among the bitterest charges that Gustave brought against the law school, among his most intense reasons for dreading to return, was the present manner of living, the present spiritual state, of Alfred Le Poittevin, and by way of vivid, frightening illustration, he read to Max from the letters which Alfred had been writing to him during the past few months:

"I have been upset these last few days. Yesterday I was drunk. . . .

"My nature is a singularly keen and sensitive one, and I think I could have done something with my life had I known how to be an artist. But what I have always lacked is any power of will. I sensed that before coming to know it definitely, and that is perhaps why I have never believed that such a thing as free will existed.

"I am weary of the present, of the past, of the future. There is something in me which has never been satisfied, I don't know what. A recollection of my past existences, perhaps? Or vague apperception of the future?"

"A strange thing: I have violent sensual appetites, but I cannot give a kiss that is not ironic. I don't know what you will think of a project which I have in mind. I plan to spend three days in Le Havre and Honfleur—places in which I was brought up and where I used to dream of love when I was very young—with a whore, whom I shall pick for the purpose. It will give me a great pleasure to take her to the places where, as a child, I *believed* in love. Then, after the three days, I will pay her off."

"I have succeeded in killing what was human in myself, and considering the state of mind I was in I think it was necessary that I do so. But perhaps I have solved the problem after the fashion of the tyrants in Tacitus: '*Solitudinem fecisse pacem appellant.*' "

"My morale is always just as low, just as vitiated: boredom and disgust seem to be incurable. If the supreme good is action, then I am certainly a long distance away from it: I must have been a statue in some former existence. I admire your serenity. Is it the result of your being less easily distracted than I, less beset by externals? Or is it because you are stronger?"

"I am leading a very disorderly life and seem lately to have lost a great deal of strength; I constantly feel that I am suffocating. Though I have been strong enough not to act against my will, the latter has never been strong enough to make me act as I should have. I ought to have travelled, been active—not content to sit stagnating by the fire. I live among people who say they love me, and who I know do love me. These people possess the means of saving me, but they would give it with such bad grace that I hesitate to ask. They will weep for me when I am dead—dead from suffocation—but they will not have done anything for me or even known that there was anything they could have done."

And, most lately, Alfred had written that he was determined, after all, to be an artist; that he had chosen a subject for a novel, but was finding it impossible to get started.

Certainly, to see a friend in such a state as this—a state into which he had entered with what he had thought to be open eyes and now recognized as mere weakness of will—and to see him doing his pitiful best to escape from it, like a man struggling in quicksand, made one feel that perhaps struggle and protest were not, after all, mere symptoms of lack of wisdom, and that Spinoza—or at least one's interpretation of Spinoza—was not a guide to go by. Gustave knew quite well that were he to return to Paris he would soon be in Alfred's present state: what steps could he take to prevent this? Only one thing had occurred to him: to approach his father boldly, frankly reveal to him the amount of writing he had done during the past five or six years, and demand—*demand*—that he be allowed to do nothing but write, since he could write so well.

At first hearing Max thought well of the plan, particularly since he had no suggestion of his own to offer in this crisis, and then after Gustave had read him *L'Education Sentimentale*, completed since his departure, he declared that it was obviously the proper procedure. He agreed with Gustave that while the *Education* hung together less well than *Novembre*, there were parts in it which surpassed anything in the earlier work, and he said he found it impossible to imagine any father's not being proud of a son for having written it. Gustave determined therefore to approach his father; and that is what he did, one Sunday after lunch—with a result that was all Alfred might have prophesied.

The doctor expressed his complete willingness to listen to some of his son's writings, and suggested that they retire to his office for the reading. They did so; each installed himself in an armchair, and as Gustave bravely set out on the first chapter of *L'Education Sentimentale* the doctor's eyes slowly began to close and before long he was dozing deeply. When he awoke, he neither apologized, nor asked to hear more, nor expressed an opinion on what he had heard, nor gave any indication of his plans for the autumn. He merely laughed, said: "If a pen had been *my* only tool, my family would have starved," and left the room; it was almost gratifying that a parent should act so perfectly in character.

Max, informed of the result, disappointed Gustave a little by doing no more than expressing his sympathy and urging him to have courage. Then he took his leave, promising to see Gustave again in the fall. Although he could not say so, Max was not over-worried. He was practical enough to feel fairly sure, from something he had seen at Croisset, that Gustave would not be sent back to Paris: during his visit he had seen Gustave in one of his attacks, and the sight of the sudden visitation, the deep unconsciousness, and the subsequent depression and lethargy of his formerly energetic friend, had so impressed him that it was impossible to imagine such a sufferer's indulging in any active life at all. But this he could scarcely tell Gustave, who bade him farewell sadly, and who felt less and less secure, as the summer drew to a close, and less and less able to do any consecutive work, even reading. The letters which Max now received were full of rancour against Dr. Flaubert, whom up to this time, because the question of writing had not been broached, Gustave had been able to admire for the eminent man of medicine that he was. Alfred, too, was the recipient of lamentations. "Every day resembles another here," Gustave wrote him, "except that there are some when I feel so empty and indolent that I am almost afraid for myself. I try to spend my time in the least boring ways possible. . . ."

In September there was a brief visit to the seashore, in October Croisset was closed; and once in Rouen Gustave gradually began to feel a little less harassed. He had Alfred's company, and Alfred was himself in better spirits; he had finally begun his novel—a metaphysical one, with the devil the leading character—and had hopes of being able to continue to write even while practising. And as the date of the opening of the university approached, Gustave's courage strengthened; it was inconceivable that his father should have delayed so long, had he any plans for this year.

Finally, the fatal date was silently and safely passed; with Alfred, Gustave exulted; and he was allowing himself to luxuriate in a feeling of at least a year's security when suddenly calamity entered the house.

One day in November Dr. Flaubert mentioned a pain in his thigh. It increased daily, and examination showed a deep and serious abscess. After treatments failed to relieve it, Achille operated; things went badly; infection, gangrene set in; for weeks the doctor suffered agony, and on the fifteenth of January he died.

Caroline, whose pregnancy had been normal and easy, came to Rouen during her father's illness; she was at his deathbed, and six days later gave birth to a daughter. At first all seemed to be well, but after several weeks her strength had not returned, and she continued to lie limply in bed. Then chills and a temperature began to appear; it was puerperal fever, and there could be but one outcome. Her long-drawn-out sufferings were even worse than her father's; for weeks she groaned and screamed in her pain, waking the baby, who she insisted be kept beside her bed. Gustave, who had gone to Paris after her delivery to attend to a mass of business following the death of his father, was not told of the gravity of her state, and was not called home until almost the end. He was aghast at what he found.

"Hamard has just left my room, where he has been

standing sobbing beside the fire," he wrote to Max, the day after his return. "My mother is a weeping statue. Caroline speaks to us, smiles, caresses us, says gentle and affectionate things to all of us, but she is losing her memory, and her ideas are confused. What a grace there is about the sick, what strange movements they make! The baby sucks and cries. Achille says nothing, not knowing what to say. What a house! What a hell! My own eyes are dry; it is strange how sorrows in fiction flood me with facile emotions, and how actual sorrows remain hard and bitter in my heart, crystallizing there as they come. Calamity is in this house, intending, it seems, to remain until it shall have glutted itself on us. Adieu! I had a premonition, yesterday, that when I next saw you I should not be gay."

Caroline died on the twentieth of March, two months after the birth of her baby. Gustave had a cast made of her hands and face and cut a lock of her hair; and he claimed as his own a striped shawl she had often worn and the table and desk on which she had often written to him.

"I watched beside her all night. I sat beside her bed and looked at her, lying there in her wedding dress and holding a white bouquet. I was reading Montaigne; my eyes kept turning from my book to the corpse, and I told myself that forms pass, that only the idea remains. Her husband and the priest were snoring. Occasionally I felt a thrill at some turn of phrase in the Montaigne, and reflected that writers, too, pass away. The night was freezing; the window was open, because of the odour; and from time to time I got up and looked at the stars, calm, gleaming, radiant, eternal. . . ."

The funeral was ghastly.

"Hamard insisted on coming with us to the cemetery, and knelt weeping beside the open grave. It had been dug too narrow, the coffin would not go in, and the gravediggers pushed and pulled, turning it in every direction, even using a pick and crowbars. Finally one of them stood on it and stamped—just over Caroline's head—to force it down. I was standing to one side, holding my hat in my hand; at the sight, I threw it down with a cry of rage. I'll tell you the rest when we're together, for I'd write it too badly. My eyes were dry as tombstones, but my anger was uncontrollable. I wanted to tell you this much, thinking it would give you pleasure. (You are sufficiently intelligent, and love me enough, to understand my use of the word pleasure. A bourgeois would laugh to see it used in this context.)"

Hamard, completely bewildered and helpless, left all arrangements concerning his daughter to his wife's family; Madame Flaubert was determined to devote herself to her as to her own child; and two days after the funeral Gustave and his mother moved out of the apartment in the hospital and installed themselves, with the child, in Croisset.

"We have been at Croisset since Sunday. What a journey it was, just my mother and the baby crying all the way. Without, the trees are still leafless, the wind is blowing, and the river is high and rough; within, the rooms are cold and bare. My mother is better than one would think she could be; she busies herself with her grandchild, putting her to bed in her room, rocking her, caring for the little thing as much as she can. She is trying to make herself into a mother again: will she succeed? The reaction has not yet set in, and I dread its coming. I am crushed, numb: grief and wretchedness are stifling me. When can I take up again my own poor life of tranquil art and long meditation?"

Such a life seemed far away, in Croisset! Suddenly he was the head of an unnatural household, an old woman and a tiny child were on his hands, the air was full of the most heart-rending grief and full of upheaval: writing was out of the question. Madame Flaubert soon lost her numbness; from one end of the day to the other she was in tears, and frequently she sat sobbing and groaning, the baby in her arms; she did not eat, and Gustave fully expected that she would die within a short time. Unable to write, he began to pretend, in his letters to Max, that the literary life was an absurdity; one slaved to produce, and then one quickly died. Better not to slave at all; better to spend one's brief life agreeably—preferably in travel, which was the most agreeable way possible. And if only—as he had so often longed before—one could travel backwards! That would be the best way to go.

"Certainly I lived in Rome in the time of Cæsar or Nero. Have you sometimes thought what it must have been like, the night of a triumph—the legions returning, the perfumes burning around the chariot of the conqueror, and the captive kings marching behind? And the circus! That is when we should have lived: then it was possible to breathe, and breathe a true poetic air, whole lungfuls of it, as on a mountain-top, until the heart pounded! Ah, some day I will get drunk on Sicily and Greece! In the meantime I have boils on my legs and keep to my bed."

"If my mother dies, my plans are made: I will sell everything and go live in Rome, Syracuse, Naples. Will you follow me? But may heaven grant me a little peace! A little peace, good God, a little quiet: nothing but that; I do not ask for happiness. . . ."

The tone of his letters to Max, during these days, was much like that of Alfred's letters of a year before, which had so distressed him; in his distress he appropriated the expression of his friend; whole phrases of Alfred's found their way into Gustave's letters. As to Alfred himself, however, he seemed somehow to have slipped away: he had been at the two funerals, but during the whole winter of grief he had been present less often than would have been natural. He had not at all wholeheartedly placed himself at Gustave's disposal, and now he almost never came out the short distance to Croisset, and did not write. In the midst of his struggles to begin a new life, Gustave wondered why. He felt abandoned; he began to head his letters to Max *solus ad solum.* Then suddenly, in June, the blow fell, the third and in many ways the hardest.

"Shall I tell you something that will make you cry: 'Oh!' followed by several exclamation points? It is the marriage —of whom? Of a young man whom you know—not me, I make haste to say!—of a young man named Le Poittevin, with a Mademoiselle de Maupassant. At this point you will give yourself over to astonishment, reverie, and other emotions. The holy nuptials will take place in a fortnight, I believe. The contract was signed last Tuesday. After the wedding the happy pair will travel in Italy, and next winter will live in Paris."

But it was impossible to keep the tone as light as that.

Alfred's marriage was more than fantastic; it was another
instance of his lack of will, for clearly he was marrying to
please his family—the Maupassants were prosperous bourgeois, good connexions—and this final surrender seemed
to Gustave a betrayal of all that their friendship had implied, all the principles they had shared.

"So here is still another person I love lost to me—and
doubly so, first because he marries and second because he
will be living elsewhere. How everything passes! How
everything passes! The leaves are budding on the trees, but
for us, where is the month of May that will renew the
bloom, the fine male savour of our youth? Are you, too,
invaded by such a mood at this news? It makes me feel
immeasurably aged, older than an obelisk. I have lived
enormously during my twenty-five years: probably when
I am sixty I shall think of myself as being very youthful—
that is one of life's bitter absurdities.

"My poor mother is always disconsolate—you cannot
conceive the extent of her affliction. If there is a God, you
must confess he is not always in a benevolent mood. Sometimes my courage weakens at carrying alone the burden
of her great despair, which nothing is able to relieve. Never
leaving the house, and seeing no one, I have thought it
sensible to furnish a study for myself, the kind I have
always wanted. I don't expect to leave it for a long time to
come, unless the wind should blow me elsewhere. . . ."

Alfred was married on the sixth of July.

But shortly before that, just when Gustave was most desperately lonely and unhappy, and when, despite his new
study, *The Temptation of Saint Anthony* or any other
work seemed a complete impossibility, everything changed
once more.

Dr. Flaubert's illness had prevented Max from paying
his autumn visit to Croisset. He had seen Gustave in Paris
in March, but after the death of Caroline, although he had
offered to come and be of any comfort he could, Gustave
had begged him to stay away. The house was too sad for
anyone to visit, and he himself was too sad to be able to
bear any demonstration of kindness and sympathy. All
spring Gustave wrote his unhappy letters and then, shortly

after Alfred's marriage, Max received a letter that did not
sound unhappy and which contained an invitation to spend
a fortnight at Croisset.

He found the house still deeply impregnated with the
tragedy of the past winter. All the flowering Norman
summer around it and the gleaming river under the terrace
could not make one overlook the expression on the white
face of its mistress. Dressed in black, Madame Flaubert
moved about the house like sorrow itself. Her voice was
flat when it was not anxiously shrill—for now almost
every event of the day alarmed her. Every headache or
exclamation of Gustave's, every whimper from the baby,
every sound louder than usual from the kitchen—all put
her in a panic. She was acutely, morbidly apprehensive.
Charming as the house was from the outside, set in its
frame of river and greenery, it was somewhat bleak and
bare within. Gustave had taken one of the best rooms for
his study—a square, good-sized chamber, with two windows on the Seine and three on the garden. He had installed his books in tall bookcases with twisted mahogany
columns; there was a green divan covered with a white
bearskin, and in the middle of the room a large round
writing table. He was proud of his room, and proud also
of the costume he had adopted. When he met Max at the
station in Rouen he was dressed like anybody else, but
after reaching Croisset he changed, and appeared in a
figured white dressing gown with a cord around the waist,
full trousers to match, and felt slippers. This garb, he
explained, allowed him greater comfort and freedom of
movement than conventional clothes, and he wore it constantly, for there were days on end when he did not leave
the property, and in the garden and on the terrace he could
wear what he chose. He seemed well—he had not had an
attack all spring; his manner was graver, more composed,
and with his mother he was tender and demonstrative. As
usual, he had things to say about the bourgeois. Achille
had been appointed his father's successor and was installed
with his wife and child in the apartment in the hospital;
and already, Gustave reported, the Achille Flauberts were
finding the completely retired life led by Gustave and his
mother exaggerated and bizarre, and from pure dislike of

the unusual were paying fewer visits than they might. Croisset and Rouen were becoming two separate factions, and Gustave's opinion of Rouen had not changed.

But none of this was what Gustave had chiefly to say; and when he finally said it, Max learned that he had been invited to Croisset not only to make a visit, but also to make the acquaintance of a remarkable young man.

His name, Gustave said, was Louis Bouilhet, and as Alfred had suddenly discovered Gustave after having known him thoughtlessly for years, in much the same way he himself had recently discovered Bouilhet. He had often seen him in the college, where he had been a scholarship pupil from an obscure village near Le Havre and had once won the first prize for rhetoric; but Louis had been so timid and retiring that Gustave had never paid him the slightest attention. Then later Gustave had seen him again among his father's medical students at the hospital. But medical students were not given much attention by Gustave and Alfred, and they could not know that this particular one carried constantly with him a little notebook in which he jotted down verses whenever they occurred to him—during lectures, in the operating and dissecting rooms, at night—and that he hated his studies, which he had undertaken only because his own father had been a country doctor and which he was continuing only because of the devotion that Dr. Flaubert habitually inspired in his students. But the coming of Achille had broken that spell. He had abandoned medicine at once, to the dismay of his mother, who kept writing him reproachful and disappointed letters from the country. With two other former collegians he had founded a tutoring school, where he now coached students for their university entrance examinations in Latin—he was, above all, a student of the classics. He was very poor, but of cheerful disposition; his literary taste was impeccable and his poetic ambitions were boundless. All week he was occupied with his pupils, but the past few week-ends he had been coming out to Croisset, arriving Saturday night and leaving Monday morning. He and Gustave were translating Aristophanes' *Lysistrata* and a comedy of Plautus. Max would certainly like him.

Max did. About dinner time he suddenly appeared in the garden, a good-looking young man who bore a considerable resemblance to Flaubert. When they were introduced, his manners were timid and provincial, but Max, always proud of not being put off by provincialism, was his most winning self; Bouilhet soon thawed—he was delightful! Beneath his timidity was not only charm, but self-confidence and a great knowledge of literature. After dinner the three young men had an excellent time in Gustave's new study over their cigars. (Max noted that Gustave had resumed smoking.) No Latin or Greek poet appeared to be unknown to Bouilhet; he recited from memory the verses of poets whom Gustave and Max had never read. Modern poetry he knew equally well, and the three of them chanted in unison from Hugo and Gautier long after Madame Flaubert had gone to bed. They argued concerning the merits of Lamartine, and decided finally that they were very few. Alfred de Musset, despite his excellent craftsmanship, Bouilhet pronounced too complaining and personal. Bouilhet's convictions were nothing if not firm; he might blush when he stated them, and his manner was modest, but he was immovable, and argued well. Evidently he was the perfect tonic for Gustave: within a few weeks he had drawn him out of the deepest, at least, of his melancholy, and Max, who had lately been trying his hand at some short stories in Paris, felt that his activities were slight indeed beside the bold projects of the young Normans. Gustave spoke as though he were on the point of embarking on something grandiose. He declared that he intended to make his debut with "a thunderclap," and Bouilhet too said he would like to defer all publication until he had prepared something solid and striking. Neither of them was more explicit, however; Flaubert seemed deliberately mysterious about his plans, Bouilhet genuinely uncertain.

At Gustave's request, Bouilhet quietly read some of his verses. Max was impressed; they were full of reminiscences of Hugo, but full of talent as well. Flaubert read others, standing in the middle of the study in his wide white wrapper, waving his arms as he declaimed. As the evening progressed, Bouilhet's timidity left him completely; he could be witty, ironic. He was revolted by the commonplace or the turgid, irritated by any literary work with a philosophical or utilitarian turn, convulsed by moralistic drama or patriotic poetry. Béranger! His poems about *la patrie!* Bouilhet made comical gestures and grimaces, declaring they were moods engendered in him by Béranger and his kind, and on the spur of the moment improvised a parody of patriotic poetry that made his friends weak with laughter.

Finally they went to bed. Max was as enchanted with Gustave's new friend as was Gustave himself. Alfred Le Poittevin (barely and bitterly mentioned these days) was not replaced—the new friendship seemed so far to be in a lighter key than the old—but at least the empty place he had left was no longer so gaping. And while *solus ad solum*, evidently, would no longer be written at the heads of letters, Max was not jealous, and he welcomed the young poet who had wrought such a transformation in Flaubert.

The next morning all three of them worked, with dictionaries, at the translations of the classical plays; in the afternoon, to the astonishment of all, Gustave proposed an outing. A carriage was got ready, and the young people rode through the brilliant green countryside. In the evening, the hilarity of the night before was repeated; the bourgeoisie and all unworthy poets were mocked; suddenly it was decided to mock in writing. Flaubert had been reading the tragedies of Voltaire: why not compose a burlesque eighteenth-century tragedy? After lively discussion, a subject was decided upon, one which Flaubert and Bouilhet felt particularly suited to their talents: *Jenner, or, the Discovery of Vaccine.* Work was begun that very night; the study resounded with laughter as they read each other lines which they thought particularly splendid.

Monday morning Bouilhet had to leave, but already the tragedy was going too well to make it possible for the others to wait until Saturday for his return. Every evening after his work was done he hurried out to Croisset, and they worked frantically, exciting each other to fresh efforts. Gradually the burlesque became broader and broader, coarser and coarser, until finally it evolved into a scabrous mass of obscenity; then, toward the end of the week, just as suddenly as they had conceived it, all three of them became bored with it, and it was put aside, never to be taken up again. The translation of the classical plays was resumed.

Throughout Max's visit Flaubert repeatedly referred, in the most vague and mysterious terms, to the great book which he had in his mind. He mentioned also another work which he planned for later: a tale about Saint Julian the Hospitaller, which he had conceived one day while staring at the Saint Julian window in the Rouen cathedral. When Max returned to Paris he felt that his friend would be resuming work very soon.

He was right. The person who was to give Flaubert the final impetus now entered the scene.

4.

James Pradier, the sculptor in whose studio Flaubert had talked with Victor Hugo that afternoon during the winter of law, was considered by many of his generation to be as great a genius as Michelangelo, and he was intensely admired as well for the violence and sensuality of his life and habits. Unlike Ingres, who treated his models with invariable courtesy and was laughed at for doing so, Pradier struck and kicked his when their poses or their bodies displeased him: that was the way an untrammelled artist should behave. He was successful, receiving frequent commissions for statues to decorate public places in Paris and in provincial and foreign cities. Crowds stood in admiration of his row of figures in front of the Chamber of Deputies; young men wrote love poems to his figures of Strasbourg (Madame Pradier) and Lille (one of his mistresses) in the Place de la Concorde; from Geneva, Flaubert himself wrote lyrically to Alfred about Pradier's statue of Rousseau on an island in the lake. Every morning, sweating, his sleeves rolled, his muscles bulging, cursing his models and uttering a stream of jokes and obscenities for the benefit of an ever-present gallery, Pradier chipped and pounded at his marble in his studio on the Quai Voltaire; and in the afternoon, when he had finished, the studio generally filled again; it was a perpetual salon. One of his most celebrated statues was entitled *Weeping Love Consoled by Voluptuousness,* and though his few hostile critics hinted that voluptuousness was exactly the quality his art did not possess, he himself declared voluptuousness and power to be the two indispensable possessions of any true artist. Pradier's studio was the one place where Flaubert had felt free to express his love of art during the year of law, and though he had gone there but seldom Pradier had claimed to sense in him vast hidden stores of the two necessary qualities, and had always jeered at him for choosing to be an obedient son rather than the creator he could be.

In the early summer of 1845, at the end of the Italian journey, Flaubert visited Pradier with Alfred, and this time he felt free to admit that he not only loved literature but was determined to create it. Pradier praised him for coming at last to his senses, and began to interrogate him concerning his past and his present and his state of health and mind. And when he learned that his young friend suffered mysterious nervous attacks, that he was frequently depressed and irritable, that he lived in the bosom of his family, that his only sexual experience had been with his mother's maid at eighteen, the young woman in Marseille, and an occasional whore in the Latin Quarter during the year in Paris, that for the past two years he had seen no women except his mother and sister, and that he intended to resume this unnatural existence and, if possible, write in it, the comments of the incredulous sculptor were scurrilous and scathing, and in the clearest of language he told Flaubert exactly what his next step should be and exactly what would be its results.

Pradier's opinion represented, of course, a common enough point of view. When a young man admits to so slight and intermittent an experience as Flaubert's, there is always someone to declare that a mistress, a prolonged, relaxing relationship, will solve everything, and Flaubert could now derive what comfort he might out of learning from one quarter that his troubles were caused by an excess of women and from another that they were the result of too few. He suspected, however, that the latter opinion might not be entirely without foundation—he knew that even his own father had had at least one mistress in his youth—and during the quiet summer that followed he gave the question more than a moment's thought.

"I have been thinking over Pradier's advice," he wrote to Alfred in July, "and it is good. But how can I follow it? And where would I be able to stop? If I went about the thing seriously, and enjoyed it in earnest, I would be humiliated! That, however, is the way it would have to be, and that is what I will not do. A normal love, regular, steady, permanent, would take me out of myself too much; it would disturb me; it would lead me into a life of action, into physical reality, into the common path; and that is just what has always been harmful to me every time that I have tried it. Furthermore, if that sort of thing were as vitally necessary as Pradier says, it would come of itself, without my having to seek it."

But as the tragic winter unrolled, this last statement began to seem less and less certainly true. Necessary as it might be, how could "that sort of thing" be expected to come of itself to a young man placed as Flaubert was placed? The thought that it might be necessary continued to occur to him, yet there seemed little to be done about it.

Shortly after Max's departure from Croisset, however, Flaubert left also to spend a few days in Paris, and almost exactly a year and a month after his last visit he again went to see Pradier in the studio on the Quai Voltaire. This time he was not merely paying a social call; he brought with him a commission. The death-mask of Caroline which he had had taken the winter before had long since hardened, and now, early one afternoon, Flaubert brought it to Pradier and asked him to make from it a marble bust. The commission was quickly accepted; out of respect for the occasion, Pradier's conversation was less gross than usual; they talked of Flaubert's work, so long delayed, but which should now begin any day; and though Pradier repeated his advice he admitted that conditions had not recently favoured the following of it.

Gradually, the habitués of the studio began to arrive; a crowd of artistic, theatrical, literary people was soon

laughing and chattering among the blocks of marble, the
Greek and Roman casts. It was the first gathering that
Flaubert had been in for some time, and he was quickly
exhilarated. Conquering the timidity which he felt as the
result of his long seclusion, he responded with all his anima-
tion and all his charm to Pradier's introductions; and when
he heard himself being presented to an extremely pretty
and beautifully dressed blonde with the words: "Here is
a young man who is going to make a name for himself in
literature; perhaps you can be of use to him," he was
unconscious of any double meaning in the phrase.

The immediate and complete amiability of this pretty
woman took Flaubert by surprise, and it was all the more
irresistible because of her delightful maturity. She was
clearly in her middle thirties, an age which had a voluptuous attraction for Flaubert at twenty-four, and he found
himself replying without restraint to her questions about
himself and avowing quite promptly the literary desires
and ambitions he had confided to less than half a dozen
people in his entire life. At the moment of presentation
he had not grasped her name; now, after they had talked
for a few minutes, he discovered that she was someone
whose name he knew very well, a celebrity: she was
Louise Colet, the poetess, the winner (at least twice) of
the Academy's poetry prize, the friend of Madame Récamier, and the mistress, even Flaubert knew, of the
philosopher, peer of France, and former minister of state
Victor Cousin, author of *Du Vrai, du Beau et du Bien.*
How doubly good of her, then, to be so attentive to an
unknown young man from the country! Despite her re-
nown and her sophistication she seemed, in fact, scarcely
less ardent and confiding than he. Deprecating her ac-
complishments so far (it did not occur to Flaubert to pretend that he had read any of her poems), she claimed to
have the loftiest possible literary standards: her aims were
high and her goals pure. Most of the literature of the day
she found mediocre, despicable. Victor Hugo was the
only living poet a person of the proper perceptions
could wholeheartedly admire; and when Flaubert eagerly
agreed, and said that he had spoken with him in this very
room, they decided that universal as Hugo's popularity

was, few people understood his true greatness. Thousands of charlatans imitated and claimed to adore him—people who wrote for money, or who wrote to put or to keep their names before the public. The world was full of literary vulgarians. Charmingly uncertain as she was concerning the possibility of ever achieving anything superb herself, Madame Colet was insistent on one point: Monsieur Flaubert understood, she hoped, that she had no use —no use whatever—for this kind of pretender? He assured her he did understand; he was enchanted to meet someone who shared his own contempt for the falsely romantic. Their conversation was quite lengthy, there amid the visitors and the marbles and the casts; then Madame Colet rose to leave. She had to go home, to her child. She had no full-time servant. She was poor. But would Monsieur Flaubert not give her the pleasure of coming to see her some day at her modest home, 21 Rue de la Fontaine-Saint-Georges? And since he was returning to Normandy so soon, would he not dispense with a formal invitation and simply stop in the next evening? He would be delighted to, he assured her, and he spoke the truth. How pretty she was! What a voluptuous, mature figure! He would certainly come. As he kissed her hand at parting all his timidity and awkwardness returned; he was astonished that she gave no sign of noticing them. She called Pradier *"mon cher Phidias,"* he noticed, as she took her leave, and Pradier replied *"ma chère Sapho."* Neither of them smiled, and this fashion of addressing each other as Greeks might have seemed to Flaubert a little absurd had he not found it indicative of something much more immediately important. Pradier treated Madame Colet with respect; clearly the woman was a rarity!

The next evening, after dinner, he presented himself in the Rue de la Fontaine-Saint-Georges. The apartment was small, as Madame Colet had lamented, but it was delightfully Parisian. A maid ushered him into a tiny boudoir, heavy with perfume and hung with blue silk; on a chaise longue, in a low-cut gown of white muslin, was Madame Colet. Giving him her hand, she apologized for her informality; she was tired; since seeing him she had been working intensively on a new poem. An alabaster lamp, hanging by a chain from the ceiling, gave out a soft, intimate glow; Madame Colet was even prettier than she had been at Pradier's; her shoulders and bosom were even whiter than her beautiful arms; her forehead was high, her hair a mass of golden curls. The room was warm; Flaubert felt pervaded by a strange, not unpleasant discomfort; she too seemed slightly ill at ease, and once again they plunged, as if by mutual consent, into literary subjects.

As they began to converse, sipping the sugared orange-flower water which the maid brought in small glasses, Flaubert found himself wondering about two things. The apartment was perfectly quiet; the child was doubtless asleep; but where was Monsieur Colet, if there was one? And, if that was an absurd reason for wonder, a provincialism, there was another question that was certainly legitimate and Parisian: where was Monsieur Cousin? At Pradier's, the day before, he had wondered the same thing. Monsieur Cousin had not been present, and yet her liaison with him was the most famous thing about Madame Colet: they went everywhere together. Where was he now?

But soon Madam Colet and her literary fervour were occupying all his attention, and, as on the day before, they united in worshipping genius. Shakespeare, that colossus from across the Channel, came in for large quantities of adoration, and Madame Colet modestly mentioned that she had translated some passages from Shakespeare into French. Flaubert begged her to read them to him, and she rose and returned with several gilt-bound volumes, whence she read passages from *A Midsummer Night's Dream, The Tempest, Macbeth,* and *King John.* Flaubert listened respectfully, but when she had finished he did not hesitate to question. Her translation was in classical French rhyming verse: was she sure that that was the most appropriate? She admitted it might not be, but attempted to defend herself: to show that she was not a slave to any one metre she rose again, and returned with other volumes. There was *Fleurs du Midi,* her first collection of poems, with a quotation from Byron ("Child of the Sun . . . Soul of Fire") on the title page and laudatory letters from Chateaubriand in the preface; there was *Penserosa,* her second collection, so called because "a great philosopher" had once baptized her by that Miltonic name—a sentimental christening which was described in the first poem in the book; there was *Charlotte Corday et Madame Roland,* verses in defence of liberty and feminism, for Madame Colet was, she announced, a liberal; there were still other volumes; there were her two prize-winning poems, *"Le Château de Versailles"* and *"Le Monument de Molière";* and finally there was her latest volume, out only a few weeks, *Les Chants des Vaincus,* containing an impassioned defence of the recent unsuccessful Polish revolution. So many books! It was almost impossible to think of so pretty a woman's having worked so hard! Choosing the poems she thought the best, she read them aloud; Flaubert commented freely. He questioned whether modern politics were worthy of an artist's attention; he found that some of the verses, while well conceived, betrayed hasty execution; others he declared totally bad; still others, very beautiful. He apologized for his frankness; she protestingly thanked him for it: praise was all the more precious when mingled with blame; only sincerity was helpful. She rose again, and returned with the manuscripts of her very newest verse, and these too were read and criticized. The young man to whom Pradier had said, the day before, that she might be of use in a literary way, was already, on the contrary, proving of great literary use to her, for she found his ideas excellent.

The apartment was absolutely quiet; the maid had disappeared; there was no hint of husband, child, or lover, and as the hours passed the candour and confidence with which young Flaubert discussed his hostess's poetry began to invade and liberate his general state of mind. Madame Colet was no bourgeoise, he was glad to find. She was not foolish or prudish, and did not insist on sitting stiffly away from him. Several times, as they bent together over a book or a manuscript, he touched her arm by accident, and she smiled at him. Suddenly, on an uncontrollable impulse and almost to his own disbelief, he found himself touching her beautiful arm not by accident at all, and to his astonishment Madame Colet made not even the slightest pretence at displeasure! Her golden curls had occasionally brushed against his face as she had lowered her head toward her papers: now he was stroking them softly with his hand! Her enormous light blue eyes, her deliciously tilted nose, were very close to his face. Could this be true? Was she really smiling still, was she really offering her lips to his? She was; and in a moment Flaubert was holding her in his arms, they were whispering ecstatic words and covering each other with kisses.

Yes, this was all incredibly true. And as he held Madame Colet in his arms, Flaubert found himself thinking once more of Monsieur Cousin. Under Alfred's direction he had read and admired *Du Vrai, du Beau et du Bien;* he had adored the glimpses of pure beauty which it contained; and here, on this chaise longue, in the Rue de la Fontaine-Saint-Georges, he was . . . It was an intoxicating thought, and he felt himself bursting with pride and manhood.

But no: it seemed that he was not quite yet usurping Monsieur Cousin's place after all. For now Madame Colet was turning her lips away, pressing him back, whispering him to stop, to leave "before it was too late," and in the same breath calling him the sweetest names, asking him when she would see him again. He released her and stood up; they would see each other the next night, they breathlessly agreed; they would dine together. Once again they fell into each other's arms; then Madame Colet kissed him solemnly on the forehead, and he rushed out, his head in a whirl.

His dreams, that night, had almost the brilliance of his visions during an attack. The next day seemed endless; there was no one in whom he could confide: Max was in Vichy with his grandmother, Alfred still in Italy with his stupid bride, Louis in Rouen, Pradier—at least as yet—not to be thought of. He wandered alone about the city, filled with impatience and with a sense of Pradier's two indispensable qualities. Finally evening came.

It was the thirtieth of July, the anniversary of the deposition of the Bourbons in 1830; all Paris was celebrating the holiday. The streets, the quays, and the bridges were filled with crowds; there were boat races and water sports on the river, fairs on the sidewalks, and music and dancing in the squares. When Flaubert called for Madame Colet he found her ready, but to his surprise he found that her little girl was ready too. She apologized: the maid was out, there was no one with whom Henriette could be left; she would promise to behave well, would she not? The child curtsied, and her mother introduced her to Monsieur Flaubert. She was six years old. Somewhat silently, he led them to the quiet restaurant where he had expected the two of them would dine in intimacy; at the beginning, they were again a little strained, a little strange, but Henriette was delighted by her outing, by the holiday noises which drifted in, and in her questions and comments they re-found their self-possession. Before long, too, it became apparent that Madame Colet was doing her best to make up for her daughter's presence; she began to tell the story of her life.

Flaubert was not surprised to learn that she had been born in the Midi: most good things, he had always known, came from places that were brilliant and sunny and as unlike his own city as possible, and it was not strange that his northern heart should have been so quickly melted by a radiant woman from the South. As a child she had been constantly filled with discontentments; poetry and romance had always entranced her; at sunset she had often hidden in a pine-wood near her parents' house and read Lamartine; for even in Provence, she assured Flaubert, a romantic can suffer from boredom. And she had always written poetry, and dreamed of knowing poets. When she had come to Paris, a shy young girl, amazing good fortune had allowed her to be presented to Madame Récamier, and had allowed that celebrated old lady to love her. Chateaubriand, who called on Madame Récamier every afternoon, had written those admiring letters Flaubert had seen in the preface of her first collection of poems, and she had quickly attained a certain modest fame. Then, a little later, she had learned that the French Academy was offering a prize for the best poem on the subject of the opening of the palace of Versailles as a public museum; when she heard the news, the contest was almost over; but she set quickly to work, finished her poem on time, and won the prize. This was the true opening of the door: her poem was read at the Academy, she became a part of Paris, she found herself holding a salon which was so frequented by Academicians that someone called it the Academy's oyster-bed. She met painters, sculptors, musicians, actors, poets, philosophers. She met the famous Victor Cousin. . . .

"Plato!" said little Henriette suddenly.

Flaubert looked his curiosity; Madame Colet repri-manded the child and explained, blushing slightly, that "Plato" was the name under which Monsieur Cousin was known in the Rue de la Fontaine-Saint-Georges; it was the counterpart of "Penserosa," the name she had mentioned the day before. Flaubert nodded; the habit of classical nicknames was evidently something to which he would have to accustom himself.

Then Madame Colet hesitated. Monsieur Flaubert knew about her—that is to say, he knew about Monsieur Cousin, perhaps?

He admitted that he did.

He knew, perhaps, that it was all over?

No! He hadn't known that!

Well, it *was* all over, in a sense, Madame Colet said re-signedly; and in terms that the child could not understand she told of the change that had come over the celebrated liaison. Monsieur Cousin (eighteen years older than her-self) had always been perfect with her; it was only re-cently—a few weeks before—that he had suddenly and unaccountably altered. Before meeting him she had always heard that he was cold, devoted only to metaphysics; she had found him otherwise; but now he had chosen to as-sume, in a certain degree, the character that the world attributed to him. For no reason that she could imagine—and he had offered none—he had informed her one day that their relationship must change. He would continue to be her "protector," there would be no rupture, he would remain her friend, he would call on her every day. Would she acquiesce? She had, of course, acquiesced quietly and without question, hiding her hurt and her bewilderment as best she could. She was not a woman to demand explana-tions or to make scenes. Besides, the beauty of her intellec-tual intercourse with Monsieur Cousin was well worth preserving, whatever the fate of their more commonplace relations. Everything, therefore, was arranged as he desired. Every day Monsieur Cousin called, grave and polite. They discussed literature, philosophy, and any personal matters in which he might be of use to her. They discussed little Henriette, in whose education he was kindly interesting himself. If, during his visit, another caller blundered in, Monsieur Cousin, after greeting the interloper courteously, would subside into absolute silence, his arms crossed in a very odd and personal fashion on his breast. And if the person was too dull to take the hint, Monsieur Cousin would himself rise quietly and leave.

That, Madame Colet said, was her new life, to which she was gradually becoming accustomed.

As to life in general, her greatest trial, her greatest burden, was her beauty. She would be absurd to pretend that she did not know that she possessed it, and she would be wrong not to recognize the grave responsibility it placed upon her. Ever since her girlhood men had swarmed about her. There had been a young man at Aix who used to stand evening after evening in a certain spot to watch her pass; she had been too young to pity him, and, because he was not handsome, had cruelly laughed; and years afterward —quite recently, in fact—two beautiful potted orange-trees had been delivered to her door: the unknown young man had left them to her in his will. In Paris, however, few of the men whom her beauty attracted behaved in as exemplary a fashion as that, and she preferred those who admired her for her mind. A charming Parisian doctor, for example—as unknown to her as the young man in Aix —had had printed, at his own expense, a princely edition of twenty-five copies of her poems, twenty-four of which he sent to her with an anonymous note saying that he was keeping one for himself and that she should give the others to her family, to her friends, to the King, to the Academy, and to the other great libraries of France. Recently she had had a series of tender meetings with Alfred de Vigny, a chaste, spiritual communion, punctuated with pure kisses, which had lasted several weeks and was as great a tribute as any woman could receive; for Vigny, all poet, was what Monsieur Cousin pretended to be—a disembodied spirit, who seldom descended as low as the earth. Such, in her language, were the varieties of experience she valued the most highly. And now, having described her own existence, she longed to hear of Monsieur Flaubert's.

It was the moment, perhaps, for him to take her hand, trace parallelisms in their lives, enlarge on his own difficulties and sorrows, and express his eagerness to lessen or share hers. But Flaubert did nothing of the kind. Completely sincere himself, it never occurred to him that others—particularly people to whom he was drawn—were less sincere than he. Madame Colet's purity alarmed him. She had changed, then, since the night before? The presence of Henriette he should have recognized as an indication of that? The continuation of the "intellectual intercourse" with Monsieur Cousin, the chaste affair with Vigny, the preference for men who "admired her for her mind": these were not the sort of thing he had expected to hear tonight. Had she reconsidered? And although Monsieur Cousin was now accounted for, she had not even mentioned Monsieur Colet in the story of her life. Had he deceived her, treated her cruelly, abandoned her? Gustave was determined to find out everything. And in carefully chosen words, as little Henriette continued to behave adorably, he neatly combined his questions by demanding of Madame Colet, looking her straight in the eye, her opinion of adultery.

She appeared to be shocked, and blushed and stammered, protesting the question; he firmly repeated it—it was something on which she certainly had an opinion, and he wanted her to state what it was; his manner was compelling, and Madame Colet was forced to reply. In principle, adultery was a crime, a horrible thing, which broke homes and hearts and harmed innocent children. But in her case—surely there was an excuse! She hoped she would be forgiven! Her marriage had been so unwise; she had married Monsieur Colet in the Midi, solely because he had a post in Paris and could transport her there. What a mistake! Once in Paris, she discovered she could easily have made her way herself, and Monsieur Colet was an obstructive nonentity. His name was Hippolyte. At the Conservatory, where he was a professor, he was despised, and owed his only advancement to the influence of Monsieur Cousin;

his books on counterpoint had excited the hilarity of
musicians; his single one-act opera had been played exactly
once: he was a failure and a fool. She was thankful, she
whispered, seeking safe words—yes, she was thankful, if
she dared say so, that her daughter had a philosopher for
a father, disappointing as that philosopher had lately
turned out to be. But would the child feel the same about
it? Later Henriette would know. What would she think
of her mother? Would the lives of both of them be
scarred? That was one of the dangers of adultery, that was
why it was a terrible thing, to be avoided except in cases
where a trapped spirit finds in it its only way of release. . . .

But Flaubert did not let her finish. He spoke sharply.
Her general opinion was wrong, bourgeois; but her particular opinion was right; her action had been correct.
Adultery was glorious, it was revolt against the most
bourgeois and detestable of institutions. He told her of
his passion for the young nursing mother in Trouville;
calf-love as it was, it was none the less intense and genuine,
and he still had an affection for the woman who had been
the object of it. When his passion for her had been at its
height, the word "adultery" had seemed to him the most
beautiful of human words, vaguely enveloped with an
exquisite sweetness, fragrant with a peculiar magic, full
of a supreme poetry compounded of voluptuousness and
blasphemy. And that was the feeling concerning adultery
which was suddenly surging up in him again, he declared,
staring at Madame Colet. The air about them became
electric; Madame Colet could not speak; when she met
Flaubert's burning eyes her head jerked as though with a
current; hurriedly, they rose and left the restaurant.

In the Place de la Concorde he hailed a cab and told the
driver to take them to the Bois de Boulogne. They turned
into the Champs-Elysées, transformed for the holiday
into an avenue of illuminated, flower-decked obelisks; in
the distance the Arc de Triomphe was blazing, and they
halted the cab to watch it. Suddenly the entire sky was
lighted; the fireworks were beginning. They drove on
past the obelisks, under the rockets and bombs. As they
left the lights and reached the darkness and quiet of the
Bois, Henriette, exhausted from joy and excitement, fell

asleep on the seat of the carriage, and in an instant her mother and Monsieur Flaubert were in each other's arms. For a time they drove among the trees, speaking softly; then they returned to the Rue de la Fontaine-Saint-Georges and Flaubert waited impatiently in the boudoir while Madame Colet put the child to bed. The rest of the night was their own.

If Gustave's new knowledge that Plato's place had been voluntarily vacated diminished slightly the particular sensation of triumph and maturity he had felt the day before, Louise's mockery of Monsieur Cousin that night afforded him considerable consolation. She extolled Flaubert's youth, and the beauty of his body and face; Monsieur Cousin she described as a tiny, homely man, dry with age and quite lacking in any distinction of appearance. She recited a bitter poem she had written—but not shown—to Monsieur Cousin, in revenge for his behaviour; and the sensation of committing a double adultery (Monsieur Colet, he finally learned, was at the moment "on vacation") assured Flaubert's ecstasy. It was his first true night of love.

They parted at dawn, and agreed to meet in Pradier's studio that afternoon.

But at Pradier's Flaubert did not appear, and Louise found him sitting miserably in his room at his hotel, doing nothing whatever. Her anger melted in his arms, under a flood of kisses and a torrent of self-reproach and confession. The story of his life, which he had not given the night before, came rushing out, and particularly a picture of life as he now led it—in Croisset with his mother and niece and his near-by friend, in a solitude which he prized above everything else in the world, deadly and wearing as it often was, because in it work would soon be possible, and in which it was his duty to stay because it had been achieved so dearly. That was why he had not come to Pradier's; since leaving her he had realized that he would bring her only misery, for though they might begin an affair it would be impossible for him to continue it; soon, he knew, he would return to his solitude, where he could never ask her to come. It would be cruel toward her to continue now. But her only answer (for she did not believe him) was to slip into his bed; and for the next week they met daily. When they were apart for a few hours they sent each other notes; they took Pradier to dinner to show him their gratitude (and Flaubert continued to be impressed by Phidias's respectful behavior toward Sapho); they drove in the Bois, they lay together in the hotel bedroom or in the boudoir, their mouths close, talking of themselves or reciting poetry. And they invented a dull nickname for the dull professor at the Conservatory: Monsieur Colet became "the Official." Flaubert would have liked to meet him: it would have made the enjoyment of adultery even greater.

Then, one day, Flaubert said he must go home. He had, he said, already stayed too long, and he seemed not even to hear her urgings to stay just a little longer. He would return to Paris "when he could"; he would write faithfully. With all his heart he thanked her for what she had given him: why had she done it? Even now he could scarcely believe his good fortune; and her acceptance of his way of life showed a generosity of soul which he found staggering. She smiled, did not protest, because she thought she had no need to, and wept. On Tuesday, the third of August, she went with him to the train; her eyes were so red that despite the heat she wore a veil. She waved as the train pulled away: she knew he would soon return.

But the letters which he at once began to send from his solitude were far from being entirely what Louise expected. Nor were her replies what Flaubert expected either. Within the next week he wrote her six times, and in his letters can be read hers as well.

Tuesday midnight
"Twelve hours ago we were still together, and at this very moment yesterday I was holding you in my arms! How long ago it seems! Now the night is soft and warm; I can hear the great tulip-tree under my window rustling in the wind, and when I lift my eyes I see the reflection of the moon in the river. Your little slippers are in front of me as I write. Here, locked away by myself, I have just taken out everything you gave me; your two letters are in

the little silk bag, and I am going to reread them as soon as I have finished mine. I am not writing to you on my ordinary writing-paper—that is edged with black and I want nothing sad to pass from me to you. I want to cause you nothing but joy, and to surround you with a calm, endless bliss—to repay you, a little, for the overflowing generosity of the love you have given me. I am afraid of being cold, arid, selfish—and yet, God can see what is going on within me at this moment. Such memories! And such desire! Ah! Our two rides in the Bois: how beautiful they were, particularly the second, with the lightning flashing above us! I find myself remembering the colour of the trees lit by the street-lights, and the swaying motion of the springs; we were alone and so happy: I kept staring at you, and even in the darkness your whole face seemed lighted by your eyes. I feel that I am writing badly; I am not saying anything that I want to say. My sentences run together like sighs; to understand them you will have to supply what should go between them; you will do that? Every letter, every turn of my handwriting will set you dreaming? When I see your little brown slippers I dream of the movements of your feet when they were in them, when the slippers were warm with them. . . .

"My mother was waiting for me at the station. She wept at seeing me return. You wept at seeing me leave. What a sombre and grotesque thought, not to be able to move without causing tears on two sides at once! Here the grass is still as green, the trees as full, the river as smooth as when I left; my books are open at the same pages; nothing is changed. Nature shames us, her serenity is a rebuke to our pride. But you and I—let us think of nothing, neither of the future nor of ourselves, for to think is to suffer. Let the tempest in our hearts blow us where it will, and as for the reefs—if they are there we shall run onto them, that's all! We shall see.

"On the train I read almost the whole of one of your books. More than one passage moved me, but of that I will write you more fully later. As you can well see, I have not yet been able to gather myself together, and my critical faculties are not with me. I wanted only to send you another kiss before sleeping, to tell you that I love you. No

sooner had I left you—and the more as I was borne further and further away—than my thoughts flew back
toward you, more swiftly even than the smoke I saw flying
back from the train. Here: a kiss, quickly—you know the
kind—and another, and another! Still another, and finally
one more, just under your chin on the spot I love, where
your skin is so soft, and another on your breast, where I
lay my heart. Adieu, adieu!"

Thursday evening

"Your letter of this morning is sad, full of a sorrowful
resignation. You offer to forget me if that is what I want.
You are sublime! I knew you were good, but I did not
know you were as noble as that. I feel humble at the
contrast I see between us. But do you know that the
things you write me are hard and harsh? And the worst
thing about them is that it was I who provoked them.
You are returning blow for blow, evidently—a kind of
reprisal. You ask me what it is that I want of you. I cannot
tell you that, but I can tell you that what I want of myself
is to love you, to love you a thousand times more, even,
than I do. Oh! If you could read my heart you would see
the place you have in it! I can see that you have been
suffering more than you admit, your letter is a little stilted.
You had been weeping, probably? Confess that you had;
admit that you had had a bad day, that it was because my
letter was delayed that you wrote as you did. Be frank,
not proud.

"Something occurs to me which I must say. I am sure
you think me selfish. The thought grieves you and you
are convinced it is true. Well, selfishness is something
about which everyone deludes himself. I am selfish like
everyone else—less so than many, perhaps, and perhaps
more than others. Who knows? Besides, 'selfish' is a word
that everyone applies to his neighbour without really
knowing what he means by it. Who is not selfish, to a
greater or less degree? Do we not all search, according
to our individual instincts, to satisfy our natures? Saint
Vincent de Paul obeyed an appetite for charity, Caligula
an appetite for cruelty. Everyone takes his enjoyment in
his own way and for himself alone. Some direct all activity

toward themselves, making themselves the cause, the center, the end of everything; others invite the whole world to the banquet of their souls. That is the difference between prodigals and misers: the first take their pleasure in giving, the second in keeping. As for ordinary selfishness (what we usually mean by the word), although it is excessively repugnant to my spirit I admit that if it could be bought I should give everything to have it. To be stupid and selfish and to have good health are the three requirements for happiness, though if stupidity is lacking, the others are useless. But there is also another kind of happiness, yes, there *is* another, for I have seen it; you have shown me, in the air, its shining light; before my eyes I have seen the glistening of its garment. I hold out my hands to grasp it—and then you yourself shake your head, and say you suspect it is but a phantom. I am beginning to feel that you have too much sadness in your heart, that deep sadness which comes of nothing, and which, infused into the very substance of being, increases as being itself is stirred. I warned you: my misery is contagious. I am infected! Woe to him who touches me!

"You would like to make me into a pagan, you who have Roman blood in your veins. But try as I might, any effort toward that would be useless, for at the very bottom of my soul are the mists of the North which I have breathed since birth. I carry within me the melancholy of the barbarians, with their instinct for migration and their innate disgust for life—which made them leave their own country as though by so doing they could take leave of themselves. They loved the sun, all those Goths who went to Italy to die; they had a frenzied longing for light, for the blue sky, for a warm, vibrant existence. I have always had a tender sympathy for them, as one might have for one's ancestors. But, alas, I am no man of antiquity: men of antiquity did not have sick nerves like mine! Nor you, either. You are neither Greek nor Latin; romanticism has touched you, too. . . . Adieu, a long kiss."

Saturday
"I feel shattered, numb. I cannot read or think or write. Your love makes me sad. I can see that you are suffering,

and I foresee that I shall make you suffer still more. Both for your sake and for my own I wish we had never met, and yet the thought of you is never absent from my mind. Ah! How much better it would have been to have stopped short, that night, after our ride in the Bois!

"You would not believe me when I told you I was old. Alas, yes, for every sensation which touches my soul turns there into bitterness, like wine poured into jars which have been used too often. If you knew all the interior forces that have consumed me, all the mad desires that have passed through my head, everything I have tried and experimented with in the way of sensations and passions, you would see that I am not so young! It is you who are a child, you who are fresh and new, you whose candour makes me blush. The grandeur of your love fills me with humility; you deserved someone better than I. May lightning strike me, may all possible curses fall upon me if ever I forget that! You ask me whether I despise you because you gave yourself to me so quickly. Have you really been able to suspect that? *Never, never:* whatever you do, whatever may happen, I am devoted to you for life—to you, to your daughter, to anything and anyone you wish. That is a vow. Remember it. Use it. I make it because I can keep it.

"Ever since we said we loved each other you have wondered why I have never added the words 'for ever.' Why? Because I always sense the future, the antithesis of everything is always before my eyes. I have never seen a child without thinking that it would grow old, nor a cradle without thinking of a grave. The sight of a nude woman makes me think of her skeleton. As a result, joyful sights make me sad and sad ones affect me but little. After our frenzied moments together have passed, my heart swoons with sadness; for I say to myself: 'She loves me and I love her, but I do not love her enough. If she had never known me, she would have been spared the tears she is shedding now.' Forgive me, my darling, forgive me, in the name of all the rapture you have given me. But I have a foreboding of immense unhappiness for you. . . .

"And you, my child, you think that you will love me 'for ever'? For ever! What presumption on human lips!

You have loved before, have you not? So have I. Remember that you said 'for ever' before. What I am saying is harsh, I know. I am offending you, but I should rather disturb your happiness now than increase it cold-bloodedly, as others would do, so that when it does end you will suffer more. Who knows? You will thank me later, perhaps, for having had the courage not to be more tender.

"For me, physical love is always secondary. You are the only woman to whom I have dared to try to give pleasure, the only one, perhaps, to whom I have given it. Thank you, thank you for that! But will you understand me to the end? Will you be able to bear the burden of my spleen, my manias, my whims? You tell me, for example, to write you every day, and if I do not I know you will reproach me. But the very idea that you want a letter every morning will prevent me from writing it! Let me love you in my own way, in the way that my nature demands. Let me continue to love you with—since you call it that—*originality!* Force me to do nothing, and I will do everything. Understand me, do not reproach me. If I thought you were frivolous, stupid, like other women, I should inundate you with words, promises, vows. That would cost me nothing. But I prefer to express less, not more, than the true feelings of my heart. . . .

"Some time this month I will come to see you. I will stay with you for an entire day. At times I think of you as you lay on my bed that night at the hotel, your hair streaming over my pillow. At other times—yesterday, for example, when I had finished my letter—the thought of you sings, smiles, glows, and dances before me like the sight of a cheerful fire, giving forth ever-changing colours and penetrating heat, and in my memory I trace the movements of your mouth when you speak. Every evening I read some of your poems. I keep looking for traces of yourself in them; I find them sometimes. . . ."

Sunday morning
"My child, your folly is carrying you too far. Calm yourself. You are only becoming irritated against yourself and against life. I told you I was more reasonable than you. Do you really think that I am not to be pitied, too? Be

more sparing with your cries; they torture me. What do you want me to do? Can I leave everything here and go live in Paris? Impossible. If I were entirely free I should do it, for with you in Paris I should not have the force to keep myself away, and, besides, ever since my youth I have wanted to live there, and some day I shall.

"You tell me that what I needed was a banal kind of love. I reply that I needed either no love at all, or yours, for I cannot imagine one more complete, fuller, more beautiful. It is now ten o'clock in the morning; your letter has just come and I have already sent you mine, the one I wrote last night. Scarcely awake, I am writing you again without knowing what I am going to say. At least you see that I do think of you. Do not be angry with me when you do not receive a letter from me. It is not my fault. The very days when I do not write you are those when I think of you most of all. What irresistible impulse drove me toward you? For an instant I saw the abyss, I realized its depth, and then vertigo swept me over. But how *not* love you, you who are so sweet, so good, so superior, so loving, so beautiful? I keep thinking of your voice, when you spoke to me the night of the fireworks. They blazed for us, that night, like a flaming beginning of love.

"Your apartment is a little like one I had in Paris for almost two years. From it I had a view out over Paris, like your view. Summer nights I used to look up at the stars, and in winter at the glowing mist of the city floating above the houses. It seemed to me, the first time I came to your house, that I was reliving my past, that I had returned to one of those beautiful, sad twilights of my youth, when, sick with boredom and my soul filled with a feeling of death, I used to leave my law books and go to my window for a breath of air. If only I had known you then! Why could that not have been? I was free, alone, without family or mistress, for I have never had a mistress. You can scarcely believe, probably, that I am not lying. But I have never been more scrupulously truthful, and this is the reason why: the grotesque aspects of love have always prevented me from giving myself over to it entirely. At times I have wanted to give pleasure to a woman, but the idea of the strange spectacle I should present at the

moment of doing so made me laugh so much that all my
desire melted under the fire of an inner irony, which sang
a hymn of mockery and derision within me. It is only with
you that I have not—not yet—laughed at myself; but when
I see you so intense, so absolutely absorbed in your passion,
I am tempted to cry out to you: 'No! No! You are making
a mistake! Take care! Not this man!'

"Do you go to Pradier's? I await a letter from him
which will give me a pretext to go to Paris for a day.
Then, toward the first of September, I will find another
pretext for going to some town between Paris and Rouen
—Mantes or Vernon—where you can meet me. After that,
we shall see. But what is the good of getting accustomed
to seeing each other, or loving each other? Why load ourselves with the luxury of caresses, if afterwards we have to
be miserable and separated? But what else can we do?

"Adieu, my darling, I have just gone down into the
garden, and have gathered this little rose which I am
sending you. I have kissed it; put it quickly to your mouth,
and then—you know where. Adieu! A thousand kisses. I
am yours from night to day, from day to night."

Tuesday afternoon

"Forget everything I said in my letter of Sunday. I was
addressing myself to your masculine intelligence; I had
thought that you would be able to detach yourself from
yourself, and understand me in your heart. You have read
into my letter much more than I put there, you have exaggerated everything I said. Evidently you think that I was
posing, you call me a materialist. . . . Let us talk no more
about that. I was wrong, stupid, I did with you what I have
done at other times with those I have loved best—turned
the sack of my *self* inside out; and the bitter dust rising
from it has choked you as it choked them. But I will torment you no longer. I will touch you softly, like a child
one is afraid of hurting. I will draw in my quills: with a
little good will, even a porcupine is tamed! You say that
I analyse myself too much. But on the contrary I feel that
I do not know myself half well enough, and every day I
discover something new. I travel within myself as in an
unknown country, though I have gone over it a hundred

times. You do not thank me for my frankness. (Women wish to be deceived; they force you to deceive them, and if you resist they reproach you!) Well, I have never lied to you, I have never set out deliberately to please you. If I have ever pleased you it happened as it should—by itself. Why do you reproach me for my phrase, 'I wish we had never met'? I know of none tenderer. What more can anyone say when his heart is faltering because it is so full? Ask yourself whether there are many men who would have written you that letter which so wounded you. Few, I think, would have had such courage, such complete self-abnegation. But, my darling, you must destroy that letter, never think of it again—or, at least, not reread it until some time when you feel stronger.

"I must ask you not to write me such commonplaces as the following: that I am unhappy because I have never had to earn my living, that I should be better off if I had to work. As though all one had to do was to become a druggist's clerk, or a baker, or a wine merchant, to escape from the boredom of this world! Too many bourgeois have told me those things over and over again, to make me want to hear them from you.

"Why were you not the first woman I ever knew? Why could you not have been the first whose ecstasies, whose transports I felt as I held her in my arms?

"Adieu. A thousand kisses, unending. Till soon, my darling, till soon!"

By "soon," however, Flaubert all too clearly did not mean what his darling would have liked him to mean, and that was the chief cause of the trouble, the chief cause of the childish petulance which, to his dismay, his mature mistress now displayed in such generous quantities. Nobody could say that his letters were not passionate and long, and Louise did not overlook the abundance of the greatest of all compliments—incoherence—which they contained; but how unbearable were Flaubert's enormities, his complete failure to understand a woman's character, and above all how unbearable was the realization that he had actually meant what he had said that afternoon in his hotel room! And his letters of the second week—for, incredible as it seemed to Louise, a second week did go by without his returning to Paris—contained things that she liked even less than those of the first.

"Beginning Thursday," he wrote, "address your letters to 'Monsieur Du Camp, care of Monsieur Gustave Flaubert,' because the letters I get from you every day are thought by everyone here to come from him, and when he is here it would appear odd if I continued to get them as usual. Questions might be asked, etc. If you have the slightest aversion to this, of course do not do it, but I am sensitive about you, and I believe that if I so much as uttered your name in anyone's presence my blushes would give everything away." And a few days later: "Du Camp arrived today—he is to spend a month. Always address your letters like the one of this morning. He brought me your portrait. The frame is of carved black wood and sets off the engraving very well. It is facing me as I write, leaning against one of the cushions on my divan in the corner between two windows—where you would be if you were here! My mother has seen it. She likes your face, thinks you are pretty. You have an 'animated, open, pleasant expression,' she says. (I have pretended to her that proofs of the engraving happened to be delivered one afternoon when I had been taken to see you, and that you presented some of them to your visitors.)"

"He is to spend a month!" "Where you would be if you were here!" "I have pretended . . . !" These were detestable phrases. Evidently the solitude was not as solitary as Gustave had pretended, and evidently it was only she who was not allowed to disturb it, and evidently this large young man of twenty-four had to account to his mother for everything he did, for everyone he knew! Louise therefore wrote at once, insisting that he come to Paris or that he allow her to come to Croisset, for it was absurd that they should not be seeing each other; Flaubert as hastily replied: he could not come, and she *must* not—and he explained once more that he must be allowed to lead his normal life. That had been understood!

What his normal life was, he described in his letters. "I am working, reading steadily, studying a little Greek, and pondering over Virgil and Horace." "I have written to a friend at the Royal Library to send me translations of Nottinger's *Historia Orientalis,* an Indian drama called *Sakuntala,* and the *Puranas.* I am also reading Chardin's travels to help me in my oriental studies." "This morning I read some of your poems with a friend who came to see me—a badly-off young man who gives lessons here for a living and who is a poet, a real poet, the author of superb and charming things." "Impossible to come to Paris now; I have a huge boil on my right cheek, and my whole head is wrapped in bandages."

Surely these were deterrents from leaving Croisset that anyone could understand? Whether they were or not, Flaubert was finding his occupations increasingly important. His correspondence with his mistress was revealing to him more clearly every day just what the most important parts of his life were. It had taken him only this short time to be sure that what he had written to Alfred after receiving Pradier's advice was true—that a "normal love" would "disturb" him; that the normal life and the prolonged relationship preached by Pradier were abnormal for him. "I can think of nothing in the world I enjoy more than a nice room, well heated, with the right books and plenty of leisure," he had written almost two years before; and ecstatic as the hours with Louise Colet had been, they did not make him change his mind. And he was bewildered that she, whose understanding had so moved him in Paris, now seemed not to understand at all, and acted as though he had never spoken a word to her about these matters.

Even his walks aroused complaint. "Today when I happened to be walking along the Rue du Collège I saw a crowd of people on the steps of the chapel. It was Prize Day. I heard the students shouting and the sound of bravos and of a band. I went in and saw everything just as it used to be in my time, the same tapestries hanging in the same places. I remembered the odour of the damp oak-leaves in the wreaths they used to place on our heads, and the delirium of joy I always used to feel on Prize Day, with two whole months of liberty ahead of me. When I left, my heart was heavy." That was wrong, letters from Paris told him. He should not wallow emotionally in the scenes of his youth and regret the past: it should be more normal to give vent to his emotions in the Rue de la Fontaine-Saint-Georges, and enjoy the present. But, he replied, he had warned her so explicitly and repeated so frequently in his letters that he was not "normal"! Why did she not believe him?

During the second week he announced that he would really come to Paris "soon." "I have just written to Pradier, and think I made it quite clear that I shall shortly be wanting to come to Paris. As soon as I get a letter from him, I will leave Du Camp here (even though it be scarcely polite) and come." What other reason could he possibly give his mother, he asked, for wanting to spend even as long as twenty-four hours in Paris, particularly when a friend was visiting him, except that Pradier wanted to consult him about the bust of Caroline? In her replies, Louise as yet gave no indication of her sentiments concerning Flaubert and his mother, but she complained that the device was a bad one because Pradier was so procrastinating. The sculptor never wrote letters; sometimes for days on end he did not even open his mail; the delay could go on for weeks.

Her reproaches and protestations demanded such long counter-protestations that there was little room in Flaubert's letters for anything else, and even what little else there was, was unforgivably qualified. He wrote: "If you knew how I thought of your voice, of the perfume of your shoulders!" But he added: "I did not want to write you this evening, I wanted to work, but as you see I had to give in." He wrote: "Au revoir! A thousand kisses!" or: "Adieu! I bite your sweet lips!" But he added: "Come, come, a little patience, my darling. We will see each other before too long." This was insulting, and she told him so emphatically.

Shortly after the end of the second week, however, he wrote that he was longing to come, that he was awaiting only the summons. His boil had disappeared. Louise must go to see Pradier at once, force him to write, under her very eyes, the necessary letter, and post it herself. That she did, and Flaubert wrote his thanks and his eagerness. For he did eagerly look forward to their meeting, and that was exactly what Louise found the most monstrous: to long with eagerness and to seek but seldom. "I shall arrive in Paris at four o'clock or quarter past," he wrote. "So, before half-past four I shall be with you. Already I picture myself climbing your stairs, I hear the sound of the bell. 'Madame is at home?' 'Yes, come in. . . .' Ah! I am savouring our twenty-four hours in advance. But why must every joy bring me pain? I am already thinking of our separation, of your sadness. You will be good, won't you? For I feel that I shall be much more melancholy than I was the first time."

He did climb the stairs, Madame was at home, she accompanied him to his hotel, and it was good. "I keep thinking of our last meeting at the hotel," he wrote, when he had once more returned to Croisset, "with your silk dress wide open, the lace winding down over your breast. You were smiling, dumbfounded with love and rapture. How your eyes shone!" Yes, it was good. Flaubert's enjoyment was as genuine as his anticipation of it; he had the true gift of voluptuousness; and while in all logic this should have outraged Louise the more, in practice it soothed her. They had a long talk, and were sure that everything was straightened out between them. Louise, reassured, became more lenient. When in his letter Flaubert added to his memories of their rapture the words, "Why must an hour of ecstasy be paid for by a month of sorrow? Count the tears you have shed for me so far. They greatly exceed, don't they, the number of kisses I have given you?" she did not protest his bad habit of emphasizing grief. And when in still another passage of the same letter he said: "Today I have done nothing. I have neither written nor read a line. I have unpacked my *Temptation of Saint Anthony* and hung it on my wall, and that is all. I am fond of this engraving, and have long wanted to own it," she was not particularly interested.

In Croisset, however, the engraving of *The Temptation of Saint Anthony* was welcomed with the most intense interest. Maxime and Louis fully grasped the significance of the purchase, and they looked at each other with pleasure as the picture was hung on the wall. Concerning the woman in Paris, whose portrait Flaubert also had in his study, they knew little. He told them, smiling, that he

had enjoyed himself during his two days; but all particulars, all mention of names—and of difficulties—he suppressed. Max and Louis were favourably disposed to the
lady for two excellent reasons: she was pretty, and less
than three weeks after having met her Flaubert had begun
definitely to work.

About *The Temptation of Saint Anthony* he was as
secretive with his friends as he was about his mistress. He
informed them that it was his subject, and that was all. He
allowed them to assume that the books he was reading
were related to the subject in hand. For his work was,
for the time being, a work of reading. Before any writ.ng
could be done, a large amount of research was necessary,
and the winter would be one of study. From the library in
Rouen he brought home the *Bhagavad-gita,* the *Nala,* a
long book on Buddhism, the hymns of the *Rig-veda,* the
laws of Manu, the Koran, and a number of books on
Chinese religion. He wrote again to the friend in the Royal
Library in Paris, asking for the loan of several of the best
existing books, or reviews of books, on the oriental
religions and on the poetry and folklore of Arabia, India,
Persia, Malaya, and Japan. Piles of books stood all over
the study, and Max and Louis were puzzled by the presence of some of them. The relevance of the writings of the
fathers of the church, the Acts of the Councils, volumes of
scholastic philosophy, the Dictionary of Heresies, and the
Golden Legend they understood quite well, but what
could a book on Chinese poetry have to do with Saint
Anthony? Why was Flaubert reading Malayan folklore?
"Watch out!" Louis could not help crying, one day. "Your
Saint Anthony was a naïve and ignorant monk: don't make
him into a scholar!" There was no reply whatever.

Max stayed on at Croisset into the beginning of September. The days quickly became cold; in the study a fire
burned most of the time. Letters kept coming from Paris
addressed to Monsieur Du Camp, but the city seemed far
away, and it was almost as though the studious, retired
winter had already begun. Flaubert worked at his round
table; at a smaller table Max worked at an account of his
eastern travels. In the evening, after dinner, they talked
and smoked, sometimes till two or three, sleeping late in

the morning. Week-ends, when Louis was there, the work
was intensified. Louis worked silently, enveloped in vast
clouds of smoke from his pipe, or taking big pinches of
snuff; he was beginning a long poem about a Roman
dancer, which meant that he too had to study. Max had
brought from Paris one of the books he needed, Lipsius's
De Gladiatoribus. Occasionally they read aloud from it,
and Flaubert regretted that they could not give gladiatorial
combats in the garden at Croisset. In thanks for the
volume, Louis wrote a poem to Max—"*Poète aux pieds
légers, aux courses vagabondes*"—celebrating his travels in
the desert.

Shortly before Max left, he and Flaubert paid a visit to
some ruined Gothic abbeys out beyond Croisset. They
wandered among the tumble-down naves and transepts and
cloisters, deciphering the half-obliterated inscriptions, Flaubert declaring that he derived a fierce, perverse joy from
the sight of the vegetation growing amid the old stones—
"nature's invasion of the works of man the minute he is no
longer there to defend them." It made him reflect that one
day he himself would "serve to make the tulips grow,"
and the thought delighted him. "Who knows?" he said.
"Perhaps I shall make a perfectly superb manure, a most
superior guano."

To these musings Max replied, as was his wont, with a
practical proposal. The following spring, he announced, he
intended to spend three or four months touring Brittany, a
province which he did not know at all but which he had
heard was still largely un-French, full of Celtic remains.
Why should Flaubert not come along? They would walk
through the countryside, stoutly shod, staffs in their hands
and packs on their backs, sleeping wherever night might
find them. Flaubert's illness now seemed a thing of the
past; by the spring he would probably have finished his
studies and be ready to write; and such a tour would be
just the thing between the two sedentary tasks.

It was, of course, a splendid idea, and Flaubert welcomed
it with enthusiasm and longing, but he was very much
afraid, he told Max, that his mother would receive such a
proposal with terror. Nevertheless, he determined to approach her, and after their return from the abbeys he did.

Max, too, was more than dubious as to whether the trip would be allowed. He had recently received the distinct impression that her son's great affection for himself and Bouilhet was regarded by Madame Flaubert not without a certain jealousy. He had had no definite proof of this, but he felt sure that it was so, and was therefore as surprised as Flaubert when the sad, nervous woman gave her consent at once. She fully realized, she said, that life at Croisset was confining for Gustave, and that after another winter he would need a change, and she was quite willing that he should make the trip if in the spring he still wished to and if his health continued to permit it. There was only one suggestion she would like to make. By the first of May— the date Max had tentatively mentioned—she, too, would be ready for a change of scene, and it would give her pleasure to accompany her son and his friend. Not that she had any intention of walking with them across the country, sleeping in peasants' huts or in the fields, but after they had got a certain distance she would set out in a carriage with the baby and meet them here and there in towns where there were good inns. In this way she would also be able to keep an eye on Gustave's health. Had they any objections?

There was but one answer, and Flaubert, to whom his mother's self-invitations were no novelty, was so delighted to be allowed to go at all that Max repressed all comment. During the winter, it was agreed, Flaubert would study the history of Brittany in addition to his material for Saint Anthony, and Max would investigate its geography, ethnology, customs, and archæology. Thus they would not travel in ignorance. They rapidly drew up a tentative itinerary, and lamented that Louis would be chained to his pupils, unable to accompany them.

Max's departure was now imminent. The days immediately preceding it were full of manœuvres: notes kept passing back and forth between Croisset and Paris.

Wednesday
"I hope that we shall be able to see each other in a few days. Du Camp is returning to Paris, and I am supposedly accompanying him as far as Gaillon to see the Château

Gaillard, which is a few miles away. But instead of that I will go on to Mantes, where I will stay until the six o'clock train, arriving back here at eight. Such is the plan which I have long been hatching. Let us hope that my brother-in-law doesn't conceive the unfortunate idea of accompanying us! Or my mother herself—for at Les Andelys, near the château, we have some old friends whom she has not seen for a long time, and she might perhaps take advantage of the opportunity. You would leave Paris at nine in the morning and be at Mantes at ten-fifty; I should arrive at eleven-nineteen. We'd have five wonderful hours together. It is little, I know, but it is at least something, and I foresee no possibility of being able to come to Paris for some time."

Saturday

"I thought you would kiss me for the idea I had of our going to Mantes, and instead you are already reproaching me in advance for not staying there longer. You thought you could find my vulnerable point in my vanity, saying: 'So you are watched over like a young girl?' If this phrase had been addressed to me five or six years ago it would have made me do something desperate—I should have got myself killed, if necessary, to erase the effect it would have had on me. But now it rolls off me like water from the neck of a swan; it has humiliated me not at all.

"As for my refusal to have you here—do you think that as far as I am concerned it would not be sweet? What would *I* risk? If my mother realized what was going on she would not say a word to me about it: I know her. She might be jealous of you, but things would stop there. It is for your own sake that I told you not to come, for the sake of your good name, your honour. I don't want you to be subjected to banal witticisms, or to have to blush before the customs men who patrol our garden wall, or to have one of our servants giggle in your face. You didn't understand any of that, of course! You are sarcastic! Thank you! Let's talk no more about it!

"No, my friend Du Camp will not stay with us; he will continue to Paris. We can do very well without him. Can't we do without the whole world when we are alone?"

. . .

At the expense of such bickerings the rendezvous was arranged, and despite them, to the delighted astonishment of both Gustave and Louise, it was a delirium of physical pleasure, orgiastic, far and away the most ecstatic of the meetings. Louise declared she had never dreamed that love could go so far; Gustave taught her sensualities which amazed and thrilled her. They debated as to whether this was debauchery or not, and decided they did not care. Occasionally, as they lay together, she noticed that Gustave seemed plunged into abstraction, thinking of other things; but those moments were few, and so rapturous were the others that Louise won a victory: Gustave spent the night.

"I made up a story which my mother believed," he wrote back from Croisset the next day, "but yesterday the poor woman was very worried. She came to the station at eleven o'clock, and lay awake all night fretting. This morning I found her on the platform when I arrived, in a state of frightful anxiety. She did not utter the slightest reproach, but the expression on her face was the greatest reproach possible.

"When shall we see each other again? Oh, I beg you, I entreat you, never reproach me with not seeing you more often. You cannot imagine how that distresses and wounds me. Is it my fault? It will never be that. But I do not see any possibility in the near future: it will be a long time until our next meeting. Let us resign ourselves in advance. Accept this idea.

"Everything was sweet, wasn't it? Nothing disturbed us, and I think I said nothing to distress you, nor you anything to me. What a beautiful memory! It deserves a commemorative Mass! I feel that we are more closely, intimately bound, that fewer external things can affect our union, and that even if there are long periods when we do not see each other that will make no difference.

"This evening I got back to work by forcing myself to it. Let us both work hard, as well as we can. We will see each other from time to time when possible, give each other a good gust of air, feast upon each other until we

nearly die, and then return to our fast. Who can be sure
that if we lived together continuously we should not grow
tired of each other? There would be suspicions, jealousies
perhaps, leading to bitterness and quarrels. We should end
by continuing to see each other out of sheer obstinacy or
merely from habit—no longer from attraction, as now.
But no, I do not believe that. For you are too good, too
sweet, too devoted, to be like other women, so selfish and
sharp with the men they love."

"I think I said nothing to distress you, nor you anything
to me." The words look pathetic, as they lie there in so
early a note between lovers. And they are even more
pathetic than they seem, for they are false, and as Gustave
wrote them he knew it. The three weeks with Louise
Colet, which had sent him to work, had also taught him to
lie. Louise had indeed, in Mantes, said something to distress
him. Perfect as her flesh had been, the imperfection of her
spirit had betrayed itself to a degree which he shuddered
to think of, and in an utterance which eclipsed the most
petulant and vituperative of her complaints. By his side in
bed, she had passionately declared that she would "not
exchange her present happiness for all the fame of
Corneille." And that statement had driven a cold blast of
air into Gustave's entrails. He had made no reply. It had
almost stupefied him. It was the cause of the fits of abstraction which Louise had perceived.
  Fame! What is fame? The external sound of the pleasure
that art gives. What rational being would sacrifice a pin or
a shoestring for the fame of Corneille? But—to be
Corneille! To feel *one's self* Corneille! For that a rational
being would sacrifice a great deal, anything at all—including, with no hesitation whatever, lying in bed with a
mistress or a lover in a quiet hotel in Mantes. The poetess
who in Pradier's studio had declared her contempt for
literary pretenders, who had claimed to prefer men who
"admired her for her mind": fame was the supreme
sacrifice which occurred to her poor imagination! It was
embittering. Much tumbled down, that day at Mantes.
"You are too good, too sweet, too devoted to be . . .

selfish and sharp . . ." Why not write easy falsehoods like that, if they made things smoother—and since all perception of the truth was out of the question?

Back in Croisset, Flaubert, more certain than ever of what a normal life was, buried himself in his books. With Max gone he had no distractions. He saw only Louis Bouilhet, who continued to come week-ends. For a brief time after the satisfaction of Mantes, Louise's letters were peaceful and amiable; and then, when their tone not unexpectedly resumed its sharpness, Flaubert retorted, with a note of carelessness not present before: "Talk to me about something else, in the name of God, in the name of myself —since you love me—than of coming to Paris." The days grew shorter and colder. He changed his white summer dressing gown and trousers for a winter model of dark brown flannel, which made him look like the monk he felt himself to be. From Florence came a letter from Alfred, depressing in its impersonality and its references to "my wife." Added gloom came to Croisset in the person of Hamard, who, his mind now wavering, settled in a house near by and did nothing but drink, wandering in and out of the Flauberts', talking nonsense. From time to time came a letter from Max, containing some such injunctions as "Don't neglect the Breton history! What have you learned about the war between Jean de Montfort and Charles de Blois?" And Gustave would reply: "The difference between a *menhir* and a *cromlech:* is it quite clear in your mind?" Madame Flaubert still spent hours alone, in tears. Caroline's baby was nearly a year old. So the winter of study for *The Temptation of Saint Anthony* got under way.

5.

But Saint Anthony—the hermit who sat weaving baskets of palm-leaves in the Egyptian mountains, the story of whose life caused Saint Augustine to burst into tears, and on whose behalf young Flaubert was now for some reason consulting books on Persian poetry—this old anchorite did not, during the winter, completely monopolize the scene at Croisset. The poetess in Paris kept sending a perfect avalanche of letters to the house beside the Seine. She was quite oblivious of having unmasked herself in a literary way before the young purist with whom she was so infatuated; and he, despite the unmasking, continued to send as steady a stream of letters to her. Since a large part of the correspondence was devoted to disputes concerning Flaubert's persistent refusal to come to Paris or even to Mantes, it would seem at first glance that he might have saved considerable time and trouble by making slightly more frequent excursions to those places, rather than writing endless letters explaining why he could not or would not come. But Flaubert was a writer above all, and at the moment he was a writer who was not writing a book. Except on rare occasions, he infinitely preferred writing Louise letters to lying beside her in a hotel bed. For correspondence with an absentee afforded constant opportunity for the feeling and expression of longing and regret—and these were subtler, headier pleasures even than those of Mantes, and pleasures which Flaubert knew how to taste to the full. Such considerations, together with his studies and the conditions of his life at Croisset, explain why he wrote Louise so often and saw her so seldom, and why he was willing to expend so much ink in attempts to calm the jealousies and temper of a woman he had so quickly ceased to esteem.

Her jealousies about Maxime Du Camp, among others. Even before the trip to Mantes Flaubert had had to write reassuringly about Max: "Do not fear that I show your letters to anyone at all. Max knows only that I write to a woman in Paris. He sees me write to you every day, but as yet he does not even know your name." And as the autumn progressed Max's role increased.

September 17

"Du Camp left Monday evening for Maine. He will be back in a month, about the middle of October. If the Official should return to Paris before that time, how shall we arrange for you to receive my letters? I think that if I were to address them general delivery to some post-office, say the Bourse, under a name which we agreed upon, and if you were to tell them there in advance that you were expecting them, they would give them to you. That would be the best thing to do until Max's return. After that, everything will be easy. I will write to him at his address, marking the envelopes so that he knows they are for you. He will be careful to deliver them to you at hours when you are alone. You would like to see him, you say, poor darling? I too should like to have someone I could talk with about you, someone who knows you, who has been in your home, who could tell me things about you, if only details about your furniture or your maid."

September 20
"You asked the other day how I spent the time with Du Camp when he was here. For three whole days we plotted on the map a grand Asiatic tour that would last six years and cost 3,600,000 and some francs. We planned every-thing—the buying of horses, equipment, tents, clothing, and guns, the pay of our guides and servants, etc. We worked ourselves up to such a pitch that we became a little deranged on the subject. Max, particularly, was in a state of fever! Isn't that crazy? But what can I do if it is in my blood? Is it my fault?"

September 27
"Do not confide your secret to anyone, and as for your letters do not trust your dressmaker any more than any-body else. One is always betrayed by such people, just as by one's friends. Although it is an appalling walk to the post-office in the Rue Saint-Jacques, it is much better that way, much safer. You'll go every other day."

October 3
"Du Camp is still in the woods, riding and hunting wild boar. He will be back about the tenth, and will call on you at once."

October 7
"The servants at Du Camp's must certainly take you for a lady who is more than kindly disposed toward him. Be patient a little longer; you will see him early next week.

Tell me: if there is someone with you when he comes,
what pretext should he give for his visit? I want to write
him about that. And what is the best time of day?"

October 14

"I am happy that you like Max. He has a good, beautiful,
and generous nature—I realized that the first day I saw
him, and it has been a godsend to me. He and I are alike at
too many points in our spirits and our very constitutions
for either of us ever to fail the other. Love him as you
would love a brother of mine who might be living in Paris.
Trust him as you would trust me—more than me, for he
is worth more than I am: he is more heroic and possesses
far more delicacy than I.

"The nobility of his manner is a product of the nobility
of his heart. I am grosser, commoner, more wavering. You
must not believe what he says of me in a literary way.
Loving me as he does, he is doubtless partial, and then I
am in a way his master, for it was I who dragged him from
the mire of journalism in which he was about to be buried
for the rest of his life and inspired him with a love for
serious study. In two years he has made great progress. He
now has a charming talent and will soon have a beautiful
one. In him feeling and taste predominate; what he writes
is moving—one of his things I cannot read without tears.
And with all these good qualities he is modest as a child."

For a time all went well. Max wrote to Croisset that he
was devoted to this pretty woman who had started Flaubert working. He found her sad, he said, because of her
lover's determination not to emerge from his solitude, and
to soothe her he talked about Flaubert as much as he could,
in an attempt to make her feel that he was with them. He
did talk a great deal about what he was convinced was
his friend's literary genius, and Flaubert had to write to
Louise: "Do not place me on a pedestal, do not think of
me as superior to other men, do not adore me so much."
But before very long, Max made a mistake—it was easy,
he discovered, to make a mistake with Madame Colet—and
Flaubert bore the brunt of it.

• • •

October 24

"Why reproach me already for my wretched trip to Brittany? How do I even know that I am going to make it? The chances are overwhelmingly that it will come to nothing, like all my other plans great and small. Between now and ten months from now how many things could happen to prevent it! Illness of Max or of myself or of my mother or of anyone else down here, lack of money, etc. I had not said anything to you about it because I was far from sure that it would take place, and I still am far from sure."

Throughout November Max's letters were somewhat less expansive on the subject of Louise, and in December, when he came to spend a few days at Croisset, it was clear that she was on his mind. He was polite and complimentary whenever she was mentioned, but it was obvious that something about her was troubling him, and by insistent questioning Flaubert learned what it was. Louise, it appeared, had been not only assiduous, but acidulous, with Max. Not content with receiving him—and the letters he bore—at her apartment every other day, she had taken to visiting him at his apartment on the days in between, to make sure that no extra letters had arrived. And one day, when she had arrived at a most inconvenient moment—for his friend's mistress was not the only woman who came to Max's apartment—and when Max had been obliged to tell his servant to say she could not possibly come in, she had gone off in a rage and had written Max a note such as he had never before received—or expected to receive—from anyone. He had not seen her since, and had been sending Flaubert's letters to the Rue de la Fontaine-Saint-Georges by his servant.

Flaubert was embarrassed, but he could not pretend to be surprised; and for the first time he began to talk with Max about Louise Colet. To excuse her conduct as best he might, he related some of the difficulties amid which she lived. He confidentially told Max about Monsieur Colet, Monsieur Cousin, Louise's want of money, and the like, and he emphasized the laudable industry, energy, and elevation of her life. What was his astonishment, however, to discover that Max was quite familiar with all these details, far more familiar with a good many than he himself, and able to correct some and supply others! Alarmed, for Flaubert's sake, by the note he had received, Max had begun to make inquiries about Louise from the people on the fringes of literature with whom he had once associated, and he confessed that he would not be doing his duty as a friend if he did not offer, at least, to repeat to Flaubert some of the information he had secured. Should he continue?

Flaubert begged him to do so, and with the best countenance he could muster listened to the tale Max had to tell.

In the first place, Max began, Madame Colet's winning of the Academy prize for her poem *"Le Château de Versailles"* had been the subject of considerable amusement and indignation at the time, for quite contrary to what she herself now declared, she had, everyone knew quite well, been more than acquainted with Monsieur Cousin at the moment of writing the poem, and everyone knew that it had been his influence that had made the prize fall where it did. Furthermore, under mysterious circumstances the amount of the prize that year had been doubled, *after* it had been awarded! And her second winning of the prize had been accomplished in the same manner. It was Monsieur Cousin who had presented her to Madame Récamier. Close inspection of the preface to *Fleurs du Midi,* her first collection of verse, would reveal that the "laudatory letters from Chateaubriand" which she had mentioned to Flaubert were in reality the great man's politely worded refusals of Louise's request that he accept the dedication of her book, and had been placed in the preface without his permission or knowledge.

Madame Colet's poverty, Max declared, existed merely in her imagination. Monsieur Colet received not only an excellent salary at the Conservatory, where his rank and pay had both been raised at the suggestion of Monsieur Cousin, but also a quite unjustified pension from the Ministry of Public Instruction, of which Monsieur Cousin had formerly been head. And Madame Colet herself was in receipt of a generous pension, many times renewed and increased, from the same source. Madame Colet was extravagant and entertained lavishly; if she was in financial difficulties she had only herself to blame; and the Ministry, with which Monsieur Cousin was no longer connected, was getting decidedly tired of her incessant requests for still further awards.

And as to Monsieur Cousin's "mysterious" and "inexplicable" behaviour in breaking off his more intimate relations with Louise, the philosopher had once been heard to remark: "I find that instead of a dove I love a lioness," and Max was convinced that the break was only Monsieur Cousin's first step in the process of dissolving the relationship entirely. Plato was acting with prudence. His daily visits to the Rue de la Fontaine-Saint-Georges probably had a double motivation: a concern for his daughter—to whose support he made generous contributions—and a fear (for the author of *Du Vrai, du Beau et du Bien* was known to be a timid man) that if he broke with Louise too abruptly she might act toward him as she had acted toward Alphonse Karr.

Alphonse Karr? Flaubert knew the name—it belonged to a trivial, often-heard-of literary man—but he was ignorant of its connexion with Louise Colet's, and begged Max to explain. Max did, producing documents, and begging Flaubert once more to remember that he was revealing all these details, painful as he realized they must be, solely for friendship's sake.

In 1839, Max related, while he and Flaubert were still in college, Alphonse Karr had started a miniature monthly magazine, called *Les Guêpes—The Wasps*—to be devoted to minor matters of literature, wit, and society. "We are going to laugh together," Karr had said in his foreword to the first number, "at a lot of people who would like to be taken seriously, and we are going to enjoy measuring the smallness of great men and of great things." In an issue early in 1840, Karr mentioned—as though in passing—that he had heard that a lady whom he knew only by reputation, "the poetess Louise Colet, *née* Revoil," had refused to be presented to him at a literary gathering, and he wondered why. Whether or not Louise recognized this as a warning, she ignored it, and in the issue of *Les Guêpes* for June of that year appeared an item which caused a stir, and which Max allowed Flaubert to read for himself:

"Mademoiselle Revoil, after several years' union with Monsieur Colet, has finally received heaven's blessing on her marriage, and is on the point of presenting the world with something other than an alexandrine. When the venerable minister of public instruction learned this news he took a noble view of his duties toward literature. He did for Madame Colet what he would doubtless do for any other woman of letters. He surrounded her with care and attentions. He allowed her to go out only in his carriage. At a dinner at the ———s', tired and eager to leave early, he none the less waited several hours for the interesting poetess to decide to take her departure, so that he might see her to her home. He recently went to Nanterre in search of a nurse for the child of letters that is soon to see the day, and it is hoped that he will not refuse to be its godfather. It is things like this that the newspapers—which should seize on them with gratitude—ignore and condemn to oblivion."

And *Les Guêpes* for July contained the sequel, entitled "Murderous Attempt of June Fifteenth":

"On the 15th of June, as I was leaving my home in the Rue de la Tour d'Auvergne, I noticed a woman walking along the opposite sidewalk. She was still young and quite handsome, although her beauty was rather massive and . . . I will not write the other word that occurs to me. When she arrived exactly opposite me she crossed the street, came straight up to me, and said: 'Are you not Monsieur Karr? I want to speak to you a moment.' I bowed and pointed to the door, which was still open, but she asked me to go first, to show her the way. Bowing again, I obeyed. My servant was out, and as I bent over to ask the concierge for the key of my apartment my unknown friend suddenly drew a long knife which had been hidden in her parasol and struck me with it in the back. The concierge screamed, but with a single movement I had warded off the blow and seized the weapon. I ordered the concierge to do nothing to prevent the woman from taking her departure, and saying: 'Madame, you will allow me not to prolong our conversation,' I bowed and entered the house. As I climbed the stairs I heard her exclaim: 'It can't be possible! He must wear a steel vest!'

"A friend arrived a few moments later, and showing him the knife I said: 'I am certainly right in thinking that women of letters are very poor housekeepers. Here is one who has just spoiled her set of a dozen table knives.' 'You're mistaken,' he said, 'this is a kitchen carving knife.'

"My friend Dr. Lebatard, who came to see if any damage had been done, told me that the wound might have been very dangerous, and that I should certainly have been badly stabbed if the lady had struck straight instead of lifting her hand high above her head like a tragic actress, doubtless foreseeing the engraving which could be made of the affair. Here is a portrait of the knife, which I accuse of being a trifle vulgar. Its honest dimensions are: length, 38 centimetres; width of blade, 2½ centimetres. It is at present hanging in my study with my pictures and statuettes, with this inscription: 'Given me by Madame Colet (in the back), June 15, 1840.' "

The day after the event, Max said, Monsieur Karr received two visits—one from the police, to whom he refused to talk, and one from the critic Sainte-Beuve, who as Monsieur Cousin's representative asked what Monsieur Karr intended to do. The answer was: "Nothing whatever," and Monsieur Cousin accepted it at once.

Louise herself, however, had the last word, in a letter to a newspaper:

"The blow fell at a moment that was particularly tender and serene. I was alone, working on the layette of my child. On first reading I was made giddy; then I uttered a terrible cry—a call for help to others, or, if others were lacking, to myself. No matter by whose agency, I knew I must procure the death of that man.

"My husband arrived during this supreme anguish, but in him I found only bewilderment, grief, and weakness. I say weakness, not cowardliness, for on two separate occasions I had been witness to my husband's courage. He was not afraid of that man, but considered him unworthy of a duel.

"Bursting with contempt, he wrote a letter into which he poured all his tenderness for me, and which he wished to send to the newspapers. I forbade it, however, and have kept the letter as a proof of the love of a man who did not know how to protect a woman. It was not my place to force him to fight!

"For me the night was a long sleeplessness and a dull stupor—apparent stupor, that is, for the blood of my revolutionary grandfather and the blood of his daughter, my proud and sainted mother, was boiling within me, and I heard the child in my bosom cry out: 'That man must die!' One does not refute an insult. To the man who attempts to dishonour, there is but one reply: death.

"I waited for daylight, counting the hours. When I was alone, I made my preparations. I chose for my arm a kitchen knife, for to have chosen an elegant weapon would have seemed to me theatrical; I thought only of acting with simplicity, as is fitting in a great sorrow.

"My home was not far from that of the man whom I meant to kill. Resolutely, I made my way thither. I found him at his door, in shirtsleeves. I uttered only these words: 'I must speak to you.' He urged me to enter, and as he bent toward the concierge's lodge I struck him in the loins. A few drops of blood spurted out; the knife had slipped. Uneasy over his infamies, he wore, I have heard, a kind of cuirass. He turned quickly and disarmed me.

"He writes: 'She was quite handsome, although her beauty was rather massive.' How atrocious! How worthy the remark of that man's withered soul! I was massive like any mother ready to bear her child! I tottered home, leaning against the walls of the houses to keep from falling.

"The frightful illness which followed was like a wall raised between the world and myself. Those who loved me and struggled to save my life stood guard over me; they kept from me all news, particularly all comment by the columnists, whether ironic or benevolent. When I was free to make inquiries, I no longer wished to do so: a more powerful preoccuptaion, a soothing love, filled my days and my heart. I was enveloped in the innocence of my lovely child."

There was little that Flaubert could reply to Max's reports on Louise, and, jolted though he might be, one who had received from her the letters that Flaubert had re-

ceived, and who had heard her speak of the *fame* of Corneille, could scarcely disbelieve them. And when Max
pointed out that the attempt on the life of the wretched
Karr was perhaps one of the reasons for Monsieur Cousin's
present cautious behaviour, reminding him that Louise
was the author of a laudatory poem on Charlotte Corday,
Flaubert thought he was probably right, and that it was the
reason for another person's peculiar behaviour also. The
great respect that Pradier—that despoiler of women—always evidenced toward Sapho, that respect which had
pleased him so but about which he had so often wondered,
was that, too, not clearly explained now? One question
remained: why had Pradier introduced him to such a
woman as that? Evidently he thought Flaubert could be
trusted to look after himself! And, as it happened, Pradier
was quite right. Max was astonished at the calmness with
which his friend thanked him for his disclosures, and
they did not cause Flaubert to change his tone toward the
lady in the slightest. "Max and I often speak of you," he
wrote to Louise a few days later. "I am always afraid my
mother will hear us, for one evening my brother-in-law
came out of her room, which is next to mine, and to my
dismay repeated to us almost word for word the conversation we had been having. Fortunately," he added, perhaps
with a smile, "we were not talking about you at that moment."

Back in Paris, Max again did not see Louise, and to her
annoyance continued to send Flaubert's letters by the
servant who had refused her admittance. Though there
was no change in Flaubert's behaviour, her suspicions concerning Max became ever stronger. She sensed that there
was something in the wind; she told Flaubert she was
sure he had been influenced against her during Max's visit,
that he had read Max the letters in which she had spoken
unfavourably of him. During the winter her letters became
more and more hysterical in their denunciation of Max,
and Flaubert was able to fight only feebly against the
strength of her intuition.

"You are falling into that mania of parents, who, seeking an explanation for their son's pranks, invariably think
that he is under the influence of some bad boy whom they

know—a supposition which is generally completely unrelated to the facts of the case. Always Du Camp! Eternally
Du Camp! That is becoming a chronic malady with you.
Frankly, you take me for an imbecile. Do you think I
act only with Max's permission? If you do, let me tell you
first that he never reads your letters when he is here—
and, by the way, he has not been here for some time—and
second that I still preserve a little of my own free
will. . . ."

Louise definitely hated Max. At Flaubert's repeated request, her attacks ceased for a time, but poor Max, conscious now of the jealousy of the mistress as well as of the
mother, did not visit Croisset as often as he and Gustave
would have enjoyed.

Another cause for disagreement was furnished by a lady
whom Flaubert had not seen for some time.

"You want me to send you something about ourselves,"
he wrote to Louise at the beginning of the second week of
their relationship. "Well, here is a page I wrote two years
ago—a fragment of a letter to a friend:

" 'From her eyes, fixed and unmoving, there seemed to
come a kind of liquid light, making them appear larger
than in life. Her bare shoulders (for the bodice of her
dress was unfastened, and fell away from her body) were
of a rosy pallor, smooth and firm as marble; her blue
veins traced patterns in her warm flesh, and her pulsating
breast rose and fell, with a stifled breathing which filled
me with emotion. That seemed to last a century: the entire
world was nonexistent. I saw nothing but the pupils of her
eyes, which grew larger and larger, and heard nothing but
her breathing, which made the only slight sound in the utter silence which surrounded us. Then I approached her and
kissed her eyes. They were warm and sweet. She looked at
me, astonished. "Is it possible that you love me?" she
whispered. "Is it possible?" I made no answer, but held
her in my arms, feeling her heart beating against
me. . . .' "

And when this extraordinary present was promptly
complained of he replied:

"You ask me whether the few lines I sent you were writ-

ten for you; you would like very much to know for whom
they were written. Jealous! They were written for no one,
like everything I write. I have always forbidden myself to
put anything of myself into my works—and yet I have put
a great deal. I have always tried not to subordinate art to
the satisfaction of one isolated personality. I have written
tender pages without feeling love, boiling pages with no
fire in my blood. I have imagined, remembered, and combined. What you read is not the recollection of anything."

But it was, of course. It was an excerpt from one of the
letters he had written to Alfred from Marseille and of
which he had taken copies when writing *Novembre;*
Louise knew very well that such a scene was more remembrance than imagination.

"You believe that another woman is still in my heart,"
he replied to her protests, "that she has remained there, and
shines so brightly that you have only passed in her shadow.
Oh, no! No! Be convinced, once and for all. You often
tell me that I am cynically frank, so be logical: believe it,
this frankness. That story is old, very old, almost forgotten
—I have scarcely a remembrance of it; it even seems to me
that it took place in the soul of another man."

The matter might easily have ended there. Louise appeared to be appeased, merely asked that when he next
came to Paris he should bring the manuscript of *Novembre*
with him and read it to her, and made no further protests.

But a little later, toward the end of September, one of
his letters contained a request. "By the way—while I
think of it, ask your cousin, since he has lived in Cayenne,
to give me news of two people: Monsieur Brache and
Madame Foucaud de Lenglade." Louise secured the information, and when she characteristically inquired who
this Madame Foucaud was, Flaubert quite calmly replied
that she was the young woman of whom they had recently
spoken, and who had moved, he had heard, from Marseille
to Cayenne.

"Is your cousin a dependable man," he inquired, "to
whom one could confide a letter with the certainty that it
would be delivered? For I should like to write to Madame
Foucaud.

"Do not be jealous of this old acquaintance. You shall

read the letter, if you like—on the condition that you promise not to tear it up. Louise, if I thought of you as a commonplace woman I should not say all this to you. But what displeases you, perhaps, is exactly that—that I treat you as a man, not as a woman. Try to use a little understanding in the relations that exist between us. I should like to make of you something entirely apart—neither friend nor mistress. Each of those categories is too restricted, too exclusive—one doesn't love a friend sufficiently, and with a mistress one is too stupid. It is the intermediate term that I am seeking, the essence of these two sentiments conjoined. What I want, in short, is that, like a new kind of hermaphrodite, you give me with your body all the joys of the flesh and with your spirit all those of the soul. Will you understand this? I fear it is not clear."

Clear or not, Louise did not like it; it was bad, and unquestionably clear was her reply. Even Flaubert's writing powers were put to the test. He besought her to listen to him.

September 30

"About ten years ago we were all at Le Havre one vacation. My father learned that a woman who had been his mistress when he was seventeen was living there with her son, and he made up his mind to go to see her. He did not do as many bourgeois would have done—he did not hide his action: he was too superior a man for that. My mother and we three children stood waiting for him below, in the street. The visit lasted almost an hour. Do you think my mother was jealous, or felt the slightest rancour? No. And yet she loved my father, loved him as deeply as any woman has ever loved a man—and not only when they were young, but up until the last day they were together, after thirty-five years of marriage.

"So, why do you take offence in advance at a token of remembrance that I intend to send to Madame Foucaud? I do more than my father did—I allow you to be a third in our conversation, which takes place across the Atlantic. Yes, I *want* you to read my letter, if I do write one and if you can understand in advance the feeling that makes me write it. You say you consider the thing shows a lack

of delicacy toward you. I should say the opposite—it
seems to me a mark of confidence far from usual. I entrust
you with my entire past! I say to you: 'See—this is the
person I *did* love, and now it is you whom I *do* love.' And
that hurts you! You're enough to make anyone lose his
mind!"

October 3
"I will not mention the worthy Madame Foucaud again,
since the subject upsets you. You will do as you like about
it."

October 4
"Here is the letter for Madame Foucaud. I should like to
be there beside you, to wipe away with a kiss each little
frown that will appear on your forehead as you read it,
for I am afraid that you will be upset again, my darling.
In writing to this woman, I have obeyed an impulse. Have
I done right? I have no idea. I am a little like Montaigne:
'I cannot suffer contradiction or argument within me.' The
idea came to me, I gave in to it, and that is all. If you do
not reproach me, I shall have done right; if you do,
wrong. Tell me frankly, my love, the effect the letter has
on you. I wrote it just now, very quickly. In rereading it,
I see that it has a rather free-and-easy air; the whole thing
is rather dashing, I think. The woman did not have a very
great intelligence, but that was not what I asked of her.
Apart from the purely mythological moments I had nothing to say to her. At the end of a week, had we lived
together, I should have been dead with boredom. Everybody is not like you, you know, ever able to exert attraction by means of new and hidden charms whose existence
has never been suspected."

October 7
"Yes, I suppose it is quite possible, as you prophesy in
your letter, that if Madame Foucaud is in need of money
she may ask me for some. And if I have some when she
asks for it, I will certainly give it to her."

· · ·

October 8

"You say you found my letter to Madame Foucaud a little tender? I should never have thought that. On the contrary, it seems to me the whole thing was light, gallant, parts of it even verging on the insolent.

"You are convinced that I loved this woman seriously. That is not true. Only, when I was writing to her, with the faculty I have of being stirred when I hold a pen, I took my subject seriously—but *only when I was writing*. Many things which leave me cold when I see them or when others speak of them, enrapture me or irritate me or hurt me if *I* speak of them, or especially if I write about them. That is one of the effects of my mountebank nature."

This fluency was finally too much for Louise, and she retired exhausted from the combat. The letter was sent to Cayenne, and Flaubert received no reply. When he came to Paris he forgot his promise to bring the manuscript of *Novembre*, and listened to some reproaches on that score; then, when he came again, he did bring it, and read it to Louise. She wept a little at the lush, romantic descriptions of the love of the virgin boy of nineteen and the beautiful older woman, and she said she found it equal to Chateaubriand's *René*. Far from arousing the author's gratitude, however, this statement caused him to ask her, with some sharpness, kindly not to commit such sacrilege. *René* was one of his and Alfred's favourite books, and nothing was to be found its equal.

The irritation caused Louise by the episode of Madame Foucaud was scarcely mitigated by the manner in which Flaubert received a memento she had sent him about a week after the meeting in Mantes. On the first page of a tiny notebook, exquisitely bound in blue morocco, she had written: "Memories of a day at Mantes, Wednesday the ninth and Thursday the tenth of September." On the next page was an excerpt from one of Flaubert's own letters describing the perfection of the day, and then followed a long descriptive and narrative poem, which reproduced and glorified their hours together down to the last thrilling detail. At the end of the little book Louise had added:

"I have written these verses for you alone, and I wish they were better, both as to sentiment and movement, so that they might please you more. In a year, if you still love me, if the memory of Mantes does not find you indifferent, I will work over line by line this poem I have written for you and try to make it worthier of you."

Flaubert pretended to be delighted with the present, but he was not very convincing in his remarks. Concerning one or two lines, particularly, Louise found his comments offensive—the unfortunate line in which she sang the crayfish they had eaten for dinner as the product of the Seine which flowed past the Hôtel du Grand Cerf, and that in which she described her passionate young lover as "an untamed buffalo from the deserts of America."

If such poetry as that made him laugh, he should certainly have hidden his laughter from the poetess. But he did not, and as a result of such behaviour toward such a mistress he found, as the months passed, that scarcely one of his actions was allowed to pass uncriticized.

During their first days together in Paris, Louise had reproachfully declined Flaubert's offer of a bracelet, saying that a present from him under such circumstances would make her feel like a prostitute. His failure to insist, however, and his failure ever to offer her a present again, she found even more blameworthy. She herself was lavish with gifts—very personal gifts. A pair of her slippers, locks of her hair, a pair of her mittens, two portraits of herself, copies of all her books, the poem on Mantes, innumerable manuscript verses, and a cigar-holder encrusted with a jewel which belonged to her mother and bore the words "*Amor nel Cor*": all came to Croisset, and finally Flaubert had to beg her to send nothing more, as the drawers of his table were becoming crowded and he feared discovery.

Even at New Year's he held to his policy.

"It is customary to make a present to those one loves. I look about me to find something to send you, something which is mine. I find nothing. So, my dear Louise, accept this—a kiss, from my very heart, in which I put my entire being and in which I take you in your entirety. I place it here, at the bottom of my letter: take it."

She took it angrily.

"Why do you reproach me with having wished to give you a bracelet after our first night and not having sent it to you, instead, for New Year's? The reason is quite simple: I had some money that day, I have none now: that is all there is to it."

A little later, when she wrote suggesting that he give her a "silken Turkish belt," which he said he had just received from a travelling school-friend, he sent it, pretending he had intended to do so all along; but apart from that, Louise had to content herself with his wish that he could buy and keep for themselves alone the carriage in which they had first driven in the Bois, and with the single bouquet of flowers he gave her on each of their rare meetings. She dried them, labelled them—"Mantes, September 10"; "Bois de Boulogne, December 1"—and put them away in a box. She was not content, and was all the more piqued by his readiness to send money to the lady in Cayenne.

She was enraged by a eulogy of solitude which he wrote on the arrival of a new armchair from Paris, in which he said he expected to spend many "long, shut-in hours . . . silent evenings in the light of the lamp, watching the fire and listening to the blowing of the wind." "Is it possible that you reproach me even for my innocent affection for an armchair?" he wrote back, astonished. "If I told you about my shoes, I think you would be jealous of them."

The picture of the life at Croisset was the most intolerable of all. Realizing that Louise had none of the understanding of his need for solitude that she had claimed to have in Paris, Flaubert ignored that aspect of the question almost entirely, and in response to her commands and beseechings that he join her, or that he allow her to join him, described the physical conditions that made it impossible. As a result, during the winter Louise secured a vivid picture of the house she was not allowed to visit and of the woman who kept her lover from visiting her. She grew to hate all mention of Croisset, and she grew to hate Madame Flaubert as she hated Max. It was not as though she could believe that the lady was one of those mothers

so brilliant and charming that they suffice for their sons,
a great beauty or wit or intellect, someone whom she
could consider a worthy rival. No—all Flaubert said
about her led Louise to think of her as a person distinguished only by her neuroticism and her incessant sadness,
and this made Flaubert's refusal to leave all the more
perverse, and accentuated in him another quality Louise
found increasingly unpleasant: his taste for death and
decay. For Louise had no suspicion that her lover was a
disciple of "a Greek of the late empire," and that most of
his qualities which she found inexplicable or perverse were,
so to speak, late-Grecian legacies.

The picture grew as the winter advanced.

"If I cannot come to Paris as you desire, it is because I
must stay here. My mother needs me; my slightest absence
distresses her. Her sorrow makes me the victim of a
thousand unimaginable tyrannies. What would present no
problem at all to some people, presents an insoluble one to
me. I cannot refuse someone who begs me for something
with a grief-stricken face and tears in her eyes. I am weak
as a child and I give in, because I do not like reproaches
or beseechings and sighs.

"In order to come to Paris I should need some pretext,
and what could it be? The second time I should need another one, and so on. Since I am now the only thing that
binds my mother to life, she spends the entire day racking
her brain for possible misfortunes and accidents that might
befall me. When I need something I never ring for a servant, because if I do I immediately hear my mother running
breathlessly up the stairs to see if I have an attack, etc.
I assure you that if I could not only go to Paris, but live
there with you—near you, at least—I should do it: but,
alas!"

"Yesterday my mother was in my room while I was
dressing, holding the baby in her arms. When your letter
arrived, she took it, looked at the handwriting, and said
half in fun as though she were addressing the baby and
half seriously to herself: 'I should love to know what is
inside.' I gave a silly laugh, trying to produce a humorous
effect, to prevent her from having any suspicion of any-

thing serious. I don't know whether she suspects or not. It is possible, for the never-failing regularity of the postman these days is something to be marvelled at."

"As for your coming here, do not think of it! The village consists of a dozen houses on the quay; there is no place where we could see each other."

"You always tell me of your sorrows, my dear Louise, and I believe you, for I have seen proof of them. Next to not being able to live with the persons one loves, having to live with a person one despises is the saddest thing in life. I feel your sorrow in myself, which is the best proof of all. But there is another sorrow which I see, too, a sorrow which is always with me here at Croisset. This sorrow never complains, at moments it even smiles, and beside it yours, great though it is, can never be anything but a fleabite beside a first-degree burn, or a momentary spasm beside a death-struggle. The two women whom I love best in the world control my heart as though with a double bit: they pull me this way and that by their love and their sorrow. Pardon me if what I say offends you. I no longer know what to say to you, and hesitate to say anything. When I speak to you I am afraid of making you weep, and when I touch you I am afraid of hurting you. But you must know this: my life is tied to another life, and will be as long as that other life lasts."

"If you knew what my life really is! When I come down in the evening after eight hours of work, my head full of what I have read or written, preoccupied and often irritable, I sit down at the dinner table opposite my mother, who sighs at the sight of the empty chairs and the baby who cries or screams. Often my mother has nervous attacks or hallucinations.

"My brother and his wife act just about as indelicately as they can. We bore them—there is nothing surprising in that—and they leave us to ourselves. They are right, I suppose. And finally, my brother-in-law has just returned unexpectedly from England, in a deplorable mental state. He plays with his child so violently that I fear some day he will kill her, and my mother is in perpetual anguish, so that I must always be there—with him, with her, with them all."

"Everything is going badly here. My niece is sick. She has vomiting spells, like her grandfather, like her mother—perhaps she will go the same way as they. I am prepared for it. This child will not live to be very old, I fear.

"Though we say nothing to anyone, my mother and I are most disturbed over the state of my brother-in-law. Grief has so shattered him that we think he is going mad. His mind cannot last much longer.

"I am afraid all this will end badly."

That was the provincial hole which Flaubert preferred to Paris, and the life which he preferred to life at her side! Part of the time she could not believe that that *was* the life he led; a young man does not neglect a pretty woman for an existence of that kind; a young literary man does not choose it in preference to a Paris salon. She did not know which she ought to consider more outrageous—to be sure that he did live in that way, or to be convinced that he was lying. When she told him her suspicions, however, he wrote back emphatically:

"Be satisfied on one point: I do not 'press another woman in my arms' here in Croisset, as you put it. None. I can live without women for years on end. It is a long time since I made a practice of spending New Year's Eve in a brothel, to inaugurate the year, and even when I did it, it was more of an affectation than a real pleasure."

The wording of the assurance was almost as displeasing as the suspicion it was aimed to dissipate.

"Come, my pet," he wrote a few days later. "You are hurt again, this time at what I said about New Year's Eve. I said it simply to amuse you—I am far from perspicacious with you, it would seem."

Perspicacious! His inability—or his unwillingness, for it seemed to Louise at times that it was impossible for any-one to be as tactless as Flaubert from pure naïveté—to put himself in the place of the person to whom he was writing was fantastic. At any time, about anything, Flau-

bert might be expected to write the most unbounded
enormities. His letters swarmed with them.

He was tantalizing:

"What joy it would be now to be alone together! Alone
in a cosy room, well shut in, curtains drawn, door bolted,
a fire blazing; and to be in bed, side by side, one against
the other, pressing against each other, feeling each other,
our limbs interlaced, arms around each other, mouth on
mouth, breast against breast."

He was brutal:

"You want to know whether I love you? Yes, I do, as
much as I *can* love. By that I mean that for me love is not
the first thing in life, but the second. It is like a bed in
which one lies to relax the heart. But one doesn't stay in
bed all day!"

"Women do not understand that it is possible to love on
different levels; they talk a great deal about the soul, but
it is the body with which they are most deeply concerned,
for they see all of love called into play in the bodily act.
A man can adore a woman and yet sleep every night in a
brothel, or have—and even love—another mistress. Come,
now, don't scowl! I am not alluding to myself. I live like
a monk!"

"I had conceived an idea of love entirely different from
yours. I thought it was something independent of everything—even of the person who inspired it. Absence, outrage, infamy—all these do not matter. When people are
in love, they can go ten years without seeing each other
and without suffering as a consequence." ("What can I
possibly think of this?" Louise wrote helplessly in the
margin opposite that last sentence.)

He was just plain tactless:

"It gave you pleasure, poor angel, the little bouquet I
sent you? It was not I who had the idea of slipping those
symbolic flowers into my letter, for I did not know their
symbolism. It was Du Camp who taught me it and advised
me to make use of it."

When she told him that she could not work or enjoy her
friends, for thinking of him, he pushed the tribute aside
and urged her to resume her normal life; when she wrote

that she found Plato's daily visits almost unbearable, he urged her to treat him kindly and to learn all she could from him, for he was a man of taste. Clearly, Flaubert was incorrigible. Those of his compliments and tendernesses which were at once properly worded and seemingly spontaneous could be counted on the fingers of one hand:

"Since knowing you, I have been in perfect health. You have been my doctor."

"Your image is always between my eyes and the lines they are reading—like a faint mist, one of those floating, lifting morning mists all luminous, airy, and rosy."

"Now I am going to hasten to read a folio which will initiate me in the composition of talismans. If I find one that will make me invisible, I will steal to the Rue de la Fontaine-Saint-Georges, slip in, and kiss you under the very beard of the Official."

There were a few like that, and Louise found herself seizing for meagre enjoyment on the equally few passages in which, though she herself was not mentioned, there were at least no blunders and which gave hints of less unattractive aspects of life at Croisset:

"The sky is clear, the moon brilliant. I hear sailors singing on the river as they lift anchor and make ready to leave on the incoming tide."

"The moonlight is brilliant on the green lawn; the sky is blue, flecked with stars."

That was scarcely enough for Louise. The passion of the August letters was decidedly absent from those of the fall and winter, and she was sure she knew the reason why: her lover did not see her enough. In a sense she was right. Even Flaubert, with all his power to evoke past and future emotions, could not write letters like his first—annoying as parts of even those had been—during separations as long as these. But the thing was less simple than Louise knew.

For if Flaubert continued to outrage Louise, Louise continued to shock Flaubert, and this was more serious for the life of their relationship.

Even after the disillusioning at Mantes, he was quite willing to pay the price of her temper for the privilege of being able to work alone in Croisset, bask at a distance in the warmth of her infatuation, see her when he needed to, and correspond with her at length. After a day of study he enjoyed nothing more than putting down more or less haphazardly on paper some of the thousand ideas that swarmed in his head—literary ideas, mostly—and it was of these ideas, in addition to stormy discussions of the difficulties between them, that the letters to Louise were compounded. The writing of such letters sharpened his ideas. Max Du Camp was a gay and sympathetic friend, and Louis Bouilhet was at Croisset to talk to on Saturdays and Sundays, but it was so far only in his intimacy with a woman—idiosyncratic though it was and despite all the difficulties that this particular woman raised—that Flaubert found again the complete ease and benefit of full expression that he had so rapturously enjoyed with Alfred Le Poittevin. If Alfred had not married, Louise would have received even less attention, for Alfred was always the person Flaubert loved most in the world—and he was a person whom he scarcely ever mentioned to Louise. Alfred had come back from Italy and was living in Paris, and this was another reason for Flaubert's infrequent visits to the city. The few times he did go, during the winter, he saw Louise and he saw Alfred, and the two contrasts—that between the past and the present in Alfred, and between Alfred and Louise—he found dispiriting.

No, it was not Louise's temper which shocked Flaubert and did most to undermine their relationship. Rather, it was Louise's literary spirit, or lack of it—her worship of the *fame* of Corneille, in diversified form—which gradually destroyed the very *raison d'être* of Flaubert's letters to her, and made her temper and her hypocrisies less and less worth tolerating. It was when Flaubert wrote about the things closest to his heart that Louise found his letters least satisfactory.

She reproached him for writing at such length of Shakespeare rather than of themselves, for talking constantly about art with her as he would "with anyone at all." "You regard that subject as secondary," he retorted, "as something amusing, between politics and the news? Not I!" When he assured her that a line of verse could cause him more joy or more anguish than any living person, she was irritated; she wrote him a poem called *"L'Art et l'Amour,"* in which she praised some *tableaux vivants* she had recently seen, declaring that she infinitely preferred them, because they were alive, to the pictures by Rubens and Titian and Raphael from which they were copied. He learned that he was wrong to spend all his time with his books and not to read the newspapers. "But politics bore me to extinction, and I have a profound feeling of disgust for the ephemeral, the passing, that which is important today and will not be tomorrow."

She kept urging him to publish something right away, to arrive, mocking him for his absurd excess of literary scrupulousness.

"Having neither cleverness, which attains success, nor genius, which conquers glory, I have condemned myself to write for myself alone, for my own personal amusement, the way one smokes or rides. It is almost certain that I shall never print a line, and my nephews will probably make three-cornered hats for their grandchildren out of the oriental tales, dramas, mysteries, and other nonsense that I write out very seriously on fine white paper."

"If I do appear in print some day," he wrote at another time, "it will be an appearance in full armour."

She was a poetess, and yet she admired Béranger, the patriot versifier who made Alfred groan and of whom Louis Bouilhet made such excellent fun.

"For my own personal consumption I like the geniuses who are a little less agreeable to the touch, more disdainful of the people, more withdrawn, more arrogant in their manners and their tastes; or the only man who can take the place of all others—my adored Shakespeare, whom I am going to take up again."

"I have to scold you for something which shocks and scandalizes me—the little concern you have for art these days. If your lack of concern were for glory, I should approve, but for art, the only thing true and good in life! You lump with the beautiful a lot of extraneous matters—the useful, the agreeable, etc. Tell the philosopher to explain to you the idea of pure beauty as he expounded it in his treatise, and as I conceive it; we will speak of it again the next time."

She said Flaubert read too much, and had no interest in causes.

"It is the mania of the present day," he replied; "writers blush for their trade. Simply to write verses or a novel, carve marble—ah, what is the use of that? It was all very well in times past, when the social mission of the poet did not exist. But now every work has to have its moral significance: a sonnet must have a philosophical implication; a play must rap the fingers of a king; a watercolour must soften the manners of the times. . . ."

Thus the picture of life at Croisset on the one hand, and the literary *gaffes* on the other, combined to turn their correspondence into a battlefield and eventually to destroy it. During the winter Flaubert accomplished most of his reading for *The Temptation of Saint Anthony*, but both to him and to Louise it was a winter of combat and disappointment. Where, wondered Louise, was Flaubert's passion of the first few days? Where, wondered Flaubert, was that literary understanding and sincerity that had so enchanted him in Paris?

As early as December Louise declared that she could not go on—a relationship which consisted of absence and of acrimonious or impersonal letters was absurd—and Flaubert consented to break everything off:

"Since you insist, I agree. Since you find nothing more to say to me, frankness demands that I confess that I can find nothing more to say to you, having exhausted all possible means of making you understand the one thing which for five long months you have persisted in not even wanting to understand. Why have you wanted to encroach upon a life which does not belong to me, and change my whole existence to satisfy your desires? I love you as much as I ever did, but I love you in *my* nature. Forget me entirely. Do not write me at all. I will never forget you, and in ten years you will find me if you call me.

"Adieu. I repeat: 'Adieu'—adding nothing more, since now you say you want no more kisses at the bottom of my letters. They revolt you, you say. They are 'the passing remembrance of an instant of physical enjoyment.' Agreed."

His easy agreement infuriated her; far from ceasing to write, she wrote more wildly, and he retorted:

"It is impossible for me to continue any longer a correspondence which is becoming epileptic. Change it, I beg. If I had betrayed you, exposed you, sold your letters, you could not write me things more atrocious or more distressing.

"What have I done, good God? What have I done? You treat me like a peasant and a miser. If despite the love that binds you to my sorry person my character wounds you too much, leave me. If you feel that is impossible, accept me from now on as I am.

"Do you know what offends me in you? It is your mania for comparing yourself to a prostitute, for talking incessantly of purity and sacrifice, or morality, of your scorn for the senses. . . .

"I will come to Paris when Pradier asks me to—in six weeks, for one day. After that, I don't know when. I lack the time, the money, and a pretext."

At New Year's, there were the recriminations concerning the lack of a present, and during the early months of 1847 the correspondence became increasingly "epileptic." Louise's letters all claimed to be letters of final adieu. Flaubert always answered them, because there was always some injustice, or some slight to literature, which he felt he could not let pass, and she quickly wrote him again, unwilling that he should have the last word, and reproaching him for not letting them forget each other.

In February he had to spend a day in Paris on business, and wrote her that he would be there, allowing her to choose whether or not they should meet. She came to his hotel; there was a violent scene; he had visions of suffering the fate of Alphonse Karr; but fortunately her screams, sobs, and vituperations brought the staff to their door; and on his return to Croisset he found already waiting for him a letter in which she reproached him for having told her he was coming to Paris at all, for "not having allowed her wound to heal." During the spring, the correspondence languished; as the first of May approached, the thought of his now definite Breton trip—three months in the company of Max, with his mother joining them here and there— made her almost incoherent. Before he left he wrote her a long letter:

"You want to know whether I love you, so that we may make a quick break and end things frankly. Isn't that what you wrote me yesterday? But that is too big a question to be answered by a yes or a no. For me, love is not and should not be in the foreground of life; it should stay in the background. There are other things in the soul, it seems to me, which are nearer the light, closer to the sun. So, if you consider love as the principal dish of existence, my answer is no. If as seasoning, yes. If you mean by 'loving' to be exclusively preoccupied with the loved one, to live only in her, to see, of everything there is to see in the world, only her, to be full of the idea of her—to feel, finally, that your life is bound up in her life and that that has become an organ of your soul, then no. I have never felt the necessity of the company of anyone. The desire, yes. The need, no.

"Forget those 'extraneous influences' which you think are acting on me. They do not exist, and not in Max any more than in anyone else. As to your dissensions with Max, you must remember that his entire relationship with you was for the purpose of serving your interests, not his own. He may very well have been hurt (he is easily hurt —unlike me, you see, despite the 'pact' which you say binds us) by a number of strong things you wrote him, or perhaps he is tired of being so continuously employed on my behalf. The role of confidant may be perfectly honourable, but it is not always amusing—nor the role of a victim of slander, either. He was devoted to you, poor chap—and if necessary he would be again."

On the first of May, very early in the morning, Flaubert and Du Camp, dressed in tramping clothes and carrying knapsacks, crossed the half-awakened city of Paris from Max's apartment in the Place de la Madeleine to the Gare d'Orléans. The winter was over. The notes for *The Temptation of Saint Anthony* were almost complete. To that last letter there had been no reply from the Rue de la Fontaine-Saint-Georges, and no good-byes were said. Flaubert had gone to Paris just three times since the ecstatic day in Mantes.

There was, however, one affecting farewell.

Since his return from his wedding-trip to Italy, Alfred Le Poittevin had been in worse health than ever. After he had practised for several months in Paris, the state of his heart made it impossible for him to continue, and late in the winter he retired with his wife to his father-in-law's property at Neuville-Champ-d'Oisel, on the outskirts of Rouen in the opposite direction from Croisset. There Flaubert visited him in February, and was distressed by his weakness and utter listlessness. Alfred made no effort to come to Croisset or even to write, and late in April Flaubert went to Neuville once more to say good-bye before setting out. "I saw Alfred last Thursday," he wrote to Max. "His spouse is going to enrich him with a son or a daughter in a few weeks. There's a little beggar that's going to make me laugh, just to look at him. His father is just the same, vegetating as always in complete idleness. It is deplorable." But just as Flaubert was on the point of leaving, Alfred did write:

"You must have some indulgence for a friend who suffers from laziness, whose disease (like most diseases) is growing steadily worse, and who, though he thinks of you often, seldom tells you so. I hope that this letter will reach you before your departure. If not, it will join you in the course of your peregrinations, and instead of being a distraction amid boredom will perhaps have the good fortune to be one of the pleasures of your journey. Kindly remember me to your travelling companion, who I trust will reciprocate by thinking of me from time to time.

"Like people who have been at sea and have experienced there nothing but a great disinclination ever to return to it, I, since my return from Naples, have been completely averse to the slightest movement. A few walks in front of the house, in the garden, and occasionally as far as the edge of the woods—such is the daily evolution of the body which it has pleased divine Providence to associate with my spirit. Not that the latter is much more active—each is slumbering.

"If you were to be asked in what respect I differ from a boa, you could reply that it is in this: that while he digests slowly he eats enormously, whereas I, in order to digest my readings even slowly, have to take them in extremely small doses. . . .

"I should be glad to be favoured by a word of reply. Meanwhile I wish you *bon voyage*, good inns, the greatest possible number of antiquities and the least possible number of things of today."

The formality, almost the affectation, of such a letter from one who had been the friend that Alfred had been was as painful as the impression of utter degeneration that it conveyed, and injected a note of bitter sadness into Flaubert's departure. Otherwise the sensation of leaving Croisset, the study with its piles of books, and the "epileptic" correspondence with Louise was one of relief and joyousness; in the train to Blois, where they were to start to walk, Flaubert was filled with exuberance, and at Tours he had an attack, the first since his father's death. Like the attack in Switzerland, he laid it to over-excitement and too rapturous delight, and like that attack its after-effects were slight. In a few days they were on the road again.

The trip was a splendid success.

"Knapsacks on our backs and hob-nailed shoes on our feet, we have walked about four hundred miles along the coast, often sleeping in our clothing for lack of sheets and making a meal of eggs and bread for lack of meat. As to monuments, we have seen them in quantity! So many dolmens and menhirs and peulvans! There is nothing more tedious than Celtic archæology: everything is so like everything else that it drives one to despair. But to balance that we have had many fine moments in the shadow of old châteaux; we have smoked many a long pipe in many an ancient moat all grassy and perfumed with broom. And then the sea! The sea! The fresh air, the liberty—I mean the real liberty—saying what you want to say, thinking aloud as you speak, letting your feet take you where they will, letting time fly behind like the smoke of your pipe!"

Madame Flaubert first joined them at Brest, bringing the fantastic news that Alfred was the father of a son, and from time to time they rejoined her in the larger towns. They had intended to keep a journal, but discovered it took too much time, and jotted down instead rapid notes on what they saw, to be expanded later. Max was a perfect companion—not a quarrel, not a disagreement, marred their three months together—and Flaubert found him so witty that his jokes found place in his notes. Tramping along the primitive roads, between meadows of broom and gorse, they sang and shouted poetry or nonsense, delighting in the astonishment of the peasants whom they met. Consulting the historical and other memoranda they had made during the winter (Max's were much the more systematic), they reminded each other of Gilles de Retz, Anne de Bretagne, the wars of the Vendée.

Flaubert was unable not to write to Paris. "If this letter, too, remains unanswered," he wrote from Nantes, "then, a long adieu! When you need a friend, Louise, remember me. Think of me at moments of intense sadness. Adieu! Tonight when your daughter is asleep, kiss her for me."

At Combourg they visited the château where Chateaubriand had lived as a boy and which he had described in *René;* stretched out on the grass at the foot of an oak, they read *René* aloud, and that night they walked round and round the château in the moonlight, reciting their favourite passages. At Saint-Malo they were rowed out to the tomb which the still living Chateaubriand had already prepared for himself on an island in the bay. There Flaubert's romanticism so overcame him that he wrote yet again to the Rue de la Fontaine-Saint-Georges:

"I send you, my dear friend, a flower which I picked yesterday at sunset on the tomb of Chateaubriand. The sea was beautiful, the sky rose, the air soft—it was one of those splendid summer evenings, flaming with colours, of a splendour so immense that it became melancholy. One of those evenings ardent and sad as a first love. . . ."

From Saint-Malo they returned slowly to Croisset through Normandy, stopping here and there to visit old friends and relations of Madame Flaubert. It was late in July when they arrived, the two young men bronzed and jubilant over the success of their long walk. After lingering a few days, to share Flaubert's pleasure in recounting the trip to Louis Bouilhet and to listen to the poems Louis had written in their absence, Max left to join his grandmother in Vichy. Flaubert answered the letter from Louise which he had found awaiting him.

"I had thought of inventing some pretext for going to Rouen, my darling, so that I might come to Paris for your feast-day. But to come I should have to be away two days (owing to the hours of the boats), and two days would be a rather long time for a simple visit to Rouen. Patience, my poor darling; this winter I hope to spend a fortnight in Paris. It is not absolutely necessary for me to go (there are a few books in the Royal Library that I should look at), but I will seize that pretext."

Louise quickly replied. She was sure that she understood. Flaubert's trip to Brittany had doubtless exhausted his slender resources, and that was why he could not come to Paris. It was absurd, however, to allow money to keep them apart on such an occasion, and she begged him to let her lend him something. But: "Thank you for your offers, for your devotedness, but at the moment I have no need of anything," he wrote, and proceeded to reinstall himself, with maddening placidity, at Croisset. Soon he was writing, with some surprise:

"You declare that I should have sent you flowers, at least, on the 29th of July. But you know very well that I do not recognize the word 'should,' my dear Louise. You demand that I forget you absolutely. I could give you the outward sign of doing so, but within, no. You have not been able to resign yourself to accepting me with the infirmities of my position, the exigencies of my life. I gave you the depths of a man's devotion. You want the surface things, the appearances, the little attentions and constant comings and goings—everything that I have killed myself trying to make you understand I cannot give you."

During the days at Croisset after the end of the trip, Flaubert and Max had sorted and divided their notes, and when Max left he took half of them with him, for it was arranged that he was to write the even and Flaubert the odd chapters of a book about their days in Brittany.

Flaubert set to work at once, and found the effort agonizing. He had written nothing in two years—the trans-

lations of Plautus and Aristophanes counted for little—
and while he recognized that he had gained in critical
perception and in taste, he had certainly lost much of his
verve and most of his facility. For the first time in his life
he found himself forced to write slowly. The difficulties
gave him nightmares. He saw himself writing slower and
slower as the years passed, becoming increasingly disgusted
with what he produced, ending by daring to write nothing
at all. This Breton book he considered an exercise in composition for *The Temptation of Saint Anthony;* there was
to be no thought of publication; it was to be a kind of
intimate journal, written for himself and Max alone. In
Vichy and then in Paris, Max too wrote out first drafts;
late in October he came to Croisset for most of the rest of
the year. The book progressed steadily, but with difficulties, and the thought of the other book which was
awaiting him and on which all his hopes were pinned sent
Flaubert into still another attack.

"I have been ill," he wrote to Louise. "I had an attack a
week ago, and am still poorly. The work I am doing—I am
finally writing—contributes not a little toward putting me
in an abnormal state. That is why I have not answered
your letter. It was still less amiable than its predecessors,
but I have so many squalls within myself that I can put up
with storms in others.

"We are now busy writing our tour, and though this
work does not demand very great refinement of effects or
preliminary arrangement of the various parts, I am so little
used to writing, and become so peevish over it—particularly toward myself—that it gives me much trouble. When
the book is finished, in about six weeks, it will perhaps be
amusing because of its honesty and its lack of ceremony.
But good? At any rate, since we are going to have two
copies made of it, one for each of us, you may read it if
you like.

"I write without interruption from morning till night,
and the further I go the more difficult I find it to write the
simplest things, the more conscious I become of the emptiness of what I thought my best work of the past. Today,
for example, I spent eight hours correcting five pages, and
I consider that I worked well. You can imagine the rest:

it is pitiable. That is what Max and I are doing. Writing in
the same room, our pens of necessity mix a little each with
the other. If I had four sous I would go to Paris next
month. I absolutely need some information that I can find
only at the Bibliothèque Sainte-Geneviève."

His New Year's present to Louise for 1848 was what it
had been a year before, a kiss; and things between them
soon became worse than ever. Each of them, at about the
same time, exaggerated his usual behaviour. Flaubert out-
did himself in tactlessness. Without meaning the slightest
offence, and speaking from a purely literary point of view,
as Louise should—of course—have well known, he informed her that the letters of a celebrated murderer which
he was reading at the moment reminded him of the letters
he had been receiving from her. "You will laugh at the
comparison," he wrote, "but I will show you that it is
just." Louise did not laugh—she wept and railed; and
then she did something even more unforgivable than ex-
tolling the *fame* of Corneille, or preferring *tableaux vivants*
to paintings by Rubens, Titian, and Raphael, or comparing
Novembre, by G. Flaubert, to *René*, by Chateaubriand.
She was reading *Candide*, another of Gustave's favourite
books, and she expressed an opinion which caused him to
reply in horror:

"What a strange idea of yours to wish that someone
would CONTINUE *Candide*! Is it possible? Who would
do it? Who *could*? There are some things so overwhelmingly great—and *Candide* is among them—that they would
crush anyone who tried to carry them. They are armour
for giants, and the dwarf who put them on his back would
be crushed before he took a single step. You possess insufficient quantities of admiration and respect. You have a
love of art but not the religion of art. Even as you are,
however, it is impossible not to have for you an involun-
tary tenderness and inclination."

Her letters became cold and stilted—because, she said,
his were like that. And she objected strenuously to the
new salutation with which he chose to address her: "Old
Friend." Letters became fewer and fewer, Flaubert's increasingly careless.

"It is because I do not force myself and whip myself

into artificial declarations to you that you find me so cruelly cold, so strangely insensible," he wrote early in the spring. "Everything is right, if others do not suffer as a consequence: that is my entire morality. But when others suffer in spite of you? When that is the result of a will that is fatal and more powerful than your own, what is there to say? What is there to do? What remedy exists?

"You had hoped I would be a fire—blazing, flaming, brightly glowing, cleansing the air, and restoring life. Alas! I am but a poor night-light, my red wick glimmering in bad oil, full of water and dust. I should have made you happy, you say. Ah, Louise—I, make a woman happy! I do not even know how to play with a child. My mother takes the baby away from me when I touch her, because I make the little thing cry. And yet, she is like you—she always wants to be near me, and keeps calling for me.

"The fault is neither in you nor in me, but in God.

"A bit of medical advice: take many baths. A little while ago when I was excessively irritable I followed this regime and improved at once."

God, now, and baths! Clearly, things were ending.

On his arrival at Croisset in October, Max had found Flaubert grief-stricken over Alfred, who he said was dying; and a few days later, when they drove out to Neuville, it was clear that he was right. Alfred was shockingly changed. He had grown bald; his hands had lost much of their flesh; his complexion, always pallid, was now a deathly grey; breathing itself seemed difficult. Scarcely had they arrived when he drew Max aside and asked him to return the manuscript of an ode he had written and given him. Max understood. The ode was obscene, and Alfred preferred not to leave it behind.

He was quite composed, and without illusions concerning the state of his health. He said he was writing, as fast as possible; during the summer he had begun a new novel, which he would like to finish. He read a few pages aloud; it concerned a disenchanted being, bewildered by life and weary of living, who finally does away with himself. "You ask me: 'Why die?' I reply: 'Why live?'" The reading of even short excerpts tired him. He spoke of a young poet whom he and Flaubert had known at college and who had died of tuberculosis a few years before at Nice—the des Hogues whose grave the family had discouraged Flaubert from visiting because it would look queer—and he recited some of his melancholy verses which were appropriate to his own approaching end. After they had talked awhile he stood up, saying he was stifling, and leaving the house they walked up and down in an alley of birches, whose yellow leaves fell about them. Despite the cold, Alfred was thinly clad. He seemed to be in pain: he said nothing, but kept pressing his hand to his heart, as though to check its too rapid beating.

Suddenly the scene changed ludicrously; they were joined by Alfred's father-in-law, the manufacturer of bricks, who began to talk politics—a subject that was anathema to the young men. The campaign for parliamentary reform had begun. Business in France was bad and a number of the more eminent liberal and radical politicians were passing from town to town, speaking at "reform banquets" organized in advance by the local liberal elements, convincing many of the bourgeois that prosperity could be regained only through the enactment of liberal social legislation and extension of the franchise. But Alfred's father-in-law was opposed to all change; he declaimed to the young men against the "dangerous agitation," the "coming revolution." Flaubert and Max exchanged smiles, when to their astonishment Alfred began to speak, and strangely and weirdly uttered a prophecy concerning things to which his friends knew him more than indifferent. "If you have government bonds, sell them. The first time a strain is put upon the government it will collapse. Louis Philippe is doomed." For a moment they were all silent with surprise, then they laughed a little awkwardly, and Monsieur de Maupassant walked away, back to the house. Alfred leaned wearily against a tree. "Look, there is rebellion here, too," he said, pointing to his breast. "And the rebel will win."

Alfred saw them to their carriage. He begged Flaubert to send him his volumes of Spinoza; his own were lost, and —"I want to read them once again."

All the way home Flaubert talked passionately to Max

of Alfred and their past together, evoking a thousand memories, speaking bitterly of Alfred's wife and child, weeping, and crying out against the death that was clearly soon to sweep this friend still further away.

Shortly afterwards, when Max had returned to Paris, Flaubert attended one of the Rouen reform banquets which so frightened Monsieur de Maupassant, and wrote his impressions to Louise:

"Lately I witnessed a sight of true splendour and am still dominated by its intense and sorry grotesqueness: I attended a reform banquet! Such taste! Such cooking! Such wines! And such speeches! Nothing has ever given me such an absolute contempt for success, considering the price at which it is to be obtained. I sat cold and nauseated with disgust amid the patriotic enthusiasm. Never will the most beautiful works of the masters of literature receive a quarter of that applause. The poems of Musset will never be received with the cries of admiration which arose from every corner of the room at the virtuous bellowings of M. Odilon Barot and at the laments of M. Crémieux over the state of our finances. And after this séance of nine hours, passed in the company of cold turkey, suckling pig, and my locksmith, who tapped me on the shoulder at the beautiful passages, I came home frozen to the marrow. No matter how sad an opinion you may have of mankind, bitterness comes into your heart at the sight of such frenzied nonsense, such unbridled stupidity, as that."

During the winter, increasing numbers of the bourgeoisie became convinced that the stagnation of trade was the fault of the stagnant government of Louis Philippe, and in February Alfred's prophecy came true: a large reform banquet in Paris was forbidden by government order, immediately whole companies of the Garde Nationale revolted and were joined by crowds of the proletariat and encouraged by public opinion, Louis Philippe abdicated and fled, his palace was sacked, and the moderate republican factions appointed Lamartine head of a provisional government.

At noon on the first day of the rioting, Max entered his apartment to find Flaubert and Bouilhet sitting beside his fire; they had come to Paris for a few days to take a look at the excitement "from the artistic point of view," and that afternoon the three of them gaily roamed the streets, taking shelter in doorways and under arcades as they watched the street-fighting. In the evening, with the city growing increasingly turbulent, they dined pleasantly in an excellent restaurant, and that night, while one of the bloodiest episodes of the revolution was taking place scarcely three hundred yards away, they were sitting around Max's fire and Bouilhet was reciting the first canto, recently completed, of *Melænis*, his Roman poem. The next morning Max and Flaubert lost Bouilhet in a thick crowd, and without him they watched the fighting at the Palais Royal and the sacking of the Tuileries; when they returned to the Place de la Madeleine at the end of the day they found him waiting; he had strayed into a proletarian quarter, where he had been forced to work at the barricades, and in the excitement he had dropped a heavy paving-stone on his own foot. He was too lame, after dinner, to accompany them to the Hôtel-de-Ville, where they heard the Republic proclaimed, and the next day he and Flaubert returned to Rouen.

Flaubert's chief revolutionary emotion was one of malicious pleasure in the discomfiture of exactly such people as Alfred's father-in-law, who out of self-interest had supported Louis Philippe and now found themselves on the wrong side, with even most of their own class against them.

"It is all very funny," he wrote to Louise on his return to Rouen. "There are many long faces—very cheering to see. I take profound delight in the sight of all the flattened-out ambitions. I don't know whether the new form of government and the resultant social conditions will be favourable to art. It's a question. Certainly they can't be more bourgeois or ineffectual than the old, and I wonder whether they can be more stupid."

Political comments were not the only contents of that letter. Following his new policy, Flaubert had informed Louise that he was in Paris, and had heard nothing from her. But back in Rouen he received, forwarded by Max, a letter she had written and which had been delayed by the interruption of the mails. He was not sorry he had not received it in Paris, for it was nothing but a long return to a theme he had hoped never to hear again.

"What is the use of coming back endlessly to Du Camp," he added, "to the grievances, well founded or not, that you may have against him? You should understand that the subject has been painful to me for some time. This persistence, which began as mere bad taste, is ending by being cruel.

"My monstrous personality, as you so amiably call it, is not such that it effaces in me every honourable feeling— every *human* feeling, if you prefer. Some day perhaps you will realize that, and repent of having wasted so much vexation and bitterness on my behalf.

"Whatever happens, you can always count on me. Even if we no longer write to each other or see each other, the bond between us will never disappear and the consequences of our past will always be alive."

His words were given a chance to be tested, for this time Louise did not reply for almost five months.

It soon became evident to the bourgeois that the proletariat with which it had allied itself in the revolution was not content with moderate republicanism, and having had a taste of success through force, was preparing to taste further and bring about the radical reforms which it desired. This caused the bourgeois to become counter-revolutionaries almost overnight; in deposing the stagnant monarchy they felt they had done all that was necessary to unfetter and stimulate trade; they had no desire to improve the lot of the masses, and in every city in France they "made public profession of good citizenship" by joining the reorganized Garde Nationale, which formed an excellent means of defence of the new *status quo* against attacks from the left. Max, who loved action and was anything but a democrat, joined the Garde at once. Louis Bouilhet astonished both his friends. Despite his injured foot, it appeared that the social idealism he had witnessed during his brief visit behind the proletarian barricades had inspired him and started him thinking, and the result was that he presented himself as candidate for the Chamber of

Deputies from the department of the Seine-Inférieure. Flaubert was aghast: this timid young poet, who was fond of saying that he wished he might always be followed by a flute-player to accompany the rhythm of his odes! But France was a republic now, Louis enthusiastically reminded him, like Rome in its most glorious days. Lamartine, a poet, was head of the provisional government; Hugo had been elected mayor of his district in Paris; the government of France was no longer divorced from the life of the spirit; it was no longer unfitting for a young literary man to enter politics. Lest popular prejudice be unduly jostled, however, Bouilhet did inscribe himself in the campaign as a "teacher" rather than as a "poet," and he proceeded to spend his spare time not at Croisset as usual, but speech-making in the neighbouring villages. Flaubert's revolutionary activity was more limited. For the moment, in fact, it took the form of a letter to Max, asking whether there was not some chance that they might both be named secretaries to one of the new ambassadors, and be sent to Rome, Constantinople, or Athens. Max wrote back mockingly, inquiring whether he were suffering from some mental disorder. His own wearing of a uniform he defended on grounds of national emergency and his distaste for the populace, but he saw no reason for others to act like himself, and he felt no personal hostility whatever toward Bouilhet for wishing that the revolution would continue to liberate still further. He wrote as mocking to him as he did to Flaubert, and Louis replied just as lightly: if he were elected, he promised, he would see that all government measures were drafted in verse.

It was on April 3, in the midst of these events, that Alfred died.

"Alfred died on Monday at midnight," Flaubert wrote to Max. "I buried him yesterday. It was I who wrapped him in his shroud, I who gave him the last kiss, I who saw the coffin nailed down. I passed two long days and nights beside him, reading Kreuzer's *Religions of Antiquity* as I watched.

"The window was open, the night splendid. I could hear a cock crowing, and a night moth circled round and round the taper. I shall never forget it, or the look on Alfred's face, or the distant sound of a hunting horn which came from the forest that first night at midnight. On Wednesday I walked all the afternoon, with a dog that followed me without being called. It had become attached to Alfred and always went with him when he walked alone. The night before his death this same dog howled frightfully and could not be quieted. From time to time I rested on mossy banks, smoking and looking up at the sky, and behind a heap of brushwood I lay down and slept a little.

"During the last night I read *Feuilles d'Automne.* I kept coming either upon his favourite passages or upon something appropriate to my present circumstances. Now and then I went over to him and lifted the veil covering his face. I was wrapped in a cloak that had belonged to my father but which he wore only once—the day of Caroline's wedding.

"At daybreak the attendant and I began our task. I lifted him, turned him, covered him. All the next day my hands were cold from the shock of the touch. Decomposition had set in rapidly; we wrapped him in a double shroud. When it was done he looked like an Egyptian mummy in its bandages, and I was filled with an indescribable sense of joy and relief on his account. Outside there was a whitish mist. As the sky lightened I began to see against it the line of the trees in the forest; the two tapers burned dimly in the dawning whiteness; the birds began to sing. . . .

"We laid him in the entry, where the doors had been removed and where the morning air poured in, freshened by the rain. He was carried to the cemetery on men's shoulders—an hour's walk. As I walked behind the coffin it seemed to sway with the movements of a boat. The service was atrociously long. In the cemetery the earth was heavy. I stood beside the grave and watched each shovelful as it fell; I thought there must be a hundred thousand of them.

"I returned to Rouen on the box of a carriage with Bouilhet under a beating rain. The horses went at a gallop, and I cried out to urge them on. The air did me good. I slept all last night and most of today.

"That is what I have passed through since Tuesday

evening. I have had marvellous intimations and intuitions and flashes of untranslatable ideas. A host of things have been coming back to me, with choirs of music and clouds of perfume.

"As long as he was capable of doing anything. he read Spinoza in bed until one in the morning. On one of his last days, when the window was open and the sun pouring in, he cried: 'Shut it! It is too beautiful—too beautiful!'

"At certain moments, dear Max, you were strangely present to me, and my mind was a confusion of mournful images.

"Adieu! I embrace you, and long to see you, for I have unutterable things to say to you."

In the weeks that followed, Flaubert was far too restless to work. His part of the Breton books was done, and while the editing and fitting-in of Max's chapters would have provided him with a task just mechanical enough, Max was too busy in the Garde to be able to finish them. And the "host of things" which had been coming back made it impossible for him to begin, just yet, the long book that was waiting. He felt the need of action, and for that reason he committed what he considered a folly—he joined the Garde Nationale in Rouen, writing ironically that he had "taken part in a review on the occasion of the planting of a liberty tree." After a few days he resigned, for as yet parading at tree-plantings was all the Rouen Garde was called on to do, and besides there was little difference, in Flaubert's eyes, between the bourgeois and the proletariat: each seemed as bourgeois to him as the other. He went to Paris, hoping that Max's company and the sight of movement would absorb some of his restlessness. But Max was so busy that he could scarcely see him, and the things he did see he did not like.

"Everything is deplorable here," he wrote to Louis. "Republicans, reactionaries, reds, blues, tricolours—all are competing in ineptitude. It is enough to make an honest soul vomit, as my old friend the Garcon used to say. Perhaps the patriots are right and France is at a low ebb. As to her spirit, that is certainly true. Politics have ravished her of the last drop of that."

He did not remain long, and was back in Croisset in time to console Louis, who was crushingly defeated in the elections at the end of the month. The results of the voting were such, however, that Louis did not require much consolation for his own defeat: the new government proved to be three-quarters bourgeois. Poets and progressives were embittered. It was becoming clear that the revolution would do little either to improve the lot of the masses or to alter the general dullness of existence. All it had done so far was to improve the condition of the bourgeois, and everywhere the Garde Nationale was ready to check the slightest leftward move. Clearly it was not a revolution with which a man of spirit cared any longer to be associated, and Louis returned to his usual occupations, resuming his week-ends at Croisset. In his presence Flaubert gradually felt his courage return, and he did the very last of his note-taking, reading Swedenborg, Strauss's *Life of Jesus,* and the writings of Saint Theresa.

The "host of things," too, the "choirs of music and clouds of perfume," which had filled his mind as he sat beside Alfred, and which had at first kept him from working, now began to have the opposite effect, and to urge him on. His thoughts were filled with Alfred. He thought of the dizzy conversations beside the fire in his room at the hospital, when Alfred had expounded to him the systems of philosophy. He thought of the laugh of the Garçon, of the *idées reçues,* of the books which Alfred had inspired and which he had written so easily. Without Alfred he would never have conceived the idea of *The Temptation of Saint Anthony.* Alfred was the first person to whom he had mentioned the idea, in his letter from Milan. Alfred seemed once more his friend: no longer separated by the barriers of existence, by wife and child, they could work together as they had in the past. Alfred's spirit was far more of a stimulant than the living, married Alfred of Neuville-Champ-d'Oisel had ever been. He would write a book of which Alfred would have approved! It would be a supreme tribute to their friendship, a book which never could have been written had each of them not known the other.

It was three years after first seeing the picture by

Breughel in the Palazzo Balbi-Senarega that Flaubert finally began to write. On "Wednesday, the 24th of May 1848, at quarter-past three in the afternoon," he set down the first words of *La Tentation de Saint Antoine.*

In June the long-expected outburst came. The masses and their sympathizers, enraged by the obstinate conservatism of the newly elected government, rose in the cities and were quickly crushed by the Garde Nationale. In Paris the June Days, the twenty-fourth, twenty-fifth, and twenty-sixth, were bloody and fierce. Maxime Du Camp received a ball in the leg while storming the people's barricades, spent some time in bed (where he finally finished his parts of the Breton book), and was made Chevalier de la Légion d'Honneur for bravery under fire.

As soon as he was well enough, he came to Croisset, bringing with him not only his Breton chapters but another book too. He had found a publisher for his account of his eastern travels, and now brought inscribed copies to both his friends. It was called *Souvenirs et Paysages d'Orient,* and was dedicated to "G. F., *s. ad s.*" In Flaubert's study he read aloud some of the passages he had written in that very room; his friends laughed at the impudent preface in which he welcomed his "unexpected reader," and congratulated Max on his appearance in print. He and Flaubert put the Breton book together and gave it to a copyist; and then, to the envy of the others, he left for a rest and vacation in Algeria. Of the three, Max was the first to have a book appear. Who would be the second?

Toward the end of July a letter came from Louise, the first since March. She announced that she was leaving Monsieur Colet, moving out of the little apartment with the blue boudoir in the Rue de la Fontaine-Saint-Georges. Under the spell of the approaching anniversary, her letter was tender, and there were enclosures. But her news was received without comment. The answer was long in coming, and when it did come it was brief:

Croisset,
August 21, 1848.

Thank you for the gift.
Thank you for your very beautiful poem.
Thank you for the remembrance.

Yours, G.

Louise could scarcely be expected to realize how little she counted for, now that Alfred Le Poittevin's spirit was at Croisset!

6.

It was curious, however, during that summer and fall, how while working under the impulse of Alfred's memory Flaubert entered under the influence of Louis Bouilhet. Alfred in death was more powerful than Alfred in his recent life, but as the book which he had inspired gradually took form, the role of Louis at Croisset and Rouen began to expand. Not that Louis exercised any control whatever over *La Tentation de Saint Antoine.* That was Alfred's book, and though at Croisset every week-end Louis wore Flaubert's dressing gowns, worked beside him, and talked with him, he remained in utter ignorance of the contents of the manuscript which he could see growing from week to week. No; Flaubert was doing no definite work under the encouragement and guidance of Louis, as he had written his four or five unpublished books under the encouragement and guidance of Alfred; but day by day, during the composition of *Saint Antoine,* he came without knowing it to depend more and more on Louis's judgments concerning literature in general. He had always admired Louis's literary perception and tact; now, unconsciously, he began to consider them infallible. From Louis's pronouncements there seemed to be no appeal, and with this intensifying confidence grew Flaubert's affection, each aiding the other. With Alfred gone, there was no disloyalty.

As to Max, there was never any question of *his* becoming a mentor. He was a gay and dependable friend, but in literature rather a pupil and admirer. The letters which Max received during his vacation in Algeria gave no hint of the pedestal onto which Louis was gradually being raised. They were gloomy: Flaubert was having attacks because of worry over what he was writing; the household had moved to Rouen for the winter and Flaubert was finding his fellow-citizens more intolerable than ever; Flaubert would like very much to know what his future life was to be.

Early in December the three friends were reunited in Rouen, and Max told of his Algerian travels, his lion hunts, his rides in the desert. Though a far more important election than the last was under way, they were now inattentive to politics—Flaubert indifferent as always, Louis because he could no longer hope that change would be brought about, Max because he need no longer fear that it would. On December 10, while Louis Napoleon Bonaparte was being elected president of France, they were once more sitting by a fire and Louis was once more reciting the stanzas of *Melænis*.

Flaubert informed them willingly that *La Tentation de Saint Antoine* was progressing with great speed, but that was all he did tell them, and for lack of information they sought satisfaction in conjecture. Max expressed the guess that Flaubert was writing the memoirs of the saint, his confessions of his temptations and near-capitulation, and that he was using that form as a means of painting a psychological portrait. Louis did not think so at all. "Remember that Saint Anthony himself is a character of no great account," he argued, "whereas his period is curious and interesting. I wager we'll find that Flaubert has tried to reconstruct the Alexandrian world, showing the simultaneous decay of the Roman Empire and rise of the Christian Church." Each of them knew that neither could be completely right, for neither of the surmises made any provision for Flaubert's books on Persian religion and philosophy, Arabian religion before Mohammed, and ancient Hindu folklore. They did not keep their guesses entirely to themselves, but Flaubert heard them without a word. Working under the impulse of his "marvellous intimations and intuitions and flashes of untranslatable ideas," he wrote as quickly as he had in the days of Alfred, and Louis seemed almost frightened by the number of pages he was covering. "Prose is like a river!" Louis said. "It keeps flowing on and on. How do you know when to stop?"

Max did not stay long, and during the entire winter Flaubert seldom left the house. "A lot of things can be done in one evening," he wrote in his notebook, one night. "After dinner tonight I talked with my mother, thought of travel, and dreamed of the various lives I might be leading. Then I wrote almost an entire chorus of *Saint Antoine,* read the whole first volume of Chateaubriand's *Mémoires d'Outretombe,* and smoked three pipes. Now I am going to take a pill . . . and I have not yet gone to sleep!" That was a fairly complete picture of his life, and as a result of it the pile of manuscript rapidly thickened.

Late in February Max came again. He was, he announced, going to the Orient once more—this time on a greatly extended tour, a slightly condensed but still glorious version of the grand journey which he and Gustave had plotted during one of Max's visits to Croisset. He was going to start in the middle of the summer, and go to Egypt and the Sudan, Palestine, Syria, Armenia, and Persia, returning eventually by way of Turkey, Greece, and Italy. The trip would take at least two years, and he was already making preparations. He exhibited books by Champollion and other eastern travellers which he was reading for the suggestions they might contain. As expected, the news sent Flaubert into the jealous lamentations with which he had greeted Max's two previous announcements of departure, but this time there was mingled with the jealousy a note which Max found new, and set him thinking. It was clear to one who had not seen Flaubert in several months that he was becoming increasingly nervous and apprehensive over the fate of the book he was writing. All question of the merit of the book aside, there was no telling whether its completion would have any practical consequences; he had no plans for anything to follow; what would he do with himself? Flaubert was not as explicit as this in his conversation, but it was clear to Max that all this was in his mind. Was Flaubert always to be a provincial recluse? Max wondered. Was he never to have any change from Croisset except Rouen, any change

from Rouen except Croisset? Were his dreams of the
Orient, of the desert, of the sun, never to be realized?
All night Max lay awake trying to solve Flaubert's problems; it seemed more and more evident to him that the
moment of the completion of *Saint Antoine* was the moment for his friend to have an important change of scene
and accomplish that which—next to writing well—he most
ardently longed to do. Madame Flaubert was well off;
there were no financial hindrances. Flaubert should accompany him. The Breton trip had shown them that they
should always travel together.

The next morning, when he told Flaubert of his
thoughts, Gustave merely made a hopeless gesture in the
direction of his mother; but later in the day, during a visit
to the hospital, Max carried the matter further. "Couldn't
you explain to your mother that a warm climate would
be beneficial for Gustave's health?" he dared say to Achille.
"You're a doctor, she'd listen to you." Achille made almost
as hopeless a gesture as his brother, but promised to try.
The very next day came a stroke of luck. Madame Flaubert received a letter from her husband's old friend, the
amiable doctor in Paris who had been so excellent a guide
for Gustave in Marseille. To her displeasure the doctor
declared, unsolicited, that he disapproved of the life Gustave was leading, and said that he should travel "much
further than merely to Brittany." The delighted friends
informed Achille at once, and pretending ignorance of the
letter he came and expressed to his mother the same opinion concerning Gustave. The house was filled with tension;
finally, two mornings later, at breakfast, Madame Flaubert
glacially said: "Since I am told it is necessary for your
health, you may go with Maxime. You have my consent."
Max could not repress a cry of triumph, which won him
a rebuking glance; Flaubert thanked his mother in a low
voice and turned very red.

During the next few days Max's glamorous prophecies of
the wonders they would see brought from Flaubert only
the briefest of responses. He seemed to have been made
inarticulate by this sudden, totally unexpected prospect of
paradise, and furthermore, to Max's bewilderment, when
he did speak it was generally to bewail the things they

would not see, rather than to rejoice in the things they would. "But we shan't see the Ganges!" he kept lamenting, and Max ended by being irritated. It was his first meeting with what Louise had come upon earlier: the Flaubertian enjoyment of not enjoying. When he pointed out a little stiffly that since according to Flaubert *Saint Antoine* would not be finished before September, he was changing his plans and postponing his departure, Flaubert scarcely thanked him. As he left Croisset he could not help wondering whether he might not have been wiser to travel alone. Max was tending more and more to dislike queerness.

A few days later, in Paris, the oddness of the Flauberts was once more made apparent to him. He received a visit from Madame Flaubert, who addressed him with no polite preliminaries at all, almost as she would a servant. "Everyone tells me that Gustave's health demands that he spend two years in a warm climate, and that the long absence would do him good in every way," she said abruptly. "I have resigned myself to the sacrifice. But Egypt, Palestine, and Persia are not the only warm countries in the world. It seems to me that the journey you plan would be excessively fatiguing, and I dread its dangers for Gustave. What I have come to ask you is this: will you do me the favour of abandoning your present plans, and go to Madeira instead? The climate is excellent there. It would suit Gustave's requirements perfectly and relieve my anxiety." With considerable surprise, Max asked her if Gustave knew she had come, and when she said he did not he took a firm tone. The journey he had arranged was the concluding part of a long plan of study, the culmination of his "long apprenticeship in the study of oriental life." For no reason would he consider abandoning it. Madame Flaubert inquired whether his decision was irrevocable; he replied that it was; and bowing coldly, she left. Flaubert never knew that she had come, and Max felt himself less loved by the lady than ever.

Throughout the spring and summer he wrote often to Croisset of the preparations he was making. He was reading constantly and securing introductions to Parisians who had travelled in the East. He was studying photography, an art which was in its clumsy infancy: he was determined to be the first man to photograph the antiquities of Egypt. Flaubert's general unhandiness made Max decide to take with them his servant Sassetti. He did vast quantities of shopping. And his master-stroke was to request, through well-placed friends, that he and Flaubert be charged by the French Republic with unremunerated but official missions, which would have the result of recommending them to the principal persons in the countries they were to visit. The request was granted. Max was charged by the Ministry of Public Instruction to do just what he wanted to do—bring back photographs of Egyptian monuments. And Flaubert—since Max had been unable to suggest any mission which he could appropriately be given— was to his stupefaction "entrusted by the Ministry of Agriculture and Commerce with the task of collecting information at the different posts and chief halting places for caravans such as he might consider useful to the Chamber of Commerce," an announcement which finally aroused some mirth in the hermit of Croisset.

During the summer Max's grandmother died, and there were legal matters of inheritance to be attended to. Fortunately he enjoyed practical planning; for Flaubert, buried in his writing, allowed him to attend to absolutely everything for both of them. Preparations were well under way when on the thirteenth of September he received from Croisset the message he was waiting for. *La Tentation de Saint Antoine* was finished. He went down at once.

It was a solemn moment when Flaubert, Bouilhet, and Du Camp gathered round the table in the study at Croisset, Flaubert thin from overwork and with a huge pile of manuscript in front of him. He had kept firm; they did not know a word that the manuscript contained. Would it be the thunderclap? That was what Flaubert was wondering; his hands were trembling, his voice was at first unsure. He solemnly declared that after they had heard the manuscript he would absolutely obey their verdict as to its disposition. He would read, he said, for periods of four hours—from noon until four, and from eight until midnight—until he had finished. And then, with his manuscript before him on the table, about to begin, he suddenly startled them by waving some of the pages in the air over his head, and uncontrollably crying: "If you don't howl with pleasure at this you're incapable of being moved by anything!" Then he calmed himself, and began.

"*La Tentation de Saint Antoine*," he announced, almost as a challenge. Then: "May 1848—September 1849. G. Flaubert. Part One. On a mountain. On the horizon, the desert; to the right, Saint Anthony's hut, with a bench beside the door; left, a small oval chapel. A lamp hangs above a picture of the Virgin; on the ground in front of the hut, baskets made of palm-leaves. In a cleft in the rock the hermit's pig is sleeping in the shade. Anthony is alone, seated on the bench weaving his baskets. He raises his head, looks vaguely at the setting sun. 'I have worked enough: now to prayer!' "

So it began. As Saint Anthony prayed, the temptations assailed him. After they had ended, the manuscript closed with the words: "Here ends *La Tentation de Saint Antoine*, Wednesday, the twelfth of September, 1849, twenty minutes past three in the afternoon. Sunny, windy weather." It took Flaubert eight sessions of four hours each to read the five hundred and forty-one large pages of his manuscript, and the four days spent listening to them were without any question whatever four of the most painful days in the lives of Louis Bouilhet and Maxime Du Camp.

"The hours during which Bouilhet and I, exchanging an occasional glance, sat silently listening to Flaubert as he sang and chanted the phrases of *La Tentation de Saint Antoine* have remained very painful in my memory," Max wrote later. "We listened with strained attention, always hoping that the action was about to begin, and always disappointed, for the situation remains unchanged from the beginning of the book to the end.

"Saint Anthony, who is utterly bewildered and rather simple—I was going to say a trifle silly—sees the various forms of temptation pass in review before him, and all he finds to do is to utter a series of exclamations: 'Oh! Oh! Ah! Ah! My God! My God!' Not only are his senses tempted by the enthralments of the flesh, but also his mind is subjected to the incitements of all the heresies and all the philosophies, which attack him with their subtlest arguments. There are not only the seven deadly sins, but also an eighth, logic, which explains and excuses them all. Saint Anthony's pig plays an important role: it is attainted by the deadly sin of pride, and dreams of attaining the rank of boar.

"As he read, Flaubert warmed, but we, though we tried to share his enthusiasm, remained cold as ice. Words, words—harmonious phrases expertly put together, full of noble images and startling metaphors, but often redundant, and containing whole passages which could have been transposed and combined without changing the effect of the book as a whole. There was no progression—the scene always remained the same, though played by different characters. We said nothing, but Flaubert could easily perceive that we were not favourably impressed, and from time to time he interrupted himself to cry: 'Wait! Wait! You'll see!' We listened to what the Sphinx had to say, and the Chimera, the Queen of Sheba, Simon the Magician, Apollonius of Tyanus, Origen, Basilides, Montanus, and Hermogenes. With even closer attention we listened to the Marcionites, the Carpocratians, the Paternians, the Nicolaites, the Gymnosophists, and the Archontics, and to Pluto and Diana and Hercules, and even to the god Crepitus. All our efforts were unavailing. We could not understand, we could not imagine, what Flaubert was driving at, and indeed he was arriving nowhere. Bouilhet and I were aghast. After each reading Madame Flaubert took us aside and whispered: 'Well? What do you think of it?' We dared not reply.

"Before the last reading, Bouilhet and I took counsel together and agreed to be perfectly frank with Flaubert. He was in great danger and it would be wrong for us to allow the danger to continue, for his entire literary future, in which we had absolute confidence, was in the balance. Thinking he was following romanticism to its logical conclusion, Flaubert was without knowing it going backwards, returning to the diffuseness of pathos. This tendency had to be checked, or he would lose his high qualities. It was painful to have to take this course, but friendship and conscience demanded it. Close to midnight that night, when he had finally come to the end, Flaubert pounded his fist on the table. 'Now!' he cried. 'Tell me frankly what you think!' Bouilhet was naturally timid, but no one could express himself more fearlessly when he had once made up his mind to speak. It was he who replied. 'We think you should throw it into the fire, and never speak of it again.'

"Flaubert jumped from his chair with a cry of horror.

"Then began one of those severe but bracing discussions possible only among those who possess one another's entire confidence and whose affection for one another is absolutely disinterested."

Like the reading, the discussion also lasted for hours.

Bouilhet and Du Camp understood, now, the presence of the Arabian, Hindu, and Persian books at Croisset. For what Flaubert had tried to do was not merely to reconstruct the Alexandrian world, as Louis had prophesied, but to dramatize the thought of the entire world, east and west, in Saint Anthony's day, to parade before the hermit all other ways of thinking and living than his own, in a diabolical attempt to force him to admit that his was not the only life or even the best. It was, though this only Flaubert himself knew, the very philosophical ballet or vaudeville that he had instantly conceived before the Breughel in Genoa, and in his own terms he had accomplished his purpose.

But it was precisely his purpose that Louis and Max attacked. "We don't deny that there are fine passages," they said. "But they are fine only in themselves. A book must be a complete structure, made up of parts that combine to produce a given effect—not a collection of beautiful but unrelated phrases."

"But *style!*" Flaubert insisted.

"Style and bombast are two entirely different things, and you have mistaken the one for the other. Do you remember La Bruyère's advice: 'If you want to say that it is raining, say: "It is raining"?' Your *Tentation de Saint Antoine* contains some excellent echoes of antiquity, but they are buried amid exaggerations and verbosity. You wanted to make music and you have produced only noise."

Knife after knife was plunged into the poor author. It was hideous, the utter collapse of all his hopes. One after another his protests were beaten down unmercifully, so that he sat silently, scarcely daring to speak. "But the things you say are bad spring from faults inherent in my temperament!" he finally cried desperately. "How can I correct them?" There was a silence which lasted several seconds. Then it was Louis who spoke. For it was, of course, only because Louis was there that Flaubert was able so quickly to admit, even grudgingly, that the work he had conceived four years before might be a failure. During the writing of *Saint Antoine* his confidence in Louis had grown to be greater than his confidence in himself. Now suddenly he began to see how great it was— so complete that even in the very midst of his distress he felt that Louis's harsh criticism must be valid.

The Temptation of Saint Anthony, Louis declared, was a failure for three reasons, and very explicitly he developed them.

The subject was a particularly bad one for Flaubert. Flaubert's greatest literary faults were lyricism and lack of precision, and these faults could only be encouraged by such a subject as *Saint Antoine.* Impossible to be precise about the parade of the civilizations past a third-century monk! And because he had been unable to endow the characters with any personality of their own, Flaubert had done what was easier, and filled them with his: to anyone who knew Flaubert, parts of the book were almost embarrassingly autobiographical. That was not art, but confession. Flaubert's earlier books had all been confessions. And confessional literature was outmoded, and must be avoided at all costs: down with *René*!

The writing itself was poor. Louis had feared for the style of the book, he revealed, as he had observed the speed with which Flaubert had written it. The five hundred and forty-one pages of *Saint Antoine* had taken him a little less than twice the time he had given to the six chapters of his half of the book on Brittany. The simple, unpretentious, graceful style of the travel book, which

Flaubert had achieved at the cost of so much time, anguish, and effort, Bouilhet admired far more than his
earlier, lush, Chateaubriandesque style, to which he had
now returned. Flaubert should write in his own style, not
in Chateaubriand's.

And third, the *Tentation* was uninteresting because it
was unoriginal. It was an imitation of imitations of *Faust,*
as Flaubert's earlier books had been imitations of Musset's
Confessions and Byron's *Cain.* It was far from a thunderclap. There was nothing arresting about it. In a sense it
was only an elaboration of *Smarh,* which Flaubert had
written when he was seventeen.

All this Bouilhet said with some courage, for he knew
that Flaubert must well realize where most of the blows
were falling. It was the taste and counsel of the fourth
young man in the room (there were really four) that were
being called into question; and although Alfred was not
once mentioned by name, Flaubert almost trembled as the
implications of Bouilhet's words became clear. "The faults
of *Saint Antoine* are there not because they are inherent in
your character, but because they were inherent in Alfred's," he seemed to be saying. "Alfred took you in
charge when you were very young, and ever since, with
one exception, you have been writing what he would have
wished you to write. The one book which bears the mark
of your own good style was written without Alfred's
influence."

Confessions, prose-poems, and pseudo-novels being outworn, Louis summed up, it was not to the romantics that
a young man in the mid-nineteenth century, with a talent
for writing prose, could profitably look for inspiration and
guidance. Such a young man, he declared, should write a
real, a realistic novel—for it was in the novel concerned
with living human beings and their daily life that the
future of prose almost certainly lay. And for that purpose
it was necessary to study the one good model available.
For there was one. A model who pointed the way to the
future; a model not without faults, yet with many virtues,
particularly for Gustave Flaubert. And Bouilhet proceeded
to name him; and as he had expected, Flaubert cried out
with horror.

Balzac!

The enemy of romanticism! The man who wrote novels about the sordid material concerns and financial machinations of the bourgeois! Why, at fifteen Flaubert had written a perfect imitation of a Balzac story! Balzac wrote with no style whatever! What had Balzac to do with Gustave Flaubert! This was too much! For an instant the whole new confidence in Louis threatened to founder.

But Bouilhet replied with calm assurance that the objectivity and precision of Balzac were precisely the antidotes that Flaubert needed, and that if Flaubert were to write a novel about the bourgeois (a class which had always interested him and which he was wrong to believe unworthy of literary treatment), emphasizing their emotional rather than their material concerns and employing a good style of his own, the result would be something new in the history of literature. It might even be the famous thunderclap, which *Saint Antoine* was not!

It took Louis some time—several hours, in fact—to say this, for he went into great detail, analysing Balzac with shrewdness and appreciation, pointing out how Flaubert could profit by a study of Balzac and at the same time develop the qualities which were original to himself. And then he stood up, said with a smile that those were all the opinions he had to offer, and suggested that since it was now eight o'clock in the morning and broad daylight, they all go to bed.

Shocked and bewildered, yet spellbound, Flaubert was the last to rise. It was Max who opened the door of the study, and as he did so he caught sight of a black dress disappearing up the stairs: it was impossible to know how long Madame Flaubert had been anxiously listening. One behind the other, silently, the three friends went to their rooms.

It was a long time before Flaubert fell asleep. Among the thousand thoughts that surged in his brain was the realization that he had changed guides. Alfred's memory would never die, but now his place was taken. The catastrophe of having *Saint Antoine* pronounced a failure was lessened by the fact of Louis's presence: confidence in his friends was Flaubert's favourite refuge.

. . .

The next evening, in the garden under the tulip-tree, the
friends briefly resumed the discussion.

"You mean," Flaubert asked, "if for example the young
daughter of a bourgeois family here in Normandy suffered
from religious mania, had mystical conversations in the
midst of the most banal surroundings, I might write on a
subject like that, painting her background exactly and
giving my imagination free rein in the emotional parts?"

"Not too free," said Bouilhet. "Even those parts gain in
being precise. Choose your subject carefully, choose one
that will fit *you;* then go ahead. And for the sake of yourself and the neighbours," he laughed, "it might be wise
to change the scene from Normandy to Picardy or
Flanders, where the bourgeois are much the same but
where they don't know you!"

"It won't be easy," Flaubert answered. "But I'll try."

The next day Louis returned to Rouen and Max too said
farewell; there was still much to do in Paris before embarking at Marseille. As he left, Madame Flaubert bowed
coldly, and as soon as he had gone she informed her son
that both his friends were jealous of him and that it was
for that reason that they had spoken of the *Tentation* as
they had. Flaubert laughed at her and put the manuscript
away in a drawer—obeying to that extent Bouilhet's recommendation that he burn it. In a drawer it would harm no
one—and some day, perhaps . . .

During the following weeks, while Flaubert was busy
with preparations for departure to the land of Saint Anthony, Bouilhet came out as often as he could, and it was
during these last talks that their affection and their understanding fully blossomed. Bouilhet was the one young
man of the four who had to earn his own living, the only
one who had had even a momentary gleam of hope in
human progress and regeneration; and it was his contact
and concern with the human race, with matters of daily
existence, that made him invaluable as a friend for Flaubert. He was the luckiest accident of Flaubert's life. And

Flaubert was the one friend in whose literary ability Louis believed. Alfred he had scarcely known, but of him he had finally given his literary opinion; and of Max, the only one so far to have put his name before the public, he had never expressed any opinion whatever. He had not, for example, pointed out that there was a difference in quality between the Flaubert and the Du Camp chapters in the Breton book, or between the Flaubert Breton chapters and Max's *Souvenirs et Paysages d'Orient.* As Flaubert packed they talked about the *Tentation* and about the kind of book the next could be. "Above all," said Bouilhet, "forget work! Enjoy yourself! See all you can! We'll talk about all this on your return!" And Flaubert resolved to obey him in this as in everything else. Bouilhet's presence still soothed his hurt, and it was not until a bit later, when Bouilhet was far away, that he was to begin to feel the real throb of the wound.

It is scarcely to be wondered at that as he prepared to leave for Egypt—that dream of all his life—Flaubert thought gloomily of himself as an unsuccessful writer. The thunderclap—what a damp rocket it had turned out to be! Almost three years' work, sixteen months' writing, gone to the devil! What he quite naturally failed to appreciate was that despite his preoccupation with *Saint Antoine* during the four years since his visit to Genoa, the writing of that book had not been his only experience in that time. The tragedies in his home, the sensuality and disillusionment of the affair with Louise, his love for his three friends, the laborious composition of the Breton book: these had been as valuable as was Louis's bitter medicine. They formed a large part of the material on which he was to draw for his future work.

Many notes of exhortation and reminder passed back and forth between Croisset and the Place de la Madeleine as October advanced. Finally the equipment was completed. It included up-to-date camping paraphernalia, Max's bulky photographic apparatus, copies of *Les Orientales* and *Feuilles d'Automne*, from which the young travellers could not bear to be separated, a supply of aphrodisiac lozenges with which to buy the good will of desert sheikhs, and a considerable number of "H. Penny's Patent Metallic Note-books—warranted if written on with his prepared pencils to be as plain and durable as Ink. They will be found of great advantage to travellers and all persons who wish to preserve their writing."

Their ship was to sail on the fourth of November.

Part Two

The Purge

The Oriental Journey

I LEFT Croisset on Monday, October 22, 1849. Of the servants who said good-bye to me as I left, only Bossière, the gardener, seemed to me to be really moved. For me the moment of emotion had come two days before, on Saturday, when I put away my pens and papers. The weather was neither good nor bad. At the station, Achille's wife and their little girl; also Bouilhet. In the coach with us, sitting almost opposite me, was the maid of the prefect of the Seine-Inférieure, a small dark woman with frizzy hair.

The next day we had dinner with Monsieur Cloquet. My mother was sad during the entire meal. Hamard was astonished that I should be going to the Orient, and asked me why I didn't prefer to stay in Paris, where I could "see the plays of Molière and study André Chénier."

Wednesday at four o'clock we left for Nogent. My uncle Parain kept us waiting and I was afraid we should miss the train, which would have seemed a bad omen. Finally he arrived, a fancy parasol (a present for his grand-daughter) hanging from his wrist.

From Paris to Nogent: nothing; a gentleman in white gloves sat opposite me. In the evening, much embracing of family, etc.

The next day, Thursday—atrocious day, the worst I have ever spent. I was not to leave till the day after the next, but I determined to go at once; it was unbearable. Eternal strolls with my mother in the little garden. I set my departure for five; the clock seemed to stand still. I placed my hat in the living room and sent my trunk on ahead to the station; I had only to run out. Farewell visits from the local bourgeois: among them Madame Dainez of the post-office. Also Monsieur Morin, the postmaster, who

as he left shook hands with me over the gate, saying:
"You are going to see a great country, a great religion, a
great people, etc."

Finally I got away. My mother was sitting in an armchair beside the fire, and in the midst of caressing her and
talking with her I suddenly kissed her on the forehead,
rushed from the room, seized my hat, and ran out of the
house. How she screamed when I closed the door of the
living room behind me! It reminded me of her scream just
after the death of my father, when she took his hand.

My eyes were dry, and I felt no emotion except nervousness and even a kind of anger; my face must have looked
set. I lit a cigar, and my cousin Bonenfant ran out and
joined me. He spoke to me of the necessity, of the advisability, of making a will, or leaving a power-of-attorney
—some disaster might overtake my mother in my absence, etc. I have never experienced such a feeling of hatred
toward anyone as toward him at that moment. God has
probably forgiven him for the wrong he did me, but the
memory of it will always remain with me. He nearly drove
me mad. I was able to shut him up without being impolite.

At the station entrance, a priest and four nuns: bad
omen! And all afternoon a dog in the neighbourhood has
been howling dismally. I envy strong men who don't notice
those things at such moments.

My uncle Parain said nothing to me at all—a proof of the
largeness and goodness of his heart. I shall always be more
grateful to him for his silence than for the greatest possible
service.

In the waiting-room there was a gentleman (a business
acquaintance of Bonenfant) who was deploring the fate of
dogs who travelled in the baggage-car. "They are with unknown dogs who give them fleas; the small dogs are
smothered by the big dogs; one would rather pay a little
more, etc." Suddenly Eugénie appeared, in tears: "Monsieur Parain! Madame Flaubert wants you, she is having
hysterics!" And they hurried off together.

From Nogent to Paris: what a ride! I closed the windows
(I was alone in the compartment), held my handkerchief
to my mouth, and wept. After a time the sound of my
own voice brought me to myself, then the sobs began

again. At one point I felt so giddy that I was afraid. "Calm yourself! Calm yourself!" I opened the window; the moon, surrounded by a halo of mist, was shining in puddles; it was cold. I thought of my mother, her face all contracted from weeping, the droop at the corners of her mouth. . . .

At Montereau I went into the station restaurant and drank three or four glasses of rum, not to try to forget things, but just to do something, anything.

Then my misery took another form: I conceived the idea of returning. (At every station I was on the point of getting out; only the fear of being a coward kept me from it.) I imagined the voice of Eugénie, crying: "Madame! Madame! It's Monsieur Gustave!" I could give my mother this enormous pleasure at once; it depended solely on me. I lulled myself with this idea; I was exhausted, and it relaxed me.

Arrival in Paris: interminable wait for my baggage. I cross the city, via the Marais and the Place Royale. I had to make up my mind before arriving at Maxime's. He was out. Aimée receives me, tries to stir up the fire. Maxime returns at midnight. I felt deflated, and completely undecided. He told me it was up to me to choose, and finally I decided not to return to Nogent. At one o'clock in the morning, after hours of sobbing and anguish such as no other separation had ever caused me, I wrote a letter to my mother.

The next two days I lived lavishly—huge dinners, quantities of wine, visits to brothels. The senses are not far removed from the emotions, and my tortured nerves needed relaxation.

FLAUBERT TO HIS MOTHER

Paris, October 26, 1849,
One o'clock in the morning.

You are probably sleeping now, my poor darling. How you must have wept tonight! So did I, I assure you! Tell me how you are; keep nothing from me; for if I should find out later that this trip of mine were really too much for you to bear I should be filled with horrible remorse.

Max is very good to me; you have no reason to fear on that score. I found our passports ready. Everything has gone smoothly—a good sign. Adieu. This is my first letter, others will soon follow. Tomorrow I will send you a longer one. And you? Write me volumes. *Overflow* into your letters! Adieu. I hug you; my heart is full of you. A thousand kisses.

FLAUBERT TO HIS MOTHER

Paris, October 26, 1849,
Later in the day.

[From the second of eight letters written to his mother between his departure from Nogent and his embarkation at Marseille.]

One day has gone by, poor darling, probably the worst. How wretched you must have been today! I keep thinking of your dear sad face. . . . Max has been kindness itself, even offering to see about trains should I decide to return to Nogent. It is understood between us that once we have seen Egypt, if we are not well, or if I feel I cannot remain away from you, or if you call me back, I will return. So do not torment yourself in advance, have no fears; I feel that the longing to be back with you will see me through everything. Oh, how I will hug you when I return, my darling!

FROM THE ''SOUVENIRS LITTÉRAIRES'' OF
MAXIME DU CAMP

We were to leave Paris on the twenty-ninth of October. Flaubert had taken his mother to her family at Nogent-sur-Seine, and on the twenty-sixth he came to stay with me. I had not been aware that he intended to come, but when I returned home that evening my servant told me he had arrived.

I did not see him at first when I entered my study, but after a moment I saw that he was stretched out at full length on a black bearskin in front of a bookcase. I thought he was sleeping, but then I heard him sigh. I have never beheld such a state of prostration, and his size and appearance of physical strength made it all the more remarkable. When I questioned him he replied with lamentations:

"Never again will I see my mother or my country! This journey is too long, too distant, it is tempting Providence! What madness! Why are we going?" I was dismayed. He told me that he had left his study at Croisset exactly as though he were going to return to it the next day—on the table a book open at the page he had last read, his dressing gown thrown over a chair, his slippers near the divan. "It is unlucky to take precautions," he told me, and then, referring to my grandmother's death, said cruelly: "You are lucky; you leave no one behind."

I gave him the night in which to recover from this state of discouragement, but the next morning before he was up I went into his room. "There is nothing that obliges you to leave with me," I said. "If you think the trip is more than you can do, you ought to give it up. I will go alone." The struggle was brief. "No!" he cried. "I'd be so ridiculous that I'd never dare look at myself in a mirror again!"

The arrival of Bouilhet and of my friend Louis de Cormenin, who came to keep us company during the last days, was a diversion for him. He threw off his languor and was himself again.

On the twenty-eighth we had a farewell dinner. Théophile Gautier, Louis de Cormenin, Bouilhet, Flaubert, and I dined in one of the private rooms of the restaurant Les Trois Frères Provençaux, in the Palais Royal, and spent the evening talking of art, literature, and the ancient world. Flaubert, very keyed up, spoke of discovering the sources of the Nile. Gautier urged me to become a Musulman, that I might wear silken robes and kiss the black stone at Mecca. Louis de Cormenin was depressed because of my departure, and Bouilhet silently gnawed the end of his cigar after enjoining us to think of him if we should find ourselves in the presence of some relic of Cleopatra. As we separated, we said affectionate farewells.

The express did not exist in those days, and it was a long journey from Paris to Marseille. On the twenty-ninth we took the stage-coach, then the steamer from Chalon to

Lyon, then the Rhône boat as far as Valence, where we
were stopped by fog, then a postchaise to Avignon, and
finally the railroad, which took us to Marseille on November 1. On the fourth, in overcast, dirty weather, we
boarded the *Nil,* a steam packet of 250 horsepower which
rolled like a drunken man and made but little headway.

I cannot say that Flaubert had no recurrence of his melancholy. He stood for a long time leaning against the side,
gazing at the coast of Provence as it gradually disappeared
into the fog. After eleven days of wind and heavy seas, we
sighted the shore of Egypt, and on the fifteenth of November 1849, we disembarked at Alexandria.

FLAUBERT TO HIS MOTHER

> *Malta. On board the Nil.*
> *Night of Wednesday–Thursday,*
> *November 7–8, 1849.*

. . . One of the most comical-looking faces is Maxime's.
He did not expect to be sick, poor boy, and recommended
me to the attention of the ship's doctor, whereas I haven't
had a moment's discomfort and he scarcely stops suffering
for a second. As to his servant Sassetti, he puts on a bold
front, but he is hardly any steadier on his feet than his
master. . . .

2.

FLAUBERT TO HIS MOTHER

> *Alexandria, November 17, 1849.*

. . . When we were two hours out from the coast of
Egypt I went into the bow with the chief quartermaster
and saw the seraglio of Abbas Pasha like a block dome on
the blue of the Mediterranean. The sun was blazing down
on it. I had my first sight of the Orient through, or rather

in, a glowing light that was like melted silver on the sea. Soon the shore became distinguishable, and the first thing we saw on land was a pair of camels led by their driver; then, on the dock, some Arabs peacefully fishing. Landing took place amid the most deafening uproar imaginable: Negroes, Negresses, camels, turbans, cudgellings to right and left, and guttural cries that hurt the eardrums. I am gulping down a whole bellyful of colours, like a donkey filling himself with hay. Cudgellings play a great role here; everyone who wears clean clothes beats everyone who wears dirty ones, and when I say clothes I mean a pair of short breeches. You see many gentlemen sauntering along the streets clad in nothing but a shirt and a long pipe. Except in the very lowest classes, all women are veiled, and in their noses they wear ornaments which hang down and sway from side to side like the face-drops of a horse. On the other hand, if you don't see their faces, you see their entire bosoms. As you change countries, you find that modesty changes its location, like a bored traveller who keeps shifting from one seat in the carriage to another. One curious thing here is the respect, or rather the terror, that everyone displays in the presence of "Franks," as they call Europeans. We have had bands of ten or twelve Arabs, advancing across the whole width of a street, break apart to let us pass. Alexandria is really almost a European city, full of Englishmen, Italians, etc. Yesterday we saw a magnificent procession celebrating the circumcision of the son of a rich merchant. This morning we saw Cleopatra's Needles (two huge obelisks on the shorefront), Pompey's column, the catacombs, and Cleopatra's baths. Tomorrow we leave for Rosetta, whence we shall return in three or four days. We go slowly and don't get overtired, living sensibly and clad in flannel from head to foot, even though the temperature indoors is sometimes 30 degrees [Réaumur]. As to ophthalmia, it is found only among people of "the most vile condition," as they say here. A young doctor who has been in Egypt for five years told me this morning that he has not known of a single case among well-to-do people or Europeans. So don't be afraid. Be brave. I'll come back in good repair.

FLAUBERT TO HIS MOTHER

Alexandria, November 23, 1849.

We set out at daybreak last Sunday, saddled and booted, harnessed and armed, with four men running behind us and our dragoman, mounted on his mule, carrying our coats and provisions. The desert begins at the very gates of Alexandria: first mounds of sand covered here and there with palms, and then dunes which stretch on endlessly.

At a place called Edku (you will find it on your map) we took a ferry and there our four runners bought some dates from a camel-driver whose beasts were laden with them. A mile or two further on we were riding tranquilly along side by side, a hundred feet in front of our runners, when suddenly we heard loud cries from behind. We turned, and saw our men in a tumult, jostling and pushing one another and making signs for us to turn back. Sassetti dashed off at a gallop, his velvet jacket streaming out behind him, and digging our spurs into our horses we followed after to the scene of the conflict. It was occasioned, we discovered, by the owner of the dates, who had been following his camels at a distance and who, coming upon our men and seeing that they were eating dates, had believed they had stolen them and had fallen on them with his cudgel.

But when he saw us three ruffians descending upon him with rifles slung over our saddles, roles were reversed, and from the beater which he was, he became the beaten. Courage returned to our men, and they fell upon him with their sticks in such a way that his backside was soon resounding with blow after blow. To escape, he ran into the sea, lifting up his robe to keep it dry, but his assailants followed. The higher he lifted his robe, the greater the area he exposed to their cudgels, which rattled on him like drumsticks. You can't imagine anything funnier than that man's black behind amidst the white foam churned up by the combat. The rest of us stood on the shore, laughing like fools; my sides still ache when I think of it. Two days later, coming back from Rosetta, we met the same camels as they were returning from Alexandria. Perceiving us from afar, the owner hastily left his beasts and made a long detour in the desert to avoid us—a precaution which diverted us considerably. You would scarcely believe the important role played by the cudgel in this part of the world; buffets are distributed with a sublime prodigality, always accompanied by loud cries; it's the most genuine kind of local colour you can think of.

At six in the evening, after a sunset which made the sky look like melted red paint and the sand of the desert like ink, we arrived at Rosetta and found all the gates closed. At the name of Soliman Pasha they opened, groaning softly like the doors of a barn. The streets were dark, and so narrow that there was just room enough for a single horseman. We went through the bazaars, where each shop was lit by a glass of oil hanging from a cord, and arrived at the barracks. The pasha received us on his sofa, surrounded by blacks who brought us pipes and coffee. After many courtesies and compliments, we were given supper and shown to our beds, which were equipped with excellent mosquito-netting. The next morning, while we were washing, the pasha came into our room followed by the regimental doctor, an Italian who spoke French perfectly and did us the honours of the city. Thanks to him we spent a very agreeable day. When he learned my name and that I was the son of a doctor, he said he had heard of Father and had often seen his name cited. It was no small satisfaction to me, dear Mother, to think that the memory of Father was still useful to me, serving as a kind of protection at this distance. That reminds me that in the depths of Brittany, too, at Guérande, the local doctor told me he had quoted Father in his thesis. Yes, poor darling, I think of you both constantly; as my body continues on its journey, my thoughts keep turning backward and bury themselves in days past. . . .

FROM FLAUBERT'S TRAVEL NOTES

First night on the Nile. Feelings of contentment, of lyricism: I make gestures, recite lines from Bouilhet, cannot bring myself to go to bed, think of Cleopatra. The water is yellow and very smooth; a few stars. Well wrapped in my pelisse, I fall asleep on my camp-bed, on deck. Such rapture! I awoke before Maxime; in waking, he stretched out his left hand instinctively, to see if I was there.

On one side, the desert; on the other, a green meadow. With its sycamores it resembles from a distance a Norman plain with its apple-trees. The desert is a reddish-grey. Two of the pyramids come into view, then a smaller one. To our left, Cairo appears, huddled on a hill; the dome of the mosque of Mohammed Ali; behind it, the bare Mokattam hills.

Arrival in Bûlâq, confusion of landing, a few less cudgel-lings than at Alexandria, however.

From Bûlâq to Cairo, road along a kind of embankment planted with acacias. We come into the Ezbekîya, all land-scaped. Trees, greenery. Take rooms at the Hôtel d'Orient.

FLAUBERT TO HIS MOTHER

Cairo, December 2, 1849.

Here we are at Cairo, poor darling, where we shall probably stay the entire month of December, until the return of the pilgrims from Mecca, which should take place in a little more than three weeks. We are going to visit Cairo carefully, and force ourselves to do some work every evening, a thing we have not yet done. Toward the first of January we shall board a Nile boat and go up the river for six weeks, then drift down it and return here. The entire journey to Upper Egypt is extremely easy and without the slightest danger of any kind, especially at this season when the heat is far from excessive. If you would like to have an inventory of what I wear these days, poor darling, here it is: flannel body belt, flannel shirt, flannel drawers, thick trousers, warm vest, large neck-cloth, with an overcoat, besides, morning and evening; and under my red tarboosh I wear two white skullcaps.

It's at Cairo that the Orient begins. Alexandria is too diluted with Europeans to have kept a very pure local colour. Here there are fewer hats. We haunt the bazaars,

the cafés, the mosques, and especially the buffoons—
strolling comedians of great talent, whose jokes are more
than indelicate. One of our first visits was to the slave
market. What contempt for human flesh! Socialism is not
very near in Egypt. I am lost in admiration of the camels
who keep crossing the streets and lying down between
the shops in the bazaars.

FROM FLAUBERT'S TRAVEL NOTES

Little street behind the Hôtel d'Orient. We are taken
upstairs into a large room. A kind of alcove projects out
over the street; on each side of the alcove, little windows
which cannot be shut. Opposite the alcove, a large window
without frame or glass; through it, a palm-tree. On a large
divan to the left, two women squatting; on a kind of
mantelpiece, a nightlight and a bottle of raki. La Triestina
came down, a small woman, blond, red-faced. The first of
the two women—thick lips, snub-nosed, gay, brutal: *"Un
poco matta, Signor,"* said La Triestina; the second, large
black eyes, straight nose, tired plaintive air, probably the
mistress of some European. She understands two or three
words of French and has heard of the Legion of Honour.
La Triestina was violently afraid of the police, begged us
to make no noise. Abbas Pasha [the viceroy], who is fond
only of men, makes things difficult for women; in this
public-house it is forbidden to dance or play music. Nevertheless she played the darâbukka on the table with her
fingers, while the other, having rolled her girdle and
knotted it low on her hips, danced; she did an Alexandrian
dance which consists, as to arm movements, in raising
the edge of each hand alternately to the forehead. Another dance: arms stretched straight out frontways, upper
arm a little bent, the torso motionless; the pelvis quivers.
Preliminary ablutions of these ladies. A litter of kittens had
to be removed from my bed. Hadely did not undo her
jacket, making signs to show me she had pain in her chest.
    Effect: she in front of me, rustling her clothes, noise
made by the golden coins in her hair—a clear-cut, quiet
sound. Moonlight. She carried a torch.

On the matting: her firm flesh. Bronze. Shaven. Fatty but dry. She helped me to get back into my clothes. Her words in Arabic that I did not understand. Questions of three or four words; as she waited for the answer, her eyes seemed to enter into mine and mine into hers; the intensity of her look was doubled. Expression of Joseph (the dragoman) amid all this. Lovemaking by interpreter.

FLAUBERT TO HIS COUSIN,
MADAME BONENFANT

Cairo, December 4, 1849.

First of all, dear relatives, let me tell you that I don't know how to thank you for the tender care you are lavishing on my poor mother. She needs it badly, I can assure you, and without you I don't know what would become of her. In a letter I received yesterday, she speaks of returning to Rouen toward the end of December. I think she would do well to stay there as short a time as possible and then come back to you; there is no place where she would be better off.

When you answer this, dear Olympe, tell me frankly how she is, whether or not she is too sad, etc. She is being very reasonable in her letters, but I am afraid she may be writing them with great care, and, out of fear of depressing me, putting on a brave front to mask her true state of mind. In any case, hide nothing from me: in this I appeal to your frankness and your kind heart. You probably took her in your arms that evening when I left: how she wept! I thank you for all the tenderness you gave her at that terrible moment. None of it is lost: I gather up every drop of it and store it in a safe place. . . .

FROM FLAUBERT'S TRAVEL NOTES

The pyramids. Set out at noon on Friday, Max mounted on a white horse that kept jerking its head, Sassetti also on a white horse, myself on a bay, Joseph on a donkey. At Giza we saw stretching out ahead of us an immense, very green meadow, with squares of black soil which are the plots most recently ploughed, the last abandoned by the flood: they stand out like India ink on the solid green. I think of the invocation to Isis: "Hail, hail, black soil of Egypt!" The soil of Egypt *is* black. Some buffaloes grazing; now and again a waterless, muddy brook in which our horses sink to their knees; soon we are crossing great puddles of water or brooks.

About half-past three we are almost on the edge of the desert, the pyramids looming up ahead of us. I can hold myself in no longer, and dig in my spurs; my horse bursts into a gallop, splashing through the swamp. Two minutes later Maxime followed suit. Furious race. I begin to shout in spite of myself; we climb rapidly up to the Sphinx, clouds of sand swirling about us. For a time our Arabs followed us, saying: "Oh! Oh! Oh!" It grew larger and larger and seemed to rise out of the ground like a dog gradually lifting itself up.

View of the Sphinx: Abu-el-Houl (Father of Terror). The sand, the pyramids, the Sphinx, all grey and bathed in a rosy light; the sky perfectly blue, eagles slowly wheeling and soaring over the tops of the pyramids. We stop before the Sphinx; it seems to fix us with a terrifying stare; Maxime is quite pale; I am afraid of becoming giddy, and try to conquer my emotion. We ride off madly at full speed. We walk our horses slowly around the base of the pyramids. Our baggage is late in coming; night falls.

The tent is raised. Dinner. Effect of the little white cloth lantern hanging from the tent-pole. Our guns are stacked. The Arabs sit in a circle around their fire or sleep under their blankets in the holes they dig in the sand with their hands; they lie there like corpses in their shrouds. I fall asleep in my pelisse, noticing all these things; the Arabs sing in a monotonous tone; I hear one telling a story. Desert life.

At two o'clock Joseph wakes us, thinking that day is breaking, but it was only a white cloud on the opposite horizon, and the Arabs had mistaken Sirius for Venus. I smoke a pipe in the starlight, looking up at the sky; a jackal howls.

Ascent. Up at five—the first—and wash in front of the

tent in the canvas pail. We hear several jackals barking.
Ascent of the great pyramid, the one to the right
(Cheops). The stones which at a distance of two hundred
paces seem the size of paving blocks are in reality—the
smallest of them—three feet high; generally they come up
to our chests. We go up at the left-hand corner (opposite
the pyramid of Khephren); the Arabs push and pull me;
I am quickly exhausted, it is desperately tiring. I stop five
or six times on the way up. Maxime started before me and
goes fast. Finally I arrive at the top.

On the side of the pyramid lit by the rising sun I see a
business card: "Humbert, Polisher," fastened to the stone
with pins. (Pathetic condition of Maxime, who has raced
up the pyramids ahead of me to put it there; he nearly
died of breathlessness.) Imbeciles have written their names
everywhere: "Buffard, 79 Rue Saint-Martin, wallpaper
manufacturer," in black letters; some Englishman has
written "Jenny Lind"; almost all the names are modern.
Easy descent at the opposite corner.

After breakfast we visit the interior of the pyramid.
Smooth, even corridor (like a sewer) which you descend;
then another corridor ascends; we slip on bats' dung. It
seems that these corridors were made to permit the huge
coffins to be drawn slowly into place.

As we emerged on hands and knees from one of the corridors, we meet a party of Englishmen who are coming in;
they are in the same position as we; exchange of civilities;
each party proceeds on its way. . . .

FLAUBERT TO LOUIS BOUILHET

Cairo, end of December 1849.
De Saltatoribus. We have not yet seen any dancing girls;
they are all in exile in Upper Egypt. But we have seen
dancing men. Oh! Oh! Oh! That was us, calling you. I
was indignant and very sad that you were not here.

Three or four musicians playing curious instruments
(we shall bring some home) took up their positions at the
end of the hotel dining room while one gentleman was still
having his dinner and the rest of us were sitting on the

divan smoking our pipes. As dancers, imagine two scoundrels, quite ugly, but charming in their corruption, in the intentional degradation of their glances and the femininity of their movements, their eyes painted with antimony and dressed as women. For costume, they had wide trousers and an embroidered jacket. The latter came down to the epigastrium, whereas the trousers, held up by an enormous cashmere girdle folded double several times, began only at the bottom of the stomach, so that the entire stomach, the loins, and the beginning of the buttocks are naked, seen through a black gauze held tight against the skin by the upper and lower garments. At every movement, this gauze ripples with a mysterious, transparent undulation. The music never changed or stopped during the two hours. The flute is shrill, you feel the throb of the tambourines in your breast, the voice of the singer dominates everything. The dancers advance and retreat, moving the pelvis with a short convulsive movement. A quivering of the muscles is the only way to describe it; when the pelvis moves, the rest of the body is motionless; when the breast shakes, nothing else moves. In this manner they advance toward you, their arms extended and rattling a kind of metal castanet, and their faces, under the rouge and the sweat, remain more expressionless than a statue's. By that I mean they never smile. The effect is produced by the gravity of the head in contrast to the lascivious movements of the body. Sometimes they lie down flat on their backs, like a woman in bed, then rise up with a movement of the loins similar to that of a tree which swings back into place after the wind has stopped. In their bowings and salutations their great trousers suddenly inflate like oval balloons, then seem to melt away, expelling the air that swells them. From time to time, during the dance, the impresario who brought them plays around them, kissing them on the stomach and the loins, and makes obscene remarks in an effort to put additional spice into a thing which is already quite clear in itself. It is too beautiful to be exciting. I doubt whether we shall find the women as good as the men; the ugliness of the latter adds greatly to the thing as Art. I had a headache for the rest of the day.

• • •

The other day I took a bath. I was alone in the depths of the hot-room, watching the daylight fade through the great circles of glass in the dome. Hot water was flowing everywhere; stretched out indolently I thought of a quantity of things as my pores tranquilly dilated. It is very voluptuous and sweetly melancholy, to take a bath like that quite alone, lost in those dark rooms where the slightest noise resounds like a cannon-shot, while the naked Kellaks call out to one another as they massage you, turning you over like embalmers preparing you for the tomb.

We chat with priests of all the religions. The poses and attitudes which the people take are sometimes really beautiful. We have them translate songs, tales, traditions—the most genuinely popular and oriental things possible. We hire scholars for this—that is literally true. We act with considerable swank, and permit ourselves much insolence and enormous liberty of language. The proprietor of our hotel thinks that we sometimes go a little far. One of these days we are to have a visit from some sorcerers—always in the hope of seeing more beautiful oriental movements.

Go to see my mother often; keep up her courage; write to her when she is away; the poor woman needs it. And in the evening, when you come home and the verses do not come and you think of me, and are bored, take a sheet of paper and write me everything, everything that comes into your head. I devoured your letter when it came, and have reread it several times.

FROM THE ''SOUVENIRS LITTERAIRES'' OF
MAXIME DU CAMP

This man was relatively learned. He knew everything about the precepts of Islamism, about Mohammedan customs, and about the cabbalistic lore which is so thoroughly interwoven with religious ceremony as to form a part of the liturgy. We made an arrangement with him. For three francs an hour he was to spend four hours with us daily, replying to the questions which we put to him. It was money well earned and wisely spent. It was I who led the questioning, for I had the intention of using the information in a book to be called *Mohammedan Morals*. Birth, circumcision, marriage, the pilgrimage to Mecca, death-rites, and the last judgment, those six points which in the Orient sum up almost the whole of life, were fully treated by Khalil Effendi, and we took notes as we spoke. Flaubert intended to use his memoranda for an oriental story he had in mind. . . .

FLAUBERT TO HIS MOTHER

Cairo, January 5, 1850.

Your fine long letter of the sixteenth arrived in time to be a New Year's gift, poor darling. I was making an official New Year's call on the French consul when the mail pouch was delivered. He opened it at once, and I seized the envelope, which I recognized among a hundred others (my fingers itched to open it, but etiquette, alas, forbade that). Fortunately, he invited us to step into his salon and pay our respects to his wife, and since in the pile of letters there was one for her from her mother, each of us granted the other permission to read his correspondence, almost before even exchanging greetings.

A few days ago I spent a fine afternoon. Max remained at home to do I forget what, and I took Hassan (a second dragoman we have temporarily hired) and paid a visit to the bishop of the Copts for the sake of a conversation with him. I entered a square courtyard surrounded by columns, in the centre of which was a little garden—that is, a few large trees and borders of dark greenery around which ran a kind of latticework divan. My dragoman, with his wide trousers and his large-sleeved jacket, walked ahead; I behind. On one of the corners of the divan was sitting a scowling, evil-looking old personage with a white beard, wearing a heavy pelisse; books in a baroque kind of hand-writing were strewn all about him. At a certain distance were standing three doctors in black robes, younger and also with long beards. The dragoman said: "This is a

French gentleman (*cawadja fransaoui*) who is travelling all
over the world in search of knowledge, and who has come
to you to converse of your religion." The bishop received
me with many courtesies; coffee was brought, and soon
I began to ask questions concerning the Trinity, the Virgin,
the Gospels, the Eucharist—all my old erudition of *Saint
Antoine* came back in a flood. It was superb, the sky blue
above us, the trees, the quantities of books, the old fellow
ruminating in his beard before answering me, myself
sitting cross-legged beside him, gesticulating with my
pencil and taking notes, while Hassan stood motionless,
translating aloud, and the three other doctors, seated on
their stools, nodded their heads and interpreted an occasional word. I enjoyed it deeply. That was indeed the
ancient Orient, land of religions and flowing robes. When
the bishop gave out, one of the doctors replaced him; and
when finally I saw that they were all somewhat flushed,
I left. I am going back, for there is much to learn in that
place. The Coptic religion is the most ancient of existing
Christian sects, and little or nothing is known about it in
Europe (so far as I know). I am going likewise to talk
with the Armenians, the Greeks, the Sunnites, and especially the Mohammedan scholars.

We are still waiting for the return of the caravan from
Mecca; it is too good an event to miss, and we shall not
leave for Upper Egypt until the pilgrims have arrived.
There are some droll things to see, we have been told: the
horses of the priests walking over the prostrate bodies of
the faithful, all kinds of dervishes, singers, etc.

When I think of my future (that happens rarely, for I
generally think of nothing at all, despite the elevated
thoughts one should have in the presence of ruins!), when
I ask myself: "What shall I do when I return? What shall
I write? What will I be good for? Where shall I live?
What path shall I follow?" and the like, I am full of doubts
and indecisions. At every stage of my life I have shirked,
in just this way, facing my problems, and I shall die at
sixty before having formed any opinion concerning myself
or, perhaps, writing anything that would have shown me
my capabilities. Is *Saint Antoine* a good book or a bad
one? That is something I often ask myself. Was I really

mistaken in it, or was it perhaps the others who were wrong? However, I do not worry about any of this; I live like a plant, filling myself with sun and light, with colours and fresh air. I keep eating, so to speak; later the problem of digestion will have to be solved, and that is the important thing.

You ask me whether the Orient is up to what I imagined it to be. Yes, it is, and more than that it extends far beyond the narrow idea I had of it. I have found, clearly delineated, everything that was hazy in my mind. Facts have taken the place of suppositions—so excellently so that it is often as though I were suddenly coming upon old and forgotten dreams.

FROM FLAUBERT'S TRAVEL NOTES

Sunday, January 6 [*1850*]. We spend the whole afternoon shooting birds of prey along the aqueduct. Whitish, wolf-like dogs with pointed ears frequent this malodorous region; they dig holes in the sand, nests where they lie. Carcasses of camels, horses, and donkeys. The muzzles of some of the dogs are purple with clotted blood that has been caked by the sun; bitches in whelp walk about with their big bellies; according to their nature they bark sharply or move aside to let us pass. A dog from another troop gets a far from friendly welcome here. A caravan of fourteen camels passes along the arches of the aqueduct while I am watching for vultures. The brilliant sun makes the carrion stink. The dogs doze or tranquilly tear at the carrion.

After shooting at eagles and kites we take a few shots at the dogs; one shot, landing near them, made them move off slowly, without running. We were on one low hill, they on another; all the hollow between us was in the shade. One white dog standing poised against the sun, ears erect. The one Maxime wounded in the shoulder half turned around, rolled on the ground in convulsions, then went off—probably to die in his hole. At the place where he was standing when hit, we saw a puddle of blood and a trail of drops leading in the direction of the slaughterhouse. The latter is a medium-sized enclosure about three hundred paces away; but there is a hundred times more carrion without than within, where there is little but entrails and a pool of filth. It is just beyond, between the wall and the hill behind it, that one generally sees the greatest number of wheeling circles of birds. All the land in this area is only mounds of ashes and broken pottery. On one piece of pottery, drops of blood.

It is along the aqueduct that one generally finds the soldiers' prostitutes, who let themselves be taken here in exchange for a few paras. During the shoot, Maxime disturbed a group of them, and I treated our three donkey-drivers to Venus at a price of sixty paras (one and a half piastres—about seven sous). That day, a few soldiers and women were smoking at the foot of the arches and eating oranges; one of them was keeping a lookout on top of the aqueduct. I shall never forget the brutal movement of my old donkey-driver as he came down on the girl, taking her in his right arm, caressing her breasts with his left hand, dragging her down, all in one movement, laughing with his great white teeth. His little black wooden chibuq attached to his back; the rags wrapped around the lower part of his diseased legs.

FLAUBERT TO HIS MOTHER

Cairo, February 3, 1850.

We shall probably leave for Upper Egypt next Wednesday; the evening of our departure we are to dine with Soliman Pasha. Our boat will be waiting at his water-gate, and if there is a wind we shall get off directly after dinner. We'll go up the river as quickly as possible, stopping only when the wind stops—a thing that doesn't happen very often—and it is on our way back, downstream, that we shall stop and visit places at our leisure.

Our boat is painted blue; its rais (captain) is called Ibrahim. There is a crew of nine. For quarters we have a room with two divans facing each other, a large room with two beds and a kind of alcove for our baggage, and a third room where Sassetti will sleep and which will serve as a storehouse as well. The dragoman will sleep on the deck. The latter is a gentleman who has not taken off his clothes a single time since we have had him; his language is incredible and his appearance even more curious. However, he is a hearty and worthy kind of fellow, with whom one could go to the Antipodes without a scratch.

This is indeed an amusing country. Yesterday, for example, we were in a café which is one of the best in Cairo, and where there were, at the same time as ourselves, in the café, a donkey voiding and a gentleman urinating in a corner. No one finds that odd; no one says anything. Sometimes a man beside you will get up and begin to say his prayers, with great bowings and exclaimings, as though he were completely alone. No one even turns his head to look, it is all so natural. Can you imagine someone suddenly saying grace in the Café de Paris.

You ask me about my mission. I have almost nothing to do and I think that I will do almost nothing, and such being the case I should need considerably more cheek than I have to ask for any compensation. I am becoming less and less covetous of anything at all. After my return I shall resume my good life of work in my study, in my comfortable armchair, near you, my darling, and that is *all* I intend to do. So, please, don't speak about pushing myself ahead. What should I push myself toward? Except for the voluptuous joy that I always feel when I sit at my round writing table, what is there that would satisfy me? Am I not already in possession of everything that the world considers enviable? I have independence, freedom of fancy, two hundred pens, and a knowledge of how to use them. And then this Orient, particularly Egypt, tends to flatten out small worldly vanities. The sight of so many ruins makes you lose your desire to build anything new; all the dust of the ancients tends to make you indifferent to fame. At the present moment I certainly see no reason (even from a literary point of view) to do anything to get myself talked about. To live in Paris, to publish, to bestir myself—all that seems unbearable, from this distance. Perhaps I shall have changed my mind in ten minutes.

FROM "LE NIL, EGYPTE ET NUBIE,"
BY MAXIME DU CAMP

Our rais was a handsome young man of twenty-five, named Ibrahim. He spent his days sitting in the bow, staring straight ahead and uttering an occasional word of command. He rarely conversed with the sailors, ate alone, and never smoked. For an Arab he was meticulously, almost elegantly, clean and neat, and despite the extreme simplicity of his costume, which consisted of a blue gown and white turban, he had a somehow lordly air which gave even greater distinction to his dark, animated features, his soft and contemplative eyes. One day when he removed his turban so that his head might be shaved, I saw that his one lock of hair came down to his waist—beautiful black hair that many women might have envied. He was harsh and haughty with his men and sometimes struck them, but if it came to giving them an example in a difficult current he would seize the oars or the poles and propel the boat himself. Like all Arabs, he had no resistance against physical pain. At Muneiha, where I went ashore to make some purchases in the bazaars, I returned to the boat to find Rais Ibrahim weeping, rolling on the deck, and uttering cries of lamentation, to the dismay of his sailors. When I hastily asked him what was wrong, he informed me in tones of death that he had just had a tooth pulled. Regularly, every day, he said five prayers, and he almost never went ashore. During the five months he was in my service, I do not remember ever having to address him a word of reproach.

The dragoman, Joseph Brichetti, was a singular individual of fifty-five, thin and alert, with a long greyish beard and, in the offing, a young wife who instantly consumed every sou the poor fellow earned. He was a Genoese, and had sought his fortune in the Egyptian army, in commerce, and in the service of travellers, without ever having been able to find it. He had arrived in Egypt after a youth replete with adventure, and he now knew the country almost to its tiniest village and its last palm. His language, a mixture of Arabic, French, and Italian, was not always easily understood. Laziness, drunkenness, and women, the usual faults in dragomans, were not present in Joseph, and despite an unparalleled vanity he was assiduous and agreeable. His cleanliness, however, was more than doubtful: every morning after having lightly passed over his eyes the slightly dampened corner of a towel, he would say with satisfaction: "*Ah, j'o fini mon tolette!*" In all the twenty-five years that the poor man had travelled in the Orient he had never been able to accustom himself to vermin. On the coast of Phœnicia, at Oum-Khaled-el-Moukhalid, where we camped at a spot which had recently been the stopping-place of a caravan, I was awakened by Joseph's groans and found him scratching and desperately lamenting: "*Quo quantité de puces qui fa, bon Dieu!*" He was unable either to read or write, an ignorance which caused him constant humiliation and regret. "At this minute I would be a colonel with the Turks or captain of a Turkish frigate, if I knew how to write," he told me one day, and he was probably right. He was never drunk, robbed me not excessively, obeyed orders quickly, and was enormously useful on the Nile. He lived on fairly good terms with my servant Louis Sassetti, who had come with me from Paris and who in his quality of Frenchman despised all the "savages" with whom he was now in contact. It is thanks to the intelligent aid of Sassetti that I was able to bring to successful termination the photographic work that I had undertaken. He distilled the water and washed the utensils, leaving me free to devote myself to the fatiguing business of making negatives. If, some day, my soul is condemned to eternal damnation, it will be in punishment for the rage, the fury, the vexation aroused in me by my photography, an art which at that time was far from being as easy and expeditious as it is today.

Every time that I visited a monument I had my photographic apparatus carried along and took with me one of my sailors, Hadji Ismael, an extremely handsome Nubian, whom I had climb up onto the ruins which I wanted to photograph. In this way I was able to include a uniform scale of proportions in every one of my plates. The great difficulty was to get Hadji Ismael to stand perfectly

motionless while I performed my operations, and I was
finally inspired to tell him that the brass tube of the lens
jutting from the camera was a cannon, which would vomit
a hail of shot if he had the misfortune to move—a story
which immobilized him completely.

The day I returned from an expedition to Dendera I
overheard the following conversation between him and
Rais Ibrahim:

"Well, Hadji Ismael, what news?"

"None, Rais Ibrahim. The thin father ordered me to
climb up on a column which bore the huge face of an idol;
he enveloped his head in the black veil, he turned his
yellow cannon toward me, then he cried: 'Do not move!'
The cannon looked at me with its little shining eye, but I
kept very still, and it did not kill me."

"God is great," said Rais Ibrahim.

"And Mohammed is his prophet," replied Hadji.

According to Mohammedan law, full and complete ablu-
tion is indispensable following certain bodily acts. When
a husband leaves the women's apartments, for example, he
must entirely submerge himself—in a pool, in a river, anywhere, so long as his head is momentarily under water.
When he emerges, he raises his hands to heaven and says:
"O Lord, I render thee thanks for the joys thou hast given
me, and I pray thee to lead in holy ways the child that
may be born. O my God, make me blind in the presence
of unlawful women!"

Very often, standing on my boat at daybreak, I have
seen fellahin run to the Nile, strip off their clothing, and
plunge into the river. At such moments my sailors would
laugh and call out to the bathers pleasantries which were,
to put it mildly, indelicate.

FROM FLAUBERT'S TRAVEL NOTES

February 6, 1850. On board. As evening fell, our first
day out of Cairo, the sky became solid red to the right,
rosy to the left. The pyramids of Sakkara cut sharp grey
triangles out of the vermilion back-drop of the horizon.

To the left, the sky paled toward the zenith from rose to yellow, then to green; then the green itself paled, and with an almost imperceptible transition through white became the blue which made the vault above our heads. An incandescence glowed in the entire right-hand side of the sky, drenching it in golden light.

Dance of the sailors. Joseph at his stoves. The boat heeling. The Nile in the middle of the landscape; and we in the middle of the Nile. Tufts of palm-trees grow at the base of the pyramids of Sakkara like nettles at the foot of graves.

Somewhere, far away, on a river gentler and younger than this, I know a white house, and I know that its shutters are closed because I am not there. I know·that the poplars, stripped of their leaves, are trembling in the cold mist, and that cakes of ice are drifting on the river and being thrown up against the frozen banks. I know that the cows are in their stable, that the espaliers are covered with their straw, and that from the farmhouse chimney white smoke is rising slowly into the grey sky.

I see the long terrace, Louis XVI, bordered with lindens, where in summer I stroll in my dressing gown. In six weeks the trees will be budding, each branch will be studded with red. Then will come the primroses—yellow, green, rose, iris—decking the grass in the courts. O primroses, my pretty things, drop your seeds carefully, that I may see you another spring!

I see the long wall hung with roses, and the summer-house beside the water. A clump of honeysuckle grows outside, climbing up over the wrought-iron balcony. At one o'clock of a July morning I like to fish there in the moonlight.

FLAUBERT TO LOUIS BOUILHET

> *On board, March 13, 1850.*
> *12 leagues beyond Syene.*

In six or seven hours we are going to pass the tropic of that well-known personage Cancer. It is 30 degrees

[Réaumur] in the shade at this moment, we are barefoot
and clad in nothing but shirts, and I am writing to you on
my divan, to the sound of the darâbukkas of our sailors,
who are singing and clapping their hands. The sun is
beating down mercilessly on the awning over our deck.
The Nile is as flat as a river of steel. On its banks are
clumps of tall palms. The sky is blue as blue. *How I miss
you!*

Every day I read the *Odyssey* in Greek. Since we have
been on the Nile I have done four books; we are coming
home by way of Greece, so it may be of use to me. The
first days on board I began to write a little, but I was not
long, thank God, in realizing the ineptitude of such behaviour: just now it is best for me to be all eyes. We live,
therefore, in the grossest idleness, stretched out on our
divans watching everything that goes by: camels, herds
of oxen from the Sennâr, boats floating down to Cairo
laden with Negresses and elephants' tusks. We are now,
my dear sir, in a land where women go naked—one might
say with the poet "naked as the hand," for by way of
costume they wear only rings. I have seen daughters of
Nubia whose necklaces of golden coins descended below
their waist, and whose black stomachs were encircled by
strings of coloured beads. And their dancing! But let us
proceed in proper order.

From Cairo to Beni Suêf, nothing very interesting. From
Beni Suêf we took a five-day trip to Lake Mœris, and at
Medinet el-Faiyûm spent the night in the home of a Christian from Damascus, who offered his hospitality. With
him, evidently as boarder, there was a Catholic priest.
Under the pretext that the Mohammedans drink no wine,
these brave Christians gorge themselves with brandy: the
number of glasses tipped off in sign of religious con-
fraternity is incredible. Our host was a man of a little
learning, and since we were in the country of Saint
Anthony we spoke of him, of Arius, of Saint Athanasius,
etc., etc. The poor fellow was delighted. Do you know
what was hanging on the walls of the room where we
slept??!! An engraving of a view of Quillebœuf and another one of a view of the abbey at Granville!!!

Travelling that way, by land, you spend your nights in

houses of dried mud, looking up at the stars through chinks in the sugar-cane roofs. On your arrival the sheikh at whose home you are staying has a sheep killed, and the leading persons of the town come to pay you a visit and kiss your hands. You let them do it with the aplomb of a sultan, and then you take your place with them at table; that is, you all sit down on the ground around a common dish into which you dip your hands, tearing, chewing, and belching to outdo one another. The custom of the country demands that you belch after meals: I do it badly.

At a place called Gebel el-Teir we had an amusing sight. On the summit of a mountain overlooking the Nile there is a convent of Copts, who have the habit, as soon as they see a boatload of tourists, of running down, throwing themselves in the water, and swimming out to ask for alms. Everyone who passes is assailed by them. You see these wretches, totally naked, rushing down their perpendicular cliffs and swimming toward you as fast as they can, shouting: "*Baksheesh, baksheesh, cawadja christiani!*" And since there are many caverns in the cliff at this particular spot, echo repeats: "*Cawadja, cawadja!*" loudly as a cannon. Vultures and eagles were flying overhead, the boat was darting through the water, its two great sails bulging. To drive off the Christian monks one of our sailors, the clown of the crew, began to dance a naked, lascivious dance, offering them his behind as they clung to the sides of the boat. The other sailors screamed insults at them, repeating the names of Allah and of Mohammed. Some hit them with sticks, others with ropes; Joseph rapped their knuckles with his kitchen tongs. It was a chorus of blows, yells, and laughter. As soon as they were given money they put it in their mouths and returned home via the route they had come. If they weren't received with a good beating, the boats would be assailed by such hordes of them that capsizing would be almost inevitable.

At Qena we had landed to buy provisions and were walking peacefully and dreamily in the bazaars, inhaling the odour of sandalwood which floated about us, when suddenly, at a turn in the street, we found ourselves in the quarter of the prostitutes. Picture to yourself, my friend, five or six curving streets lined with hovels about four feet high, built of dry grey mud. At the doors, women standing or sitting on straw mats. The Negresses had dresses of sky-blue; others were in yellow, in white, in red—loose garments fluttering in the warm wind. Odours of spices. On their bare breasts long necklaces of golden coins, so that when they move they rattle like country carts. They call after you in drawling voices: "*Cawadja, cawadja,*" their white teeth gleaming between their red or black lips, their metallic eyes rolling round like wheels. I walked through these streets and walked through them again, giving baksheesh to all the women, letting them call me and catch hold of me; they took me round the waist and tried to pull me into their houses. I resisted, quite deliberately, having made up my mind not to destroy the mood of melancholy induced by the scene. I left completely dazzled, and have remained so. There is nothing more beautiful than the sight of such women calling you in the sunlight. If I had gone with them another image would have taken its place, lessened its splendour.

I have not, however, always been so stoically artistic; at Esna I visited Kuchiouk Hanem, a very celebrated courtesan. Her confidante had come to the boat in the morning, escorted by a pet sheep all spotted with yellow henna, with a black velvet muzzle on its nose, which followed her like a dog; very droll. . . .

FROM FLAUBERT'S TRAVEL NOTES

March 6 [1850]. Esna. House of Kuchiouk Hanem. Bambeh precedes me accompanied by her sheep; she pushes open a door and we enter a house with a small courtyard and a stairway opposite the door. On the stairs, opposite us, surrounded by light and standing against the background of blue sky, a woman in rose-coloured trousers. Above, she wore only a dark violet gauze.

She had just come from the bath, her firm breasts had a fresh odour, something like the smell of sweetened turpentine; she began by perfuming our hands with rose water.

Kuchiouk Hanem is a tall, splendid creature, lighter in colouring than an Arab; she comes from Damascus; her skin, particularly on her body, is slightly coffee-colored. When she bends, her flesh ripples into bronze ridges. Her eyes are black and enormous, her eyebrows black, her nostrils slit, broad heavy shoulders, full, apple-shaped breasts. She wore a large tarboosh, ornamented on the top with a convex golden disk, in the middle of which was a piece of green glass imitating emerald; the blue tassel of her tarboosh was spread out fanwise and fell down over her shoulders; just in front of the lower edge of the tarboosh, fastened to her hair and going from one ear to the other, she had a small spray of white artificial flowers. Her black hair, wavy, unruly, pulled straight back on each side from a centre part starting at the forehead. She has one upper incisor, right, which is beginning to go bad. Two bands of gold, twisted together and interlaced, around one wrist. Triple necklace of large hollow golden beads. Earrings: golden disks, slightly convex, circumference decorated with small golden seeds. On her right arm is tattooed a line of blue writing.

She asks us if we would like a little entertainment, but Max says that first he would like to entertain himself alone with her, and they go downstairs. After he finishes, I go down and follow his example. Ground-floor room, divan covered with a caftan.

The musicians arrive: a child and an old man, whose left eye is covered with a rag; they both scrape on the rebfabeh, a kind of small round violin with an iron leg which rests on the ground, and two horse-hair strings. The neck of the instrument is very long in proportion to the rest. Nothing is more discordant or disagreeable. The musicians never stop playing for an instant unless you shout at them to do so.

Kuchiouk Hanem and Bambeh begin to dance. Kuchiouk's dance is brutal. She squeezes her bare breasts together with her jacket. She puts on a girdle fashioned from a brown shawl with gold stripes, with three tassels hanging on ribbons. She rises first on one foot then on the other—marvellous movement: when one foot is on the ground, the other moves up and across in front of the shinbone—the whole thing with a light bound. I have seen this dance on old Greek vases.

Bambeh prefers a dance on a straight line; she moves with a lowering and raising of one hip only, a kind of rhythmic limping of great character. Bambeh has henna on her hands. She seems to be a devoted servant to Kuchiouk. (She was a chambermaid in Cairo in an Italian household and understands a few words of Italian; her eyes are slightly diseased.) All in all, their dancing—except Kuchiouk's step mentioned above—is far less good than that of Hassan el-Bibesis (the male dancer in Cairo). Joseph's opinion is that all beautiful women dance badly.

Kuchiouk took a darâbukka. When she plays it, she takes a superb pose: the darâbukka is on her knees, or rather on her left thigh; the left elbow is lowered, the left wrist raised, and the fingers of the left hand, as they play, fall separately on the skin of the darâbukka; the right hand strikes flatly, marking the rhythm. She leans her head slightly back, in a stiffened, scornful pose, the whole body slightly arched.

These ladies, and particularly the old musician, imbibe considerable raki. Kuchiouk dances with my tarboosh on her head. Then she accompanies us to the end of her quarter, climbing up on our backs and making faces and jokes like any Christian tart.

At the café. A hut with sunlight filtering through the branches and making luminous patches on the matting where we are seated. We take a cup of coffee. Kuchiouk's joy at seeing our shaven heads and hearing Max say: "*La illah Allah Mohammed rassoun Allah.*"

Second and more detailed visit to the temple.

Dinner.

We go back to Kuchiouk's house. The room was lighted by three wicks in glasses full of oil, inserted in tin sconces hanging on the wall. The musicians are in their places. Many glasses of brandy are quickly drunk; the liquor and the fact that we wear swords have their effect.

Arrival of Saphiah Zougairah, a small woman with a large nose and eyes that are black, deep-set, savage, sensual;

her necklace of coins clanks like a country cart; she kisses our hands.

The four women seated in a line on the divan singing. The lamps cast quivering, lozenge-shaped shadows on the walls, the light is yellow. Bambeh wore a rose-coloured robe with large sleeves (all the costumes are in light colours) and her hair was covered with a black kerchief such as the fellahin wear. They all sang, the darâbukkas throbbed, and the monotonous rebecks furnished a soft but shrill bass; it was like a rather gay song of mourning.

Coup with Saphiah Zougairah (little Sophie). She is very corrupt and writhing, extremely voluptuous, but the best was the second with K. Feeling of her necklace between my teeth. I felt like a tiger.

Kuchiouk dances the bee-dance. First, so that the door can be closed, the women send away Fergalli and another sailor who up to now have been watching the dances and who, in the background, constituted the grotesque element of the picture. A black veil is tied around the eyes of the child, and a fold of his blue turban is lowered over those of the old man. Kuchiouk shed her clothing as she danced. Finally she was naked except for a handkerchief which she held in her hands and behind which she pretended to hide, and at the end she threw down the handkerchief. That was the bee-dance. She danced it very briefly and said she does not like to dance that dance. Joseph, very excited, kept clapping his hands: *"La, eu, nia, oh! eu, nia, oh!"* Finally, after repeating for us the wonderful step she had danced in the afternoon, she sank down breathless on her divan, her body continuing to move slightly in rhythm. One of the women gave her huge white trousers striped with rose, and she pulled them on up to her neck. The two musicians were unblindfolded.

When she was squatting on the divan, the magnificent, absolutely sculptural design of her knees.

Another dance: a cup of coffee is placed on the ground; she dances before it, then falls on her knees and continues to move her torso, always clacking the castanets, and describing in the air a kind of gesture with her arms as though she were swimming. That continues, gradually the

head is lowered, she reaches the cup, takes the edge of it
between her teeth, and then leaps up quickly with one
bound.

She was not too enthusiastic about having us spend the
night with her, out of fear of thieves who are apt to come
when they know strangers are there. Some guards or pimps
(on whom she did not spare the cudgel) slept downstairs
in a side room, with Joseph and the Negress, an Abyssinian
slave who carried on each arm the round scar (like a burn)
of a plague-sore. In bed. She insisted on keeping the outside. Lamp: the wick rested in an oval cup with a lip;
after violent caresses, *coup.* She falls asleep with her
hand in mine. She snores. The lamp, shining feebly, cast
a triangular gleam, the colour of pale metal, on her beautiful forehead; the rest of her face was in shadow. Her little
dog slept on my silken jacket on the divan. When she
· coughed, I covered her with my overcoat. I heard Joseph
and the guards talking in low voices; I gave myself over
to a nervous intensity full of reminiscences. Feeling her
stomach against my buttocks. The *mons,* warmer than the
stomach, heated me like a hot iron. Another time I dozed
off with my fingers passed through her necklace, as
though to hold her should she awake. I thought of Judith
and Holofernes sleeping together. At quarter of three,
awakening full of tenderness. We told each other a great
many things by pressure. (As she slept she kept con-
tracting her hands and thighs mechanically, like involun-
tary shudders.)

I smoke a chicheh, she goes down to talk with Joseph,
brings back a bucket of burning charcoal, warms herself,
comes back to bed. *Basta.*

How flattering it would be to the pride, if at the moment
of leaving you were sure that you left a memory behind,
that she would think of you more than of the others who
have been there, that you would remain in her heart!

In the morning we said farewell very calmly.

March 9 [1850]. Aswân. Aziza. This tall girl is named
Aziza. Her dancing is more expert than Kuchiouk's. For
dancing she takes off her flowing robe and puts on a cotton
dress of European cut. She begins. Her neck slides back

and forth on her vertebræ, and more often sideways, as though her head were going to fall off: terrifying effect of decapitation.

She stands on one foot, lifts the other, the knee making a right angle, then brings it down firmly. This is no longer Egypt; it is Negro, African, savage—as wild as the other was formal.

Another dance: putting the left foot in the place of the right, and the right in the place of the left, alternately and very fast.

The blanket which served as a rug in her hut became wrinkled; she stopped from time to time to pull it straight.

She stripped. On her stomach she wore a belt of coloured beads. Her long necklace of coins descended to her vagina, and she passed the end of it through the bead belt.

Furious jerkings of the hips. The face always expressionless. A little girl of two or three, affected by the music, tried to imitate her, and danced likewise, making no sound.

This was in an earthen hut, scarcely high enough for a woman to stand erect, in a section outside the city, all in ruins, razed to the ground. In the midst of this silence, these women in red and gold.

March 29 [*1850*]. *Abu Simbel.* Reflection: the Egyptian temples bore me profoundly. Are they going to become like the churches in Brittany, like the waterfalls in the Pyrenees? Oh, necessity! Necessity of doing what you *ought* to do; of always having to be, according to the circumstances (and despite the aversion of the moment), what a young man, or a tourist, or an artist, or a son, or a citizen, etc., *ought* to be!

April 4 [*1850*]. Left Es-Sebû'a at four a.m. About eleven o'clock we meet the boat of the effendi whom we had already seen at Wâdi Halfa and who is the nazir charged with extorting the taxes from Aswân to Wâdi Halfa. He surprised and forcibly seized a village sheikh who had not given a sou of the tax demanded; the old man was chained to the bottom of the boat; we could see only his bare black head shining in the sun. The effendi's boat keeps close to ours for a while, then touches ours bow on; a man hands over a small bleating sheep, a present from the effendi, who is clearly not sorry to be with us, in case of trouble. All day, as a matter of fact, we see men and women from rebellious villages following us, or rather following him, on the bank.

He pays us a long visit, we make him a present of a bottle of Cyprus wine and one of raki. The sheikh will be taken to Ed-Derr, where after four or five hundred blows he will be left fastened to a certain large sycamore-tree until someone goes bail for him.

We talk bastinado with the nazir. When a man is to be killed, four or five blows suffice—his thighs and neck are broken; when he is only to be punished, he is beaten on the buttocks: four to five hundred blows is the usual number; the patient is sick for five or six months after—it takes that long for the old flesh to be replaced by new. The effendi laughed as he added the last detail. In Nubia the bastinado is usually given on the soles of the feet. The Nubians greatly dread this punishment, since after it they are never again able to walk.

FROM THE "SOUVENIRS LITTÉRAIRES" OF
MAXIME DU CAMP

To Flaubert one temple seemed precisely like another, the mosques and the landscapes all the same. I am not sure that when gazing on the island of Elephantine he did not sigh for the meadows of Sotteville, or long for the Seine when he saw the Nile. At Philæ he settled himself comfortably in the cool shade of one of the halls of the great temple of Isis to read *Gerfaut*, by Charles de Bernard, which he had bought in Cairo. The thought of his mother continually drew him in the direction of Croisset, and the disappointment of *Saint Antoine* continued to distress him. Often of an evening, when the water murmured gently around our boat and the Southern Cross shone out among the stars, we would talk over his book which was so close to his heart.

FLAUBERT TO HIS MOTHER

Philæ, April 15, 1850.

Here we are, back from Nubia in as good condition as
we set out for it, if one can say such a thing after having
spent two long months without receiving a word from
those one loves most in the world. We arrived at Philæ
yesterday as night was falling. I at once set out with
Joseph on a donkey for Aswân (a league from here), in
the hope of finding a package of letters: nothing! I
imagine that you missed one mail and that all the other
letters are at the chancery in Cairo, where I have just
written to ask them to send them on to Qena; otherwise I
should be without letters from you until our return to
Cairo, the end of May. That will make, or would make,
almost four months without knowing what has become
of you.

The sky was beautiful last night, the stars were shining,
the Arabs singing on their dromedaries. It was a real oriental night, the blue of the sky hidden beneath the profusion
of the stars. But my heart was very sad, poor beloved
darling. Write me twice—even a hundred times—rather
than just once, by every mail. A letter is easily lost—
several of Max's have disappeared. If only I knew that
mine were reaching you, I would not complain. But that is
my greatest anguish. When I think of you fretting I am
miserable. Perhaps you are ill, my darling, perhaps at this
moment you are weeping, looking with those lovely
eyes I so adore at the map which represents to you only
an empty space in which your son is lost. No, no; I will
come back; you cannot be ill, for a strong desire preserves
life! It will soon be six months that I am gone; in six more
it will not be long before my return—that will probably be
next January or February.

Last night the effendi had letters for Maxime and even
for Sassetti, who never receives any. But nothing from you,
nothing from Achille, who should certainly be sending me
some news of you, it seems to me; nothing from Bouilhet;

nothing from Uncle Parain, who should occasionally get up early of a morning and write me, in any spelling at all: "Your mother is well." That is all I ask: it seems to me little enough. But perhaps no one thinks of me any more?

FROM FLAUBERT'S TRAVEL NOTES

Edfu. The temple of Edfu serves as public latrine for the entire village.

FLAUBERT TO HIS MOTHER

Thebes, moored to the Luxor bank,
May 3, 1850.

It is half-past four in the morning. I have got up hastily, poor darling, to send this letter off to you via the French agent at Qena, who will forward it to Cairo. A special messenger is leaving on horseback to take it, and to bring back letters from you, if there are any. Will I be more lucky at Qena than at Aswân? I hope so!

We arrived at Thebes last night at nine. We walked about Luxor in the light of the moon which was rising behind rows of columns, illuminating the great ruins. Ah, how beautiful the sky is here, my darling—such stars, such nights! We have seen nothing of Thebes as yet, but it must be superb. We will stay here a fortnight, I imagine, for it is immense.

Between Qift and Qena,
May 16, 1850.

I thought constantly of Alfred at Thebes. If the system of the Saint-Simonians is true, he was perhaps travelling with me, and it was not I who was thinking of him, but he thinking in me. And I often think of the others, too, my darling! I cannot admire in silence. I need to shout, to gesticulate, to expand; I have to bellow, break chairs— anything to call others to share in my pleasure. And what others should I call, if not those I love best?

When I take a sheet of paper to write you, I have no idea of what I am going to say. Then it begins to come of itself, and I find myself chatting away. I enjoy it; line follows line. And when I have no more to say I read it over in a sort of farewell, and whisper to it in my thoughts: "Go quickly! Kiss her for me!" Lines of handwriting kissing! You see my stupidity these days!

Qena, May 17.

Joy! Joy! My heart is leaping with it, Mother darling: ten letters for me, among them one from Bouilhet and one from Parain. I kiss you till you suffocate: I see that you are well, that you are being sensible! I love you a thousand times more for that. How darling your letters are! I devoured them like a starving man. Adieu—a thousand more kisses!

FLAUBERT TO LOUIS BOUILHET

Between Girga and Asyût,
June 4, 1850.

I have pondered on many things since we parted, Louis. Sitting in the bow of our Nile boat, watching the water flow past, I ruminate on my past life with deep intensity. Many forgotten things come back to me, like snatches of songs sung by one's nurse in childhood. Am I beginning on a new period? Or am I arriving at complete decadence? And from the past I go dreaming into the future, where I see nothing, nothing. I am without plans, without ideas, without projects, and, what is worse, without ambition. Something—the eternal "what's-the-use?"—always places its bronze barrier across every avenue that I open up in the realm of hypothesis. Travelling has not made me gayer. I don't know whether the sight of ruins inspires great thoughts, but I should like to know the source of the profound disgust that fills me these days when I think of making myself known and talked about. I don't feel within me the physical strength to publish, to run to the printer, to choose paper, to correct proofs, etc. And what is that, beside the rest? Better to work for one's self alone. The public is so stupid. Who reads? And what do they read? And what do they admire?

Ah, blessed peaceful times of the past, blessed eras of powdered wigs! You lived with complete assurance, poised on your high heels, twirling your silver-headed canes! Beneath us the earth is trembling. Where can we place our fulcrum, even admitting that we possess the lever? The thing we all lack is not style, nor that dexterity of finger and bow known as talent. We have a large orchestra, a rich palette, a variety of resources. We know many more tricks and dodges, probably, than were ever known before. No; what we lack is the intrinsic principle, the soul of the thing, the very idea of the subject. We take notes, we make journeys: emptiness! Emptiness! We become scholars, archæologists, historians, doctors, cobblers, connoisseurs. What good is all that? Where is the heart, the verve, the sap? Where to start out from? Where to go to?

Yes, when I return I shall resume—and for a good long time, I hope—my tranquil old life at my round table, between my fireplace and my garden. I shall continue to live like a bear, caring nothing for my country, for critics, for anyone at all. These ideas revolt young Du Camp, whose head is full of quite different ones; that is, he has very active plans for his return and intends to throw himself into a demoniacal activity. At the end of next winter we will talk about all this.

I am going to make you a very frank confidence: I pay no more attention to my mission than to the king of Prussia. To "discharge my duties" exactly I should have had to give up my journey—it would have been absurd. I make blunders now and then, but not of that size I trust. Can't you see me in every town, informing myself about the crops, about production, about consumption? "How much oil do you make here? How many potatoes do you eat?" And in every port: "How many ships? What tonnage? How many arrivals? How many departures?" And ditto, ditto, *ad nauseam.* Ah, no! Frankly—was it possible? And after committing a sufficient number of such turpitudes, if I took certain steps and if my friends spoke for me and if the ministry was well disposed, I should have won the Legion of Honour! Tableau! Great satisfaction for my uncle Parain!!!

As for you, I gather that the establishment is flourishing and that your pupils acquit themselves not too badly. So much the better: try to make some money and live well. That's always something.

I have seen Thebes, Louis; it's pretty fine. We arrived one night at nine, in a moonlight that was flooding down on the columns. Dogs were barking, the great white ruins had the air of phantoms, and the moon on the horizon, completely round and seeming to touch the earth, appeared to be motionless, resting there expressly. Karnak gave us the impression of a life of giants. I spent a night at the feet of the colossus of Memnon, devoured by mosquitoes. The old scoundrel has a good face, and is quite covered with inscriptions. Inscriptions and bird-droppings are the only two things in the ruins of Egypt which give any indication of life. The most worn stone doesn't grow a blade of grass; it falls into powder, like a mummy, and that is all. Often you see a tall, straight obelisk, with a long white stain down its entire length, like a drapery —wider at the summit and narrowing toward the base. That is from the vultures, who have left their mark there over the centuries. It is a very handsome effect and has a curious symbolism. It is as though nature said to the monuments of Egypt: "You will have none of me? You will not nourish the seed of the lichen? Well, then, I will shit upon you!!!"

At Esna I saw Kuchiouk Hanem again; it was sad. I found her changed. She had been sick. The day was heavy and cloudy; her Abyssinian servant was sprinkling water on the floor to cool the room. I stared at her for a long while, so as to be able to keep a picture of her in my mind. When I left, we told her we would return the next day, but we did not. I intensely relished the bitterness of the whole thing; that is what I principally valued, and I felt it in my very bowels.

I saw the Red Sea at Kosseir. It was a journey that took four days for the going and five for the return, on camelback, and in a heat which in the middle of the day rose to over 45 degrees Réaumur. That was a bit scorching: oc-

casionally I longed for some beer, especially since our
water smelled of sulphur and soap in addition to the taste
of goat given it by the skins. We rose at three in the
morning and went to bed at nine at night, living on hard-
boiled eggs, dry preserves, and watermelons. It was real
desert life. All along the route we came upon the carcasses
of camels that had died of exhaustion. There are places
where you find great sheets of sand which seem to have
been turned into a kind of paving, areas smooth and
glazed like the threshing-floor of a barn: those are the
places where camels stop to piss. The urine, aided by
time and the sun, varnishes the sand and levels it like a
floor. We had taken some cold meat with us, but in the
middle of the second day had to abandon it. The odour of
a leg of mutton we left on a stone immediately attracted
a vulture, which began to fly around and around it.

We met great caravans of pilgrims going to Mecca
(Kosseir is the port where they take ship for Jidda,
whence it is only three days to Mecca). Old Turks with
their wives carried in baskets; a whole veiled harem called
out to us like magpies as we passed; a dervish wearing a
leopard-skin.

The camels in a caravan go sometimes one behind the
other, sometimes all advancing on one broad front. When
you see, foreshortened on the horizon, all those swaying
heads coming toward you, it is like a horde of ostriches
advancing slowly, and gradually drawing together. At
Kosseir we saw pilgrims from the depths of Africa, poor
blacks who have been on the march for a year, even two
years. There are some curious sights. We also saw people
from Bukhara, Tatars in pointed caps, who were preparing
a meal in the shade of a shipwrecked boat made of red
Indian wood. As for pearl-fishers, we saw only their canoes.
Two men go in each canoe, one to row and one to dive,
and they go out onto the open sea. When the diver returns
to the surface of the water, he is bleeding from the ears,
the nostrils, and the eyes.

The day after my arrival I swam in the Red Sea. It was
one of the most voluptuous pleasures of my life; I lolled in
its waters as though I were lying on a thousand liquid
breasts which were caressing my entire body. Because of

all the shells, shellfish, madrepores, corals, etc., the bottom of the sea is more brilliant than a spring meadow covered with primroses. As for the colour of the surface of the water, all possible tints passed through it, glistening side by side and melting together, from chocolate to amethyst, from rose to lapis lazuli and the palest green.

As to any change which may have come about during our separation, I do not think, Louis, that if there is one it will be to my advantage. You will have gained as the result of your solitude and concentration; I shall have lost by diffusion and reverie. I am becoming very empty and very sterile. I feel it. It increases in me like a rising tide. Perhaps it is because my body is constantly moving; I cannot do two things at once. Perhaps I have left my intelligence behind, with my dressing gowns, my leather divan, and your society, dear sir. Where will all this lead us? What shall we have accomplished in ten years? As for myself, it seems to me that if I fail in the next thing I undertake, I might as well jump into the sea. Formerly so dauntless, now I am becoming excessively timid—and in the arts timidity is the worst possible thing and the greatest sign of weakness.

June 5 [*1850*]
Tomorrow is the sixth—the birthday of Corneille! What a session at the Rouen Academy! What speeches! The fine costume of those gentlemen: white ties, pomp, sound traditions! A brief report on agriculture!

Cairo, June 27, 1850.
A bizarre psychological phenomenon, my good sir! Back in Cairo (and since reading your good letter), I have been feeling myself bursting with intellectual intensity. The pot has suddenly begun to boil! I feel a painful need to write! I am wound up tight.

You speak of the pleasure my letters give you; I find it easy to believe, from the joy I get from yours. I usually read them over three times, I stuff myself with them. What you tell me of your visits to Croisset touched me to the quick. I felt that I was *you*. Thank you, my dear

Louis, for the visits you pay my mother; thank you, thank you. She has only you to talk with about me as she would like to talk, for you are the only person she knows who really knows me. Her heart tells her that. But don't feel yourself obliged to spend every Sunday at Croisset; don't bore yourself out of devotion. . . .

You won't believe that Max and I talk constantly about the future of society. For me it is almost certain that at some more or less distant time it will be regulated like a college. Teachers will make the rules. Everyone will be in uniform. Humanity will no longer commit barbarisms as it writes its insipid theme, but—what wretched style! What lack of form, of rhythm, of spirit!

FROM FLAUBERT'S TRAVEL NOTES

Monday, July 1 [*1850*]. *Cairo.* Last day. Farewells. My sadness at leaving makes me realize what elation I must have felt on arrival. Fellahin I shall never see again. A child bathing in the little canal of Sakieh.

Bûlâq. Farewells of the sailors. The real emotion was yesterday, when we said good-bye to Rais Ibrahim and embraced him.

Our last night. Up until three in the morning. Dawn. Cocks crow, my two candles are lit. I am sweating, my eyes are burning, I have early morning chills. In four hours I leave Cairo. Adieu Egypt! Allah! as the Arabs say.

From Alexandria to Beirut. We board the *Alexandra* at one o'clock, but don't leave till the next day—engine trouble. The boat left while I was sleeping; I was unable to see the land of Egypt disappear at the horizon, I did not make my last farewells. . . . Will I ever return?

3.

FLAUBERT TO LOUIS BOUILHET

Jerusalem, August 20, 1850.

Jerusalem is a charnel-house surrounded by ramparts. Everything in it is rotting, the dead dogs in the streets, the religions in the churches. There are masses of dung and ruins. The Polish Jew in his foxskin cap glides silently along the dilapidated walls, in whose shade the drowsy Turkish soldier tells his Mohammedan beads and smokes his cigarettes. The Armenians curse the Greeks, who detest the Latins, who excommunicate the Copts. All that is even sadder than it is grotesque. Or perhaps it is more grotesque than sad. Everything depends on the point of view.

The Holy Sepulchre is the agglomeration of all possible maledictions. In so small a space there are an Armenian church, a Greek church, a Latin church, a Coptic church. Each insulting the others, cursing them from the bottom of its soul, encroaching on their rights to candlesticks, rugs, and pictures—such pictures! It is the Turkish pasha who has the keys to the Holy Sepulchre; when you want to visit it, you apply to him. I find that titillating; as a matter of fact, it is for humanitarian reasons, for if the Holy Sepulchre were given over to the Christians they would massacre each other without fail. Events of this kind have happened already. "*Tantum religio,*" etc., as our friend Lucretius remarked.

After my first visit to the Holy Sepulchre I returned to the hotel in a state of fatigue and depressed to the very marrow of my bones. I took up Saint Matthew and read the Sermon on the Mount with a virginal swelling of the heart, easing the cold bitterness I had been feeling. They have done everything possible to make the holy places ridiculous; the whole thing is disgustingly whorish. Hypocrisy, greed, falsification, impudence—there is plenty of those, but of holiness not a trace. I resent not having been emotionally moved. I wanted nothing better—you know me well enough to believe that. . . .

FROM FLAUBERT'S TRAVEL NOTES

Jerusalem. Holy Sepulchre (second visit). The Greek priest took a rose, threw it on the sacred stone, sprinkled it with rose water, blessed it, and gave it to me: it was one of the bitterest moments of my life—it would have been so rapturous for a believer! How many poor souls would have longed to be in my place! How it was wasted on me! How keenly I felt the inanity, the uselessness, the grotesqueness, the very essence of the moment!

FLAUBERT TO HIS MOTHER

Jerusalem, August 25, 1850.
The country (as opposed to the holy places) seems to me superb. One never stops thinking of the Bible for a moment; sky, mountains, appearance of the camels (oh, the camels!), the clothing of the women—everything is there. At every moment new pages come to life before you. So, poor darling, if you want to have a good idea of the world in which I am living, reread Genesis, Judges, and Kings. Two days ago we returned from a trip to Jericho, the Jordan, and the Dead Sea. Two or three times I thought I was losing my mind. We had an escort of eight horsemen; we raced each other, galloping at top speed under an ultramarine sky like lapis lazuli. At Jericho we slept on the terrace of a Turkish fortress, built on the top of a hill. The moon was shining so brightly that one could see to read without strain. Below the wall jackals were crying; around us, on mats, ragged Turkish soldiers smoked their pipes or said their prayers. The next night we slept at Saint Saba, in the midst of the mountains in a Greek monastery more fortified than a castle, for protection against the bedouins. All night I heard the monks

chanting in their church and the tick-tock of the great clock perched on a rock above the monastery.

FROM FLAUBERT'S TRAVEL NOTES

Jerusalem, August 19 [*1850*]. Visit to the French consul, with Sheikh Mohammed. Siesta. Dinner. After dinner, Beethoven sonata; it brings back my poor sister and our little living room, with Miss Jane bringing in a glass of sugar-water. A sob filled my heart; this music, so badly played, harrowed me with sadness and pleasure. These feelings lasted all night, and gave me a nightmare.

FLAUBERT TO LOUIS BOUILHET

Damascus, September 4, 1850.

You too, Brutus! (Which doesn't mean that I'm a Cæsar!)

You too, my fine friend, whom I so admired for your immovable faith! In the midst of my lassitudes and my discouragements you were always the seltzer water which enabled me to digest life. I used to soak myself in you as in a tonic bath. When I was alone and full of self-pity I used to say to myself: "Look at him!" and then I would return, vigour renewed, to my work. You were my most moral example, my continual edification. Is the saint now to fall from his niche? I beg you—do not abandon your pedestal!

Are we fools, perhaps? Maybe so, but it is not up to us to say so, still less to believe it. However, we should by now have finished with our migraines and our nervous exhaustions. One thing is our ruin: "taste"—good taste. We have too much of it—or rather, we worry about it more than we should. Fear of bad taste engulfs us like a fog (a foul December fog that suddenly appears, freezes your guts, stinks, and stings your eyes), and not daring to advance, we stand still. Think how captious we are becoming, how endless our criteria, our principles, our preconceived ideas, our rules. What we lack is daring. Our scruples make us like those poor believers who scarcely live for fear of hell and who wake up their confessor at dawn in order to accuse themselves of having had amorous dreams during the night. Let us worry less about the results of our efforts. Let us love the muse and love her and love her. The child that may be born is of minor importance: the purest pleasure is in the kissing.

If we do badly, if we do well—what is the difference? I have stopped thinking of posterity—a wise move. My stand is taken. Unless some excessively literary wind begins to blow in a few years, I have resolved not to "make the presses groan" with any elucubration of my brain. You and my mother and others (for it is a wonderful thing, how no one will allow anyone to live as he likes) used to scold me for my manner of life. Just wait a bit till I come back, and see whether I don't resume it. I'll dig into my hole, and—though the world crumble—I will not budge. Activity—unless it be truly frenzied—is becoming more and more distasteful to me. I have just sent back without even looking at them several silk scarves which were brought me to choose from; I had only to raise my eyes and decide, but the thought of the effort so overpowered me in advance that I sent away the merchants without buying anything. Had I been a sultan, I should have thrown them out of the window: I was full of rancour toward anyone who was seeking to force me into any activity whatever.

If you think that your troubles bore me, you are mistaken. I have shared greater burdens of the same nature; I am afraid of nothing in that line. If my room in the hospital could tell of all the boredom and worry that two young men used to give vent to within it, I believe it would collapse on the heads of the bourgeois who now inhabit it. My poor Alfred! Astonishing how much I think of him, and how numerous the unshed tears in my heart with regard to him! How we used to talk! How complete our confidence and our understanding! We flew high.

But watch out for one thing: take care lest you *enjoy* being bored, for that is dangerous. What is your trouble,

Louis? How I should like to be there to implant a kiss on your brow and a kick on your behind! What you are feeling now is the result of the long effort you have made for *Melænis*. Do you think that the brain of a poet is like a loom for weaving cotton, able to keep on producing indefinitely without fatigue or intermission?

I too occasionally feel momentary twinges of adolescent anguish. *Novembre* sometimes comes into my head. Am I approaching a renascence? Or perhaps decrepitude resembles the period of blooming. However, I have recovered (not without difficulty) from the terrible blow of *Saint Antoine*. I do not say that I am not still occasionally giddy when I think of it, but at least I am no longer sick about it as I was during the first four months of this journey. I saw everything through the veil of distress with which that disappointment had enveloped me, and I kept repeating to myself the inept question which you send me now: "What's the use?"

I am, however, maturing(?). (Probably you'd rather I talked about my trip, the open air, horizons, blue sky?) From one day to the next I feel myself growing more sensitive, more emotional. A mere trifle brings tears to my eyes; utterly insignificant things twist my bowels. I fall into reveries and abstractions without end. I always feel as though I had drunk too much, and am more and more inept and inapt at understanding anything which is explained to me.

And now and again I have great waves of literary ambition: I promise myself some writing orgies when I return. *Voilà*.

You do well to think of my idea for a *Dictionnaire des Idées Reçues*. Such a book, fully and amply executed, and preceded by a good preface in which we would indicate just how the work was intended to reconcile the French public to tradition, to order, and to conventional morality, and written in such a way that the reader couldn't tell whether or not we were pulling his leg—that would perhaps be a strange book, and it might very well have some success, for it would be made up entirely of topics of the hour.

God, the beautiful women at Nazareth! At the fountain,

their jugs on their heads. In their robes, belted tight across the hips, they describe Biblical movements. They walk royally, the edge of their striped and coloured garments fluttering in the wind. Around their heads they wear bands of gold or silver coins. You see them in profile, passing by like phantoms. . . .

Adieu, old Louis.

FROM FLAUBERT'S TRAVEL NOTES

Baalbek, September 14 [*1850*]. The stones of Baalbek give the impression of being immersed in deep thought. Olympian effect. I stayed there two days, walking about alone, the air filled with bits of white fluff from the dry thistles growing amid the ruins; sometimes there was a sudden beating of wings high above me—a bird darting from his hiding-place in the capital of one of the columns. While I was in the naos, looking at the beautiful red colour of the stones, a large painted bird came and alighted at my left, on the capital of the second column. A falcon? Reddish body, the tips of the wings black; it stayed there calmly, ruffling its neck feathers; it had a superb air. It made me think of the eagle of Jupiter. How handsome, on its Corinthian capital!

FROM THE "SOUVENIRS LITTÉRAIRES" OF MAXIME DU CAMP

At Beirut I met with a serious disappointment.

My intention had been, after resting in Beirut, where I received some much-needed cases containing linen and other clothing, to continue my journey by way of Antioch and Baghdad, then go down as far as Basra and make an excursion into Persia, finally reaching Constantinople by way of Armenia and the old Greek colonies on the shores of the Black Sea. This was an extensive programme, but there was no real obstacle in the way of my carrying it out.

The very day of our arrival, however, Monsieur de Lesparda, the French consul-general, took me aside and said: "Here is a letter I have been asked to give you confidentially, without the knowledge of your companion." As soon as I saw the handwriting, I guessed the contents. It was a six-page letter from Madame Flaubert, which may be summed up as follows: "Instead of going further away, come nearer home. It almost kills me with anxiety to think that Gustave intends to go beyond the Euphrates and that I shall be without news of him for months at a time. The thought of Persia terrifies me. What difference can it make whether you are in Persia or in Italy? I beg you to have pity on me."

I did not have a good night. At daybreak the next day I saddled my horse and rode out into the country. I asked myself whether I had the right to exact such a sacrifice from Gustave and his mother. I told myself that I was only twenty-eight, that there were many years before me, and that alone and master of my actions I should be able one day to make the expedition I now felt morally bound to abandon. I made my decision, but it was hard. Had I known then that the circumstances of my life would be such that it would never again be possible for me to execute the project which I was postponing, would I have had the courage to turn toward the west, when all my desires urged me eastward? I doubt it; I should probably have gone ahead with the adventure, allowing Flaubert, perhaps, to return alone to France if he wished to. My journey across Mesopotamia and Persia is buried under the mound where sleep so many dreams that will never waken. Through this disappointment I learned a lesson by which I myself was unable to profit but from which others may gain: it is well for tourists to travel in groups, but real travellers travel alone if they wish to gain the objectives they have set for themselves.

I announced my decision to Flaubert, who drew a long breath, as though a weight had been lifted from him. "I should have gone with you to Persia had you wanted me to," he said. I was sure of it, and it was for that reason that I could not bring myself to take him upon an excursion which would have removed him too far from his mother. But we never referred to the subject again. We

quickly made out our new itinerary, and on the evening
of the first of October boarded the Austrian steamship
Stamboul. On the fourth at dawn we cast anchor in the
port of Rhodes.

FROM FLAUBERT TO HIS UNCLE,
MONSIEUR PARAIN

From quarantine, Rhodes,
October 6, 1850.

It appears that young Bouilhet is giving himself over to
immorality in my absence. You see him too often. It is you
who are corrupting this young man. If I were his mother,
I should forbid him your society. There is nothing worse
for youth than association with aged debauchees. Nevertheless, my good friends, continue to drink my health
now and again when you are together. Even pickle your-
selves in my honour if it pleases you: I give you absolution
in advance.

Have you sometimes reflected, old Uncle, on the limitless serenity of fools? Stupidity is immovable; nothing can
attack it without being shattered against it. It has the
nature of granite, hard and resistant. At Alexandria a
certain Thompson of Sunderland has written his name in
letters six feet high on Pompey's column. It can be read a
quarter of a league away. There is absolutely no way of
seeing the column without seeing the name of Thompson
of Sunderland, and consequently without thinking of
Thompson of Sunderland. The imbecile is incorporated
into the monument and is perpetuated with it. Nay, more
—he overwhelms it with the splendour of his gigantic
letters. Is it not admirable, to have the power to force future travellers to think of you and to remember you? All
fools are more or less Thompsons of Sunderland. How
many of them we meet in life—in life's most beautiful
squares, in its purest corners! They are always bursting in
upon us: they are so numerous, they come back so often,
their health is so excellent! In our travels we have met
many, and already we have a handsome collection of them

in our memory; but since they pass quickly by, they amuse us. It is not as in ordinary life, where they end by driving you crazy.

The Holy Land is no place in which to become pious. There is an Arab proverb which says: "Beware the pilgrim." That is wise, I assure you. In the Garden of Olives, I saw three Franciscans partaking of a slight collation in the company of two damsels whose white breasts were gleaming nakedly in the sun. The good fathers were caressing them with visible satisfaction. We left just at the moment a bottle of brandy was being passed. Nevertheless, I am bringing back a formidable collection of rosaries as presents for good souls. All this does not prevent Syria from being a superb country, and our hearts were heavy when we left Beirut. We lived a fine vagabond life for two months.

I must inform you that we no longer wear any socks in our shoes. We suddenly realized that by omitting them we could save on laundry and have cooler feet. The weather is growing colder now, however. We still sleep out of doors, but in heavy clothing. Since last January we have not had a drop of rain, but we shall get some at Constantinople.

I missed you one day about two weeks ago. It was at Esdud, in the centre of Lebanon, about three hours distant from the cedars. We dined with the local sheikh. To get to the room where we were to be entertained we had to push through a crowd (I use the word literally) of forty or fifty servants. As soon as we were seated on divans, we were perfumed with incense and sprayed with orange-flower water. The sprayer was followed by a colleague carrying a long fringed towel, on which we wiped our hands. The master of the house, a young man of about twenty-four, wore a coat embroidered in gold, and wound round his head was a red silk turban thickly encrusted with tiny golden stars. There were at least thirty dishes on the table for the four of us. To do honour to so much honour I ate in such a way that if I did not have indigestion that night it was because my stomach is made of iron. It would, of course, have been a great impoliteness toward our host to have refused. At Kosseir, on the shores of the Red Sea, under similar circumstances, Maxime almost passed away from indigestion.

Adieu, old Uncle. Don't you and Bouilhet indulge in too many indecencies. Write me often, and accept the best embrace ever given by nephew to uncle, or by friend to friend. Yours from the bottom of my heart.

FLAUBERT TO HIS MOTHER

Rhodes, October 7, 1850.

Maxime abandoned photography at Beirut. He sold all his equipment to an ardent amateur. In exchange, we have acquired more than three yards of silk-and-wool cloth embroidered in gold, enough to make two couch-covers such as kings do not possess. It will be *chic*. Adieu, dear old lady; your Gustave covers your poor hollow cheeks with kisses.

FROM THE ''SOUVENIRS LITTÉRAIRES'' OF MAXIME DU CAMP

For thirteen days I was kept at Smyrna by an attack of intermittent fever, which returned daily. . . . Flaubert nursed me with incomparable tenderness and lavished on me the feminine attentions which the sufferings of others always aroused, as though for the sake of contrast, in his robust nature.

FLAUBERT TO HIS MOTHER

Constantinople, November 14, 1850.

As to the idea that is troubling you, that I'll be bored when I return, be reassured. I have passed the age of boredom (and with it I left a part of myself behind). Besides, I shall have too much work to do to be bored. Something new is preparing itself within me—a second manner, perhaps? Before long I shall have to give birth. I must know what I am capable of producing. Will I be able to find again, for another work, all the energy that I put—so mistakenly—into *Saint Antoine?*

FLAUBERT TO LOUIS BOUILHET

Constantinople, November 14, 1850.

Of Constantinople, where I arrived yesterday morning, I shall tell you nothing today, except to say that I have been struck by the idea of Fourier, that some day it will be the capital of the world. It is really enormous as *humanity.* You know that feeling of being crushed and overwhelmed that one has on a first visit to Paris: here you are penetrated by that feeling, elbowing so many unknown men, from the Persian and the Indian to the American and the Englishman, so many separate individualities which, in their frightening total, humble your own. And then, the city is immense. One gets lost in the streets, which seem to have no beginning or end. The cemeteries are like forests in the middle of the city. The oriental cemetery is one of the beautiful things about the East. It does not have that profoundly exasperating quality of cemeteries at home—no wall, no ditch, no separation, or enclosure of any kind. It is situated anywhere, in the country or in a town, here and there and everywhere, like death itself alongside of life, and given no attention whatever. You walk through a cemetery as you walk through a bazaar. All the graves are alike; they differ only in age, and as they grow old they sink and disappear, like one's memory of the dead. The cypresses planted in the cemeteries are gigantic, and give the places a green light full of peace.

Where have you got with the muse? I expected a letter from you here with something in verse enclosed. What are you reading? How I should love to see you!

As for me, literally speaking, I don't know where I'm at. At times I feel paralysed (the word is weak); at other times my unborn style passes through me and circulates within me with intoxicating heat. Then it leaves me. I meditate very little, day-dream occasionally. My type of

observation is preponderantly moral. I should never have
suspected that side of the journey. The psychological,
human, comic side abounds. One meets splendid specimens.

From time to time, in a town, I open a newspaper.
Things seem to be going at a dizzy rate. We are dancing
not on a volcano but on the rather rotten seat of a latrine.
I am engrossed by the idea of studying the question. After
my return I should like to burrow into the socialists and
do, in theatrical form, something very brutal, very farcical,
and—of course—impartial. I have the words on the tip of
my tongue, and the tone of the thing at the tips of my
fingers. Many subjects for which I have more definite plans
are less eager to be born than that one.

As for subjects, I have three; perhaps they are all the
same, a thought that bothers me considerably. One: *Une
Nuit de Don Juan*, which I thought of in quarantine in
Rhodes. Two: the story of Anubis, the woman who
wished to be loved by a god. That is the loftiest of the
three, but is full of atrocious difficulties. Three: my
Flemish novel of the young girl who dies a virgin and
mystic, having lived with her father and mother in a small
provincial town at the end of a garden of cabbages and
fruit-trees, beside a stream the size of the Robec. What
irritates me is the kinship of idea of these three plans. In
the first, insatiable love in the two forms: earthly and
mystical. In the second, the same story, but the character
gives herself, and the earthly love is less exalted because
it is more precise. In the third they are both united in
the same person, and the one leads to the other; only, my
heroine dies of religious exaltation. Alas! It seems to me
that when one is as good as this at dissecting children
which are to be born, one is not sufficiently vigorous to
create them. My metaphysical clarity terrifies me. I must
abandon my pretensions in that direction. I need to know
my own measure. In order to be able to live at peace, I
must have an opinion of myself, a considered opinion
which will regulate me in the use of the powers which
I possess. I have to know the quality and the limits of my
land before beginning to plough it. I am experiencing a
need, with relation to my personal literary problem, that
everyone in our age feels to some extent with relation to

the life of society: I feel the need of "establishing myself."

To return to the antique in literature has been done already. To return to the Middle Ages has also been done already. The present is the only hope for literary subject matter. But the present offers a trembling foundation: at what point can one safely attach the first beams? But it is entirely on that that the vitality and durability of modern literature depend: on being able to find a secure point of attachment in the present. All this troubles me so much that I have come not to like to have to speak about it. I am irritated by it sometimes, like an ex-convict listening to a discussion of the penal system; especially in conversation with Maxime, who strikes hard and is not one to be encouraging—and I badly need to be encouraged. On the other hand, my vanity is not yet resigned to receiving encouragement-prizes only!

I am about to reread the whole of the *Iliad*. In a fortnight we are to be in the Troad, and in January we shall be in Greece. I fret at my ignorance: if only I knew Greek! I have wasted so much time over it without really learning it! The man who retains the same self-esteem when he travels that he had as he looked at himself every day in the mirror in his room at home, is either a very great man or a very sturdy fool. I don't know why, but I am becoming very humble.

Passing Abydos, I thought of Byron. That is his Orient, the Turkish Orient, the Orient of the curved sword, the Albanian costume, and the grilled window looking on the blue sea. I prefer the baked Orient of the bedouin and the desert, the depths of Africa, the crocodile, the camel, the giraffe.

I lament not having gone to Persia (money! money!). I keep dreaming of Asiatic journeys, of going overland to China, of impossibilities, of the Indies or of California—the latter always excites me on the human side. At other times I become so choked up with tenderness that I could weep, thinking of my study at Croisset, of our Sundays. Ah, how I shall miss my days of travel, how I shall keep reliving them, how I shall keep repeating the eternal monologue: "Fool! You did not enjoy it enough!"

I keep thinking of the *Dictionnaire*. Medicine would

provide material for good articles; also natural history.

Why has the death of Balzac affected me so strongly? One is always saddened by the death of a man one admires. I had hoped to know him later, hoped he would like me. Yes, he was a stout fellow, one who completely understood his age. He, who had studied women so well, died just after he had married—and when the society which he knew had begun its denouement. With Louis Philippe, something disappeared which we shall not see again.

Why have I a melancholy desire to return to Egypt, to go back up the Nile and see Kuchiouk Hanem? All the same, it was a rare night that I spent there, and I tasted it to the full. How I missed you, Louis!

Tomorrow I am going to have your name, *Loue Bouil- hette* (Turkish pronunciation), written on a sheet of blue paper in letters of gold—a present which I expect you to hang on your wall. It will remind you that you have been with me every day of my journey.

FROM FLAUBERT TO HIS UNCLE,
MONSIEUR PARAIN

Constantinople, November 24, 1850.

Ah, my licentious old Uncle, if you were here how you would stare at the women one sees in the streets! They have themselves carted about in old spring coaches, gilded on the outside like snuff-boxes, and you can see them inside lolling on divans as in their homes. Over their faces they wear transparent veils, through which you can see the red paint on their lips and the black arches of their eyebrows. In a slit in the veil appear their eyes, which seem to burn you when they turn in your direction and dart their fixed pupils right at you. From a distance the veil itself is not visible but gives them a strange pallor which stops you in your tracks and fills you with astonishment and admiration: they look like phantoms. Their veils fall to their hands, and through them gleam their diamond rings. To think—oh, misery!—that in ten years they will be in hat and corset, imitating their husbands who already dress like Europeans, in shoes and overcoats!

One evening in November 1850, at the French Legation in Constantinople, General Aupick, then our ambassador, said to me after dinner: "Has any worthy recruit been added to the ranks of literature since you left Paris?"

I mentioned Murger's *Vie de Bohème*, which recently had some success at the Variétés, and added: "A few days ago I received a letter from Louis de Cormenin in which he said: 'I lately met at Gautier's a man named Baudelaire, who is certain to be talked about. His originality is a trifle self-conscious, but his poetry is vigorous and he has the true poetic temperament, a rare thing these days.'" The moment I uttered the name Baudelaire, Madame Aupick hung her head, the General glared at me as though he were accepting a challenge, and Colonel Margadel touched my foot as if to warn me that I was on dangerous ground. I was considerably embarrassed, realizing that I had made some blunder but not knowing what it was. Ten minutes later, when the General and Flaubert were arguing about a book by Proudhon, both talking and neither listening, Madame Aupick approached me, and in a very low voice said: "He really has talent, hasn't he?"

"Who?"

"The young man whom Monsieur Louis de Cormenin praised in his letter."

I nodded affirmatively, but said nothing, for I was more in the dark than ever.

Colonel Margadel took leave at the same time as we. "My God!" he said. "You nearly caused an explosion by talking of Charles Baudelaire-Dufaïs; he is Madame Aupick's son. The General and he have often come close to blows, and the General does not allow his name to be mentioned in his presence. I have warned you: don't repeat the mistake. . . ."

Constantinople, December 15, 1850.

When am I to be married, you ask me, apropos of the news of E——'s marriage. When? Never, I trust. As far as man can answer for what he will do, I reply in the negative. Contact with the world, with which I have been steadily rubbing shoulders now for fourteen months, makes me feel more and more like returning to my shell. Uncle Parain, who claims that travel changes a man, is wrong. As I set out so shall I return, except that there are a few less hairs on my head and considerably more landscapes within it. That is all. As far as my ideas of behaviour are concerned, I will keep the ones I have always had until I see a reason to change. And, seriously, if I had to say how I really feel, deep down, and if I am not presumptuous in saying it, I will tell you that I feel I am too old to change. I have passed the age. When one has lived as I have, a life so inward and secret, full of turbulent analyses and re-pressed impulses, when one has so frequently excited and calmed one's self by turns, and employed all one's youth in learning to manage one's soul, as a horseman manages the horse which he forces to gallop, to walk, to jump, to trot, and to amble—all simply to provide himself with entertainment and to learn more about such things; well, what I was going to say is, if one doesn't break one's neck at the beginning the chances are one won't break it later. Like a married man I, too, am "established," in that I have found my equilibrium in life. And I don't imagine that there will be any internal disturbance to make me change my mind. For me, marriage would be an apostasy which it appals me to think of. Alfred's death has not erased the memory of the irritation which his marriage caused me. It was as though pious folk were to hear the news of some great scandal caused by their bishop. When, in a big way or a small one, one wishes to meddle with God's works, one must begin—if only from the hygienic point of view —by putting one's self in such a position that one cannot be made a fool of. You can depict wine, love, and women

on the condition that you are not a drunkard, a lover, or a
husband. If you are involved in life, you see it badly; your
sight is affected either by suffering or by enjoyment. The
artist, in my way of thinking, is a monstrosity, something
outside nature. All the woes with which Providence
showers him come from the stubbornness with which he
denies that axiom. His refusal to admit it brings suffering
not only to him, but to those with whom he is in contact.
Ask women who have loved poets, or men who have loved
actresses. So (and this is my conclusion) I am resigned to
living as I have lived; alone, with a throng of great men
instead of a social circle, with my bear-rug (being a bear
myself), etc. I care nothing for the world, for the future,
for what people will say, for any kind of established
position, or even for literary fame, which in my early days
I used to stay awake so many nights dreaming about. That
is what I am like; that is my character.

No, no; when I think of your sweet face, so sad, so
loving, and of the joy I have in living with you, who are
so full of serenity, so full of a serious, grave kind of charm,
I know very well that I shall never love another as I do
you. You will never have a rival, never fear! The senses
or the fancy of a moment will not take the place of that
which lies enclosed in triple sanctuary. Some will perhaps
mount to the threshold of the temple, but none will enter.

When I know the date of your departure, I will send
you a list of things to bring me.

FLAUBERT TO LOUIS BOUILHET

The Piræus, December 19, 1850.
. . . I saw the mosques, the seraglio, Santa Sophia. In
the seraglio there was a dwarf, the Sultan's dwarf, playing
with white eunuchs outside the throne-room. The dwarf
was richly dressed, European style, spats, overcoat, watch-
chain—hideous. As for eunuchs, the black ones (which
were the only ones I had seen up to now) had no effect on
me. But the white eunuchs! I was not prepared for them.
They look like nasty old women. The sight irritates the

nerves and torments the imagination. You are filled with a devouring curiosity, and at the same time a bourgeois feeling makes you hate them. There is something so anti-normal in them, physically speaking, that your virility is shocked. Explain that to me. Nevertheless, they are one of the most curious products of the hand of man. What would I not have given, in the Orient, to become the friend of a eunuch! But they are completely unapproachable.

FROM FLAUBERT'S TRAVEL NOTES

The Piræus, Thursday, December 19 [1850]. Stormy weather Wednesday morning. Toward noon we double Cape Sunium. The columns. The coast, grey-violet, arid, without trees or vegetation of any kind, just rock (the evening before, passing Chios, the fields were black and the mountains covered with clouds). The Acropolis of Athens stands out alone, dazzlingly white in the sun, Ægina to the left, Salamis opposite, Philopappos behind the Acropolis. The frigate *Pandora* and the brig *Mercury* decked with flags for the feast of Saint Nicholas—full-dress shakos of the Russian sailors. Joy at being in Athens. In Greece! But I can stay all too short a time.

How sad, last Sunday, strolling in the courtyard of the mosque of Top-Hana! Adieu, mosques! Adieu, veiled ladies! Adieu, good Turks in the cafés!

FLAUBERT TO HIS MOTHER

Athens, December 24, 1850.

I am in Olympian mood, inhaling great gusts of antiquity. The sight of the Parthenon is one of the things which has most profoundly penetrated me in my entire life. Let people say what they will—Art is not a lie. Good luck to the bourgeois! I do not envy them their gross felicity!

FROM THE ''SOUVENIRS LITTÉRAIRES'' OF
MAXIME DU CAMP

At Thermopylæ we lunched off a haunch of goat, and afterwards washed our hands in the hot spring Minerva brought forth from the earth to refresh Hercules when he was wearied after his combat with Antæus.*

We stayed there some time, rereading Plutarch's account of the battle. On the lower slopes of Œta a herd of goats was browsing. To the north the walls of Zeïtuni were visible, and beyond the bay the peaks of the Negropontine mountains.

Flaubert was in ecstasy. " 'Wayfarer, go tell them in Sparta . . .' " he quoted.

"How is it," he asked me, "that this brief encounter over-shadows all the great battles, all the butcheries of antiquity? It was really just an engagement of the vanguard of an army, such as takes place in every campaign. Why were these Spartans such heroes? They were three hundred bourgeois, three hundred *gardes nationaux* who had left their shops and come here because it was their turn to be called out. They were all killed because they were attacked from front and rear, and could not escape on either side. What a marvellous narrative one could make of it!"

We had to cross Mount Cithæron, whose reputation is anything but good. In the afternoon the rain began to come down in torrents, and was succeeded by fine, blinding snow, driven against us by a north wind. Night was approaching; the trees about us were shrouded in low-lying clouds which seemed to be resting on the earth itself. Ahead, the mountain, white with snow, seemed to be cut in half by them. Not a living creature was visible; the solitude was complete.

* I picked up some crystals I found at the edge of the spring and this is the result of an analysis made in Paris: carbonate of chalk, 94.50; carbonate of magnesia, 1.75; sulphate of chalk, 1.45; organic matter, 0.94; sand and water, 1.23. [Note by Du Camp.]

Soon darkness closed in, but the reflection of the whiteness of the snow still lighted us a little. One hour, two
hours passed; from time to time we shook the snow off our
clothes. Our horses hesitated; we felt that they were
treading on clumps of underbrush. Suddenly the gendarme
and our dragoman halted. We had lost our way. The road
was indistinguishable under the snow. The gendarme fired
some revolver shots in the hope of getting an answer, but
complete silence reigned. Our horses were restless, as if
they feared they might be buried under the steadily falling
snow. We spent an hour looking vainly for the road; our
clothes were saturated, we were cold. The prospect of
spending a night on Cithæron in such weather was scarcely
agreeable, but we were full of good spirits and our laughter
kept us warm and encouraged our men. We resolved to
turn our horses about and find our way back to the plain
we had crossed that morning. There, as least, were villages,
and perhaps we might be lucky enough to find one.

We rode cautiously, holding in our horses to avoid falls
and vainly searching the horizon for a light. We were
beginning to imagine that this dismal ride would last all
night, when suddenly the gendarme said: "Listen!" We
stopped; in the far distance we heard the barking of a dog.
Then we discovered that our dragoman possessed an accomplishment we had not suspected. He was a fellow with
large prominent eyes like a lobster's, and had not made
himself useful in any way during the expedition, being
unable even to cook decent meals, but now he evinced an
extraordinary talent. He could bark like a dog, and he set
to work to do so vigorously. We listened; on our right we
heard answering barks, and for more than half an hour we
progressed in this fashion, barking and being barked at.

Finally, through the night we perceived a house, then a
village. All the lights were extinguished; everything was
closed. In the middle of the street dogs barred our way.
The gendarme knocked at the closed shutters with his fists
and with the butt of his revolver, demanding hospitality.
Furious and terror-stricken voices from within bade us go
to the devil. The replies came before the questions; the
very walls seemed to cry out against us.

Flaubert was enraptured. " 'The stranger is a guest sent by the gods,' " he chanted. "You can read it in Homer!"

Flaubert was in excellent humour. At Megara he scoured the city in search of the birthplace of Aspasia; at Corinth he lamented that the thousand sacred courtesans who served the temple of Venus were no longer alive to dance before us to the sound of flutes and crotala. In the Argive Plain, between Argos and Nauplia, he longed to discover the spring Canathy, where Juno bathed every year to renew her virginity. On the other side of Argos he reviled the Hydra of Lerna for descending so low as to turn the wheels of a mill. He was gay.

FLAUBERT TO HIS MOTHER

Athens, January 26, 1851.

The other day we had with us, at the table d'hôte in the hotel, a group of English naval cadets, aged about nine to fourteen, who had come with perfect poise, exactly like their elders, to give themselves a treat. In their uniforms which were too big for them, you could imagine nothing more amusing and charming. The smallest of all, who sat next to Maxime and was no taller than the table itself, kept knocking his nose against his plate. These gentlemen drank toasts with the sang-froid of lords, and smoked cigars. They were greatly intrigued by me. They took me for a Turk (most people do in these parts), and told the hotel-keeper they were sorry they were leaving in the morning, for otherwise they would have liked to pay me a visit and chat with me.

Patras, February 9, 1851.

We have arrived at the end of our travels, Mother darling. In four days we shall embark for Brindisi, and there we shall return to conditions of ordinary touring. The real journey is at an end.

We shall see each other the end of next month! From now on I count no longer by months, but by weeks and days! I am afraid that you will be cold during your journey. Take good care not to be. Profit by my experience: have no confidence in the heat of the so-called warm countries. Do me the favour, I beg of you, of having some woollen body-belts made. Take along a foot-bag, for you will certainly freeze in the coach from Paris to Marseille. Be well supplied with warm clothing, muff, thick coat, etc. If you were completely reasonable, you would make yourself a present of a little fur pelisse. Remember that the steamboats are unheated, and that at the end of March the weather will still be cold. Believe me, Mother, I am not exaggerating; follow my advice. Good health while travelling is maintained only at the price of all these precautions.

We are in pitiful state. Our socks are without heels, our shirts in rags, and our shoes all patched. With my beard and my goatskin (the latter patched with fox-tails), I have terrified the entire population of the Peloponnesus. I shall have my beard cut off at Naples—my splendid beard which caused me to be taken for a pasha and a bandit by turn. You will see me as before, smooth-chinned. My face, up to the middle of my forehead, is burned almost to the colour of liquorice. My hair is growing back a little, but in a year or two I shall have a completely naked dome. I think I have grown heavy.

Francis, our dragoman, was made prisoner by the Turks in the war of independence, but escaped. As we rode he told us good stories about the war and his flight. We have been pleased with him. I am bending all my efforts now to add the howling dervish to my repertoire of imitations. Francis gives me lessons. It drives Maxime almost insane, but I continue none the less. One evening my chest was literally staved in, and in the house where we were staying everyone rushed to my door to see what was going on.

Here in our hotel the *kiques* (as they are called) are next to, or rather in the middle of, a hen-house which occupies one of the rooms. You have to fight your way past the turkeys to get to the seat. And what a seat! I suspect the hotelkeeper of fattening his poultry with dung; the cooking would indicate it.

FLAUBERT TO LOUIS BOUILHET

Patras, February 10, 1851.

As we gazed at Parnassus, we thought of the exasperation that the sight would have caused a romantic poet of 1832, and of the harangue he would have addressed to it.

The Parthenon is the colour of brick, with, in spots, tones of bitumen and ink. Whatever the weather, it gleams gloriously. Birds come and perch on the dismantled cornice—falcons, crows. The wind blows between the columns; goats browse amid the broken pieces of white marble underfoot. Here and there, in the hollows, heaps of human bones, reminders of the war. Small Turkish ruins amid the great Greek ruin; and then, in the distance and always, the sea!

Among the pieces of sculpture found on the Acropolis I noticed especially a small bas-relief representing a woman fastening her shoe. There is only a fragment of the torso, just the two breasts, from the base of the neck to above the navel. One of the breasts is draped, the other uncovered. What breasts! Good God! What a breast! It is apple-round, solid, abundant, detached from the other: you can feel the weight of it in your hand; the fecund maternity and the sweetness of the love which it invokes make you almost swoon. The rain and the sun have turned the white marble to yellow, a tawny colour, almost like flesh. It is so tranquil, so noble! It seems to be about to swell; one feels that the lungs beneath it are about to expand and breathe. It knew how to wear its sheer pleated drapery! How one would have lain upon it, weeping! How one would have fallen on one's knees before it, hands joined in worship! A little more and I should have prayed.

FROM THE "SOUVENIRS LITTÉRAIRES" OF
MAXIME DU CAMP

We had lived for sixteen months in lands which western peoples often refer to as barbaric—Egypt, Nubia, countries ruled by the Sublime Porte or overrun by Turkoman nomads, Greece. Everywhere we had gone unimpeded, receiving every assistance from the authorities, respected by the population, protected by officials. With what assiduous attentions would we not meet in setting foot on Italian soil, which likes to think of itself as a soil civilized beyond all others? We were not long in finding out. Immediately on disembarking at Brindisi, still suffering from the effects of an unusually rough passage, we entered the custom-house for the examination of our luggage.

In the room in which we were confined there were only customs officials; the police were awaiting us elsewhere. The doors were guarded by gendarmes. It appeared that the accuracy of our descriptions on our passports had to be verified. But the passports had been issued by the Ministry of Foreign Affairs and bore no descriptions. Grave difficulty; the prefect was called and questioned us closely. Our baggage was pitilessly gone over; our old coats were turned inside out, our slippers thoroughly shaken, our pistols confiscated, and it was found necessary to read through our papers, which were voluminous and totally incomprehensible to these gentlemen. They were greatly intrigued by a plan of the pilgrimage to Mecca, which I had reconstructed at Constantinople from the ordinances of Sultan Soliman; all my explanations were useless; they mistook the hill of Merwa for Vesuvius, and confabulated among themselves. Flaubert's great beard bothered them.

That went on for more than two hours. Finally we were taken to police headquarters, where for the price of a few piastres we were given a permit to stay twenty-four hours in Brindisi, a permit to go to Naples, a permit to hire a carriage, a permit to take the stage-coach, a permit to engage post-horses. Each of these documents bore our complete description. In addition, we had to explain exactly why we were going to Naples, what our address there was to be, and how long we intended to remain. We knew that letters were awaiting us at the Brindisi post-office, and I insisted on going for them; very graciously, the Prefect of Police handed them to us himself. They had been transmitted to him and he had saved us the trouble of opening them.

At Pompeii we had trouble with some veterans who tried to prevent us from taking notes; at Pæstum the police insisted on escorting us and then exacted an indemnity. Flaubert and I vainly tried to escape from everything political, but politics forced themselves upon us in a thousand and one interfering annoyances on the part of the authorities, who followed us into museums, watched us as we lunched on Cape Misenum, and listened to our conversations in the galleries of Herculaneum. In Rome we were left in peace.

[Flaubert and Du Camp remained together as far as Florence. There they separated; Du Camp returned directly to Paris and Flaubert continued to Venice, where he was joined by his mother. With her he returned to Croisset in June. During the twenty months of his journey Flaubert had suffered no attacks.]

Part Three

Realism

Madame Bovary

As far as appearance was concerned, the Flaubert who returned to Croisset in 1851 had little in common with the young man of twenty-eight who had left it two years before, and almost nothing with the handsome youth who had stood in the Genoese gallery in 1845. He no longer looked young. He had lost much of his hair, and that which remained he allowed to grow long, almost to his shoulders. His body was heavy, with a large paunch, and his face was heavy, too, and crimsoned over with a network of veins. Despite his written warnings, his mother had been aghast when she had met him in Venice. On his arrival at Croisset he insisted on waking the five-year-old Caroline from a deep sleep, and frightened her by laughing loudly at her tininess in her trailing white nightgown. She drew away from this stranger, who kept telling her he was her uncle but of whom she had no memory whatever.

To Louis Bouilhet, Flaubert's new appearance was even more astonishing. Louis had also grown somewhat bald and heavy during the two years of separation, and he too wore a long moustache, which was the same colour as Flaubert's: the instant they met, each of them saw himself in the other; they burst into exclamations; they had always looked alike, but now they were as alike as brothers! Their reunion was all the more emotional—more passionate, even, than either of them had expected! Each of them poured forth his laments that they had not travelled together and, after the first transports were over, Louis read aloud a present in verse which he had prepared for his friend. "*Kuchiouk-Hanem*," it was called; it was dedicated to Flaubert and began:

> *Le Nil est large et plat comme un miroir d'acier,*
> *Les crocodiles gris plongent au bord des îles . . .*

All the palms, vultures, sand, and flies in all of Flaubert's Egyptian letters had found their way into the poem. Bambeh's hennaed sheep, Kuchiouk Hanem's tarboosh, her rose-coloured trousers, her emerald (Louis did not specify, as Flaubert had specified, that it was of glass), her odour of turpentine—all were there; and as the poem closed, Kuchiouk Hanem was sitting sadly at her window, listening and longing for the sound of *cawadja's* boats on the Nile. Bouilhet had read not only those of the letters from the Orient which had been addressed to him, but those sent to Madame Flaubert as well; Flaubert's travels on the Nile, and particularly the night with Kuchiouk Hanem, had captivated his imagination, and his poem, which delighted Flaubert, was a symptom of his disgust with his own workaday life.

Despite his drudgery in the tutoring school, however, he had at last finished, after three years' work, the long Roman poem, *Melænis.* This, too, Flaubert insisted on hearing, and during the several sessions required for the reading of the three thousand lines he kept interrupting with enthusiastic compliments. There was no doubt as to the excellence of *Melænis!* Bouilhet's classical learning had filled the poem with a thousand interesting details, his poetical skill had made it mellifluous, his taste had kept it sure. But Louis was inclined to speak cynically of it. It was finished, nothing quite like it had ever been done before— and yet, there it was, three thousand lines written on several hundred sheets of paper and likely to remain there. Publication was out of the question; he had no literary acquaintances at all who could aid him and no publisher would even read a long poem by an utterly unknown young man who as far as the world was concerned was not a poet at all but a mere provincial Latin tutor. No: he had written *Melænis* for himself and for Flaubert and Max; Max would read it when he next visited Croisset and would be the last person to read it. To that Louis claimed to be resigned: but the futility of continuing to write tortured him. Should he begin another long work? What was the use? And yet, would it not be cowardly to stop?

Flaubert's affection overflowed into protests; as he had lectured Louis in his letter from Damascus, so he lectured

him now: indeed it would be cowardly to stop! Even if
Melænis were to remain in manuscript for ever there could
be no doubt about its beauty, but as it happened there was
no reason to suppose that it would remain there. Louis
was wrong in saying that he had no literary acquaintances.
The night of the departure of Flaubert and Max he had
met no less celebrated a literary man than Théophile
Gautier and conversed with him for several hours. Gautier
had been charming, he was the easiest man in Paris to see
—but had Louis ever called on him, ever pressed the advantage? Of course he had not; he was too timid; another
young man would have shown Gautier the poem even
before it was completed, and by now it would be on sale
in all the bookshops of Paris. Unquestionably *Melænis*
would be published. Max, who knew Gautier so well, and
who was himself so practical, would know exactly what
to do with it, and with *Melænis* in print Louis would feel
like beginning something new at once. In the meantime,
why should he not continue to write whatever came into
his head? His short poems were beautiful, too; there could
be a book of those some day. And why, as a matter of fact,
should Louis complain at all? He had finished something
of major importance, had he not? Whereas Flaubert—!
Flaubert didn't even know how to begin, what subject to
choose, what story to write!

Now it was he, rather than Bouilhet, who gave way to
complaints, and his complaints extended over a number of
meetings. As in his letters, he lamented his uncertainty, and
he described the feeling of terror which had come over
him at the sight of his writing table at Croisset. In his mind
were still the three subjects he had listed in his letter from
Constantinople: *Une Nuit de Don Juan, Anubis*, and the
Flemish novel which they had all discussed two years
before. The first two he had partly conceived. In Rome,
in fact, he had written down a few sentences of an outline
for *Don Juan*, and planned now to continue it, and to plot
out *Anubis* as well. But the Flemish novel remained completely vague. The mystical virgin who would be the
heroine assumed no reality or possibility as a character. He
could think of no story, no title, no details, and in fact the
words "Flemish novel" were to him a mere symbol of the

type of realistic book which Max and Louis had decided
he should write. Was this not, perhaps, an indication that
this kind of book was not for him? Soon he must decide;
for he must work. What was he to do? He talked on—of
writing in general and of his problem in particular. Should
he really begin by finishing the synopsis of *Une Nuit de
Don Juan* and writing one of *Anubis?* Would he not, in
such things as those, fall into the old errors of *Saint
Antoine?*

One day, however, in the midst of his monologue of
lament and querying, he noticed that Bouilhet had assumed
a far-away, inattentive look—very different from his own
when Bouilhet's difficulties had been under discussion. He
was saying nothing. He seemed to be weary of the whole
subject of Flaubert's perplexities, for when he finally did
speak, after a long pause, it was about an entirely unrelated
matter. Unaccountably, he began to talk about the visits he
had paid, in Gustave's absence, to Madame Flaubert at
Croisset.

Generally, he said, he had found her alone, with only
little Caroline and the servants; few of her Rouen friends
ventured as far as Croisset to call, contenting themselves
with seeing her during the winter, when she moved into
the city and lived in a few rooms near the hospital; only
Achille and his wife drove out to the house beside the
river, and even they, Louis gathered, very seldom. One
day, however, his visit had coincided with that of an old
lady of rustic manners—clearly not a Rouennaise—who
treated Madame Flaubert with considerable deference and
who was accorded, in turn, more warmth than Madame
Flaubert was accustomed to bestow on non-relations.
When Bouilhet was presented to her, and heard her name,
Madame Delamare, he knew at once who she was. He had
known her son, and when he said so the old lady immediately began to weep and to bewail his untimely end,
the tragedies which had overtaken him, the woman who
had caused his ruin. Madame Flaubert and Bouilhet did
their best to repair the damage which Louis's well-in-
tentioned remark had caused, but the old lady's grief had
recalled to Bouilhet the whole story of Eugène Delamare
and his misfortunes, which had recently been the subject

of much comment in that part of Normandy. And now he reminded Flaubert of it. Why he should do so Flaubert could not imagine: he was quite familiar with the story himself. He had known Eugène Delamare, he knew Madame Delamare and had seen her at Croisset. The only detail new to him was Delamare's death, which had occurred during his travels. But Louis went over the tale from beginning to end.

Delamare, a few years older than Flaubert and Bouilhet, had been an impecunious and mediocre medical student at the Rouen hospital under Dr. Flaubert. He had never passed all his examinations, and like many another young Frenchman of the time who could not afford to continue his medical studies to the end, had contended himself with becoming not a full-fledged doctor, but an *officier de santé* —an inferior category of licensed medical man then in existence. He had become the local health officer in a country town near Rouen, and after the death of his first wife, a widow older than himself, he had married a charming young girl of seventeen or eighteen, the daughter of a near-by farmer. She was pretty, had been educated in a Rouen convent, where she had read romantic novels, and was delighted to escape from her father's farm until she discovered that marriage with an adoring nonentity and life in a small country town were even more oppressive. She quickly came to despise her husband, longed for a more vivid life, began to spend too much money on clothes, her neighbours, took lovers, sank even more deeply into debt, boredom, and nymphomania, and finally poisoned herself. During the nine years of their marriage, Delamare had been perfectly blind to his wife's extravagances and infidelities; he could not endure life without her and the revelations of her behaviour, and he too killed himself. Their child, a little girl, had been taken in by old Madame Delamare, who had always hated her unbalanced daughter-in-law. They lived in poverty in a village near Croisset, and from time to time the old lady paid a visit of respect to the widow of the great man under whom her son had studied, and accepted Madame Flaubert's gifts.

Such, in brief, was the story of Eugène Delamare's tragic marriage. Bouilhet, however, recounted it to Flaubert in detail. He reminded him of the black-and-yellow striped curtains in young Madame Delamare's parlour, which had first caused her to be thought pretentious and extravagant by her mother-in-law and her neighbours and had been gossiped about all over the region; of the way she had instructed her peasant servant to address her in the third person; of her prettiness, her *chic*, her haughtiness and nervousness, her at-homes Friday afternoons which she herself was the only one to attend, the unpaid bill she had left at a lending library in Rouen. He recalled Delamare's heavy appearance and manner, his good-natured mediocrity, his satisfaction with his situation in life, the confidence, almost the affection, with which he was regarded by his country clients.

And then, after mentioning all the details of the Delamare case that he could remember, Bouilhet returned, as abruptly as he had left it, to the subject of Flaubert's literary perplexities. The story of a marriage like the Delamares', he announced without preamble, was the story for Flaubert to write. He had decided that while Flaubert was away. And when Flaubert jumped to his feet with the same cry he had uttered two years before on hearing the verdict on *Saint Antoine*, Louis asked him to sit down, and to listen, and continued.

He pointed out the advantages of the story. He had been quite wrong, he said, to suggest shifting the scene of a realistic novel to Flanders; Flaubert knew Normandy to the last detail, that knowledge he must exploit, and Normandy must be called Normandy, not Flanders. Some Normans would complain, but that was a minor matter. The background of the story of Delamare was utterly Norman. Life on Norman farms and in small Norman towns, a rural Norman medical practice, Flaubert could describe with brilliant effect. What was Eugène Delamare but the incarnation of all that was dullest in the bourgeois? What was his wife but a bourgeois victim of romanticism? And what categories of humanity were better suited to Flaubert's pen than those? The whole thing would give him an opportunity to paint provincial life as it deserved to be painted. And he repeated what he had said two years before: there was no need for Flaubert to concern himself,

as Balzac had chiefly concerned himself, with bourgeois
money matters. Young Madame Delamare had run into
debt, but precisely because she had had no thought of
money. A novel on non-material bourgeois themes, written with style, would unquestionably be something new.
And now that Balzac was dead, and there were no novelists
of any power or originality writing in France, such a book
might very easily be the thunderclap with which Flaubert
had always sworn he would appear.

But the vulgarity of it! Flaubert protested. That, although he made many other objections as well, was his
loudest cry when Louis finally allowed him to speak. Even
if he could ever bring himself to admit that a drama which
could be enacted in a Norman town was fit to take the
place of *Saint Antoine*, that dramatization of the thought
of the entire world, it would scarcely be such a story as
the Delamares'. In the Flemish novel, at least, the heroine
was to have been visited by religious mania, to have
entered into mystical trances, suffered from hysterical
afflictions; and all this, her character once determined,
would have given Flaubert scope. Whereas with the
Delamares everything was commonplace, even the vices
were mediocre! How could he bear to spend several years
describing such people as those? The prospect revolted
him.

Even so, Bouilhet insisted, the idea was good—not only
good in itself, but good for Flaubert. Delamare was mediocre, his mediocrity was the mediocrity of the bourgeois;
about the mediocrity of the bourgeois Flaubert always had
much to say; he had lampooned it in the Garçon, he had
written from Damascus about a *Dictionnaire des Idées
Reçues;* why should he not express himself in a novel,
which would be more effective than either? And a character resembling young Madame Delamare had even
greater possibilities. Flaubert could show what there was
—not only in her, but in the very air of the times—to lead
her to her fate; the essence of the tragedy was her disgust
with the surroundings in which she found herself, and
beyond which she had somehow learned, however futilely,
to look; it was the infection of romanticism, and that too
was one of Flaubert's favourite topics.

But even admitting the excellence of the themes, Flaubert demanded, how could he write the story? The husband did not baffle him; the medical background and the mediocrity he could describe—but the wife! A woman unbalanced in no mystical way but in regard to the matters of daily life, a woman who was pretentious, nervous, discontented, burdened by a dullard of a husband, a George Sand heroine without the halo of nobility: how could he paint *her?*

To this question Bouilhet made no reply, letting it hang in the air as oddly as he had previously seemed to be avoiding all mention of Flaubert's problems. The subject was changed as though by mutual consent; during the next few weeks, whenever they met, they conversed about other things—chiefly about the Orient; and Flaubert quietly set to work and finished the synopsis of *Don Juan.*

"Opening very animated," it began. "Tableau: two riders arrive on winded horses. . . . Don Juan opens his coat and throws down his sword, which is jolted out of the scabbard as it hits the ground. He has just killed the brother of Doña Elvira. They are fleeing."

Later: "Jealousy in desire . . . jealousy in possession . . . jealousy in remembrance. . . . Envy of other men . . . two kinds of love . . ."

At the end he made a list of eleven principles according to which he would have to remember to make Don Juan behave, and when he read the outline over he found that the principles all but outnumbered the actions! Clearly, *Don Juan* abounded in pitfalls all too similar to those of *Saint Antoine!* Generalities concerning sexual pleasure and jealousy were no less general than speeches by all seven of the deadly sins. *Une Nuit de Don Juan* would not do. His despair returned—and all the more strongly, for he felt that despite himself he was being pushed in the direction indicated by Bouilhet.

There remained, however, *Anubis*, the story of a woman loved by a god, and this, too, Flaubert was on the point of beginning to outline, in the desperate hope that it might satisfactorily materialize, when—abruptly—an item in his morning mail decided the issue. It was an envelope addressed in a well-known hand, and within it were two communications, one in prose and one in verse. Louis Bouilhet, it seemed, was not the only person who had verses awaiting the returned traveller: Louis had been quite right in making no reply to Flaubert's laments about the lady!

As Maxime Du Camp had indicated in his revelations concerning Alphonse Karr and the rest, there had been nothing particularly remarkable, in 1846, in the ease with which Flaubert had been admitted to the intimacy of Louise Colet, celebrated though she was. At the very instant when Flaubert had met her, the general knowledge that her relationship with the influential Monsieur Cousin had recently become less close was diminishing her prestige. She was finding that her latest book was being reviewed with less speed and less respect than her previous volumes, and that the Ministry of Public Instruction was showing itself quite firm, as it had never been firm before, in withstanding her continued demands for additional grants. The story of Alphonse Karr had always caused people to be careful in Louise's company even during the period of Plato's most complete protection, and the appearance, at the moment of her decline, of a handsome young man from the country who not only knew nothing about Karr but also was dazzled by his meeting with the celebrated poetess, was a soothing and consoling compensation, not to be disdained.

Financially, Louise had been well off. Income from writings, her pension, Monsieur Colet's salary and pension, and Monsieur Cousin's contributions to the support of little Henriette all combined to make a respectable sum, and in 1848, when she finally decided to leave Monsieur Colet, no financial necessity had tied her to him. She was surprised and indignant to discover that he was even more eager for the separation than she, and a lively acrimony marked the procedure. In the autumn she moved with Henriette to an apartment far distant from the Rue de la Fontaine-Saint-Georges; there was no longer any reason to be near the Conservatory, and the Rue de Sèvres had the advantage of being in a quarter which contained both Sainte-Beuve and Madame Récamier, from whose proximity many advantages were to be hoped for.

While she had been Flaubert's mistress, Louise had found it impossible to behave with any politeness whatever to Monsieur Cousin during his daily visits, and in consequence he had made them somewhat less than daily, and gradually called more and more rarely. He continued his contributions—his chief function—and Louise knew that he was always there and always influential should she be in the slightest need. But no sooner had she separated from Monsieur Colet and installed herself in her new home, than she received from Monsieur Cousin a letter which, had she only known it, proved Maxime Du Camp to be an acute diagnostician, and which made her feel that perhaps she had been too impetuous in her impatience with the philosopher.

"I have not written you sooner," it began, "first, because I knew that such a delay on my part would cause you, these days, no concern, and that your silence was sufficient indication that you had no thought for me whatever; but particularly because before writing I desired to have refashioned my life and to have established it on the new basis where it must henceforth remain. I have made my decision: I am not presenting myself in the elections, I am abandoning any further thought of a political career, and I am restricting my activities, I will not say to my literary career (there is no literature today), but to the obscure tasks whose fruits will be apparent only after I am gone. I see only a small number of old friends, and am ending—without violence—all unnecessary contacts. You know in what state ours have been since last October. I had thought that an utterly disinterested friendship such as mine, which demanded nothing and provided, together with many positive services, the most assiduous attentions, would be welcome and agreeable to you. Vain hope! Your habits have not changed, and at our last meeting the most trifling of occasions brought forth, once again, that lamentable vocabulary which is unprecedented in woman's mouth and which I am determined no longer to tolerate.

"I am no longer one of the leaders of a powerful opposition destined to replace the ministry; I am neither ambassador nor minister—I am nothing. For that very reason,

perhaps, I am entitled, now, to more particular consideration. In other words—if you agree—the end of my prosperity and of my services is also the end of our relations.
If you will adopt that viewpoint, I shall warmly do the
same; for what greater happiness exists than the loss of a
false friendship? Or, to be more precise, I propose that
we continue our relations, but that they be rare, feeble,
and polite. As such, they will always be agreeable to me,
and in cases of extreme need could still be of service to
you. Seek another friend, another protector, another
Providence upon whom your character may exert itself.
I can no longer be the protector or the Providence of
anyone.

"I shall come to see you some evening before long. Let
us avoid thorny subjects; let our contacts be as smooth as
possible. Allow me, at rare intervals, thus to pass half an
hour or an hour in your company. . . . An affectionate
politeness—such can be the bond between you and me. It
will spare you, at very little cost, the bitter thought that I,
too, have been forced to separate from you."

This was a blow indeed! It was clear that Monsieur
Cousin meant what he said, and it was clear, despite the
care which he took not to break completely, that he
would examine with cold suspicion any "cases of extreme
need" which she might put before him: being no longer
in the public eye, he need have less fear than formerly of
difficulties in his private life. The almost simultaneous departure of her lover, her husband, and her protector
resulted in Louise's standing almost alone: how fortunate,
at least, that she was well provided for with money, and
that she had Sainte-Beuve and Madame Récamier as neighbours!

But to her dismay even the best efforts of Sainte-Beuve
on her behalf did not result in the acceptance by any
theatre in Paris of her play *Madeleine*, a drama of the
French Revolution which she considered particularly
timely. And in the early months of 1849 Madame Récamier died, stricken with cholera. During her lifetime
Madame Récamier had allowed Louise to see some precious and unknown letters written to her by Benjamin
Constant, and a few weeks after her death a newspaper

announced the publication of these letters—edited by Madame Louise Colet, who had been allowed by Madame Récamier to make copies of them and had been entrusted with the posthumous publication. But the heirs of Madame Récamier and those of Benjamin Constant lost no time in bringing joint suit to prevent publication, contending that it was most unlikely that Madame Récamier had ever given Louise any such permission at all, and though Louise considered this a case of sufficiently "extreme need" to implore the assistance of Monsieur Cousin, his intervention was unavailing. The case dragged on for a year and was marked with angry testimony on both sides; in the end Louise lost and was forced to pay a large part of the costs.

Scarcely was that odious verdict handed down when another disaster loomed on the horizon: Monsieur Colet fell dangerously ill. With full realization of the possible consequences, Louise flew to his side and nursed him with energy and hope; but he died on the twenty-first of April 1851, and with him—far greater loss—died his salary from the Conservatory. There was just a chance that his pension from the Ministry of Public Instruction might be salvaged. Louise quickly composed and published a poem mourning her loss, and then, as a grief-stricken widow, she addressed a request to the ministry that Monsieur Colet's pension be continued for ten years in the name of "his daughter Henriette." The pension was immediately stopped.

Such was Louise's position at the moment of Flaubert's return. Her rejected play, *Madeleine,* she had published in several instalments in a Parisian newspaper, but she had published no book in five years—nothing since the meeting in Pradier's studio. If she had been in a mood to welcome Flaubert in 1846, what must she have felt in 1851, when she learned from Pradier that he had returned from the East!

Her financial position was all the more uncomfortable at this moment, because she had always spent extravagantly and never put aside any money at all. She possessed only one investment, of a dubious nature. Ever since her arrival in Paris, she had assiduously kept an autograph album; in it the Academicians and others who frequented her house were made to sign, and from time to time she purchased specimens of the handwriting of great Frenchmen with whom she was as yet unacquainted. It was, she told everyone, an investment for Henriette; should the child ever be in need, she would have only to offer for sale this precious collection, which would bring her a fortune: Louise estimated its value at ten thousand francs. Not all her friends were sure that an autograph album was the best possible type of investment. "In ten years it may have no value at all," Béranger told her. "You should be putting aside thousand-franc notes for your daughter, not the signatures of the so-called great men of a period of transition." Now Louise herself was in need of the money which the album would bring, and it must be sold. Not in France, however. Great French names were even more glamorous abroad than at home; after her recent shocks Louise would enjoy a brief change of scene; England was full of wealthy collectors. Taking with her the album and Henriette, therefore, Louise sailed to London. She placed the book in the hands of an autograph dealer who said he would do his best. She visited the Elgin Marbles, the Tower of London. And then, knowing that she would pass through Rouen on her way back to Paris, she sent to Croisset the double communication which Flaubert received at the moment of his despair concerning *Une Nuit de Don Juan.* There was a letter, announcing that Louise would be in Rouen on a certain day, and there was a lengthy poem, entitled *"Ressouvenir Païen"*:

> *Ami, racontez-moi votre belle odyssée,*
> *Que poursuivit deux ans ma jalouse pensée.*
> *Dans votre style, net et vrai comme un miroir,*
> *Ce que vous avez vu, faites-le-moi revoir!*

Had the synopsis of *Une Nuit de Don Juan* been more encouraging, or had there seemed any possibility that a synopsis of *Anubis* would have produced better results, it is possible that the appeal of *"Ressouvenir Païen"* might have been rejected and the rendezvous asked for in its accompanying letter refused. As it was, however, Flaubert and Louise met.

They met, and conversed. They embraced, and said

farewell. Louise continued on to Paris with Henriette, and Flaubert returned to Croisset. It was a brief interview, but a decisive one: their correspondence was quickly resumed. For a time their letters were less abandoned than of old; they began by calling each other *vous* instead of *tu;* but certain familiar notes were struck at once.

"At Rouen, the other day," Flaubert muses in the very first of the new series, "you must have found me very cold, though I assure you I was as warm as I found it possible to be. I made every effort to be kind, tender— no: it would have been infamously hypocritical, an outrage to the truthfulness of your heart. . . . Read, do not dream. Plunge into long studies—there is nothing continually good but the habit of stubborn work. I should like you to be in such a state that we could see each other calmly. I like your society when it is not stormy: the tempests which give us so much joy when we are young are wearisome when we have attained the ripeness of years. . . ."

And the second is even more reminiscent. "I shall have to postpone a little the rendezvous I gave you, dear friend. Circumstances independent of myself, and which I will explain to you, make it impossible for me to see you until the end of next week. You ask me to bring you something I have written. I have nothing to show you. In more than two years I have not written a single line of French, and what I wrote before my departure is illegible and uncopied. Furthermore, considering the state of disgust for myself in which I am at present existing, this is scarcely the moment. Some day, if I find that in my ship I have some undamaged cargo worthy of being seen, some beautiful thing brought back from distant shores or discovered by chance—who can tell?—you will be one of the first to see it, I promise you."

To Louise this promise which Flaubert sent her instead of manuscripts seemed beautifully phrased, but vague; it was, however, considerably less vague than she realized. A "beautiful thing brought back from distant shores" and something else "discovered by chance" had been disputing for possession of Flaubert's mind and attention, and it was the sudden reappearance of Louise herself—the sudden appearance, one might say in a certain sense, of young Madame Delamare in the flesh—that directly decided the day. The rendezvous in Paris, though postponed, took place. They became lovers once more. The synopsis of *Anubis* was never written. And it was with satisfaction that Louis Bouilhet heard his friend bring up voluntarily and for the first time since the original discussion, the subject of the realistic Norman novel.

Despite long talks with Bouilhet, however—long discussions as to the best setting for the story, the best names for the characters, the best types of minor characters, the best sequence of events—the novel took shape but slowly in Flaubert's mind, and too fragmentarily to make possible the drawing up of an outline or synopsis. Several things did become clear. First, it was obvious that the book would be concerned far more largely with a lady suggested by Madame Delamare than with the lady's husband, who would form, rather, a part of the general background which she found so intolerable. Second, the opportunity of painting a scathing picture of the bourgeois, and of describing various aspects of the romanticism which had always so fascinated him, already offered itself as certain consolation for the loss of the colour, magnificence, and antiquity in which he loved to bury himself. And third, the task might be less intolerable if he remembered to think of the book as an exercise. If it taught him the lessons of exactness, simplicity, and force which Bouilhet felt it would, and which he knew he needed, then later he could return to the themes which he loved, and his writing on them would be all the stronger. To concern himself with the bourgeois in a novel that would take at least two years to write would be an ordeal, but he would suffer it. Since discipline was needed, he would discipline himself.

But even though he realized these things, and realized that this novel was worth far more, as an idea, than either of the other more exotic subjects which he had considered, it was still an unattractive and depressing prospect, and he welcomed the arrival of an excuse which allowed

him to forget about it for at least a short time: he welcomed the arrival of Maxime Du Camp, who came down
to Croisset for a visit.

It was an excessively brisk Max this time, a young man
whose very busy manner the two young Normans found
a trifle startling even in their always efficient friend. He
quickly silenced Flaubert's sighs for the Orient—for their
Nile boat, their dragomans, the bazaars of Damascus—by
reminding him that he had often longed for Norman
scenes while there. He was displeased when he learned
that Flaubert was once again seeing Louise, he made it
clear that he thought him quite mad in continuing to
live at Croisset instead of moving to Paris, and he had
not been at Croisset many hours before he revealed that
he now was a man of affairs, and that one of his affairs
was of the deepest interest not only to himself but to
Flaubert and Bouilhet as well. Since his return from the
Orient he had been intensely occupied—copying and ex-
panding his notes, preparing his photographs for presentation to the ministry which had charged him with the mission, writing a number of short stories inspired by eastern
scenes. All these, however, he said, were as nothing beside
the most recent and important of his projects: with Louis
de Cormenin (one of the young men present at the farewell dinner at the Trois Frères Provençaux), Théophile
Gautier, and another young literary man who had had
editorial experience, he had purchased a monthly magazine, the *Revue de Paris*. Together with theirs, his name
was to appear as editor; together with them he was to
judge, accept, or refuse articles submitted. The first issue
was to appear on the first of October; the format and
contents had already been selected, and it was to include
one of Max's oriental stories, entitled *"Tagahor,"* which
he now submitted to his friends for correction and approval and which they found good. They also applauded
the energetic manifesto with which the first number of
the *Revue* was to be headed. Two paragraphs were particularly fine:

"We have but one literary principle: absolute liberty.
It may occur—it will certainly occur—that the same volume of the *Revue* will contain two articles diametrically

opposed as to execution and doctrine. We shall not undertake to reconcile them. No one on our staff is answerable for any page which he does not sign. Each author
will bear the responsibility for his own work. The public
will judge. Every piece of writing will be scrupulously
respected. We shall refuse manuscripts, but we shall not
deface them: to remove a word from ⅃ sentence is as
culpable, as barbarous, as to break the nose from a statue
or chip a figure from a bas-relief. Those who write for
the *Revue* will feel no need even to exercise that preliminary self-censorship which ⅃orestalls correction—a practice of even the proudest and freest minds when writing
for periodicals. Let the poet spread the wings of his
strophe to their fullest width: we shall not clip them.
Rather, to allow him his full span we shall enlarge the
Revue.

"What we desire, above all, is to have every author,
obscure or famous, in his own idiosyncratic form, in his
own characteristic originality, in his own frank and free
nature, without timidity or reticence, with his own bitter
or sweet savour . . . as though he were writing, for himself and in solitude, a work which was never to see the
light. . . . We desire the anarchy and the autonomy of
art."

After reading this they wondered a little at Max when
he informed them that he was going to remove from
"*Tagahor*" two passages which, though good in themselves, he considered somewhat risqué for publication.
But their wonderment was quickly swept away. For already, Max said, he was in quest of material for the
November issue and subsequent ones. And though Bouilhet had confidently expected Max to read *Melænis* whenever he should come to Normandy, he was left stunned
and breathless when, after having read it, Max not only
praised it, but announced that he would print it, entire,
in the November issue of the *Revue de Paris*, and that
Bouilhet's literary reputation was as good as made.

There was no doubt as to whether this was a matter of
the deepest interest! Many a magazine was born in Paris
every month, and few of them lived beyond the first one
or two issues; but few were launched by four men of

whom two were wealthy, one a celebrated writer, and the other an experienced editor. Furthermore, the name of the *Revue de Paris* was not unknown; under previous editors the magazine had at times had considerable success, and in good hands and with vigorous contents it would certainly attract attention. In addition to taking part in the editing and management, Maxime declared, he intended to make frequent contributions; Gautier would write many articles, he was delighted to be able to publish Bouilhet, and he confidently expected contributions from Flaubert as well. "From me!" Flaubert exclaimed, and when Max assured him that he meant what he said, and Flaubert replied that Max knew very well what his stock of manuscripts was and that at the moment he was too confusedly beginning the conception of a large work to be able to write anything of magazine size, Max took a surprising, even a peevish and reproachful, tone. He wished that Flaubert would do as he himself had done— outgrow his youthful feeling that it was necessary to begin with a "thunderclap." It was all very well for Bouilhet to have done so—in fact, greatly to his advantage that he had—but he had begun early. For Flaubert to begin only now, at almost thirty, on the long process of manufacturing a thunderclap, was a mistake. Max himself was quite willing to make his entry into the kingdom of letters in humble style, hoping to arrive, eventually, at great things, but travelling by easy stages—via travel books, the editorship of a magazine, articles and short stories, even photographs. Why should Flaubert not do the same? Why, instead of beginning on a long work, of which the very conception was already causing him difficulties and of which the composition would require years of obscure toil, should he not begin to put his name before the public at once? Why, for example, should he not write an account of his travels in Greece, where he had been so happy and where he had had adventures of a dozen kinds and feelings of a thousand? Such a work could be short and interesting, and was just the kind of thing for a literary beginning: Flaubert could write it excellently and the *Revue de Paris* would publish it at once.

But Flaubert, though he might be at sea concerning the

nature of the great work he was about to begin, had no doubts about his feelings in this matter, and he did not spare Max in his reply. He remembered, he said, his excitement when he had received his inscribed copy of Max's travel book three years before; but now his opinions had changed. Incidents gathered in a foreign country, he thought, should be used only in stories or in novels; they should never be presented in a bald travel recital; an account of a trip, travel notes edited for publication, anything of that sort he now considered literature of a low type, and it did not interest him. He would continue in his efforts, vague and difficult as they might be, to produce the thunderclap. He would persist in the ambition which Max now thought so immature.

After a few more remarks on each side, Max could only smile, and shrug, and let it be seen that he thought Flaubert intransigent and impractical. He did not insist, and he soon returned to Paris and his new duties. Bouilhet, though bursting with expressions of gratitude on the acceptance of *Melænis*, had none the less stubbornly refused to take one side or the other in the discussion, saying that Flaubert must act as he saw fit.

Flaubert did. He wrote nothing whatever for the *Revue de Paris*, but he wrote nothing on his novel, either. He had persuaded Max to leave behind him at Croisset the recently rewritten and expanded copy of the rough notes he had made during their travels; and making use of them, of his memory, and of the letters he had written to his mother and to Bouilhet, Flaubert went over his own notes, adding details here and there and copying the whole for his own pleasure, reliving, as it were, his beloved travels. Besides, his mother had recently conceived the whim of paying a visit to the Great Exhibition in London —with him, of course, and with little Caroline—and Flaubert hoped that by filling up the intervening weeks with the travel notes he could postpone work on the unattractive but compelling novel for an indefinite time.

But such—alas!—was not the case. When the notes were done, and Max's mailed back to him in Paris, Madame Flaubert suddenly announced a three weeks' postponement of departure. It was like a command from invisible powers. Forcing his will more strongly than he had forced it since his days in law school, Flaubert chained himself to his table and ground out a synopsis—bare, but containing a beginning, a middle, and an end—of a possible novel based on the marriage of Eugène Delamare. "I began my novel yesterday evening," he wrote to Louise, "and already I foresee terrifying difficulties of style. It is no small thing to be simple. I am afraid of falling into Paul de Kock or of writing a kind of Chateaubriandized Balzac." The outline done, he flung it at Bouilhet and quickly fled with his mother and his niece; it was like escaping from a gathering of oppressive Rouennais. The one thing that had come easily in the outline was the names of the principal characters. Charles Bovary was quickly baptized; Marie, Flaubert's first choice as a name for his heroine, became Emma almost immediately; and since the book would doubtless be concerned largely with Madame Bovary, *Madame Bovary* would be its name. But Flaubert had still to convince himself that he would write it.

In England he walked all over the Exhibition with his mother, carrying on his shoulders his ecstatic niece—who was by now madly in love with her uncle; they visited English friends whom they had formerly seen in Trouville; he thought of his novel as little as possible; and at Louise's request he called on the autograph dealer with whom she had left her album. "He tells me that it is a bad time of the year," he had regretfully to write her. "All the nobility is in the country." And he could only leave the album hopefully there when he returned.

For, much too soon, it was time to return. The Great Exhibition was splendid—"splendid even though popular," as Flaubert put it—but three or four weeks was quite long enough for Madame Flaubert to be away from Croisset. And, once back, the terrible project had to be taken up again. To Flaubert's surprise and dismay, he found that Bouilhet considered the scenario very promising. Flaubert's complaints that the characters had as yet no reality for him, that he could not feel that he was actually engaged in composing a book, he said were due to the fact that the outline was insufficiently detailed, and

he urged him to write another, filling it with details of
Norman small-town life in general and of the Bovary's
life in particular. This he tried to do, but it was torture;
it would not come at all; and since Bouilhet was so utterly
convinced that it would eventually come, and that perse-
verance was the only programme, Flaubert relieved his
feelings in a letter to Max, who had recently written
blaming him again for continuing to live an ingrown provincial life and tempting him anew by asking whether,
even though he would not write a travel article for the
Revue de Paris, he would not consider publishing in the
magazine a few of the best parts of *Saint Antoine:*

"I keep longing that you were here, so that we might
have a long and serious talk which would perhaps enable
me to reach some decision. Last Sunday Bouilhet and I
read various bits of *Saint Antoine.* It would be very difficult to publish fragments. There are some beauties, but—
but—they are not complete in themselves, and I think that
'queer' would be the judgment of the most indulgent,
even the most intelligent, readers. Bouilhet's objection is
that I have put all my faults and only a few of my vir-
tures into *Saint Antoine,* and he thinks I should be unfair
to myself where I to publish it. Next Sunday we are going to read all the speeches of the gods; perhaps they
would make the best selection. But I don't know what to
think. In this question of publication—the most important, perhaps, in the life of an artist—I feel no conviction
whatever; my entire personality seems to disappear. Not
that I don't try—I do everything I can to find some opinions, and I am completely devoid of them. The arguments
for and against seem to me equally good, and if I were
to decide by tossing a coin I should be perfectly content
to abide by the outcome.

"If I were to publish now it would be for the most
stupid reason in the world: because I have been told to
—not from any initiative of my own. I feel neither the
need nor the desire to publish. And don't you think that
one should do only what one feels urged to do in one's
own heart? Yes, what I dislike particularly is that it is
not my idea but someone else's—a proof, perhaps, that I
should be wrong to give in.

"You well know that I am a man of sudden fervours and sudden faintnesses. But even you little know all the invisible nets of inertia that encircle my body, all the mists that float in my brain! I often feel the most killing and stupefying fatigue at the idea of having to perform the slightest action; and only with the greatest effort, sometimes, do I grasp the clearest idea. The opiate of boredom in which I was steeped in my youth will affect me to the end of my days. I hate life. Yes, life, and everything that reminds me that life must be borne. It tortures me to eat, to dress, to stand on my feet. I have dragged this misery about with me everywhere—at college, in Paris, in Rouen, on the Nile, throughout our travels. You, so clear and precise by nature, have often objected to these vague *normandismes* which I have always been so clumsy in trying to excuse, and you have not spared me your reproaches! But must one not follow one's path? If movement is repugnant to me at the moment, it perhaps means that I do not know how to proceed. There are times when I think I am wrong in trying to write a rational book at all, and in not abandoning myself to all the lyricism, violence, and philosophico-fantastic eccentricities which would come to me so easily. Who knows? At least, some day I shall produce a book which will be truly mine.

"Yesterday I talked about all this at length with my mother. She is like me; she has no opinion. Her final words were: 'If you have written something you think good, publish it.' That scarcely helps. I give you all that precedes as a theme for meditation. Only, when you meditate, consider my whole self. Despite my sentence in the *Education Sentimentale*—'Even in the most intimate confidences there is always something that remains unsaid'— I have told you everything, in so far as a man can be sincere with himself. I am showing you my very bowels. I am putting my trust in you. I will do as you wish. I entrust you with my individuality, for I am weary of it. I had no idea, when I began my letter, that I was going to tell you all this. It came of itself, and I send it off. Adieu."

But from Max, now feverishly busy with the *Revue de Paris,* no reply arrived for almost two weeks, and in those

two weeks everything changed at Croisset. No sooner had
the laments been written than a load—a load of irresolution
—suddenly lifted from Flaubert; a moment of fervour
followed the weeks of faintness; and, taking up his original synopsis, he worked it over, filling it with details. For
the first time he felt that he was working on something
that he was going to continue. He visited the village which
he had decided would be his model. He took notes on it
and on the landscape. He thought out the Bovarys: all at
once they were people who were capable of living and
of being described. The new outline was long and rather
rough*—Bouilhet agreed that there was no need to polish
it, for the story would depart widely from it during the
writing, if the story was any good!—and when it was done
and Louis approved it Flaubert felt challenged to undertake the actual writing.

He began his book. He wrote the first sentence, the
first paragraph, a dozen times: it was a kind of terrible,
unfamiliar ecstasy!

"I'm tormenting myself, scratching myself," he wrote
to Louise. "My novel is having a frightful time getting
started. I have abscesses of style, I itch with sentences that
never appear. What a heavy oar the pen is, and what a
difficult current ideas are to row in! I'm so disconsolate
about the whole thing that I greatly enjoy it. Today I
passed a fine day at it in the greatest serenity in the
world, the window open and the sun shining on the river.
I have written one page and sketched three others. In a
fortnight I hope to have ploughed the first furrow; but
the tone in which I am steeping myself is so new to me
that I keep opening my eyes in astonishment."

Max's answer finally came, and it was that of a very
privileged—or very presumptuous—editor to a young author of whose entire conduct he disapproves. It was not
life in general, he declared, that Flaubert hated, but his
own life, and his own life should be changed. Absurd to
live in a provincial hole, at the beck and call of an old
lady and a child! Such an existence kept turning Flaubert
in upon himself, jeopardizing his development. It had
been because of necessity, because of illness, that he had

* See Appendix.

begun his seclusion, but it was perverse to continue it now. He refused to make Flaubert's decision about publishing; that he must do himself. "I have made my own success," he wrote, "and I am going to make Bouilhet's. Write me something good and I will make yours. I say this perfectly solemnly, perfectly seriously. I know I can do it, but I cannot give you a single bit of advice." And at the end he struck a note of particular severity and gloom. "Whom do you know who began with a better situation than your own? No one. You had none of the anxieties of existence, you had plenty of money and were generally thought to have even more, you had the shelter of your mother's house, you could count on great sacrifices being made to sustain you, from your father you had an illustrious name to which the public was already accustomed: what have you done with all those advantages? Nothing, and you are thirty years old! If you haven't begun within two more years, I don't know what will become of you."

Flaubert found Max's letter offensive, and he did not answer it. One could wish that he had. It would look well, today, a brief word of assurance: "Dear Max, I *have* begun. I have begun a book called *Madame Bovary!*"

He had been back only a few months, and already *Madame Bovary* was under way. So recently returned from eastern scenes, he was plunged far more intimately than ever before into the depths of Norman life, the life which hitherto he had always avoided by seeking refuge in some exoticism of time or space. It was, of course, Louis Bouilhet who had achieved Flaubert's rapid return to work. Had it not been for him, *Madame Bovary* would doubtless never have been begun. But could even Louis have persuaded him actually to undertake and pursue a subject so lacking in glamour, had it not been for the oriental journey? The two years in the East had been a purge, so to speak, of Flaubert's romantic longings: of his lusts after exoticism in all its forms, of his need for brilliant colour, heat, violence, grandeur, and filth. Now, with those boiling desires drawn off—at least for the moment—he had for the first time in his life the courage to concern himself with the details of daily existence in a

small French town, which he saw with new eyes. Never
before could he have endured the company of the
Bovarys!

2.

What Max did not understand, of course, was that it
was precisely the retirement which he so castigated and
considered so perverse that would make possible for Flaubert the continuous composition indispensable to his project. It was true that the retirement had been originally
entered into for reasons of necessity; but whether or not
necessity now demanded the continuation of it, it had
become through long habit a necessity in itself, and this
Flaubert recognized very well. And he recognized, too,
now that after such travail *Madame Bovary* was finally
begun, that it was necessary not only to continue the life
of retirement but to organize it—to adopt a schedule
which would allow the writing of the book to be steadily
pursued. Croisset, although it still isolated Flaubert from
intellectual companionship, was somewhat less quiet and
dreary these days than it had been before the oriental
journey. Caroline was no longer a baby whom one could
put out of the way whenever it was convenient to do so,
but a very determined and intelligent little girl of more
than five who demanded constant attention; and although
she had an English governess, engaged in London during
the visit to the Exhibition, and although Madame Flaubert
herself was teaching her to read and write, it was time
that she be given instruction in other things as well. Uncle Parain, too, was now frequently in residence at Croisset, preferring the company of his favourite nephew and
of his grandniece to that of his more immediate family
in Nogent; the charming, irresponsible old man spent
most of his time playing with Caroline. A child, a governess, an old man—even such company as this made a
routine obligatory; and Madame Flaubert kept the pattern
of life at Croisset subordinated to the needs of her son.

As the first chapters of the novel were slowly written,
the routine became fixed. Mornings, until ten o'clock,

were quiet hours; not until Flaubert's bedroom bell rang
were the members of the household allowed to talk in
anything but low voices or to perform noisy tasks; it was
as though their complete awakening were deferred until
his. In response to the bell a servant hurried upstairs with
the mail, the newspapers, a glass of cold water and a filled
pipe; the water was drunk, the pipe lighted, a few puffs
taken, the letters opened. Then, as he read, Flaubert
pounded vigorously on the wall; his mother appeared
from her adjoining room and sat beside him until he got
up. By eleven he was dressed and downstairs for the meal
which combined breakfast and lunch, and after it everyone accompanied him as he strolled, smoking and chatting, on the terrace. Along one side there was a hedge of
old lime-trees, pruned straight like a high green wall, and
a walk along it which led to the summerhouse beside the
water, the summerhouse with the wrought-iron balcony,
the honey-suckle vine, and the fish-pole, which had been
so well remembered on the Nile. Or they all walked up
the hill behind the house to another terrace—this one
with rows of yews and a garden-seat under a clump of
chestnut-trees. From either place they looked out onto
the wide river, the plumes of smoke from the steamboats,
the convoys of sailing vessels being towed up to Rouen;
and at one o'clock, when a steamboat leaving the wharf
of a near-by village gave a sharp blast of its whistle, they
all went back to the house and Caroline's lessons began.
In her uncle's study she flung herself on the white bearskin on the divan, covered its head with kisses, and then
paid attention. At times Flaubert talked to her about history, making her repeat the classical myths and tales he
had told her the day before; or they talked about geography, sometimes adjourning to the garden with a pail
and shovel, making models of islands, peninsulas, mountains, bays. "After the geography lessons I give my niece,
sometimes I sit looking at the map with silent and sombre
melancholy," he wrote to Louise. For the rest of the afternoon, until dinner time at seven, he worked at the
round table whose sight had so frightened him on his return, sitting in the armchair which had aroused the jealousy of Louise. Looking out the windows he could see

the passing masts of invisible ships. There were new things in the study now: Egyptian necklaces and amulets, arrows from the Sudan, oriental musical instruments, Turkish lanterns, two mummy's feet stolen from a tomb. After dinner he sat talking with his mother; at nine, or ten at the latest, he was back at work, and interrupted himself only to kiss his mother good-night when she was installed in her bed; then he worked steadily until two, three, or even four in the morning. These hours were his real day: a long, solitary night, perfectly quiet except for the sound of his own voice as he repeated his sentences aloud, was the achievement of the routine.

Sundays, as usual, Bouilhet appeared. He liked to play games with Caroline or cards with Madame Flaubert and Uncle Parain; sometimes it was difficult for Flaubert to draw him into the study until the evening. But Sunday night, invariably, Flaubert read him what he had written during the week—sometimes only a page, or two, or three. Questions of style, of content, of treatment were threshed out: it was some time before Bouilhet was satisfied with the sentence rhythms which Flaubert was to employ. Long and oratorical sentences were of course taboo, and while the simplicity of the style of the Breton book remained a model up to a certain point, the poet now thought that *Madame Bovary* should be written in prose that was more distinguished, more originally beautiful. Together they read over sentences dozens, even hundreds, of times; and then, when each sentence seemed right, they read over the paragraphs into which they were combined. Gradually, out of single sentences that were simple and direct, Flaubert learned how to construct paragraphs and pages that were also simple and solid, but shimmering and rich as well; inversions, shifts of emphasis, variety in sentence length resulted in a style that was more compelling and stronger than the monotony of the romantics. In the end, Bouilhet was delighted by the impact of the result, and so was Flaubert; but it soon became clear that this new style was not something which once conquered could thereafter be employed with ease and swift carelessness. Every sentence, every paragraph, it seemed, would have to be forged painfully, read aloud, and worked over again

and again, like lines of verse; the book could advance
only at a snail's pace; it would take years! It was a staggering prospect!

Sometimes, in fact, particularly at the beginning, the
prospect was almost unbearable: the unexalted subject, the
stubborn style, the fewness of the pages so far written
filled Flaubert with desperation, and in the letters to
Louise with which he varied his solitude as he had done
in the past he cried out his difficulties. "I am advancing
so painfully, spoiling so much paper, scratching out so
many lines! My sentences are slow to come, for it is a
very devil of a style that I have adopted. A curse on all
simple subjects! If you knew how I torture myself you
would have pity on me, and if you knew the utter flatness
of the monotony in which I live you would be astonished
that I notice even the difference between winter and summer, day and night."

This complete resumption of daily monotony, so soon
after the ever-changing Orient to which it formed such a
contrast, and the terrific effort of forging a style and beginning a novel, became literally unbearable during the
month of November, and with the approval of Bouilhet
—who was in a lenient mood now that *Madame Bovary*
was definitely launched—Flaubert left his work and spent
several weeks in Paris, enjoying for a time the life he
knew he must not live permanently. He saw something
of Max despite his editorial busyness and despite the lessened confidence each now had in the other; he saw the
other editors of the *Revue de Paris* and the literary circle
that was forming around them. He increased his acquaintance with Gautier and learned a lesson from him, for
Gautier, charming though he was, had in Flaubert's opinion changed lamentably from the young man who had
worn his scarlet waistcoat to the opening of *Hernani*
twenty years before. He had been the wildest romantic of
them all; in *Mademoiselle de Maupin* he had made savage
fun of literature that was written to be "useful," saying:
"the most useful place in the house is the water-closet";
and now he was a journalist, a dramatic critic, laughing
at the days when he had given publishers "two volumes
of prose in exchange for the publication of one volume of

verse which sold seventy-five copies," and saying that his
only advice to young authors was to "sell a book as soon
as it is finished, for as much money as possible." But Flaubert knew that, unlike Maxime Du Camp, Gautier would
not have become a journalist at all if the necessity of
earning his living had not existed; Gautier made it clear
that he envied a young man like Flaubert, who was able
to undertake a long work and proceed as slowly as he
thought necessary and who was not forced to "sell his
copy as a linen merchant sells handkerchiefs"; and this
contact with an old idol made Flaubert realize, more than
Max's letter, the advantages that accrued from an income.
But it was not only poverty—it was also society, a hectic
life in the midst of literary Paris—that had kept Gautier
from doing as great things as he had perhaps been capable
of, and Flaubert felt more strongly than ever that it
would be necessary to remain beside his fire at Croisset,
composing for himself alone, if he was to accomplish
what he wanted to.

He saw Louise, who was somewhat cheered by the
arrival of a small legacy from a distant relative; he even
delighted her by consenting for the first time to attend
her Sunday salon, where the artistic people and the Academicians found him charming; at her request he read her
parts of *L'Education Sentimentale*—as several years before and under slightly strained circumstances he had read
Novembre—and left the manuscript with her to finish;
and he assisted her in a bit of flummery. She was going to
offer to some magazine the verses she had had waiting for
Flaubert on his return, and for the sake of interest she
planned to add, after the title *"Ressouvenir Païen,"* the
words *"A Monsieur —— après son voyage en Orient."* In
the past, under previous editorships, the *Revue de Paris*
had accepted quantities of Louise's verse, and now that
Max was where he was it would be advantageous for her
to be reconciled with him if possible; so, Flaubert suggested, why not say "Monsieur Maxime Du Camp" instead of merely "Monsieur ——" and send the poem to
the *Revue de Paris?* Louise was enchanted by the idea,
and the poem was promptly dedicated to Max and sent
off.

He saw Caroline's father, who was drinking more than ever and who would clearly have to be dealt with, before long, in a legal and unpleasant manner. He was in Paris on the second of December, and witnessed Louis-Napoleon's *coup d'état;* and it was in Paris that he celebrated his thirtieth birthday, an occasion which filled him with more serious thoughts than the change in the government of France. "There is something solemn taking place within me these days," he wrote a few days before. "I am in a critical period: I am shortly going to be thirty, time to choose one's road and not turn back." He spent New Year's Eve with Maxime and a group of his friends, and a few days later returned to Croisset, to his *"longue vie habituelle."* "I have set to work again like a rhinoceros," he wrote to Uncle Parain. "The good old days of *Saint Antoine* have returned. Heaven grant that the result may satisfy me more!"

But the return of the good old days was brief. It was not long before Bouilhet, one Sunday night, was forced to remind Flaubert that as the writing progressed the scenario would have to undergo changes; for, though Flaubert had not realized it, something was beginning to go badly, and Bouilhet saw that the fault was in the plan itself. From now on, it seemed, not only would the long scenario be necessary, but frequent amendments to it— shorter, very detailed scenarios of each successive scene or at least of each successive chapter! Bouilhet even suggested drawing a plan, as detailed as possible, of the village in which the Delamares were to live. Such things as these made progress even more tortoise-like. To realize that the plan must be changed was one thing, but to be pulled up when things seemed to be going comparatively well and to be told that he was on the wrong track—that was enough to make Flaubert weep. "I feel as dreary as a corpse," he wrote to Louise, "completely stupefied. My accursed *Bovary* torments and confounds me. Last Sunday Bouilhet made several objections concerning one of my characters and concerning the plan; I am quite unable to refute him, and yet, though there is some truth in what he said, I feel that the opposite is true also. Ah! I am utterly weary, utterly discouraged! You call me a master—what a sorry master I am! The whole thing has not been worked out sufficiently, perhaps. Everything depends on the conception. But I am going right ahead as rapidly as possible, in order to form an ensemble. There are moments when it all makes me want to die like a dog. Ah—I shall know the pangs of art before it is done!' "

Louise's pen, too, seemed these days to be less light and facile—as well as less profitable—than formerly, and during his stay in Paris Flaubert had spent considerable time going over her verses. It was time, she felt, that she should publish another volume, and she hoped that the young man who had originally been presented to her so that she might be of some use to him would now be of some use to her. After his return to Croisset she sent him drafts of new poems, with numerous passages underlined for comment; he wrote back fully and frankly, criticizing them strongly, particularly when she used words for rhyme rather than for sense or included expressions which were trite and worn, and he warned her against beginning a play she had in mind before she had thought it out sufficiently. To her dismay, the English autograph dealer reported that no one was interested in her album, and Flaubert wrote to his mother's English friends asking them to do what they could. In the meantime, since she continued to complain of poverty, he offered to send her five hundred francs, half of a sum which he was keeping in reserve; she gratefully declined, but he urged her to consider that the money was at her disposal, "in a drawer at Croisset," should she need it.

Small gifts she accepted. In the past she had often asked him in vain to send her something which had been associated with his daily life; now she set her heart upon having his signet ring, and since there was no longer any risk of compromise he agreed to give it to her, but requested a slight delay. "I use it as a seal," he wrote. "I am having an Egyptian scarab mounted to take its place, and as soon as I have that I will send you the other." And in the meantime he sent her other things: a paperweight which he had always used, and "a little bottle of sandalwood oil —two-thirds of my entire supply. Pour half a drop on anything at all and you'll see what a fragrance it has. It

is the best and the most precious of the oriental perfumes. I have some on my hands now—I have just been
preparing the bottle for you—and the scent brings back
to me the bazaars of Cairo and Damascus." As to the paperweight, it was, though she did not know it, a gift
which he could easily spare, for in going over his father's
effects he had come upon another paperweight, one with
a hilarious history, which had always been used by Dr.
Flaubert and which he was now delighted to have on his
desk. It was a simple block of wood, a piece of a ship's
mizzenmast, and it had been extracted by Dr. Flaubert
with a delivery forceps from an old seaman who had
come to him in bewildered discomfort, able to offer no
explanation whatever as to how so large and obstructive
an object had arrived where it was.

Louise's literary opinions, as usual, Flaubert found val-
ueless. "I am astonished by the excessive enthusiasm you
express for certain parts of the *Education.* I consider them
good, but not so far above the other parts as you say. The
pages which impressed you (those on art, etc.) don't seem
to me the sort of thing that is very difficult to do. I think
I could do them better now, though I have no intention
of touching them. However, the book contains one chapter that I still find very good indeed, and that you don't
mention—the flight of my characters to America and their
subsequent boredom with each other. . . . There exist
within me, speaking from a literary point of view, two
distinct persons: one in love with eloquence, with lyricism, with the soaring of eagles, with all sonorities of
phrase and mountain-peaks of idea; another seeking and
probing the truth as much as he can, liking to state the
small fact as forcefully as the large, wanting to make you
feel almost tactilely the things he describes; the latter
loves to laugh, and takes pleasure in man's animalities.
Unknown to me, the *Education Sentimentale* was an effort to fuse these two tendencies of my mind. I failed."

And of *Saint Antoine,* which Louise now asked to see,
he wrote her warningly, after saying that he was afraid it
might be lost in the mail, and that that would be a definitive judgment of Providence. "*Saint Antoine* was another
experiment. The subject was completely suited to my

temperament, leaving me entirely unrestricted as to lyricism, movement, excesses of all kinds; all I had to do was to let myself go. Never again will I write with such recklessness and abandon as during the eighteen long months of the composition of *Saint Antoine.* How ardently I carved the stones for my necklace! I forgot only one thing—the thread. It was a second attempt, even less successful than the first. Now I am busy on my third—and this time it is a question of succeeding or jumping out of the window. What I should like to write is a book about nothing at all, a book which would exist by virtue of the mere internal strength of its style, as the earth holds itself unsupported in the air—a book which would have almost no subject, or in which, at least, the subject would be almost imperceptible, if such a thing is possible. The finest books are those which have the least subject matter; the more closely the expression approximates the thought, the more beautiful the book is. I believe that the future of art lies in this direction. I see it, as it develops, becoming increasingly ethereal, evolving from the pylons of Egypt to the lancets of the Gothic, from the twenty-thousand-line poems of India to the effusions of Byron. Form becomes attenuated as it becomes more adroit, abandoning all liturgy, all rule, all measure, abandoning the epic for the novel, verse for prose, denying all orthodoxy, and being as free as the will of each of its creators. It is for this reason that there are no such things as either beautiful or ugly subjects, and that it would almost be possible to establish as an axiom—speaking from the point of view of pure art—that there are no such things as subjects at all, style being in itself an absolute way of seeing things. I should need a whole book to develop what I mean. I shall write all that in my old age, when I have nothing better to scribble. Meanwhile I am working courageously on my novel. I go slowly: in four days I have done five pages, but so far I enjoy it. I have found serenity in this work."

Undaunted by the rebuffs which her praise of his work had so far brought, Louise wrote fulsomely about *Saint Antoine,* and this time Flaubert was glad to accept even her compliments. "So you are truly enthusiastic about

Saint Antoine!" he wrote, in delight. "I shall always have
one admirer for that book—that's something, at least.
Though I don't accept everything you say about it, I do
think that my friends did not want to see everything that
was in it. It was lightly judged. I don't say unjustly, but
lightly. I am in a completely different world now—the
world of attentive observation of the most unexciting details. My gaze is fixed on the mould of the soul—a long
way from the mythological and theological flamboyance
of *Saint Antoine.* And, just as the subject is different, I
am writing in an entirely different manner. I want my
book to contain not a single agitated page, and not a single observation by the author. I think that it will be less
lofty than *Saint Antoine* as to ideas (a fact that matters
little to me), but it will perhaps be more extraordinary
without appearing so. It seems to me that there are things
which I alone sense, and which others have not said, and
which I can say. However, let us talk no more about *Saint
Antoine.* It disturbs me; my mind becomes filled with the
subject and I waste time thinking about it."

And in these letters written while the first chapters of
his book were taking shape, he wrote as candidly as before about the nature of his feelings for Louise, no longer
fearing her reactions, whatever they might be. Knowing
Louise as he did, in fact, it seems almost as though he were
inciting reactions. Soon he would be painting, would he
not, with a wealth of tiny detail, the full-length portrait
of a pretty woman who was a discontented wife and an
insistent mistress? "I feel for you a mixture of friendship,
attraction, esteem, tenderness of heart, and sensual impulse
—a complex which I cannot define but which seems to me
sound. You occupy a corner of my heart, a sweet place
exclusively your own. If I love others, you will remain
there none the less (it seems to me); you will be like the
spouse, the favourite, the one to whom one returns. Would
it not be sophistry to pretend the contrary? Observe yourself carefully: of all the feelings you have ever had, has a
single one disappeared? No—every one of them is preserved, is it not? Every one. The mummies in one's heart
never fall into dust, and when you peer down the shaft

there they are below, looking at you with their open, unmoving eyes."

When weeks went by and he did not come to Paris and
she accused him of considering her only as a means of distraction, he admitted the charge: "Yes—you are a relaxation for me, but in the best and deepest sense. A relaxation
for my heart, because the thought of you makes me tender,
and my heart lies upon the thought as I upon you. You
have loved me deeply in the past, dear Louise, and now
you admire me and love me still. Thank you for all that.
You have given me more than I have given you, for what
is most exalted in the soul is the enthusiasm which comes
from it."

But the principal subject of his letters was the book, the
terrible novel which was torturing him so, the exacting
exercise set him by Louis Bouilhet. Week by week he
informed Louise of its progress.

"I have been working with great spirit. In a fortnight I
shall be in the middle of Part One. From the day that style
was first invented, I think that no one has ever taken more
pains than I. Every day I see my way more clearly; but
what good is that if the imaginative faculty fails to keep
pace with the critical!"

"Bad week," he wrote a week later. "Work hasn't gone
well at all; I reached a point where I had little idea of what
to say next. It was all *nuances* and *finesses*, in which I
couldn't see my way, and it's very hard to make clear in
words what is still unclear in your head! I made outlines,
spoiled them, floundered about. I shall perhaps find myself
again now. Oh, what a slippery customer style is! You
have, I think, no idea of the type of this book. To the same
extent that I was slovenly in my other books, in this one
I am trying to be impeccable, to follow a straight geo-
metric line. No lyricism, no observations; personality of
the author absent. It will be dismal to read; there will be
atrocious things in it—wretchedness, fetidness. Bouilhet,
who came last Sunday at three o'clock just as I finished
writing to you, says that I have found the right tone and
hopes that it will be good. May the gods be favourable!
But it is taking on formidable proportions from the point

of view of time. I shall certainly be nowhere near the end
by the beginning of next winter. I do no more than five or
six pages a week."

The more he wrote, the more clearly he saw what the
book was to be. Its general tone was to be that of mould:
its characters were to live in an atmosphere the colour of
mould. Madame Bovary herself was to be a woman of
perverted character, a woman falsely poetical, of false
feelings. The book would be full of Norman patois. He
became more and more intense, wound up; he could not
sleep, but felt no fatigue; his task appeared ever longer.
Part One, which he had thought would be finished by the
end of January, now threatened to take until the end of
May (actually it took until August); and at the end of
February, after almost six months of work, he had reached
in his text only the third paragraph of the first part of
the long scenario. It was, however, an important point:
Charles Bovary was educated, married, and widowed; and
his second wife was about to enter the scene. Her girlhood
was about to be described. Flaubert read old keepsakes,
old children's books, grew emotional over his own childhood, and wrote to Louise: "For two days I have been
trying to enter into the dreams of young girls! I am
navigating in a milk-white ocean of literature about castles
and troubadours with white-plumed velvet caps. Remember to ask me about this when I see you. You can
give me some exact details that I need." And Louise—who
(as she herself had told Flaubert that night in the restaurant, five years before) during her childhood had been
constantly filled with discontentments, had always been
enchanted by poetry and romance, had hidden in the
woods at sunset to read Lamartine—replied quite un-
suspectingly that she would be glad to give him any information she could.

In the meantime, Maxime Du Camp had been as good as
his word. He published the entire three thousand lines of
Melænis, dedicated to Flaubert, in the second issue of the

Revue de Paris, and although Bouilhet was paid nothing
for this lengthy contribution his name became known at
once to the six thousand readers of the magazine and his
poem was mentioned by a goodly number of the critics.
The most influential of them all, Sainte-Beuve, urged
Louis to stop "picking up Alfred de Musset's cigar-butts,"
but in general they wrote favourably, and the poem, re-
printed in pamphlet form at the author's expense, brought
him complimentary letters from several celebrities, including Delacroix and Hugo. *Melænis* also caused a coldness between Bouilhet and his mother. The lady had been
considerably dismayed when her son had given up medicine for literature in the first place, and now she was
shocked by the Roman lubricities which his poem contained and which strained her relations with her curé and
with the ladies of the local château. Flaubert was delighted
by the reproachful letters which Madame Bouilhet sent
her son. "If I had had any doubts as to the value of his
poem and as to his own value as a man," he wrote Louise,
"I should have them no longer. Impossible to have a finer
consecration than denial by one's family and one's birthplace. There he is, for his future biography, classed as a
great man according to all the rules of history."

Louise Colet, on the appearance of *Melænis,* wrote Flaubert a long letter praising it in detail, and shortly thereafter, during his midwinter visit to Paris, he brought
Bouilhet and Louise together for the first time. Bouilhet
was somewhat hesitant about the meeting, for the impression he had formed of Louise over the past several
years had not been a completely favourable one, and he
was forced to confess to Flaubert, after the meeting had
taken place, that he had not been surprised to find the
Muse—as Louise was now generally known—"just naturally lacking in naturalness." Louise, on the contrary, was
pleased with Bouilhet. He was a decidedly provincial-
looking and -acting young man, and in Louise's small salon
his habitual aroma of garlic was even more pronounced
than usual—he smelled, indeed, "like a whole coachload of
Southerners"—but Louise declared that she liked his mixture of timidity and sturdiness, the same qualities which
had first endeared Flaubert to her. Bouilhet did not revisit

Louise during his brief stay in Paris, and enjoyed considerably more his visit to the home of Gautier, where—
although he found Gautier, too, somewhat affected—he
revelled in the Spanish paintings, Chinese porcelains, and
Japanese prints, admired Théo's twelve cats, and conversed
with an exiled mandarin who was teaching young Mademoiselle Gautier Chinese.

But as the winter progressed and Louise showed herself
indefatigable in campaigning for good reviews not only for
Melænis but also for the shorter poems of Bouilhet which
the *Revue de Paris* printed, always without payment, from
time to time, Louis was gradually won over by her good
will; and in March, during Flaubert's next Parisian visit,
she arranged a soirée in Bouilhet's honour which made it
impossible for him to remain hostile any longer. It was
seldom that women were included among the guests in
Louise's salon, but on this evening, in addition to a select
group of Academicians, there was present a charming
young lady who, to Bouilhet's confusion and rapture, rose
at a prearranged signal and read to the assembled company
a canto of *Melænis*, provoking enthusiastic applause. It was
the first social success of Bouilhet's life; it intoxicated him;
all that night he sat up in his hotel room writing a sonnet,
"A Ma Belle Lectrice"; and this, in turn, resulted in an
affair that dazzled the incredulous young man from the
country almost as much as his sudden appearance in print.
But Louis, though a young man of considerable appetites,
had little genius for flirtation, and an affair as understood
by a Parisian actress he was disappointed to find more
confusing than satisfactory. During Flaubert's travels he
had taken to live with him in Rouen a young peasant
woman who provided him with every domestic comfort;
Flaubert found it impossible to understand how he could
bear the continual company of someone who understood
neither his work nor his interests, but Bouilhet found the
humdrum arrangement completely agreeable and was glad
to resume it when the unaccountable advances and retreats,
surrenders and resistances, of the lady in Paris finally
became too bewildering. In her desperate attempts to hold
him the actress even let him know that she was undertaking
the study of Tacitus; but this, which she had intended as a

conclusive evidence of devotion, Louis merely found as incomprehensible as her other, less literary moves, and the difficulties of correspondence brought the affair to a natural end.

Flaubert was almost as exhilarated as Bouilhet by the reading of *Melænis* before the Academicians; he hoped that a series of such intimate successes might eventually bring to his friend some post more congenial and less demanding than the tutoring in Rouen, some sinecure which would allow him more time for composition, and he wrote gratefully to Louise for her kindness. During the March visit she had been not only kind to Bouilhet but also even more useful than Flaubert had expected in helping him document Madame Bovary's dreams and discontentments as a young girl, and after his return to Croisset his letters were longer than any since their reconciliation, and devoted less exclusively to his own work. He did not fail to keep her informed of the progress of *Madame Bovary*, telling her: "The entire value of my book, if there is any, will consist in having been able to proceed straight ahead on a hair suspended over the double abyss of lyricism and vulgarity, the two qualities I want to fuse in a narrative analysis"; or crying: "How I hope that Buffon was right when he said 'Genius is but a long patience'!"; or lamenting: "Only twenty pages done in a month, working at least seven hours a day!"; or revealing that "Last Wednesday I was obliged to get up and look for my handkerchief; tears were streaming down my face. I had moved myself deeply as I wrote, and was deriving a delicious kind of enjoyment from the emotion of my idea, from the sentence which was expressing it, and from the satisfaction of having found it." But he also professed the greatest respect for her opinions concerning *Par les Champs et par les Grèves*, the Breton book, which he had left with her to read; he sent her, when once again she won the Academy poetry prize, "great kisses on the heart," declared that his visits to her were oases in the desert of his life, sent Henriette presents of jam and candy, and finally prevailed on Louise to accept a loan of five hundred francs, two hundred of which she was later able to return. In the two months between the March visit to Paris and the fourth of June, which they spent together in Mantes, he scolded her for only four things. He reproached her for having written a miserable comedy called *The Governess,* during one entire scene of which, a drawing lesson, the heroine stood quite still in the centre of the stage, holding a bird—it would have to be a stuffed bird—on her wrist. "That scene alone would kill a masterpiece," Flaubert informed her. He deplored another comedy, equally poor, entitled *Love Letters,* which covered Monsieur Cousin with ridicule. That, he felt, was not the way to treat the father of one's child. He wondered that she should have so little taste as to admire Musset's speech on his reception to the Academy, the fatuousness of which had made Flaubert's flesh creep. And finally he commanded her not to worry about a series of boils with which she was afflicted, and which she claimed to have caught from him. "Boils are *à la mode,*" he wrote unfeelingly. "My sister-in-law is studded with them, and does nothing whatever about it, an example which I urge you to follow instead of throwing your money away in pharmacies and doctors' offices. This brief list of reproaches was something of a record for Flaubert, and in the comparative absence of checks Louise's letters were all the more unrestrained in their lyricism about life and in their admiration for all that was turgid in literature.

On the very day they spent in each other's arms at Mantes, Pradier died of apoplexy at a country spot not far away, in the embrace—it was said—of one of his models with whom he had momentarily retired from a picnic, and this death, "*si douce et si rapide,*" inspired Louise to write a funeral ode which Flaubert found excellent. Everything she wrote, these days, she submitted to him; indeed, many of her poems were writen on themes broached in the letters which Flaubert wrote her (there was one, for example, entitled "*Fantômes,*" based on Flaubert's words: "Of all the feelings you have ever had, has a single one disappeared? No . . ."), and late Sunday nights, after the weekly reading from *Madame Bovary,* he and Louis sometimes spent several hours correcting the latest verses of the Muse.

His letters were usually written late Saturday nights and

early Sunday mornings, after the week's work was done. "You live," he told her, "in the back room of my heart, and come out on Sundays."

"The clock has just struck three," he wrote her one of these Sunday mornings. "The day is beginning, my fire is out, and I am going to bed. How many times in my life I have looked up to see the green light of dawn stealing through my windowpanes! In between the branches of a great acacia outside my little room in the hospital in Rouen, over the Luxembourg in the Rue de l'Est in Paris, from stage-coaches and boats on my travels . . ." Now dawn frequently surprised him as he struggled with the sentences of his book, describing the emotions of Madame Bovary at her ball, yet trying to avoid the banality of the ball scenes that infested romantic novels, and deciding that it would, after all, be more subtle and sober not have her seduced at the ball; reflecting that the one hundred and twenty manuscript pages now done represented only those that had been retained of at least five hundred that had been painstakingly written. It became more and more apparent that if the book succeeded at all it would be a prodigious *tour de force;* for he felt, while writing it, "like a man playing the piano with leaden balls attached to his fingers."

Life at Croisset was eventless. Caroline made her first communion, there were visits from the Nogent cousins, there was a dinner party at Achille's—"*Dîner de scheik!* Champagne! Birthday of the mistress of the house! Family celebration! Tableau!" ("Nothing new at the Achilles'," he wrote his uncle Parain, "except new governess, new cook, new groom, new boils on the behind of Madame—at least so I was told, I saw nothing of them myself.") Madame Flaubert paid for the repairing of the billiard table in Achille's apartment in the hospital, since (as Achille, seconded by the boil-sufferer, quite rightly pointed out) it was not he, but Gustave and his friends, who had ruined it almost twenty years before with theatrical performances, and now there was another generation who wished to enjoy it properly. From Paris came frequent bottles of patent hair-tonic, sent by Louise to arrest if possible the ever-increasing baldness, and she also sent offerings of tooth-powder. Flaubert laid in a supply of English rum, and enjoyed Baudelaire's articles on "Edgar Poë" in the *Revue de Paris.* All was calm, and at the moment there was only one person upon whom Flaubert was directing the blasts of his contempt, usually so prodigally bestowed.

Since Max's admonishing letter of the previous fall and Flaubert's long stay in Paris shortly afterward, there had been no communication between the two friends. Max had not written; in March he had been too busy to see Flaubert at all, and Flaubert, hurt, requested Louise not to speak of Max in her letters, as the subject distressed him. At bottom he considered Max's busyness even more absurd than offensive. For apart from Bouilhet's poems and the pieces by Baudelaire the *Revue de Paris* was a barren sheet, very far indeed from the excellent magazine promised by Max and the principles so proudly set forth in the manifesto. Max's own stories in subsequent issues were far below the level of *"Tagahor"*; his modern poems, *Les Chants Modernes*, devoted to the praise of steam-engines and machinery, Flaubert found grotesque; the whole magazine was unworthy of serious consideration. And now, in June, when Max sent him a copy of his book of oriental photographs, which had finally appeared in splendid format— "accompanied by an explanatory text and preceded by an introduction by Maxime Du Camp, entrusted with an archæological mission in the East by the Ministry of Public Instruction"—and when the gift was accompanied by a letter in which Max once again allowed himself to "deplore bitterly" Flaubert's self-burial in the country, and even declared that such an existence could scarcely result in anything but softening of the brain, Flaubert did not accept the criticism in silence.

"You seem to have a mania with regard to me," he replied. "But don't think that it worries me—I have long since made up my mind on the matters you mention. I shall tell you merely that all the words you use—that I should 'hurry,' that 'it is time' I came to Paris, that my 'place will be taken,' that I should 'become established'— are for me a vocabulary devoid of sense. It is as though you were talking to an Algonquin. I don't understand. At what should I hasten to 'arrive,' as you put it? At the

eminence of MM. Murger, Feuillet, Monselet, Arsène
Houssaye, Taxile Delord, Hippolyte Lucas, and seventy-
two others? Thank you. To 'become known' is not my
chief concern—that can afford complete satisfaction only
to very mediocre vanities. And besides, can celebrity be
considered a proof positive of the value of one's work?
Even the most widespread fame during one's lifetime may
not suffice to endure afterwards, and seldom can anyone
but a fool be sure of posthumous glory. Thus even to one's
self illustriousness is no proof that one has accomplished
great things, and obscurity no proof that one has not.
I am aiming at something better—to please myself. Success
seems to me a result, not an end in itself. I have conceived
a certain manner of writing and a certain beauty of
language which I wish to achieve. When I think that I
have gathered the fruit of my efforts I shall not refuse to
sell it, and I shall not forbid applause if it is good. If on
the other hand when it is gathered no one wants it, that
can't be helped. I assure you I agree with you in wishing
I had greater facility and that I could accomplish more
with less labour. But I see no remedy for that state of
affairs. If a work of art is good, if it is authentic, it will be
recognized some time—and if one has to wait for recognition six months or six years or until after one's death,
what is the difference?

"You tell me that it is only in Paris that one breathes
the breath of life. In my opinion your Parisian 'breath of
life' often has the odour of rotting teeth. In that Parnassus
one is visited more often by a miasma than by divine madness, and you'll agree that laurels gathered there are apt to
be somewhat spattered with dung. I am sorry to see a man
like you go one better than the Marquise d'Escarbagnas in
Molière, who thought that 'outside of Paris there is no
salvation for gentlemen.' This judgment itself seems to me
provincial, in other words, narrow. Humanity exists everywhere, my dear sir, though I agree that there is more nonsense in Paris than elsewhere. And there is unquestionably
one thing that one does acquire in Paris—and that is im-
pertinence. . . .

"As for deploring so bitterly my sodden way of life, it is
as though you were to reproach a shoemaker for making

shoes or a blacksmith for striking his iron or a painter for living in his studio. Since I work from one o'clock in the afternoon until one o'clock in the morning every day, except from six to eight in the evening, I scarcely see how I could make use of the remaining time. If I led a genuinely provincial or rural existence, devoting myself to dominoes or melon-raising, I could understand the reproach. But if I am becoming brutish you will have to lay the blame on Lucian, Shakespeare, and novel-writing. I told you that I shall move to Paris when my book is done and that I shall publish it if I am satisfied with it. My resolution has not changed in the slightest. That is what I can say, and I can say nothing more. . . ."

And when Max quickly replied in a wounded and paternal tone, persisting in his advice, Flaubert wrote again:

"I am sorry you should be so sensitive. Far from wanting to make my letter offensive, I tried to make it the opposite. To the extent that I could I kept within the limits of the subject, as they say in rhetoric. But why do you begin all over again? Are you always going to preach diet to a man who is pretentious enough to consider himself in good health? I find your distress on my account comical, that's all. Do I reproach you for living in Paris, for having published, etc.? Have I ever advised you as to how to lead your life? Each of us must live in the way that suits him. All plants don't require the same care. And besides, if destiny is not with us, you will strive in vain in Paris and I shall strive in vain here; if we haven't the vocation nothing will come of our efforts, and if on the contrary we have it why torment ourselves about the rest?

"Everything that you can tell me, I assure you, I have already told myself—whether it be blame or praise, bad or good. Everything added by you will be merely a repetition of a mass of monologues that I know by heart. But there is one thing I must say. I deny absolutely the existence of the literary renascence which you announce. I see no new writers, no original books, no ideas that aren't outworn. Everyone is trailing at the backsides of the masters, as in the past. The same old humanitarian or æsthetic saws are repeated over and over again. I don't deny that the young men of today really want to create a school, but I chal-

lenge them to do it. I should be glad to find myself
mistaken—I should profit from the discovery. As for my
'position,' as you call it, of man of letters, I abandon it to
you willingly. I decline the honour of such a title and I
refuse to admit that I have any mission. I am simply a
bourgeois living quietly in the country, occupying myself
with literature, and asking nothing of others, neither consideration nor honour nor even esteem. . . .

"You and I are no longer following the same route, we
are no longer sailing in the same skiff. May God lead each
of us where he wishes to go! I am not seeking port, but
the high seas. If I am shipwrecked, you have my permission
not to mourn."

There was no reason to critize Max for having fulfilled
his mission and there was no denying that his photographs
were handsome; but Flaubert considered the most beautiful collection of photographs even less worthy of a
literary man than a collection of travel sketches, and as to
the introduction which opened the volume he was dismayed to find that Max had concocted it out of the
writings of others, out of books by Lepsius and Cham-
pollion-Figeac, whole passages of which were cited between quotation marks but without the names of the
authors. Of the twenty-five pages of the introduction less
than three were in Max's own words. And while it was
easy enough to see how during the course of their travels
together Max had acquired the habit of managing Flaubert's life as well as his own, it was time for him to realize that their travels were over and that Flaubert was
now engaged on something which he understood better
than he had ever pretended to understand itinerary-
planning, camp-pitching, dragoman-hiring, or provision-
buying. Despite what he had done for Louis Bouilhet—and
the excellence of Louis's verse had in turn done much for
the *Revue*—Max was not to be encouraged in his im-
pertinence. To Flaubert's second letter he made no answer,
and to the glee of Louise the friendship begun in such high
spirits in the students' quarter ten years before and whose
motto for a time had been *solus ad solum*, appeared no
longer to exist.

Louise's poem, *"Ressouvenir Païen,"* with the revamped

dedication, had been politely acknowledged by a rather surprised Max, but despite the trickery it had never been published in the *Revue de Paris,* and in fact nothing by Louise was ever accepted by Max's magazine. This was all the more offensive because the *Revue* published frequent contributions not only by George Sand, whom Louise considered as her deadly rival in the field of letters, but even by the infamous and detested Alphonse Karr; and in revenge Louise decided that when *"Ressouvenir Païen"* was published in the new volume of collected verse she was now preparing it would appear with its proper dedication, *"A Monsieur Gustave Flaubert, après son voyage en Orient."* She was astonished, when she informed Flaubert of this, to be told that she must not think of doing any such thing, and she was equally astonished when he refused to listen to a scandalous morsel she had dug up from Maxime's past. Such behaviour after the end of a friendship she found quite incomprehensible. Louise had hoped to reap affectionate benefits from this long-desired break between the friends, but unfortunately Flaubert was at this very moment in a state of considerable exasperation with her as well.

Ever since meeting Musset the day of his reception into the Academy, Louise had given him every evidence of the confidence with which genius always inspired her, admitting him alone into her house at all hours of the day and night as one would a brother, walking with him in the moonlight as she had previously walked with Vigny, and finally having to leap from a moving cab when the drunken poet ("Musset's genius," Flaubert once remarked, "like the Duke of Gloucester, is drowned in a tun") began ignobly to pretend to misunderstand the exalted character of their relations. After this incident Musset did not call again, and when Louise charitably called on him, in an effort to repair the friendship and set it firmly on a spiritual basis, she discovered to her mortification that he had placed in his concierge's lodge the engraving of herself which Louise had given him, and had ordered the concierge to say, should the original of the portrait appear: "Monsieur de Musset has gone to Lake Como, in America." Such, at least, was the account of the affair which Louise gave Flaubert. She kept him fully informed concerning the sequence of events, even sending him some of Musset's too intimate letters, which she said it had never occurred to her to take amiss; but the anger with which the story filled Flaubert did not spring from the jealousy she had counted on arousing, and was directed against Louise herself rather than against the poet. What infuriated him, he told her, was not so much that she should have been placed in so ridiculous a position—though in some ways the affair did her as much harm as the story of Alphonse Karr— but that she should have put herself at the mercy of someone for whom he had so little respect from a literary point of view. That aspect of the affair caused him to form an "odious image" of her. "Musset has never separated poetry from the sensations which it brings to perfection. . . . His inspiration is always too personal. . . . I was formerly excessively enthusiastic about him; he humoured the vices of my spirit—lyricism, vagabondism, swagger of idea and expression. . . ." As usual, Louise's crime was a literary one.

Louis Bouilhet, too, as the year 1852 advanced, was discovering that Louise was after all not so very different from what he had always supposed her to be. Although he had written her his thanks for the evening which she had arranged, she seemed to be offended that his sonnet had been addressed to the young actress rather than to herself. In several letters written during the spring and early summer, and in a sonnet of her own addressed to him on Saint Hyacinthe's day, the sixteenth of August—his name was Louis Hyacinthe Bouilhet—she continued coyly to regret that she did not inspire him. The fact that this second sonnet arrived just a week before Saint Louis's day, the twenty-fifth of August, which was also the feast-day of Louise, was too significant to be ignored, and in reply Louis finally wrote her the lines which she desired. They were not very good—he knew it, he had not spent much time on them—but a few weeks later it became apparent why Louise had wanted the poem so particularly: it suddenly appeared in the *Revue de Paris*, and Louise joyfully confessed that she had sent it in as coming directly from him, and asked to be congratulated on having secured the publication of a poem which, although her name was not mentioned, was a tribute to her, in the magazine which seemed to make an editorial principle of snubbing her. She also explained that her action was intended in part as a blow against Max for Flaubert's sake, but to her annoyance Flaubert declared himself no more amused or pleased than Bouilhet. And about the same time, when Louise began to write Bouilhet long letters complaining of the indifference and coldness which Gustave was at present displaying toward her, and begging him to urge his friend to treat her with greater consideration, he began to realize that at no time, perhaps, had her kindness in his direction been altogether disinterested, but that rather she had hoped to make Flaubert the more tender by doing what she could for his beloved friend.

The last twenty pages of the first part of *Madame Bovary* were written with particular care, but even so Flaubert discovered on reading them over with Bouilhet that they were full of "monstrous negligences." Revision would take a good two or three weeks. He worked well in the heat—it had on him, he said, "the effect of brandy"— and he kept the blinds of his study closed against the sun and wore only a vast, cool white Nubian shirt, one of two he had brought back for himself and Bouilhet. Week-ends they worked side by side in their eastern garments—"white as phantoms," Louis said, "and calm as gods." The week's revision of *Madame Bovary* was read aloud and criticized. Flaubert often cried out in objection or protest, for a sentence on which he had worked an entire day Bouilhet might quite calmly pronounce superfluous, irrelevant, or false in tone. There were generally too many metaphors. "I am devoured by them, as by vermin," Flaubert wrote, "and spend my time crushing them." Changes in the scenario were discussed and made. Louis read the poems which he had been able to write after tutoring hours, consulting with Flaubert as to whether they were good enough to send to magazines. He was sending verse to other editors now, as well as to Max and his friends, for Max had lately begun to imply that without the *Revue* Louis would have no market at all. Later, when work was done,

they talked of history, metaphysics, literary theory, or
swam in the river in the moonlight. Once they spent four
hours regaling each other with imaginative descriptions of
their old age—they pictured themselves as ancient, miserable patients in a home for incurables, or as street-sweepers,
clad in tattered garments and reminiscing wretchedly of
their past and of their week-ends together. They were so
eloquent that they convulsed each other with laughter and
nearly put each other into tears. There was little possibility
that Flaubert would end his days in misery (though it was
apparent that if Dr. Flaubert had invested his savings
differently the family would be considerably richer), but
Bouilhet's future was uncertain. He had earned a reputation with *Melænis,* but no money whatever; so far no
Academician had offered him a post; and now in the hope
of financial return he was undertaking a new project, a
play in verse about the court of Louis XIV, to be entitled
Madame de Montarcy. Had he been independent, he
would have preferred to write non-dramatic poems on
Chinese subjects—the mandarin at Gautier's had inspired
him, and he had bought a Chinese grammar and was
seriously studying the language—but there was always
the chance that a play might be profitable, and playwriting
was at least preferable to tutoring.

One day Flaubert spent at an agricultural show in a
near-by town: the scene in which he was to describe it
would not be written until the winter, but the show was
given in summer, and notes must be made now. Another
afternoon he spent staring at the Norman countryside
through pieces of coloured glass, to be able to describe the
effect. Evenings, after dinner, he sat with his mother and
Caroline on the wrought-iron balcony of the summerhouse
beside the river; night gradually fell; on the towing path
across the Seine they could distinguish from time to time
the silhouette of a horse pulling a noiselessly slipping boat;
the moon was reflected in golden spangles in the still
blackness of the river; eel-fishers' boats drew quietly away
from shore. They sat there peacefully until Flaubert rose,
saying: "Time to get back to Bovary," and then all returned to the house. To Caroline the meaning of the word
Bovary was not quite clear; it seemed to be a term sig-

nifying work, or writing, and her uncle assured her that
this was so. Bovary, work, writing, was his life. Reading,
too: this summer he read Rabelais, *The Golden Ass,* and
Le Rouge et le Noir, which he found badly written and
incomprehensible as to characters and intentions. He read
Shakespeare's *Pericles:* "What a man Shakespeare was!
How small all the other poets are beside him—how slight
they seem! He had the two elements—imagination and
observation—and in him they are always so copious! I
think that if I were to see Shakespeare in the flesh I should
perish with fear." Beside the boisterousness and flow of
Shakespeare, Lamartine's *"Graziella"* was unbearably hypocritical, Gautier's new poems feeble and pitiable, and
Uncle Tom's Cabin, which he was reading on the enthusiastic recommendation of Louise, considerably less than
perfect.

The revision of Part One was finally done; on the first
of September he began Part Two, and as though there had
been no interruption resumed his letters to Louise.
"Work is endless! Endless! My arms sometimes drop to
my sides from fatigue. When shall I be able to rest, only
for a few months? When shall you and I taste of each
other, freely and at leisure? Here is another long year
ahead of us, the whole winter to be lived through—you in
Paris with the buses in the muddy streets, the red noses,
the greatcoats, the wind blowing in under the door; I here
amid the leafless trees, with the steamer passing six times
a day on the white Seine."
Part Two frightened him: he wished the next five or six
months were over. He wished he were living in the time of
Pericles, or Nero, or Ronsard, or even Louis XIV, "with
the society of Monsieur Descartes"; he wished he were
travelling in India and Japan. His sentences succeeded
one another "at the pace of a tortoise," and he described to
Louise the frightful difficulties of the scene on which he
was engaged, the scene at the inn the evening of the
Bovarys' arrival in their new town:
"Never in my life have I written anything more difficult
than what I am doing now—trivial dialogue. I have to portray, simultaneously and in the same conversation, five or

six characters who speak, several others who are spoken about, the scene, and the whole town, giving physical descriptions of people and objects; and in the midst of all that I have to show a man and a woman who are beginning (through a similarity in tastes) to fall in love with each other. If only I had space! But the whole thing has to be rapid without being thin, and well worked out without taking up too much room; and many details which would be more striking here I have to keep in reserve for use elsewhere. I am going to put the whole thing down quickly, and then proceed by a series of increasingly drastic revisions; by going over and over it I can perhaps pull it together. The language itself is a great stumbling-block. My two characters are completely commonplace, but they have to speak in a literary style, and politeness of language takes away so much picturesqueness from any speech! They will talk about literature, about the sea, the mountains, music—all the well-worn poetical subjects. It will be the first time in any book, I think, that the young hero and the young heroine are made mock of, and yet the irony will in no way diminish the pathos but rather intensify it."

The later chapters in Part Two, which were to be concerned with Madame Bovary's first adultery, he thought would write themselves swiftly and with ease—for, ever since his encounter in Trouville, and particularly since his first meeting with Louise, he had always expressed himself with no difficulty whatever on the subject of adultery; but the opening scene continued stubborn, going sometimes well, sometimes not at all. It took him more than two months to complete the conversation in the inn, which covered three hours, and he was so discouraged by the time it was done that he was sure it was poor. Bouilhet, however, pronounced it excellent. "Now I have forty or fifty pages more before I'll be in the midst of adultery," he wrote to Louise, "and my little lady will give herself up to it, I promise you!" Every one of these forty or fifty pages gave him a "*mal de chien*," as he tried to make his narrative "proceed in cascades, carrying the reader along amid the shaking of sentences and the foaming of metaphors," and in November he was glad to interrupt his work and journey to Mantes, carrying with him his Grecian travel notes and several books on Greece, for the Academy had announced "The Acropolis of Athens" as the subject of its next poetical composition, and Louise expected him to be of much assistance.

It had been even longer than usual since their last rendez-vous, and this one was as orgiastic as the first of the Mantes meetings, six years before, enabling Flaubert to recapture some of the rapture of adultery which he had felt while Monsieur Colet was still alive and which he would soon be describing in his novel. A week later, however, he received from Louise a letter that filled him with terror; his agony lasted for three weeks; and then finally another letter arrived, saying all was well.

"I begin by devouring you with kisses," he wrote, bursting with relief, "for I am transported with joy. Your letter of this morning has lifted a terrible weight from my heart. It was time, too: yesterday I was unable to work all day; every time I moved (literally) my brain throbbed and pounded in my skull, and by eleven o'clock I had to go to bed. All these weeks I have been suffering horribly from worry, and have not stopped thinking of you for a second —but in a way that has been scarcely agreeable. I should need a whole book to develop my feelings in a comprehensible manner. The idea of causing the birth of someone horrifies me. I should curse myself were I to become a father. I, have a son! Oh, no! No! No! I desire my flesh to perish, and have no wish to transmit to anyone the humiliating impotencies and the ignominies of existence. I also had a superstitious thought. Tomorrow I shall be thirty-one. I have just passed that fatal thirtieth year, the year that ranks a man. It is the age when a man takes his future shape, settles down, marries, chooses a trade. There are few people who do not become bourgeois at thirty. Paternity would have confined me within those ordinary ways of living. Why did you desire this bond between us?

"I breathe again! The day is fine, the sun is shining on the river, at this moment a brig is passing with all sails unfurled; my window is open, my fire blazing. Adieu! I love you more than ever, and I kiss you to suffocation in honour of my birthday."

And he wrote her, too, of his complete scorn for a novel by Max which was appearing serially in the *Revue de Paris*, called *Le Livre Posthume* and purporting to be the memoirs of a romantic young man the author had met in Egypt and who had since committed suicide. Flaubert found it pitiable, "odious in personality and in pretensions of all kinds"; it was exactly the kind of book Max had joined with Bouilhet in urging Flaubert not to write— romantically lush, filled with confessions and containing more than one suggestion of *Novembre*. Flaubert even found one phrase which he felt had been written for him —"solitude, bearing egotism and vanity at its sinister breasts"—and the romantic hero dreamed a dream which Flaubert himself had dreamed in Egypt, in which his mother had turned first into a Turk and then into a hyena and sprung at his throat. "Max is following his own path," he wrote to Louise, "but in literature he will remember me for many a day."

As the winter grew colder, he took pleasure in writing summer scenes, for as usual he enjoyed thinking of sur-roundings which were the opposite of those in which he was; and as he approached nearer and nearer to the adultery which he longed to describe, he became increas-ingly tense. "My nerves were so vibrant tonight that when my mother came into my study at ten o'clock to say good-night I uttered a cry of terror which startled her considerably. My heart palpitated for some time afterward, and it took me a quarter of an hour to recover myself." Now he did not give way to despair even when one page was five days in the writing, or when he discovered that Balzac's *Louis Lambert* began with a scene similar to the opening scene of *Madame Bovary* and that *Le Médecin de Campagne*, also by Balzac, contained a scene similar to the one on which he was working at the moment. "What a man Balzac would have been, if he had known how to write!" he exclaimed to Louise. "But that was the only thing he lacked. An artist, after all, would not have produced so much, would not have had such fecundity." And in January, when he learned that in reward for his album of photographs Max had been promoted at the age of thirty from *Chevalier* to *Officier* in the Legion of

Honour, he was not unduly sarcastic, remarking merely: "When he compares his situation with mine he must certainly consider that he has gone far ahead." In *Madame Bovary* he was now too near to the climax, or at least to the part which he thought would "make the whole effect of the book," to be deeply concerned with anything else.

The looming threat of one annoyance, however, he was forced to recognize. Presuming on his recent letters, which he now began to fear were considerably warmer than they should have been, Louise was falling back into some of her old habits, renewing some of her old demands. "No doubt my mother would have been perfectly affable had you happened to meet in one way or another," he had to write warningly, "but as for being *flattered* to meet you (and don't take this for a gratuitous brutality), I must tell you that she is flattered by nothing whatever."

If that kind of plaguing was going to begin again, things would have to end once more as they had already once ended.

4.

Like the inauguration of most dictatorships, the *coup d'état* of Louis Napoleon Bonaparte in December 1851 entailed a political purge and literary censorship. Much the greater number of Frenchmen, however, both in private and in public life, showed a most obliging readiness to accept the new regime—"My hair is falling like the political convictions of my contemporaries," Flaubert remarked during the winter—and though there was a certain amount of underground work, almost the only person of prominence to protest defiantly was Victor Hugo. He fled to Brussels to escape arrest, nothing that he wrote from his exile was admitted into France, and letters addressed to him were confiscated. Flaubert, who considered censorship "a monstrosity, a thing worse than homicide, treason against the soul," spoke with scorn of a regime which "decorated photographers and exiled poets." To him Hugo was the greatest writer of the century and his exile a disgrace to France.

Louise Colet shared these opinions—particularly since some years earlier Hugo's favorable vote in the Academy had helped her win one of her poetry prizes—but she was prevented from expressing herself with any freedom by the thought that her pension from the state would almost certainly be discontinued were she to do so. In June, however, when the contents of Hugo's Paris house were sold at public auction, Louise was too moved to remain silent. She wrote a poem entitled *"La Maison du Poète Exilé"* and sent it to Hugo, mailing it under cover addressed to French friends in London, and with it she sent a letter thanking him for his past kindness and lamenting the times, and a copy of her new collection of verse, *Ce Qui Est dans le Cœur des Femmes.*

Late in September, after a delay due in part to his removal to the Isle of Jersey and in part to his difficulties in finding a safe channel of communication, the great man replied in the flowery and flattering style which he was accustomed to use with his admirers: "I have found all kinds of new pearls in the golden sand of your poetry. If I had you here I should make for you, from all these pearls that are yours, a necklace which would be mine. Each one of these tender and ravishing lines I should address to you." Delighted with this, Louise quickly wrote again. Recently, she said, she had read to two young literary men, named Louis Bouilhet and Gustave Flaubert, Hugo's attack on the Emperor, *Napoléon le Petit.* " 'In these days the admiration of every writer, every poet, must go out to Hugo, the master of us all, in his exile,' " she reported the young men as saying. "They blush to see some writers make their bows at the Elysée: Sainte-Beuve, Mérimée, and Musset *admire* Napoleon III!" And she offered a suggestion. If Hugo would care to have her do so, she would be glad to communicate with him regularly through her London friends, sending him French news and any information or enclosures he might desire. And he, in turn, could reply through the same intermediaries, enclosing, if he chose, letters to be forwarded to friends in France. The people in London, however, would send his communica-

tions not directly to her—her prominence made her an
easy target for suspicion—but rather via young Monsieur
Flaubert. Living in rural retirement, on a "ravishing estate"
which Louise implied she knew very well, he could receive any correspondence with impunity, and he was enthusiastic to serve the cause. (Actually, Flaubert's enthusiasm had consisted in writing to Louise: "I don't mind
Hugo's sending me letters for you if they come via London, but directly from Jersey would be too transparent.")
Hugo accepted the offer with gratitude, and shortly Brit-
ish envelopes, containing letters written on thin paper and
generally unsigned, began to arrive at Croisset. When the
first one came, Flaubert sent it on to Louise unopened—
an action which she found offensive. "There is no reason
for such delicacy—you know quite well that Hugo has
never made love to me," she wrote indignantly, and he
had to assure her that no such thought, but rather simple
politeness, had directed his action, and that since she
seemed to prefer it he would henceforth open everything.

Hugo was not always discreet. Sometimes he ignored the
London intermediaries and through friends in Jersey sent
communications directly to Croisset. This was dangerous
—a young man whom Flaubert had known at college in
Rouen had recently been fined five hundred francs and
sentenced to a year in prison for distributing copies of
Napoléon le Petit—and Flaubert worked out a system
which would be more sure in every way. All correspondence, in both directions, was to pass through both Croisset
and London. Louise's letters were no longer to be sent
through her French friends—they did not seem like reli-
able people and, besides, any dealings with Frenchmen
abroad were best avoided. They were to be enclosed in
two envelopes, the inner blank and the other addressed to
Flaubert. At Croisset the outer envelopes would be
changed and addressed in the handwriting of Caroline's
English governess to some English friends of Madame
Flaubert, some *"braves gens complètement confinés dans
leur commerce"*; thus they would seem merely to be letters sent by the governess to her own family or friends. In
England the outer envelopes would be changed again and
sent on to Jersey. A similar technique was to be used by

Hugo in the opposite direction, and Flaubert begged
Louise to ask him to observe all possible precautions. Even
so, however, all did not go perfectly smoothly. The Grand
Crocodile, the Supreme Alligator—as Hugo was variously
referred to by the conspirators—used the address of Mrs.
Farmer only when he chose to; he insisted on using
strange-shaped envelopes, and on addressing the inner
coverings himself in bizarre handwritings, forcing Flaubert
to open, re-enclose, and readdress everything before sending it on to Louise; when the governess was dismissed for
neglecting Caroline it was Madame Flaubert who addressed the letters to Mrs. Farmer.

Occasionally Hugo inserted in his envelope a brief line
of thanks to Flaubert, and Louise urged Gustave to reply,
assuring him that the notes were meant as invitations to
begin correspondence. But he had a horror of receiving
long letters expressing gratitude in pompous language—
"The sun smiles on me and I smile at the sun," the poet
had recently written to Louise—and of having to return
long letters in kind, and he merely asked Louise to assure
Hugo that he was entirely at his service and to beg him
once more to use the London address. Finally, though, a
series of letters coming directly to Croisset from Jersey
made him feel that he must take action, and he did so.
"The letter was not easy to write," he confided to Louise,
"because of the moderation of tone which I wished to
preserve. He has been guilty of too many abominations
for me to be able to express unqualified admiration—his
encouragement of literary mediocrities, for example, his
joining the Academy, his political ambitions—but on the
other hand he has afforded me many fine hours of enthusiasm. It was difficult to keep half-way between stiffness
and adulation, but I believe I succeeded in being polite
and sincere at the same time—a rare achievement."

FLAUBERT TO VICTOR HUGO

Croisset, June 2, 1853.
"I think, Monsieur, that I should inform you that your
communication dated April 27 arrived here badly dam-

aged. The outer envelope was torn in several places and bits of your handwriting exposed. The inner envelope (addressed to Madame C.) had been torn along the end, and its contents were visible—two other letters and a printed sheet. Was it the customs who opened the envelope, hoping to find a bit of lace? It would be naïve, I think, to suppose that: the indiscretion must be laid at the door of the saviours of society. If you have something of importance to transmit to me, Monsieur, I believe that the following procedure would be the most sure: you could address your letters from Jersey to a family of honest merchants whom I know in London; they would open the outer envelope and enclose the inner in one which would thus bear their English handwriting and a London postmark. I should then forward enclosures to Madame C. Your later envelope, dated May, has arrived intact.

"I beg of you, Monsieur, to allow me to thank you for all the thanks you have sent me, and to accept none of them. The man who has occupied the greatest and best place in my restricted life may indeed expect some service of me, if what I have done you choose to call service. The shyness which one feels in declaring a genuine passion will not allow me, despite your exile, to tell you at length of the bond that links me to you. In brief, it is my gratitude for all the enthusiasm you have offered me. But I do not wish to become entangled in phrases which would serve me but badly in attempts to enlarge upon it.

"I have seen you in person; we have met several times— you unaware of me, I gazing eagerly at you. It was in the winter of 1844, in the studio of poor Pradier. There were five or six of us; we drank tea and played a game; I even remember your big gold ring, with its etching of a rampant lion, which we used as a forfeit. Since then you have played for higher stakes, and in more terrible games; but in whatever you do, the rampant lion plays its part. *He* bears on his brow the mark of its claws, and when he passes into history the centuries will know him by that red scar.

"As for you, who knows? Future makers of æsthetic will perhaps thank Providence for this monstrousness, for this consecration. For is it not by martyrdom that virtue is brought to perfection? Is it not by outrage that grandeur is rendered yet more grand? And in you there is lacking neither inherent grandeur not that conferred by circumstance.

"I send you, Monsieur, together with all my admiration for your genius, the assurance of my entire devotion to you."

VICTOR HUGO TO FLAUBERT

Marine Terrace, June 28 [*1853*].

"Since you desire no thanks, Monsieur, do you know how I shall prove my gratitude? By my indiscretion. Here is a new enclosure for Madame C. Allow me to send with it, *for you,* my portrait; it is the work of my son, done in collaboration with the sun. It should be a good likeness: *solem quis dicere falsum audeat?* In it you will recognize the ring which you mention in your charming letter. I well remember that winter of 1844 and those evenings at Pradier's. A part of all of that is dead, but it is still alive at the bottom of my soul; I am glad that a memory of you should be mingled with it, for you are now one of my friends.

"I find it difficult to explain the intention of the good Lord in removing the sun from us this summer in our exile; perhaps he will compensate us by removing Bonaparte from us next winter. If such be so, all praise to the mysterious All-Powerful!"

FLAUBERT TO VICTOR HUGO

Croisset, July 15 [*1853*].

"How am I to thank you, Monsieur, for your magnificent gift? What am I to say—unless perhaps I echo the dying Talleyrand when visited by Louis Philippe: 'This is the greatest honour ever conferred upon my house!'? There that parallel ends, for all kinds of reasons, but I shall not hide from you that you have profoundly 'touched the proud weakness of my heart,' as Racine

would have said. Noble poet! How many monsters he
would find now to depict, all of them a hundred times
worse than his dragon-bull!

"Exile, at least, spares you that sight. Ah, if you knew
into what filth we are plunged! Private infamies proceed
from political turpitude, and it is impossible to take a step
without treading on something unclean. The atmosphere
is heavy with nauseous vapours. Air! Air! I open my window and turn toward you. I hear the powerfully beating
wings of your muse as she passes by, and I breathe, as the
perfume of forests, the incense that rises from the depths
of your style.

"All my life, Monsieur, you have been for me a charming obsession, a long love that has never weakened. I have
read you during sinister wakes and on beaches beside the
sea in the summer sun. I carried you with me to Palestine,
and it was you who consoled me, ten years ago, when I
was dying of ennui in the Latin Quarter. Your poetry became a part of me, like my nurse's milk. Some of your
poems will remain in my memory for ever, for they have
been the great adventures of my life.

"Here I shall stop. If sincerity exists, it is in what I have
just written. From now on, I shall molest you no longer,
and you may make use of the correspondent without fear
of his correspondence. But since you stretch out your
hand across the ocean, I take it and grasp it. I grasp it
proudly, the hand that wrote *Notre-Dame* and *Napoléon
le Petit*, the hand that has hewn colossi and fashioned
poison-cups for traitors, that has culled the most glorious
delights from the loftiest reaches of the intellect, and that
now, like the hand of Samson, alone remains raised amid
the double ruins of Art and Liberty!

"I am, Monsieur, yours, with once again a thousand
thanks."

("I have written a monumental letter to the Grand
Crocodile," he told Louise. "It is truly in the grand style,
I think—perhaps even too grand. I shan't pretend that it
didn't give me a good deal of trouble, so much in fact that
I now know it by heart. If I still remember it when we
meet, I will repeat it to you.")

Marine Terrace, September 18 [*1853*].
"I need the correspondent and I exact his correspondence. So much the worse for you, Monsieur. It is your
own fault: why do you write me the wittiest and noblest
letters in the world? You have only yourself to blame;
from now on you *must* write me.

"Would you believe that I have stupidly lost the address
in London? Hence the delay of this reply; hence the tardy
mailing of the enclosed speech.

"We are full of hope and faith here. Everything goes
well for the moment. I give the man two more years.
Thereafter, eternity will belong to the people."

From now on, with every letter for Louise, Hugo enclosed a word to "the correspondent," but for a long time
Flaubert kept his resolution not to reply. "Nevertheless, it
was kind of him to send the photograph, and I shall treas-
ure it," he wrote Louise. "It would have driven me nearly
insane with ecstasy, formerly!"

The letters which Louise sent to Jersey were long,
journal-like documents concerning literary and political
life in Paris, so vituperative and bitter that the extreme
sharpness of Hugo's first volume of poems from his exile,
Les Châtiments, has been laid in part to the ferocity of
Louise's opinions. Her letters were far from impersonal.
More than once she pointed to Musset's constant drunkenness as a symptom of the present low state of literature in
France; she mocked the tawdry literary taste displayed by
the Emperor and the Empress; and she frequently enclosed poems of her own, which Hugo praised ever more
fulsomely. "A Corneille is crowned with laurel: you are
crowned with stars," he informed her on one occasion, and
he paid her the greatest compliment in his repertoire by
professing not to understand how she escaped exile. "I
wish for you the glory of exile; and I wish for us the joy
of your presence with us here." He conscientiously used
Mrs. Farmer's address when he did not lose or forget it,

and although a few more of his letters arrived opened they were fortunately never those which he had signed, and Louise was able successfully to escape the form of glorification which he desired for her.

Eventually the long series of gracious notes from Jersey caused Flaubert to begin to worry—not about the danger which the correspondence always entailed, but about the opinion, perhaps false, which Hugo had of him—and he began to feel that honesty required that he write again. "I now want to write him everything I think," he told Louise. "Would that hurt him? But I simply cannot let him go on thinking that I'm a republican, that I admire the people, etc." He did write the letter—"I am in the midst of writing another monumental letter to the Crocodile," he told Louise a few weeks later—but perhaps he did not send it; there is no trace of it or of any answer from Hugo, no trace of any further correspondence between them until later. That is a pity; one would like to see that letter, for Flaubert's expressed opinions concerning society and even concerning the Second Empire and Napoleon III are so often greatly at variance that a carefully written letter containing "everything I think" would be an achievement worth admiring.

The two self-conscious letters to Hugo contain Flaubert's loftiest pronouncements on themes that are not narrowly literary. In the letters which he wrote before beginning *Madame Bovary* there is nearly always a complete absence of social comment, and even now he announced—at times—that social matters should not preoccupy such a person as himself. "I believe that at the present time a thinker (and what is the artist if not a thinker in every possible sense of the word?) should have neither religion nor fatherland nor even any social conviction. Absolute scepticism seems to me now so clearly indicated that to want to formulate it would be almost an absurdity." But whereas in the past this had been his constant opinion—not even expressed, so lacking had been his interest in all social manifestations except the absurdity of the bourgeois—now he was no longer either consistent or silent. The increased interference of the government in daily life, and his own daily concern with the characters and scenes of *Madame Bovary*, kept his eyes fixed on the spectacle of society, and his letters abound in clashing comment.

As in his remarks concerning censorship and the exile of Hugo, he frequently expressed dislike of the imperial authoritarianism. "I shed no tears for Lamartine," he announced in April 1853, "that writer without rhythm, that statesman without initiative. He is responsible alike for the plague of consumptive lyricism and for the advent of the Empire." Louis Napoleon's slogan, "We must re-establish the principle of authority," he declared to be as absurd as the "fear of the Reds" during the Revolution of 1848. "I hear that some first-class misery is expected this winter," he remarked in the autumn. "Is it possible, with a government as clever as ours? After caring so beautifully for the 'material interests,' and having 'given so much work to the people,' it discovers to its surprise that the people haven't a sou! Charming!" And he laughed at the Emperor for resenting critical disapproval of a play which he had sponsored and which he had intended to brighten the dimming lustre of the Comédie Française: "As though it wasn't enough to have restored order, religion, the family, private property, etc., without wanting to restore the Comédie Française! What a mania for restoration!"

At other times he spoke quite differently of the regime. "I can never forgive men of action for not succeeding," he once wrote to Louise, "since success is the only measure of their merit. Napoleon, they say, was 'betrayed' at Waterloo—a sophism: I know nothing about it, of course, but the fact remains, *he had to win*. I admire a winner, whoever he is." This being the case, the consolidation of the Empire made it impossible for him not to extend admiration to Napoleon III. "Yes, I am growing old, I am not of this century, I feel as foreign in the midst of my compatriots as I felt in Nubia, and I am beginning seriously to admire the Prince-President, who is grinding this noble France under the sole of his boots. I should even go and kiss his behind, to thank him personally for doing so, if there weren't such a crowd there already that I couldn't get near." "The Emperor's success," he said, "is explained

by the fact that he conserved and combined all his resources, didn't squander his strength in trivial actions divergent from his end. He was like a cannonball, suddenly
bursting out and causing everyone to tremble. If Hugo had
done the same, he might have accomplished in poetry what
the other has done in politics—something very remarkable
indeed. But no—he kept flying off on all kinds of impassioned tangents. Passion is the ruin of us all." And when he
found the newspapers and magazines particularly stupid he
swore: "If the Emperor were to abolish printing tomorrow, I'd crawl to Paris on my hands and knees and kiss his
behind in gratitude."

In general, however, he considered—along with Bouilhet, whose hope in the people had long since vanished—
that in the present state of society the greatest good was to
have as little contact as possible with one's fellow-citizens.
" '89 destroyed royalty and the nobility, '48 the bourgeoisie, and '51 the people. There is nothing left but a
bestial and imbecile rabble, and the only way to live in
peace is to place yourself above the whole of humanity,
to be a simple spectator. Yes, I am becoming a furious
aristocrat. Though I have never suffered, thank God, at
the hands of man, and though my life has never been lacking in cushions on which I could curl up in corners and
forget everyone else, still I detest my fellow-beings and
do not feel that I am their fellow at all." The contempt
he had always had for the bourgeois he now extended to
the entire human race, for "the bourgeoisie now *is* all of
humanity, including the people." He took as his patron
saint Polycarpe, "who had the custom of stopping his ears,
fleeing from wherever he was, and crying: 'In what a
century hast Thou caused me to be born, O my God!' "
He demanded in despair: "What is to be expected of a
population such as that of Manchester, which spends its
life making pins?" Socialism was anathema to him: "What
is equality if not the negation of all liberty, of all superior-
ity, and of nature itself? Equality is slavery. That is why
I love art: there, at least, all is liberty in a world of fic-
tions."

In art, too, he was a "furious aristocrat": "The task of
modern criticism is to restore art to its pedestal. The

beautiful cannot be popularized—merely degraded. What have we done with antiquity in desiring to render it accessible to children? Something profoundly stupid. But it is so convenient for everyone to use expurgated versions of the classics, résumés, translations! It is so pleasant for dwarfs to be able to contemplate truncated giants! What is best in art will always elude mediocre natures, that is to say, seven-eighths of the human race. So why denature truth for the benefit of the vulgar?"

His work on *Madame Bovary* gave him visions, vivid and confused, of the art of the future: "I am turning toward a kind of æsthetic mysticism. . . . When there is no encouragement to be derived from one's fellows, when the exterior world is disgusting, enervating, corruptive, and brutalizing, honest and sensitive people are forced to seek somewhere within themselves a more suitable place to live. If society continues on its present path I believe we shall see the return of such mystics as have existed in all the dark ages of the world. The soul, unable to overflow, will be concentrated in itself. The time is not far off when we shall see the return of world-sicknesses—beliefs in the Last Day, expectation of a Messiah, etc. But all this enthusiasm will be ignorant of its own nature, and, the age being what it is, can have no theological foundation: what *will* be its basis? Some will seek it in the flesh, others in the ancient religions, others in art; humanity, like the Jewish tribes in the desert, will adore all kinds of idols. We were born a little too early: in twenty-five years the points of intersection of these quests will provide superb subjects for masters. Then prose (prose especially, the youngest form) will be able to play a magnificent humanitarian symphony. Books like the *Satyricon* and the *Golden Ass* will be written once more, containing on the intellectual plane all the lush excesses which those books have on the sensual. That is what all the socialists in the world have not been willing to see, with their eternal materialistic preachings. They have denied pain, they have blasphemed three-quarters of modern poetry, the blood of Christ that quickens within us. If the feeling of human insufficiency, of the nothingness of life, were to perish (the logical consequence of their hypothesis), we should be more stupid than the birds. . . . Perhaps beauty will become a feeling useless to humanity, and art something half-way between algebra and music."

"The time of the Beautiful has passed," he declared on another occasion. "Humanity may come back to it, but it has no interest in it for the moment. The further it goes, the more scientific art will become, just as science will become artistic. Separate at their beginnings, they will meet toward the top. No human thought can picture the dazzling psychical suns in which the writings of the future will flower. In the meantime we are in a shadowy passage, groping in the dark."

And in other letters he proclaimed, as he chose, his passionate belief in "race rather than education" or his equally fervent conviction that "race no longer exists," or that "the idea of fatherland is about dead, thank God." And alongside regrets that he would not live to see the glorious blossoming of literature which he foretold, he declared that "in twenty years everyone will be so completely stupid that a bourgeois of the time of Louis Philippe will seem like an elegant aristocrat, and the liberty, art, and manners of that period will be praised to the skies."

Such were some of the hundreds of generalities which Flaubert wrote down, almost helter-skelter, in dozens of contradictory letters, on Saturday nights and Sunday mornings, after the week's work on the concrete details of *Madame Bovary* was done. The ability vividly to express a host of different points of view, always in accents of passionate sincerity, is perhaps the opposite of a handicap to a young man whose set task is the gradual bringing to life of the elaborate and solid plan of a novel with a large cast of characters. Flaubert considered *"ne pas conclure"* —"draw no conclusions"—to be the only motto for a sensible man, and the amusing thing is that even when he was talking about his work he could not help differing with himself.

"You should write more coldly," he informed Louise one Sunday morning. "We must be on our guard against that kind of intellectual over-heating called inspiration, which often consists more largely of nervous emotion than of muscular strength. At this very moment, for example, I am keyed up to a high pitch—my brow is burning, sentences keep rushing into my head; for the past two hours I have been wanting to write to you and haven't been able to wrench myself away from work for an instant. Instead of one idea I have six, and where the most simple type of exposition is called for I find myself writing similes and metaphors. I could keep going until tomorrow noon without fatigue. But I know these masked balls of the imagination! You return home with death in your heart, done up, having seen only falsity and uttered nothing but nonsense. Everything should be done coldly, with poise."

Later, however, when he was finally in the midst of the adultery he had so longed to reach, and which he knew would "make the whole effect of the book," the story was different. "This has been one of the rare days of my life passed completely in illusion from beginning to end. At six o'clock this evening, as I was writing the word 'hysterics,' I was so swept away, was bellowing so loudly and feeling so deeply what my little Bovary was going through, that I was afraid of having hysterics myself. I got up from my table and opened the window, to calm myself. My head was spinning. Now, at two in the morning, I have great pains in my knees, in my back and my head. I feel like a man who has been making too much love—a kind of rapturous lassitude. Will what I wrote be good? I have no idea—but one thing is sure, that my book has been going at a lively rate for the past week. May it continue so, for I am weary of my usual snail's pace. I fear the awakening, however, the disillusion that will come from the recopied pages. No matter; it is a delicious thing to write, whether well or badly—to be no longer yourself but to move in an entire universe of your own creating. Today, man and woman, lover and beloved, I rode in a forest on an autumn afternoon under the yellow leaves, and I was also the horse, the leaves, the wind, the words my people spoke, even the red sun that made them half shut their love-drowned eyes. . . ."

It was scarcely an echo of moments of coldness or poise when he declared that he was "nauseated by the vulgarity of his subject." At times his disgust for the people he was describing was so great that he wrote brutal scenes, full of contempt, which it was impossible to keep but which relieved his feelings. And he was least cold of all, perhaps, when to his delight the veracity of some part of his creation was demonstrated. "I had a great success today. You know that yesterday Rouen was 'honoured' by a visit from the Minister of War. Well, I discovered in this morning's *Journal de Rouen* a phrase in the Mayor's speech of welcome which I had written the day before, textually, in my *Bovary* (in a speech by a prefect at an agricultural show). Not only were the idea and the words the same, but even the rhythm of the style. It's things like this that give me pleasure. When literature achieves the accuracy of an exact science, that's something!"

Indeed, it was only when he was composing his novel—and not even when he was talking about it, and certainly not when he was talking about other things—that the power of Flaubert's writing, with its constantly shifting points of view, was enhanced rather than vitiated, one indication among others that he was a born novelist. He thought about politics and society, these days, more than he had before beginning *Madame Bovary*, and he had ever more ideas about art; but it was undoubtedly his realization that it was *in his book* that he was consistent and always in touch with reality that caused him to make, with regard to *Madame Bovary*, a claim he was never to make with regard to any of his utterances on society or politics or art: "Everything one invents is true, you may be perfectly sure of that. Poetry is as precise as geometry. Induction is as accurate as deduction. And besides, after reaching a certain point one no longer makes any mistake about the things of the soul. My poor Bovary, without a doubt, is suffering and weeping at this very instant in twenty villages of France."

Emma Bovary had begun, perhaps, as young Madame Delamare, and there was no question but that she had subsequently taken on a resemblance to Louise Colet. The scenes of adultery, in particular, contain whole phrases and passages of feeling that had been born in Paris or Mantes. And other details concerning adultery and debts seem

to have been taken by Flaubert from the life of the unfortunate Madame Pradier, whom he had seen cast out by
her sculptor husband for misconduct. But by now the
largest part of Emma's character was being modelled on
that of someone whom Flaubert knew far better than he
knew any of those ladies. "*I* am Madame Bovary"—
"*Madame Bovary, c'est moi!*"—the retort he would soon
be making to anyone who asked him the identity of his
model, could have been made now. "One no longer makes
mistakes about the things of the soul": that was why
Madame Bovary was coming true.

The book was now half done.

One of Flaubert's favourite books was the *Golden Ass*.
For him it was among the greatest of the masterpieces;
when he read it he felt "giddy and dazzled," and he was
enchanted by the way in which it combined "incense and
urine, bestiality and mysticism." During the first two years
and a half of his work on *Madame Bovary*, when he was
seeing Louise about once every three months and writing
her at least one long letter a week, he became fairly well
acquainted—though chiefly by hearsay—with the men
who frequented her salon or whom she saw about Paris;
and he fell into the habit of getting her to inquire, of each
new person she mentioned, his opinion of the *Golden Ass*.
He made the book a kind of criterion, and the results of
the census, as reported back by Louise, he found cause for
hilarity and scorn. He considered that the worth of a book
could be judged by the "strength of the punches it gives,
and the length of time it takes you to recover from them,"
and the failure of Louise's literary gentlemen to value the
good punches of the *Golden Ass* lessened considerably the
already mediocre opinion he had of most of them. For it
was, in general, the writers who failed to appreciate the
book. Plato, whose style Flaubert now considered turgid,
was pained, on one of his rare visits, that Louise should
even mention the *Golden Ass;* Musset loftily declared that
he "preferred wit to dung"; and Leconte de Lisle, whose
ink Flaubert found "pale," admitted to feeling ill at ease in
Apuleius's company. A certain Captain d'Arpentigny, on
the other hand and to Flaubert's delight, one of Louise's

less literary admirers, an authority on "the art of recognizing the tendencies of the intelligence from the shape of the hand, etc.," claimed to love the book above all others. And there was a gentleman named Babinet, a physicist and astronomer, who declared himself an enthusiast for it, and offered to lend it to Louise; failing to find it, however, he brought her instead a volume entitled *Le Musée Secret de Naples*—a collection of pictures which, as Flaubert joyfully pointed out, was seldom lent to ladies. "I adore Babinet," he wrote. "The conjunction of ideas which must have taken place in his head is superb. He looked for the *Golden Ass.* 'I can't find it,' he said to himself. 'Let me see, what shall I bring her instead? Something dirty and antique. Ah! The *Musée Secret!*' And he put it in his pocket. Don't be surprised if Babinet attempts certain moves in your direction one of these days."

The distaste of Louise's literary friends for what Flaubert considered literary vigour provoked him to many comments. He avowed his love for dung in literature, "particularly when it is lyrical, as in Rabelais," and reminded her that the bacchanal scenes of Rubens show men pissing on the ground, that in Aristophanes characters defecate on the stage, and that Sophocles portrays Ajax weeping amidst the blood of newly slaughtered animals. When she wrote him admiringly about the delicate sensibilities of Leconte de Lisle, who had confessed to her that he had never been able to enter a brothel, he exploded. "Let me tell you that *I* have often been able to! It is perhaps a depraved taste, but I love prostitution, and for itself, too, quite apart from what there is underneath. My heart begins to pound every time I see one of those flashily dressed women walking under the lamplight in the rain, just as monks in their corded robes have always excited some deep, ascetic corner of my soul. The idea of prostitution is a meeting point of so many elements—lust, bitterness, complete absence of human contact, muscular frenzy, the clink of gold—that to peer into it deeply makes one reel. One learns so many things in a brothel, and feels such sadness, and dreams so longingly of love! Ah, makers of elegies, it is not amid ruins you should linger, but on the breasts of these laughing women!" And he said that a man

of Leconte de Lisle's delicacy could have but a mediocre
relish of Shakespeare, and that *"ce brave organe génital"*
is the seat of all human affections.

Such remarks as these frequently offended Louise. And
when she was rash enough to request, and then to insist
over his demurrings, that Flaubert allow her to read his
travel notes, she was offended anew. "You wish that I
might have written your name more often in my pages.
But note that I didn't write anything reflective. I merely
set down, as briefly as possible, what was indispensable—
sensation, not thought or reverie. You may be sure that I
thought of you often, very often. If I did not come to say
farewell before I left, it was because I was already up to
my ears in emotion! Besides, I was exasperated with you;
you had long irritated me and I preferred not to see you
again, though many a time I longed to. Flesh called but
nerves forbade. As for Kuchiouk Hanem—ah, set your
mind at rest, and at the same time correct your ideas on
the Orient! Be convinced that the woman had no sensation at all—emotionally, I know, and even physically, I
strongly suspect. She found us excellent *cawadja* (*sei-
gneurs*) because we left a goodly number of piastres behind
us, that's all. Bouilhet's poem is very fine, but it is poetry
and nothing else. The oriental woman is a mere machine;
she makes no distinction between one man and another
man. Smoking, bathing, painting her eyelids, and drinking
coffee—such is the circle of occupations in which her
existence turns. Her physical pleasure in love must be
very slight, the organ which makes it possible being tam-
pered with surgically at an early age. And you tell me that
Kuchiouk's vermin degrade her in your eyes; for me they
were the most bewitching touch of all. Their nauseous
odour mingled with the perfume of the sandalwood oil
that was smeared on her skin. I like a touch of bitterness
in everything—always a jeer in the midst of our triumphs,
a dash of desolation even in moments of enthusiasm. That
reminds me of Jaffa, where as we approached the town I
smelled at the same moment the odour of lemon-trees and
that of corpses; half-crumbled skeletons lay about in the
caved-in cemetery, while over our heads golden fruit hung
from green branches. Don't you feel the consummate

poetry of this, that it is the grandest possible synthesis?"

Louise felt nothing of the kind, of course—as Flaubert should well have known. And indeed, during the period of the composition of the middle chapters of *Madame Bovary* the feeling she had most of the time was one of even greater dissatisfaction than usual with Flaubert and with life in general. Her peace of mind, never very stable, was troubled by many matters.

There was the matter of *"L'Acropole d'Athènes."*

Not only had Flaubert supplied most of the ideas for the content of this poem, with which Louise had great hopes of capturing the two thousand francs of the Academy prize, but he and Bouilhet worked for hours at a time—one week-end, for example, from two o'clock Sunday afternoon until half-past four Monday morning—cutting, smoothing, rewriting. But though Flaubert was willing to work hard for her, in matters of criticism he was his usual ungracious self; he praised the drafts she sent only when he found things in them worth praising; that was seldom, and most of his comments were merciless. "This line is bad, but it is at least clear," was his most favourable opinion in one long letter of dispraise, and he did not hesitate to say: "You naturally write lines that are stiff and pompous (when they are not flabby and banal)." When Louise complained he replied: "My first inclination was to send you back your manuscript without a word, since our observations are of no use to you and you will not (or cannot) understand them. What is the use of asking our advice and wearing us out if the only results are a waste of time and recriminations on both sides? If your protests were in defence of poetical eccentricities, flashes of originality, that would be one thing—but no, it is always the banalities that you fight for, silly phrases that drown your thought, bad assonances, trite expressions." The result was that the poem was allowed to go off to the Academy in a form satisfactory to no one, and despite the hours of work in Croisset, despite the fact that Flaubert spoke a good word for Louise to a friend whose cousin was the doctor of the prefect of the department of the Seine-Inférieure, and despite the support of Hugo (who though in exile remained a member of the Academy), Louise's entry did not win the prize. And she was even deprived of the consolation of being able to protest that the prize was awarded elsewhere through favouritism, for it was not awarded at all; none of the poems submitted, it was judged, was good enough, and once again "*L'Acropole d'Athènes*" was announced as the subject for the competition of the following year. "Gustave will have told you of the unfavourable outcome of the competition, dear brother and friend," Louise wrote to Louis. "It has caused me a series of painful and violent emotions which I desire never to experience again at any price. I have been made completely ill by it, and fear that my inspiration will not return for a long time. I am becoming dreary as a tomb. This spring weather, so bitterly cold, is very difficult for me to bear. I scarcely leave my fire." Flaubert, indignant at the defeat, was certain it was because he and Bouilhet had filled the poem with too many classical details. "Not one of the Academicians, unless perhaps Mérimée, knew as much as your poem contained, and you must remember we are all apt to feel resentment against someone who teaches us something—especially if we pretend that it is our place to do the teaching." He advised her to work the poem completely over with him and Bouilhet and Leconte de Lisle, to make it into a perfect thing that the Academy could not ignore, and submit it again. Louise, however, doubted that she cared to have anything more to do with "*L'Acropole d'Athènes*." And once again she had to borrow five hundred francs from Flaubert, having counted a trifle too heavily on the prize.

There was the matter of "*La Servante*."
Since the episode of the portrait in the concierge's lodge, Louise had nursed her rage against Musset. She was not without suspicion that his presence in the Academy might have contributed to the failure of "*L'Acropole*," and she now set about avenging herself thoroughly in a poem entitled "*La Servante*," in which Musset was portrayed as a drunkard and seducer of servant-girls. This Flaubert found abominable. "I have something intimate to say to you. You will be indignant, but I should be a swine were I to hide

what I think. It is this: this poem is not publishable *as it is,* and I beg you not to publish it. Why insult Musset? Does his personal conduct concern you? Who has made us censors? Do you hope to reform him? Why do him a greater wrong than he did you? Think of posterity, and meditate on the sorry figure cut there by the insulters of great men. When Musset is dead, who will know that he drank too much? Posterity is very indulgent toward such crimes as that. It has practically forgiven Rousseau for having put his children in an orphanage. And after all how do such things concern us? *This poem is a bad deed, and you have already been punished for it because it is a bad poem as well.* Try to read coldly what I say. If it makes you too angry, keep these pages and reread them in six months, a year (wait that long before publishing), and you will see that I am right. You wrote *'La Servante'* with a personal emotion that distorted your outlook and made it impossible to keep before your eyes the fundamental conditions for any imaginative composition. It has no æsthetic. You have turned art into an outlet for passion, a kind of chamber-pot to catch an overflow. It smells bad; it smells of hate! In short, I find this poem improper in its purpose, poor, and badly executed. And if Musset were to reply? If he did nothing but write a tiny squib that covered you with ridicule? Remember the unlucky story of the knife and how it hurt you. One has to say all these things to you, though by now I blush to do so. But nothing anyone says does you any good. You take life against the grain; you are perpetually confusing life and art, your emotions and your imagination, each of which does harm to the other. You may be sure that others think as I do, and don't dare to tell you so."

Louise found this letter unkind and abusive, accused Flaubert of bringing up the story of Karr only with intent to wound, and resented his suggesting that it was in Musset's power to cover her with ridicule. "Ridicule is none the less the only word to fit the case," Flaubert replied. "We are always ridiculous when the laughers are against us."

There was the matter of the phantoms of Trouville.

During the summer that marked the first anniversary of the beginning of *Madame Bovary* Flaubert had taken no vacation at all, but a year later, in 1853, weary of the unending struggle with style and exhausted by the growing excitement of his story, he was glad to accompany his mother and Caroline to Trouville and spend three or four weeks in the sea air, swimming, sleeping, and riding on the sand. He had not been there since the summer preceding the death of his father and sister, and the evening after his arrival he wrote to Louise: "For the past thirty-six hours I have been navigating amid the earliest memories of my life, and feel an almost physical lassitude." He was flooded with memories of the summers of his adolescence, of the young mother with whom he had been so desperately in love (she and her husband now lived in Germany), of Alfred Le Poittevin. "The mud on the bottom is stirred," he wrote; "all kinds of melancholies, like frogs disturbed in their sleep, lift their heads above the water and make strange music; I listen. Ah, how old I am, how old I am, poor dear Louise!" Alfred's widow, recently remarried, was at Trouville with her new husband; Flaubert would not see them, but thought continually of his old friend. "We lived in a hot-house of the imagination, where poetry heated our disgust for life to a temperature of 70 degrees Réaumur. There was a man! Never have I so voyaged across space! . . . ." His letters were so full of nostalgia for his youth, Alfred's name appeared so frequently, he lamented so constantly the transformation of the peaceful seaside village of his youth into a busy and ugly resort, that Louise reproached him bitterly for his obsessions.

"You complain about the phantoms of Trouville," he replied. "But I have written you often since arriving here; the longest interval between my letters was six days, and ordinarily I write you only once a week. Have you not realized that it is precisely because I am here that I have had such frequent recourse to you, in the midst of this intensely personal solitude in which I am living? I cannot take a step without running upon some youthful memory. Each wave as it breaks reawakens within me impressions of long ago. I hear a roar of days that are past, and an unending surge, like the surge of the sea, of vanished emotions. I keep remembering my old spasms, fits of melancholy, gusts of desire blowing like a wind in a rigging, and vast vague longings whirling in darkness like a flock of wild gulls in a stormcloud. On whom should I lean if not on you? My thought, weary of all this ancient dust, comes to rest on your image more softly than on a bank of grass."

And to Bouilhet he wrote: "This visit to Trouville has made me review the course of my own intimate history. I have been musing at length on these scenes of my early passions, and I bid them farewell, I hope for ever. . . . I have had two or three good afternoons all alone in the sun on the sand, where I mournfully came upon other things than broken shells. But now I have finished with them, thank God!"

The vacation refreshed him; he was invigorated by "the contemplation of the waves, the grass, and the trees," and he felt that on his return he would be able to work with increased force. On their way back to Croisset the Flauberts passed the spot on the road between Honfleur and Pont-l'Evêque where Gustave had had his first attack ten years before. Now he fully understood the relation between his old illness and his work. "If my mind had been better balanced in the first place," he told Louise, "I should not have fallen ill from studying law and being bored. I should have turned the experience to good account, instead of having been worsted by it. My unhappiness, instead of remaining in my brain, overflowed into all parts of my body, and convulsed it. . . . You first knew me when my nervous, sentimental period had just ended and I had arrived at manhood. Earlier, though, before that, I had believed in the reality of poetry in life, in the plastic beauty of the emotions, etc. I had had an equal admiration for uproars of all kinds; but I was deafened by them, and thereafter learned to distinguish between them."

Flaubert seemed quite unconscious of the fact that Louise expressed no more interest in these details of his illness than she had in those of his adolescence. He was delighted to be back in his study. He found that during his absence everything had been "brushed, waxed, and varnished"—his servant had even polished the two mummy's feet, thinking them somewhat shabby as they were—and before long the procession of identical, laborious, eventless days began again.

By now, both Louise and Flaubert were repeating their old story, making mistake after mistake. After a stroll in the country outside Mantes, she wrote him a passionate poem, "*Paysage et Amour*," and though she sent it to him he neglected to make any mention of it whatever; nevertheless, he informed her that during that very walk he had found her more irritating, perhaps, than at any time previously. "Your voice calling me every minute, and especially the way you kept tapping my shoulder to make me look at things! How I had to restrain myself to keep from speaking savagely, telling you to get out and leave me in peace! During my travels I often felt like that." He kept promising her that the instant *Madame Bovary* was done he would take an apartment in Paris, but *Madame Bovary* gave no indication of being done for a long time. It kept going at its usual rate—four days for a page, thirty-nine pages in three months, one hundred and fourteen pages in ten months, three-hour discussions with Bouilhet over individual scenes—and in the meantime, though he always promised to see her more often, he did not do so. She upbraided him on the rare occasions when he told her of having received a visitor, and through incessant plaguing she finally made him promise to try to bring about a meeting between her and his mother.

This she never let him forget. "What a strange creature you are, dear Louise, to keep sending me these diatribes— as my pharmacist would call them. You ask something of me, I say yes, I promise you again, and you still scold! Well, since you hide nothing from me (and I'm glad of that), I'll not hide from you that to me this idea seems like a mania. You want to establish, between two people whose affections for me are of entirely dissimilar natures, a relationship of which I cannot see the sense, and even less the use. I cannot see that the courtesies you do me in Paris place my mother under any obligation whatsoever. For eight years Bouilhet has been coming here every Sunday, for lunch, for dinner, and to spend the night, and we have never had a single glimpse of his mother, who comes to Rouen almost every month. And I assure you that mine is by no means offended. However, it shall be as you wish. I promise, I swear, that I will give her your reasons, and will urge her to make it possible for you to see each other. More than that, with the best will in the world, I cannot promise. Perhaps you will get along very nicely, perhaps not at all. The good woman is far from sociable, and has stopped seeing not only all her former acquaintances, but even her friends. So far as I know, she now has only one, who lives some distance away."

He reported what progress he could. "I read your poem to my mother," he could write, "and she was quite affected by it." Or: "Do you know what I talked about with my mother all last evening? About you. I told her many things that she did not know, or that she had half guessed. She appreciates you, and I am sure that this winter she will see you with pleasure." But that was as far as he seemed to be able to get, or as much as he seemed to be willing to say, and he was much more apt to write Louise whatever amusing stories he happened upon, as though in an effort to put her in good humour—for her bad humour and her insistence on the subject of Madame Flaubert were now almost continuous, and almost always went together.

"We used to have as a servant a poor devil who now drives a cab; and lately he has had—or has thought that he had—a tapeworm. He talks of it as of some very animated person who is in constant communication with him and who speaks its mind, and in his mouth the word 'it' always designates this interior being. Sometimes he is suddenly stricken with whims, and he attributes them to the tapeworm. 'It' wants this or that, and the fellow obeys at once. Lately 'it' wanted to eat thirty sous' worth of brioches; another time 'it' had to have white wine, and the next day 'it' would be indignant if it were offered red. (Literally.) The poor man had got to the point where he had sunk, in his own opinion, to the same social level as the tapeworm; they are equals, and engage in relentless combat. 'Madame,' said he recently to my sister-in-law, 'that scoundrel has it in for me; it is a duel to the death; he humbugs me, but I'll have my revenge. One of us is going

to have to win.' Well, it looks as though it would be the
worm who would win, for, with the express purpose of
killing 'it' and exterminating 'it' absolutely, our friend has
lately swallowed a bottle of vitriol, and is at this very
moment dying like a dog in consequence. I don't know
whether you sense everything that is profound in that
story. Do you see this man ending by believing in the
almost human, conscious existence of what is perhaps only
an idea, and becoming the slave of his tapeworm? It
staggers me. What a comical thing the human brain is!"

But despite such stories as this, and his entertaining ac-
counts of the incredible kitchen and garden thieving that
Madame Flaubert was discovering almost daily in her servants, and his description of his mother's cook, "twenty-five
years old and a Frenchwoman to boot," who didn't know
that Louis Philippe was no longer King of France and that
there had been a republic and was now an empire, Louise
was never diverted for long from her demands and her
reproaches, and Flaubert had continually to scold her for
her "eyes so often filled with tears," and to write her im-
ploringly. "There is a pact between us," he reminded her,
"one that is independent of us. Did I not do all I could to
leave you? Did you not do all you could to love others?
We came together again because we were made for each
other. Let us love one another in Art, as the old mystics
loved one another in God."

That was how things stood when Louis Bouilhet moved
to Paris.

Louis had not made much progress with his play. He
had found himself hampered and harassed at every turn by
theatrical necessities, and in disgust had put it aside and
returned to poetry designed to be read, not acted. He
began a long poem, with the somewhat uninviting title of
Fossiles, on antediluvian and evolutionary subjects—a
project of which Flaubert thoroughly approved because it
was on the track of the scientific poetry of the future. As
Louis brought one section of the poem after another with
him to Croisset Sundays, Flaubert was enthusiastic about
its content and its quality; it showed, he thought, a great
increase of power over *Melænis.* One passage, a picture of

a mastodon ruminating in the moonlight, he thought especially moving, and he also particularly admired a scene of love-making among prehistoric birds.

The *succès d'estime* of *Melænis* had not had the slightest echo in Rouen—a fact which was for Flaubert another proof of the poem's greatness—and despite Louis's quiet tastes and the pleasure he derived from the composition of *Fossiles* he began to feel that his life of cramming Latin down the throats of young Rouennais had become definitely intolerable. Louis wrote with extreme slowness— "He recently spent ten days changing two lines," Flaubert told Louise, "the most beautiful way in the world to die of starvation"—and even if he were eventually to sell his non-dramatic verses he could never hope to live on what they would bring. Once again the play seemed the thing, and Louis resolved to borrow money, abandon the school, and resume his dramatic efforts. But it might well be impossible, he and Flaubert decided, to write in Rouen a play which would succeed on the Parisian stage; he must move to Paris, soak himself in the theatre of the day, learn what would and what would not be tolerated by an audience, and do his work in the surroundings in which it would have to be judged. For him, a life unlike Flaubert's was necessary; they had to separate. A friend in his native village lent him two thousand francs, and in November 1853 he established himself in an apartment which Louise had found for him in the Faubourg Saint-Germain. "This is the beginning of my old age," Flaubert lamented. "Now I shall be alone, alone. I am desolated with grief and humiliated at the thought of my impotence. Each of us served as a kind of semaphore to the other in his work; when one of us raised an arm the other knew that the way was clear and he could go ahead."

In the city, Louis felt utterly uprooted. He was homesick for his peasant companion, who wrote him sorrowful letters; until he should feel more at home, he did nothing on his play but continued *Fossiles;* and it was not long before he had resumed relations with the "infamous coquette," as Flaubert called her, who had read his verses in Louise's salon, and begun relations with another young actress whom he met in the same place. Louise promised to try to find him private lessons, and, though he did not know it, was offended that Flaubert should be completely without jealousy at the thought that Bouilhet was near her. To establish him in Paris, she arranged for several more readings of his verses at her Sunday evenings, and was hurt by his lack of enthusiasm—caused, as Flaubert had to explain to her, by Bouilhet's dislike of seeming to make his Parisian entrance from beneath her petticoats. He saw Gautier, studied Chinese with his daughter, and even saw something of Max, though he found the group around the *Revue de Paris* in general uncongenial and frivolous, given to pun-making and publicity-seeking rather than to serious literary pursuits. Max was cordial, invited him several times to lunch, expressed eagerness to see *Fossiles,* and deplored the misunderstanding which had grown up between Flaubert and himself. Flaubert was wrong, he said, to despise him for busying himself with a magazine, for that magazine would be a very convenient place for the serial publication of *Madame Bovary*—if indeed *Madame Bovary* was ever finished. Later in the winter, when *Fossiles* was finally done, Bouilhet allowed Louise to arrange a reading by one of the actresses, and in a spirit of reconciliation she allowed him to invite Max, who might thus make the acquaintance of the long poem under the best possible conditions. Max came and applauded, and accepted *Fossiles* for the *Revue;* but he allowed himself several gratuitous criticisms which Bouilhet found vapid, and the letters passing between Paris and Croisset were full of sarcastic references to the *Revue de Paris* and its editors. Particularly singled out for disdain was Max's account of the Egyptian and Palestinian journey, which he had recently written and was now appearing serially in the magazine; it contained, rather obviously, no mention of Flaubert whatever, and gave the impression that Max had made the trip alone; quite apart from that, however, Flaubert and Bouilhet agreed that it was worthless and flat, equally devoid of beauty of style and interest of content, and that Max had fallen into complete literary decadence.

In an effort to supplement her income, Louise was now writing articles on clothes for Parisian fashion magazines. Her descriptions of hats were particularly esteemed by the trade, and the best milliners presented her with their models in exchange for eulogistic paragraphs, which were generally signed "Cléophée"; Louise was coming to be considered one of the best-hatted women in Paris. She kept her millinery collection in her bookcase, and had the habit of inducing gentlemen friends to buy a few models as presents for other acquaintances. The evening of the reading of *Fossiles*, the first time Louise and Max had met in a number of years, Max was his usual poised self, and it was without the slightest brusqueness or sign of astonishment that he declined Louise's suggestion that he buy some of her stock, or try to interest ladies whom he knew. His refusal, he records, "appeared to cause the Muse considerable surprise."

Since by this time Louise had so very little except dissatisfaction to express to Flaubert, she began to write less often to Croisset and to complain more often to Bouilhet. Flaubert was an egoist; he was a monster, neurotic and unhealthy in his ideas. He was stingy with his money, lacking in all generous impulses. His friends in England had sold her album for a fraction of its worth, and he had made no protest. For the sake of affording him mere physical pleasure and relaxation from his toil she had compromised the future of her charming daughter: several years before, she now revealed, she had declined a tardy but genuine offer of marriage from Plato; Flaubert's lack of gratitude for this action was repulsive; she felt scorned and bitter.

It was without pleasure that Bouilhet listened to such tirades as these. They were scarcely intended to be kept as confidences, but he did keep them to himself as long as he could, and Flaubert wondered at the infrequency of Louise's letters. "How is the poor Muse?" he wrote to Bouilhet. "What have you done with her? What has she been telling you? She writes me less often these days. I think that at heart she is tired of me. Whose fault is that? The fault of fate. For I have a perfectly clear conscience about the whole affair and see no reason that I should feel self-reproach. Anyone else in her place would be tired of me too. I have no amiable traits—and I use 'amiable' in its true sense, meaning lovable. She is certainly the only woman who has ever loved me. Is that a curse sent her by heaven? If she dared, she would say that I do not love her. She is mistaken, however."

Was Louise mistaken? A little, undoubtedly, if she really thought that Flaubert did not love her at all. And he was aware of one of the causes of the love he felt for her, unclassifiable though that love might be: it did exist partly as a result of her less fantastic love for him. That she should love him had taken his breath away at first, and some of his wonder always remained. Her company he could do without. Even when he assured her that he had often thought of her in the East he did not pretend that he had missed her, and her absence did not desolate and cripple him like Bouilhet's, or her image haunt him endlessly like Alfred's. But when they were together their physical union was perfect, and in addition to that they spoke, despite the shrill discord of their accents, the same general language. "Don't let's pity ourselves!" he wrote her soon after Bouilhet's move. "We are the privileged! Our minds are lit by gas! There are so many people who are shivering in attics without even candles!" Flaubert had travelled in exotic scenes, but his knowledge of the society of his own country was decidedly limited all during his liaison with Louise, and it was not until he had stopped seeing her and begun to see others that he realized she belonged to a well-recognized category—the bluestockings. But Louise was a good deal prettier than most bluestockings, and perhaps, after all, it was her beauty, even more than his own inexperience, that kept him from such a dismal realization for so long.

Eventually Louise's denunciations and Flaubert's wonderment at her silences became too uncomfortable for Bouilhet to put up with, and he wrote to Croisset to explain exactly how things stood: "It is certain that the Muse wants—and hopes—to become your wife. I have thought so for some time, without daring to formulate the idea to myself, but now I have been told so quite clearly —not by the Muse herself but by someone who heard her say so. That is why she refused the Philosopher. Recently she learned from me that your mother was in Paris. (She came to invite me for dinner that day, and I saw no reason to keep your mother's presence a secret.) At once she urged me—in a note which I received half an hour after her visit—to speak of her to your mother, to tell her how she loves you, etc. I told her clearly that I would do nothing of the kind, and that I wanted no such commissions. As for me, I am so exasperated by her that I don't know whether I shall go on seeing her. She has certainly been kind to me, but now I am so conscious of the purpose behind it all that I am ashamed. I shall make her some kind of gift in return for her attentiveness while I was getting settled here, and then, little by little, very quietly, I think I shall drop her. The poor woman is making enemies of all her acquaintances, past and present. No one here takes her seriously; she makes herself wantonly ridiculous. It hurts me to see it, because at bottom I like her, and a disappointment is always painful."

Marriage! The appearance of that word on the horizon was of course all that was needed to kill the relationship stone-dead; and Flaubert now determined to end it. Like Bouilhet, he proceeded with his execution "little by little, very quietly." He reminded Louise, as in the past, that "the passions, for the artist, should be the accompaniment of life, art its song. If the lower notes creep up into the melody, everything is spoiled." He began to suggest that her love for him was lessening, that she was beginning to see him as he really was, and that unfortunately, to his own bitter regret, he was incapable of reform. He confessed that he was beginning to feel himself sexless. Occasionally he suggested that they kiss, cease quarrelling, and love each other as their natures and the circumstances allowed; but he could not keep his temper when she sent him a wretched poem on her daughter—"So much sentiment! So many tears!"—or when she untiringly pursued the subject of Madame Flaubert: "Yes, you have guessed it. It is because I am persuaded that if she saw you she would be very cold and unbending, as you suggest, that I do not want you to meet. You keep bringing up this subject, and it is always irritating to me; I beg of you once more, stop it."

He had been in Paris in November, while Louis was

getting settled, and there had been a series of violent scenes. Toward the end of December, going through his boxes and cupboards at Croisset, he came upon her early letters and "the green spray that was on your hat that first day in Mantes, the slippers you wore the first evening, one of your handkerchiefs." But in Paris in February she reproached him for seeing too much of Bouilhet and too little of her. And then one evening in April, when she began to scream abuse at him and to kick him and slap him, he was suddenly filled with so overpowering a desire to assassinate her with a log that was burning in her fireplace that he fled the house, his mind full of visions of arrest, trial, and prison. After that he dared not see her again.

5.

Before Bouilhet's departure for Paris Flaubert had created Homais, the pharmacist who lived across the square from Madame Bovary and from whose "capharnaum" she was to steal the arsenic for her death. Homais was Flaubert's final crystallization of the Garçon, of the sententious and absurd bourgeois with a little learning and a head full of *idées reçues*, and he painted him as "at once comic and disgusting, essentially and personally fetid." The man became so completely alive that Flaubert was soon quoting him in his letters. "As my pharmacist would say . . ." he wrote, or: "In the probable words of Homais . . ." He delighted in writing Homais's report on the local agricultural show for a Rouen newspaper: "Why these festoons, these flowers, these garlands? Whither was it bound, this crowd rushing like the billows of a raging sea under a torrential tropic sun that poured its torrid rays upon our fertile meadows?"

When he was not actually writing, he was studying and observing. He read books on popular beliefs, books of popular medicine. He attended the funeral of the wife of an old friend of his father's, a botanist, one of the few people in Rouen whom he respected. "The poor old man will be pitiable. Perhaps I shall find something there for

Bovary. Such exploitation as this would seem odious if I
were to talk about it, and yet is there anything wrong in it?
I hope to make others weep with this man's tears, which I
shall transmute by the chemistry of style."

He was finding, to his own intense interest, that he must
not always be completely truthful and accurate in detail.
To secure greater vividness and verisimilitude for the
whole, some parts had to be distorted; strolls in the countryside had to take a longer time, journeys to Rouen a
shorter, than they did in life—or else the general action
would appear to be telescoped or tenuous. If the stroll or
the journey was the vehicle of the action, he learned to
lengthen it, filling it with conversation, incident, and
significance; if, on the contrary, it was merely a transition
between more important scenes, it was compressed, subordinated; hours and minutes were blandly lied about. The
transitions were at times more difficult to write than the
scenes which they linked: "Bouilhet was satisfied with my
horseback ride, but before this passage I had one of transition which contains eight lines and took me three days.
There is not a superfluous word in it, nevertheless I have
to cut it down still further because it drags." The policy of
reading everything aloud was adhered to: it was the only
way to test sonority and tempo. And just as he struggled
to make the style smooth and harmonious with no loss of
vigour—he wanted "not a single flabby phrase"—so he
realized that the action, too, must move smoothly, and
with ever-increasing speed and complete inevitability,
toward the closing tragedy. In life, the story of the Delamares might conceivably have had a different ending; but
in *Madame Bovary,* even in the earliest chapters, Flaubert
mentions details whose presence has no meaning apart
from their relationship to the catastrophe. The end is
inevitable, none other is conceivable, considering the
details out of which Flaubert made up his narrative. He
gave much effort to the precise description of objects and
of tiny events, but before being carefully described they
were just as carefully chosen.

Abandoned drafts—like the manuscript of *Saint Antoine*
—were not destroyed but put aside; Flaubert kept every
sheet of paper he ever touched, and his study became filled

with quantities of manuscript, crossed out, interlined, used on both sides. Scarcely for an instant did the writing of *Madame Bovary* go easily—"What a miracle it would be if in one day I were to write two pages!"—and after any interruption, such as a trip to Paris or Mantes, it took him days to get back even into that snail's pace. "The erections of thought are like those of the body; they do not come at will! And then I am such a heavy machine to set moving! I need so many preparations, and so much time, to get started!" After solving each difficulty he hoped that the rest would be easier, but there were always new obstacles. "I shall finish it some day or other," was all he could say. He longed for the ease with which he had written *Saint Antoine:* "The eighteen months I spent writing its five hundred pages were the most profoundly voluptuous of my life." Even Madame Bovary's ecstasy in her adultery, which he had so looked forward to describing, which he had felt boiling within him and ready to rush out, proved far less easy to write than to feel: "I had to lash myself till I bled, before my heroine could sigh with love," he said. At times he feared that, despite the excellent construction of each paragraph, the thing did not form a perfectly joined whole, that "the bolts holding together the planks" were visible; and such fears were dissipated only by assurances from Bouilhet. And at other times he despised his work for the very carefulness of its construction. "What is more badly built than many a thing by Rabelais, Cervantes, Molière, or Hugo? But what swift punches! What power in a single word! We have to pile up a lot of little pebbles one on top of the other to make our pyramids; theirs, a hundred times greater, are made in one huge block. But to try to imitate the methods of such geniuses as those would be ruinous. They are great, in fact, because they have no method."

"Finally I am beginning to see my way in my damnable dialogue between Madame Bovary and the curé," he wrote to Louise early one morning. (The model for the curé was a priest he had known years before in Trouville.) "But frankly, there are moments when I feel almost a physical desire to vomit, the whole thing is so *low*. I want to express the following situation: my little Bovary, in a sudden access of religion, goes to church; she finds the curé at the door, and in a dialogue (subject as yet undetermined), he shows himself to be so stupid, flat, inept, that she goes away disgusted and quite cured of her piety. My curé is a very fine fellow, even an excellent one, but he thinks only of the physical side (the sufferings of the poor, lack of bread and firewood), and has no conception of spiritual crises, vague mystical aspirations; he is perfectly chaste, and fulfils all his duties to the letter. All of that can take up at the most six or seven pages—without a single observation by the author, without any analysis, and all in direct discourse. Furthermore, since I consider it cheap to write dialogue without putting in 'he said' and 'he answered,' etc., you will see that it is not easy to avoid repetitions of phrase. Now you are initiated into the torments I've been undergoing for the past fortnight."

In the rewriting, there were always repetitions to be suppressed—especially of "all," "but," "for," and "however." He chafed to be finished, so that he could turn his attention to more sympathetic subjects—he still wanted to write *Anubis,* and he was full of ideas for a *History of Poetical Feeling in France.* He compared his work to the slowest and most painful kind of mountain-climbing, tolerable only because of the infinite perspectives and Olympian breeze waiting at the summit. Even his mother upbraided him for his growing impatience with everything outside his work, and said that his "rage for phrases was drying up his heart." He began to refer to his heroine as "my shrew of a Bovary." Chained to his desk, he took less exercise than ever, no care of himself; he was seldom in bed before three in the morning; he suffered from fever, constipation, headaches, toothaches, nausea. Some days he almost frightened himself when he looked in his glass, he was so covered with wrinkles, so weary and old-looking; more than once he came almost to the point of refusing to go ahead with his heart-breaking work. In the midst of his labours he was filled with sadness and with a rush of childhood memories: Uncle Parain, the foolish, charming old man, who was now beloved not only by Flaubert but by little Caroline, fell into senility and died, talking deliriously of his nephew and of literature, and thinking at the end that Bouilhet was reading him his poems. And it was finally necessary to summon a family council to agree that Caroline's father be declared incompetent and deprived of the power to spend his money and be the guardian of his child.

It was Bouilhet, on Sundays, who had kept up Flaubert's morale, and the outlet provided by the letters to Louise was more than ever useful.

When Bouilhet moved away and the correspondence with Louise dwindled, morale was lower and progress if possible even slower. Now it was necessary to write to Bouilhet the questions that had formerly been asked on Sundays. "What is the medical term for 'nightmare'?" he inquired. "I absolutely insist on a fine-sounding Greek word"—for it was Homais who was to employ it. When it came to the scene of the operation on the club-foot, Flaubert read all available books on the subject, consulted with Achille, and went to Paris to do the same with Bouilhet. And Louis sent him a long letter full of details concerning eye maladies and preposterous means of curing them which might be proposed by Homais. "It is not easy to render such technical details as these literary and amusing!" Flaubert lamented.

It was, nevertheless, during the first winter and spring of Bouilhet's absence that *Madame Bovary* first began to seem like an actual book, and Flaubert began to enjoy in advance the indignation of Rouen at the unflattering intensity and accuracy of the Norman local colour. He even began to talk of publication. A new school of novelists, calling themselves the "Realists," was rising, and its leader, Champfleury, who defined realism as "the choice of modern and popular subjects," had recently published a novel, *Les Aventures de Mademoiselle Mariette*, and a novelette, *Madame d'Aigrizelles*, the announcements of which had somewhat worried Flaubert. Once he had read the books he had been reassured: though like *Madame Bovary* they did deal with modern and popular subjects, there the resemblance ended. They lacked style. They lacked art. And particularly they lacked power, interest, detail, with the result that to a great extent they lacked realism. Some of their characters, however, were well drawn, and Flaubert would have liked to have *Madame Bovary* ready now, before the new school should have time to make a louder and more realistic noise which might lessen the effect of the thunderclap.

In Paris, Bouilhet had done his best to drop Louise as planned, "little by little, very quietly," but it was not an easy thing to accomplish. He declined her invitations, or most of them, but the less he called on her the more she called on him. She invariably talked of Gustave, and quizzed Louis about him without mercy; unaccustomed to subterfuge, he could not always parry her questions about his friend's movements, and Flaubert, on his rare visits to Paris, adopted the habit of travelling about the city in a curtained cab—a device which promptly inspired a scene in *Madame Bovary*. He did not always escape. Occasionally he found Louise in wait as he emerged from a shop or a house; and once, pouncing on him just as he was boarding the train for Rouen, she made a scandalous scene in the station. Another time, one evening early in the summer, she burst into a private room at the Trois Frères Provençaux. She knew that through Bouilhet Flaubert had become acquainted with a young actress—a friend of one of those whom Bouilhet had met in her salon—and Bouilhet had not been able to keep her from learning that he and Flaubert would be dining that evening "with friends" at the Trois Frères. She threw open the door like a fury, ready to fly at the throat of her successor, but she was somewhat disconcerted to be greeted, after a moment of silent surprise, with a shout of laughter: the friends were Maxime Du Camp and one of his fellow-editors, and the young men had chosen a private room because under the Second Empire it was preferable for literary men and journalists not to assemble in public. Louise withdrew with what dignity she could command.

She had, after all, followed Flaubert's advice with regard to "*L'Acropole d'Athènes*"; she had allowed him and Bouilhet and Leconte de Lisle to revise it completely, she had resubmitted it, and in April, shortly after Flaubert's flight from her fireside, the Academy had awarded it the

prize. Although the public reading of the poem in August
was unfortunate—it was greeted with catcalls and cries
of "Enough! Enough!" and a very Flaubertian scene describing the sacrifice of three hundred bulls on the banks
of the Ilissus was accused of "smelling like a slaughterhouse"—still the victory, together with her undying determination to meet Madame Flaubert, prolonged her te-
nacity. It now seemed injudicious, as well as humiliating,
to lose Gustave's intimacy, and throughout the summer
and early fall she besought Bouilhet, who was vacationing
in Normandy, to make possible a reconciliation. But his
replies, some of them written directly from Croisset, were
not encouraging, and in them she was addressed as *"chère
Madame,"* instead of *"chère Muse"* or *chère Sœur"* as in
the past. In September appeared Louise's newest volume of
collected verse, entitled *Ce Qu'On Rêve en Aimant.* It contained a poem on Bouilhet, several poems on Mantes, and
many based on ideas from Flaubert's letters, and most of
the poems had been corrected by Flaubert, but though she
sent a copy to Croisset there was no reply.

In November Flaubert moved to Paris for two months
with his mother and Caroline—with Louis away and without the gaiety of Uncle Parain to amuse the child the
gloom of Croisset was not to be faced for an entire winter;
and throughout his stay in the city Louise kept hurling
herself against his unyielding resistance. A letter he wrote
her at this time has survived—perhaps the last he ever
wrote her:

"Madame:
"I have been informed that you went to the trouble,
last evening, of coming here three times.
"I was not in; and since I greatly fear that further
persistence on your side would expose you to affronts
from mine, good manners force me to warn you: I shall
never be in.

                                        "My salutations.
                                              "Fl."

Tuesday morning.
Mme Colet, Rue de Sèvres, 21, Paris.

And the sheet of blue paper bears three additional, eloquent French words in Louise's furious hand: *lâche, couard,* and *canaille.*

Then—so the story goes—one day in January, when he had returned to Croisset, he was interrupted in his work by a loud knocking at the door and the shrill sound of an all-too-well-known voice in the hall: it was not to be believed, but it was true. Louise had her wish: she saw Croisset, and she saw Madame Flaubert, who came rushing to the scene of the disturbance; but the presentation was scarcely a formal one, and Louise was immediately ejected by Flaubert himself.

That, definitely, was the end.

In a novel of revenge which she wrote soon after, Louise painted a picture of Madame Flaubert: "Her long cold face reminded me of the carven faces of figures on tombstones. From her severe and unrelieved garb of black, one sensed that she was a widow who had not laughed since the death of her husband. . . . She appeared hard and harsh, like someone who derives consolation from the sufferings of others." Louise did not know that Madame Flaubert was less offended, that January day, by her than by Gustave. The old lady found her son's merciless expulsion cruel, and declared that she felt as though she had seen him "wound her own sex." Flaubert was taken aback. "It remains the only thing between my mother and me," he told a friend, years later.

Despite the pursuit by Louise, Flaubert had worked better than he had expected during the two months in Paris. With Bouilhet again available and with the end clearly in sight it was possible to go a trifle faster, especially since it was now less perpetually necessary to set the stage for later scenes. He enjoyed a little society—evenings with Bouilhet and the two actresses, literary evenings at Gautier's, where he made the acquaintance of Baudelaire and where the faces of Gautier and Flaubert, in their denunciatory conversations about the bourgeoisie, grew as red as the scarlet waistcoat of Gautier's youth. The move back to Croisset and Louise's irruption delayed him somewhat, but by the first of May there remained only between

one hundred and twenty and one hundred and forty pages
still to be written.

The spring was a particularly beautiful one. "You are
right, poor fellow," he wrote to Bouilhet, "to envy me the
trees, the river-bank, and the garden—everything is splendid here. Yesterday my lungs were tired from smelling
lilacs, and tonight in the river the fish are cutting incredible
capers, like bourgeois invited to tea at the Prefecture." He
took many walks in Rouen, for it was Rouen which he
was now describing: the scenes of Madame Bovary's
second affair had in life been enacted in the Hôtel du
Grand Cerf at Mantes, but Rouen was their setting in the
novel. "I am singing the cafés, the taverns, the wineshops
at the foot of the Rue des Charrettes. I am in the midst of
my Rouen scenes, and have been making tours of inspection of the brothels, the green bushes before the cafés, the
smell of absinth, cigars, and oysters." Homais considered
Rouen a Babylon, and it enchanted Flaubert to write in
such terms of the city which he found so dreary. Rouen
became almost one of the characters. "What a look Rouen
has—is there anything more heavy and depressing? At
sunset yesterday the walls were oozing such ennui that I
was almost asphyxiated as I passed!" Taking his notebook,
he spent a morning on a hill to the south of the town,
observing the view over its spires and chimneys and the
winding river that Madame Bovary had from her carriage
as it reached the summit of the hill after the journey from
the country beyond, in the afternoon he sketched out the
description, and it was eventually rewritten five times.
To give to these chapters the unmistakable stamp of
Rouen, he found a place in his text for an object which
existed nowhere else—the *cheminot*, a kind of Rouennais
breakfast roll in the form of a turban, for which he en-
dowed Madame Homais with a particular fondness.

As before, he found himself littering his pages with
metaphors—this easy method of giving colour to a drab
subject remained a temptation until the end. And it was
all too easy to fall into analyses of character, a device of
Balzac's which Flaubert considered a blemish in any work
of fiction and a confession of weakness in any author—
characters should reveal themselves, in their actions. When

he could, he read his beloved classics, and he railed as usual against the age in which he lived. "I have lately been astonished to find in Buffon's *Préceptes du Style* our own theories on the said art," he wrote to Louis. "How far one is from such ideas nowadays! In what an æsthetic void exists this glorious nineteenth century!" And as two of the least æsthetic objects of the unæsthetic century he pointed to Queen Victoria and Prince Albert, who were that summer the guests of France at the Exposition Universelle in Paris.

The autumn was as beautiful as the spring. "The leaves are falling. The garden paths, as you swish along them, are full of Lamartinian sounds which I like extremely. My dog Dakno lies beside the fire the whole day, and from time to time I hear the tugs on the river." Even with Bouilhet away, he had almost never enjoyed Croisset so much as this autumn before the completion of *Madame Bovary*. In September, on the date which marked the fourth anniversary of the beginning of the book, he hoped that "in a month Bovary will have her arsenic in her belly," but it took a little longer than that. He ran into difficulties in calculating his heroine's debts, and had to proceed slowly, consulting frequently with Rouen notaries. The exact effects of arsenic poisoning had to be studied. "I am sinking under the burden!" he cried to Bouilhet; but he had to keep working steadily all the lonely winter. "When I was describing the poisoning of Emma Bovary," he recorded later, "I had such a taste of arsenic in my mouth and was poisoned so effectively myself, that I had two attacks of indigestion, one after the other—two very real attacks, for I vomited my entire dinner." For his description of the wake around Madame Bovary's bier he drew on his memories of his watches beside the bodies of his sister and of Alfred; and his portrait of Dr. Larivière, the famous physician who was called to Madame Bovary's bedside too late, is said to be a portrait of his father, who in life had been the head of the hospital in which Eugène Delamare had studied.

The book was finished in April 1856.

Flaubert went up to Paris at once, taking his manuscript

with him, and there he wrote a letter to the ten-year-old Caroline:

"My dear Liline,

"Thank you for writing me such a nice letter. The spelling is better than in any of your others and the style is also good. If you sit long enough in my armchair, lean your elbows on my table, and hold your head in your two hands, perhaps you will end by becoming a writer.

"I have with me here a lady whom I found on the boulevards and who is at present living in my study, lying indolently on a shelf of my bookcase. Her costume is excessively light, consisting merely of a piece of paper which covers her from head to foot—the poor girl's only possessions are her hair, her chemise, and shoes and stockings. She is waiting impatiently for my departure, because she knows that at Croisset she will find some clothes more suitable to the modesty of her sex. Please give my thanks to your other child, who was so kind as to send me her regards. I send her mine, and advise her to follow a strengthening diet, for I have lately thought her a trifle pale, and am somewhat worried as to her health.

"Yesterday I was at an exhibition of pictures, and thought of you a great deal. There were many subjects which you would have recognized, thanks to your erudition, and some portraits of great men whom you also know. I even saw several portraits of rabbits, and looked in the catalogue to see if I could find the name of Monsieur Lapin, of Croisset. But he was not there. Good-bye, my darling. Kiss your grandmother for me.

                                    "Your uncle who loves you."

He stayed in Paris about two weeks. He read the entire novel aloud to Bouilhet. They made large cuts, some of them painful to Flaubert. The very first sentence of the book was completely changed. Then he returned to Croisset and had the whole manuscript copied by a copyist.

6.

As though the *Livre Posthume* and the account of the travels in the East had not been bad enough, Maxime Du Camp published in 1855 a collection of *Les Chants Modernes* which had been appearing in the *Revue* and which Flaubert found so contemptible. The streak in Max which had caused him to subject to chemical analysis the waters of the spring of Hercules at Thermopylæ was prominent in this volume. Science and industry, he announced in a militant preface, were striding ahead, whereas literature was stagnant. In an age of steam and electricity poets were still writing of Venus and Bacchus. Literature was out of touch with life: the Academy set *"L'Acropole d'Athènes"* as the subject for its poetical competition; at the Beaux Arts the most recent sculptural subject was *Hector et Astyanax.* It was time to turn to other themes. The invention of photography had not harmed painting— in fact, it had benefited it, for more than one mediocre painter, realizing his lack of genius, had turned to photography. The poetry of a great modern foundry! The masses! The colours! The muscles of the nude workers! For the love of God, Max begged, look further than antiquity! The golden age is ahead, not behind!

> *Poètes, croyez-moi! ne dites plus "Ma lyre!"*
> *Ne dites plus "O Muse!" Oubliez ces vieux mots!*
> *Imitez Rabelais quand il disait: les pots!*
> *Au lieu "du dieu Bacchus et de son saint délire"*
> *Chantez la liberté, l'amour et le progrès!*

So he commanded in verses entitled *"Aux Poètes,"* and most of the poems that followed were indeed devoted to the praise of *le progrès,* being addressed to steam, to a bobbin, to a locomotive, to Australia, land of the future, and the like. It is true that at the end of the volume he included some of his earlier verse, addressed to a rainbow or to *"Le Palais Génois"* or *"Femmes Turques";* there were also a few poems on not very clearly defined political

themes, reproaching the government for exiling Hugo and
at the same time glorying in the defeat of the people in
1848; and the preface contained implied dispraise of Gautier, who had recently offended Max by withdrawing
from the *Revue de Paris* and transferring himself to another magazine, *L'Artiste*. The quality of Max's poetry
was about on the level of Louise's at its worst, but it was
his subject matter that particularly outraged Flaubert. To
be revolutionary in literature was completely desirable—
Madame Bovary, Flaubert hoped, was a revolution in itself; but to think that literature could ignore mankind and
concern itself with manufacturing and mechanics was
idiotic. Max was guilty of "turpitudes."

What, however, could be expected from an editor of the
Revue de Paris? For several years Flaubert had filled his
letters to Louise and to Bouilhet with his contempt for
that magazine. He was pleased when he heard that the
bookstalls on the Paris quays were full of uncut remainder
copies of the *Revue;* in one issue a story by Laurent-
Pichat, a gentleman who fancied himself as a poet and was
the new managing editor of the magazine, was so commonplace that Flaubert removed a phrase from *Madame
Bovary* simply because Laurent-Pichat had employed it.
It was, in fact, impossible for any magazine at all to be
self-respecting and disinterested. "A review is a shop," he
said. "That being the case, each particular book is given
greater importance than books in general, and sooner or
later questions of business and subscription come to domi-
nate all others. It is impossible to publish anywhere at the
present time. All existing magazines are infamous whores.
I should no more like to be on the staff of a review, or of
any club or society or academy, than to be a municipal
counsellor or an officer in the National Guard." "No! In
God's name, no! I shall never try to publish in any magazine. Everything is so low these days that to become a
part of anything at all is a dishonour and a disgrace." As
to Max himself, Flaubert wrote: "For Max I am now incapable of the slightest feeling. The part of my heart
which he once occupied has been eaten away by slow
gangrene; there is nothing left of it." "I still love him at

bottom, but he has so irritated me, repulsed me, disowned
me, and in general acted toward me so odiously, that as
far as I am concerned he is already dead."

But during these years Max considered himself to be the
injured party, the hurt but forgiving friend. From time to
time he sent Flaubert an affectionate note, and always a
copy of his latest book—even *Les Chants Modernes*—
which was invariably coldly acknowledged and never
commented upon. His lament to Bouilhet about the misunderstanding and his reminder that the *Revue de Paris*
stood ready to publish *Madame Bovary* as soon as it might
be finished he repeated to Flaubert himself the first time
they met after the long interval—the evening of Louise's
irruption into the Trois Frères Provençaux. There would
be no delay, he promised; as soon as the book was finished,
the *Revue* would publish it; he knew without seeing it
that it was good.

Flaubert received the overtures coolly, but when the
book was finished, and he brought it to Paris, Max was
none the less allowed to see it—and when he had read it
there was no further mention of the folly of living in retirement, or of the "softening of the brain" induced by a
country existence. He did not hesitate to point out many
passages which should be omitted—his list of advisable
cuts was far longer even than Bouilhet's—but he covered
Flaubert with compliments and said that the novel would
be an ornament to the *Revue*. Despite Max's presumptu-
ousness, which was now less shocking because it was expected, Flaubert found the offer of such easy and rapid
publication irresistible after so many years of toil, and accepted. Publication was to begin August 1. The manuscript
was delivered early in June.

Almost the moment the manuscript of *Madame Bovary*
was out of his hands Flaubert returned, with rapture and
relief, to the exoticism of *Saint Antoine*. He was determined to make it publishable, and began to "scratch out
the ultra-lyrical movements." And he took out of the
Rouen library books on medieval domestic life and hunting, for he was also making notes for the tale of Saint
Julian the Hospitaller which he had conceived long ago

in the Rouen cathedral. How fine it was to be back in Alexandria, and back in the Middle Ages! For by now the purging effect of the oriental journey had about worn off.

"I am finding all kinds of wonderful new details," he wrote Bouilhet about "*Saint Julien.*" "I think I'll be able to give the thing an amusing flavour. What do you say of a pâté of hedgehogs? Or a squirrel pie? But don't worry that I'll drown myself in notes. In a month I shall have finished my reading, meanwhile working at *Saint Antoine.* If I were the man I should be, I'd come to Paris in October with *Saint Antoine* finished and '*Saint Julien l'Hospitalier*' as well, thus presenting the public with something modern, something medieval, and something antique all in the same year!"

In less than two weeks, however, he was interrupted by a letter from Max, who said that he had read the recopied manuscript and was disappointed to find that Flaubert had not made the cuts he had suggested; and that although the other editors had not yet seen it he would take full responsibility for saying at once that such cuts absolutely must be made; and he would like Flaubert to come to Paris immediately to discuss them with him. But Flaubert quickly replied that since he had no intention of making any further cuts whatever, he saw no reason to come to Paris before October, when he intended to move there for the winter anyway; he said the novel should be published as it was, and he wrote to Bouilhet in lamentation: "The corrections we made in *Bovary* finished me, and I confess that now I almost regret having made them—but, as you see, Signor Du Camp finds that I haven't made enough. Will everyone think the same, perhaps? Or will some agree with me that there are too many? I have acted like a fool in doing as others do, in deciding to live in Paris, in wanting to publish. As long as I was writing for myself alone, I lived in a perfect serenity of art. Now I am full of doubts and uneasiness."

And then, three weeks later, came a letter from Max which was as fantastic as *Les Chants Modernes:* "Laurent-Pichat has read your novel and I enclose his remarks about it. As you will realize when you read them, I agree with them absolutely, for they are almost the very observations that I made before you left Paris. I sent the book on to Laurent with no comment except a warm recommendation —it is not by collusion that we think so nearly alike. The advice he gives you is good—the only advice, in fact, that you should follow. Let us take full charge of the publication of your novel in the *Revue;* we will make the cuts that we think are indispensable; and later you can superintend the book publication yourself, restoring anything you choose. My private opinion is that if you do not do this you will be compromising your entire career and making your first appearance with a work which is confused and muddled and to which the style alone does not give sufficient interest. Be brave, close your eyes during the operation, and have confidence—if not in our talent, at least in the experience which we have acquired in such things and also in our affection for you. You have buried your novel underneath a heap of details which are well done but utterly superfluous; they hide the essentials, and must be removed—an easy task. We shall have it done under our supervision by someone who is experienced and clever; not a word will be added to your manuscript, it will merely be cut down; the job will cost you about a hundred francs, which will be deducted from your cheque, and you will have published something really good, instead of something imperfect and padded. You are doubtless cursing me with all your might at this very moment, but you may be sure that in all this I have only your own interest at heart."

This from the man who a few years before had brought to Croisset the manifesto of the *Revue de Paris!* "We have but one literary principle: absolute liberty"! "We shall refuse manuscripts, but we shall not deface them: to remove a word from a sentence is as culpable, as barbarous, as to break the nose from a statue or chip a figure from a bas-relief"!

There was nothing to do but to scrawl *"Gigantesque!"* on the back of that letter, and to send off another posthaste to Max, to say that if the *Revue* did not want *Madame Bovary* as it was written it was quite free not to take it at all. Indeed Flaubert almost asked for the return of his manuscript, and would certainly have done so had the editors persisted in their demands; but somewhat to his surprise they agreed, after a certain delay and much against their judgment, to print all but one of the passages which they found so faulty, and they merely stated what was now obvious—that owing to the unforeseen delays publication of the first instalment would have to be postponed until September 1. Flaubert contemptuously agreed to the one omission and wrote scorching letters to Bouilhet, and he carefully preserved the list of the other cuts which Laurent-Pichat and Max had suggested. Most of the condemned passages were those which a bourgeois magazine reader might find shocking or "too real," and they included the one which had been inspired by Louise's trackings in Paris and which Flaubert thought among the best in the book—the long itinerary of a curtained cab, inside which Madame Bovary was (all too clearly, the *Revue* evidently feared) surrendering to her second lover.

The first advertisement of the novel appeared in the *Revue* for August 1. "*Madame Bovary*," it announced, "by Gustave Faubert," without an "l." "Gustave Faubert is the name of a grocer in the Rue de Richelieu," he cried to Bouilhet, "opposite the Comédie Française! This debut seems far from auspicious to me! What do you think? Even before I appear, they skin me. I am not without forebodings. This damned 'Faubert' makes me much more disgusted than indignant." How would the magazine print the novel, if it could not even print the author's name? Perhaps it would not print it at all! By now Flaubert's opinion of his editors was such that this began to seem quite possible; he began to suspect that the whole thing was some huge farce, of which he understood nothing. Particularly did he feel so during the last days of August, when he had as yet received no proofs; and he was not surprised when the September 1 issue of the *Revue* appeared with no sign of *Madame Bovary* whatever, and no word from Maxime or anyone else. He wrote in inquiry and Max calmly replied that at the last minute there had been no space, but that the first instalment would appear "October 1, without fail, I hope." Flaubert thereupon reminded Max of his promise of rapid publication, and pointed out that he had now been waiting three months; then he returned to his studies, and waited some more. He was reading *Macbeth*, which he adored for the profusion of its metaphors, and he was poring over ancient works on the heresies for *Saint Antoine*. Some of the heretical material that he had decided to use seemed scandalous even in the nineteenth century, and he feared that if *Saint Antoine* were ever published it would cause him to be prosecuted in the courts.

Finally, late in September, came definite word from the *Revue. Madame Bovary* would absolutely appear October 1. The entire first part was already at the printer's, and though there would be no time to send the proofs to Flaubert, Max promised that everything would be respected. The book would appear in six instalments in the now bimonthly *Revue*, from October 1 to December 15, inclusive. "The winter announces itself well!" Flaubert wrote gaily to Louis, and to a young man whom he had known at college he declared: "I lose my virginity as unpublished writer a week from Thursday, October first. May *Fortuna virilis* be favourable to me!"

The first instalment of *Madame Bovary* did appear October 1 and no cuts had been made. But Flaubert was shocked by the number of typographical errors which had slipped by the eyes of the editors and printers, and even more shocked by the large number of repetitions of words which had slipped by his own. One page, full of "which's" and "who's," was especially ugly, and the sight of his work in print, far from exhilarating him, filled him with disgust. "It seems utterly flat to me," he wrote to Louis. "Everything in it seems bad. This is literally true. It is a bitter disappointment, and the success of the book will have to be deafening indeed to cover the voice of my conscience, which keeps shouting: 'Failure! Failure!'"

During the delay over the magazine publication of *Madame Bovary* and even during the months just preceding the completion of the book, Louis Bouilhet had been having troubles of his own. Despite the devotion of his young actresses, he did not enjoy living in Paris. It was not only that he was excessively poor—for it took him much longer to finish his play than he had expected, and as he neared the end of his funds he had to sell some of his few possessions—but also that he disliked the bustle, the impersonality, and the hard, metropolitan brilliance of the city. Flaubert wrote him incessantly in an effort to keep up his spirits, but he became increasingly sombre, and eventually went so far as to complain that he "missed Rouen." The idea of anyone's missing Rouen caused Flaubert an instant of hilarity, but such a confession revealed as none other possibly could the extent of his friend's dejection. Louis sometimes expressed himself in desperate cries which called for swift and peremptory replies. "In the name of God," Flaubert wrote one day, "what do you mean by such a phrase as the following: 'And so I shall gradually efface myself from the world'? Good God! I feel like giving you a kick somewhere. What do you want *me* to become, poor wretch, if *you* falter, if you destroy my faith in you?" And he frequently reproached Bouilhet for not using the assets which he had—the fact that his name was already known from *Melænis*, that he had friends, such as Gautier, who would be delighted to see more of him than he allowed them to, and who could be of use to him, introducing him to others who would smooth the way for *Madame de Montarcy* when it was finished. In fact, he scolded Bouilhet for not pushing himself in much the same way that he himself had been scolded by Max five years before—a fact which he recognized and laughed at. But a dramatist, he insisted—at least a dramatist who had to earn his living—had to do many things which a novelist with an income did not have to do; and instead of continually moaning, and thinking of returning to Rouen, Bouilhet should set out to impose himself on Paris.

When *Madame de Montarcy* was finally done, Louis took it to the reading committee of the Comédie Française, which promptly refused even to look at it. The committee did not read the plays of all and sundry; introductions were necessary, and besides there existed in the world of the theatre a traditional, complicated ritual of requests for support and protection, presentations and prereadings, with which Louis was entirely unfamiliar. He had thought it unpleasantly commercial even to write a play in the first

place, and had done so for purely financial reasons, thinking at least that if it were produced it would be produced
on its merits; now he found himself running about Paris,
waiting in outer offices, begging aid from people for whom
he cared nothing, peddling a manuscript which interested
him but little. He was not entirely unaided, however. To
his astonishment, Flaubert suddenly revealed that he possessed a genius for intrigue. From the house at Croisset he
wrote Louis letters filled with details of just whom to see
in Paris, exactly what steps to take; he pointed out in just
what way Gautier could be of most benefit, just how
Louis could best utilize Maxime and his associates, just
how the actress friends would count for most, just how he
could enlist the support of all the critics who had spoken
favourably of *Melænis* and the other poems. When Louis
expressed his surprise, Flaubert revealed that he was an old
hand at the game. It did not interest him, he said, but he
could play it well when he wanted to. He had been of
the greatest use to his brother Achille in the matter of his
appointment as his father's successor in the hospital; and
Maxime's first decoration, after the street-battles of 1848,
had also been engineered in part by his devices. It was not
for nothing that he had been born in Normandy; ruse,
trickery, and smooth dealing were parts of the Norman
character, and the only wonder was that Louis, who was
even more Norman than he, had been born so guileless.

By following Flaubert's directions, Bouilhet quite
quickly achieved his immediate goal: the reading committee of the Comédie Française consented to consider *Madame de Montarcy*. But its verdict was unfavourable, and
Louis collapsed from fatigue and disappointment. The entire day following the arrival of the bad news he spent
lying prostrate on the floor—much like Gustave on the
eve of his departure for Egypt; and he sent a letter of such
desperation to his mother that she came to Paris at once,
fearing that her son was on the point of committing suicide and hoping that if he did not, the blow would cause
him to renounce the unholy worlds of poetry and the
theatre. Flaubert doubled the length and strength of his
letters, suggesting new proceedings and overtures, de-
nouncing the behaviour of Madame Bouilhet and ordering

Louis not to give way but to continue his efforts at once.
The next most desirable theatre to the Comédie Française
was the Odéon, the second national theatre, of which one
of Max's associates on the *Revue* was director; this was a
great advantage, but Flaubert urged Louis not only to
cultivate the gentleman and his assistants, but also to learn
the names and characteristics of all the members of the
Odéon's reading committee, to secure introductions to
them, to insinuate himself among them, discover their
weak points—some he would be able to seduce most effectively by flattery, others by fine foods and wine. Louis set
to work once more; he plunged shamelessly and recklessly
into the toadyings which were so necessary and so expen-
sive; and in June, almost to his horror, the Odéon accepted
Madame de Montarcy. Flaubert was jubilant. "Go out and
paint the town red—if you can! Continue to work! Satisfy
your unquenchable ardours, fill your incredible stomach,
parade your monstrous personality! Those are the qualities
that give you your charm! You are superb! I love you!"
     The première was scheduled for the first week in No-
vember; and in the middle of October, when Flaubert installed himself in his apartment on the Boulevard du
Temple, rehearsals were under way. Flaubert attended
them all. He spent every afternoon in the theatre. *Madame
Bovary* was appearing these days; everyone knew who he
was and treated him with consideration; he was allowed to
roam over the theatre and the stage, to take part in the
coaching and direction. He remembered the billiard-table
theatre, the days when his father had forbidden him to do
his repulsive imitations; he found the Odéon glamorous
and stimulating. The fate of *Madame de Montarcy*, he
knew, was a question of life and death for Bouilhet: if it
were to fail, Bouilhet would feel that *he* had failed, and
would return to Rouen and the tutoring school, an atmosphere which Flaubert thought withering for a poet. He
began to do what he could to ensure the success of the
piece. He had himself presented to dramatic critics and
talked to them smoothly and flatteringly; he mingled with
students in the cafés near the schools, telling them of the
fine play they might soon expect—for the Odéon was in
the students' quarter and drew a large part of its public

from their ranks, and their interest counted for much in the success or failure of an Odéon play. Poor Bouilhet followed Flaubert about like a shadow, allowed him to do whatever he wished, and felt no confidence whatever. He was even more timid than usual and in a constant state of bewilderment; sometimes, if he was asked an unexpected question, he burst into tears.

On the evening of November 6 his state was pitiable. Max and Flaubert sat beside him in the wings; at their slightest change of position he clutched them and begged them not to leave. He was beside himself. When the audience applauded, he was sure they were hissing; all went well, but to him all seemed disaster. His lines were beautifully spoken and the house was sympathetic, so many spontaneous bravos ringing out that the claque was superfluous; but half-way through, Bouilhet could stand the disgrace and the fiasco no longer, and begged his friends to walk with him out in the streets. They left the theatre, walked down to the river and out onto the Pont Neuf, watching the lights in the water; Bouilhet talked of jumping in, but they calmed him as best they could and returned to the theatre in time to hear the second half of the last act and the tremendous applause which greeted the final curtain. Clearly, *Madame de Montarcy* was a success. Even a long series of curtain calls failed to convince the author of the fact, however, and at supper at Foyot's afterwards he kept asking whether there was not perhaps some faint chance that the play might catch on later. His friends took him home more dead than alive, and it was not until he had rested for two days and read the reviews that he realized the degree of his good fortune. The play was given seventy times—a large number in a Parisian repertory theatre. The imperial censor was indulgent and paid no attention to a line which could easily have been interpreted as a denunciation of the regime, and the Emperor and Empress attended and applauded.

A week or so after the opening, the newspaper *Figaro* had occasion to make fun of Bouilhet. Somewhat tardily, the leading citizens of Rouen and other prominent Normans realized that the obscure tutor who had coached their sons was a literary man of some value, and a group of seventy of them came to Paris in a body, purchased a block of seats, and cheered their compatriot. Following the performance they insisted on giving a banquet in Louis's honour. There was much toasting, and a gentleman who was a power in the Rouen judiciary read a poetical compliment of his own composition.

Figaro insisted that during the course of the banquet Bouilhet's admirers from the birthplace of Corneille placed on his head a golden wreath, bearing the words "*Cornelio Redivivo.*" This is scarcely likely, but it is true that the next day they requested him to show them the sights of Paris, with which he was now so familiar, and more than one newspaper was pleased to describe the spectacle of poor Louis, followed by seventy Rouennais, acting as guide to the tomb of Napoleon, the Panthéon, and the column in the Place Vendôme.

Bouilhet's success and Flaubert's were simultaneous; for, from the moment of the appearance of the first instalment, and despite Flaubert's own opinion, *Madame Bovary* was unquestionably a success. Bouilhet was proven right again: since the death of Balzac, no novel had so impressed the public. It was the thunderclap.

When the *Revue* for October 1 went on sale, Laurent-Pichat wrote in complimentary style to Flaubert and said that he was confident that the novel would meet with a good reception; with his congratulations he expressed once more some of his reservations about the detailed realism of the book and mentioned the cuts he would like to see made. "Do you think that this ignoble reality, so disgusting to you in reproduction, does not oppress my heart as it does yours?" Flaubert inquired in his reply. "If you knew me better you would know that I abhor ordinary existence. Personally, I have always held myself as aloof from it as I could. But æsthetically, I desired this once—and only this once—to plumb its very depths. Therefore I plunged into it heroically, into the midst of all its minutiæ, accepting everything, telling everything, depicting everything, pretentious as it may sound to say so. I am expressing myself badly, but well enough, I think, for you to understand the general trend of my resistance to your criticisms, judicious as they may be. You were asking me to turn it into another book."

As the first several instalments appeared, the impact of the book on its readers became apparent. The editors of the *Revue* reported that all the critics, littérateurs, and salon habitués were talking enthusiastically about it among themselves. The publisher Michel Lévy wrote to Flaubert, offering to publish it in book form as soon as the last instalment should have appeared in the magazine. Unlike the *Revue* (despite Max's mention of a cheque), he actually offered some money for it; "*Fantastique!*" the author exclaimed. Flaubert began to receive letters from acquaintances, schoolmates, and friends of his father's of whom he had seen nothing for years and who had mourned his illness, retirement, and seeming idleness. Like Bouilhet, he sprang into local, as well as Parisian, fame. On the fourth of October the *Journal de Rouen* published a eulogistic article, calling the attention of the inhabitants of Normandy to this masterpiece written by one of their compatriots. A few days later the second Rouen newspaper, the *Nouvelliste de Rouen*, began to publish the book in instalments, heading the first with an announcement which treated the name of the book much as Flaubert's name had been treated in the advertisement in the *Revue:*

"Our fellow townsman, M. Gustave Flaubert, is publishing in the *Revue de Paris* a most remarkable novel entitled *Madame de Bovery*. This composition, which combines with literary merit the attraction of a conscientious study of provincial manners, is enjoying considerable success. It is of particular interest to our readers, not only because of the celebrity of the author's name but also because of his choice of subject; they can appreciate more than readers elsewhere the accuracy of the details and local descriptions."

During the succeeding weeks there were a few specifically Norman outcries—especially from pharmacists—but in general the objection raised against the book was the same everywhere: its ultra-realism, the pleasure which the author seemed to take in displaying the sordid, the dreary, the hypocritical. Praise of the book continued, and it was read avidly, but this objection grew. "Everyone thinks I

am in love with reality," Flaubert remarked, "whereas
actually I detest it. It was in hatred of realism that I under-
took this book. But I equally despise that false brand of
idealism which is such a hollow mockery in the present
age."

"Only the ladies consider me a 'dreadful man.' " he
wrote to one of his cousins in Nogent. "They think I am
too true to life. That is the basis of their indignation. *I*
think that I am very moral, and that I deserve the Mont-
yon prize for virtue. My novel teaches a very clear lesson,
and if 'no mother could think of allowing her daughter to
read it'—as I have heard stated—I think that husbands
would do very well to give it to their wives. But all this
leaves me completely indifferent. The morality of art consists in its beauty, and I value style even above truth. I
think that into my picture of bourgeois life and my exposition of the character of a woman who is naturally corrupt, I have put as much literature and as much decorum
as the subject allows. I have no desire to repeat this work.
Vulgar society disgusts me, and it was because it disgusts
me that I chose to depict the society in *Bovary*, which is
so ultra-vulgar, so ultra-repugnant. This book has served
to train my hand: now to other things!"

He had almost completed the new version of *Saint Antoine*, and Gautier had offered to publish four long passages from it in four successive issues of *L'Artiste*.

But though the complaints of the ladies might leave
Flaubert completely indifferent, there were those whom
they did not—the editors of the *Revue de Paris*. For "the
ladies" were more numerous and more powerful than
Flaubert seemed to realize. "As soon as the first chapters
had appeared," Max later recorded, "our subscribers rose
in wrath, crying that it was scandalous, immoral. They
wrote us letters of doubtful courtesy, accusing us of slan-
dering France and disgracing it in the eyes of the world.
'What! Such women exist? Women who deceive their
husbands, pile up debts, meet their lovers in gardens and
hotels? Such creatures exist in our lovely France, in the
provinces where life is so pure? Impossible!' " Max understood quite well that such complaints came from the type

of person who will "drop a book in disgust because one of the characters has horse-dung on his shoes," and to such people as that it was useless to insist that the book was a masterpiece. Flaubert, when he was shown the complaining letters, and reminded that perhaps the *Revue* had been right, after all, to demand more cuts, simply said that the outraged readers were "all crazy"—and went back to *Saint Antoine.*

Things did not stop there, however.

A decree passed by the Napoleonic government soon after the *coup d'état* had abolished freedom of the press. "It had been aimed at political journalism," in Max's words, "but it had all kinds of reverberations, ruining writers who had supported themselves by writing dramatic and art criticism, scientific reports, and serial novels for the newspapers. For many of the papers were suppressed; in all of Paris only thirteen were allowed to exist. It was at that period that the exclusively literary papers were created, in which men of letters could at least try to print and sell their work. But many of these small sheets, though they were concerned only with art, science, and literature, failed to survive: the boundaries of 'politics' were so vaguely defined that it was quite possible to be accused of having set foot on the forbidden domain when you spoke of a museum (since museums are nationally administered) or of the Comédie Française (which is controlled by the Ministry of Public Instruction), etc. In such a case, the guilty were brought to court, fined, and the paper suppressed. The number of humble sheets which thus disappeared was considerable; it was a difficult period for writers. Gérard de Nerval, who was far from a rebel, said to me: 'I should like to write the story of Haçanben-Sabah-Homaïri, the Old Man of the Mountain; but I don't dare —people would find allusions to the Emperor.' The Sûreté Générale employed all its skill in the hunt for allusions."

Now, several articles in the *Revue de Paris* had at various times been suspected of this very crime of allusion. Had not Max, one of the editors of the magazine, deplored the exile of Hugo in *Les Chants Modernes?* Were not several of its contributors professors who had been dismissed from the universities during the purge, or even individuals who had been ministers under the Republic? The *Revue* claimed to be unconcerned with politics, but about it hung a suspicious aura of liberalism; it had already received several warnings, and its next misstep would undoubtedly result in suppression. Max's alarm was considerable, therefore, when, after several numbers of *Madame Bovary* had appeared, a friend who knew what was taking place in the *"hautes régions du pouvoir"* whispered that he had heard on good authority that the *Revue*, and Flaubert as well, were about to be prosecuted for "outrage of public morals and religion."

There was no reason to doubt this information. The dismay of "the ladies" provided an all-too-excellent political pretext. But there was, perhaps, still time to escape the attack by removing its pretended reason. The *Revue* acted quickly. When Flaubert opened his copy of the issue of December 1, he found to his consternation that the newest instalment of his novel was headed by an editorial note:

"The editors find themselves obliged to omit from this instalment a passage which they consider unsuitable for publication in the *Revue de Paris*. They hereby advise the author of their action and assume full responsibility for it." The omitted passage was the description of the wanderings of the curtained cab.

Max was apologetic, of course. He said there had been no time to warn Flaubert; instant action had been the only thing; Flaubert must understand the gravity of the situation. And he must consent that the final instalment of the novel, which was to appear in the next issue, be trimmed of a large number of its passages: only in this way might prosecution possibly be averted.

But Flaubert was adamant. He would not make the slightest concession. If his novel exasperated the bourgeois, it was all the same to him. If he and the editors were called into court, he would accept the call. If the *Revue de Paris* was suppressed, it would be too bad. He would not mutilate *Madame Bovary* to save any magazine. The *Revue* urged him to reconsider; Max even called on Madame Flaubert, who had come to Paris, asking her to intercede with her son; she replied coldly, indicating her belief that Max was deliberately destroying the beauty of *Madame*

Bovary because he envied its greatness as compared with his own works. And Flaubert wrote again to Laurent-Pichat, stating his position. "The omission of the passage about the cab," he ended, "did nothing to lessen the grounds of the scandal, and the omission of what you want to omit in the next number will be equally futile. You have seized upon details, whereas it is the book as a whole that is to blame. The brutal element is everywhere, not merely on the surface. Negroes cannot be made white, and it is impossible to change the blood of a book. It can be thinned, but not altered."

Unfortunately, the *Revue* had the law on its side. A magazine or newspaper could, it appeared, suppress any passage it chose of a work which it was publishing, and Max informed Flaubert that the editors intended to take advantage of their right. Flaubert begged them to cancel the last number entirely; they refused—such a step would injure the prestige of the magazine. Flaubert had to give in. Max offered him the opportunity of heading the instalment with any kind of note which he chose, and furious but trapped he wrote as follows:

"Considerations which it is not in my province to judge compelled the *Revue de Paris* to omit a passage from the issue of December 1; its scruples having been again aroused on the occasion of the present issue, it has thought proper to omit several more. In consequence, I hereby decline responsibility for the lines which follow. The reader is therefore asked to consider them as a series of fragments, not as a whole.

"Gustave Flaubert."

In the *Revue* the last instalment was shorn of a dozen passages. The *Nouvelliste de Rouen* cancelled publication of all remaining chapters.

Flaubert was right, however: the *Revue de Paris* accomplished nothing by its suppressions. It was too late and the affair was, after all, political: *Madame Bovary* was but an excuse. Despite the cuts, Max's friends in the government told him that prosecution was unavoidable; the government police were determined to destroy the magazine.

Three people would be summoned to court: Laurent-Pichat as managing editor, Flaubert as author, and one Pillet, the printer. Max warned Flaubert to take steps to protect himself, and he rebelliously did so. To his wrath, his fate was bound up with that of a magazine for which he had nothing but contempt. If he went to prison, it would be because of his connexion with the *Revue de Paris;* if he won his case, he would save the *Revue.* He was filled with disgust; the world was quickly proving to be what he had always said it was. With all his heart he regretted publishing.

Nevertheless, he was active. He put himself in the hands of an eminent lawyer—Maître Sénard, a Rouennais well acquainted with the Flauberts. He wrote to Achille to seek the support of the prefect of the Seine-Inférieure, for in such a case as this it was exactly the bourgeois solidity of the Flaubert family, which Flaubert always thought he considered so antipathetic, that might save the day: "The important thing is to bring pressure to bear on Paris by way of Rouen. An indication of the influential position which Father had and which you now have in Rouen is our best means of preventing the thing from coming to a head. They thought they were attacking some penniless devil, and when they learned that I had something to live on they opened their eyes. The Ministry of the Interior must be made to learn that we are, in Rouen, what is called 'a family'—that we have deep roots in the city and the department, and that in attacking me, especially on grounds of immorality, they will offend many people. I expect great results from the prefect's letter to the minister of the interior. As I told you, the whole thing is political, and what will stop it is to make evident the political disadvantages of continuing—dangerous effect on the coming elections in our department, etc."

Meanwhile he was receiving compliments on his book from all sides. Even the director of the Beaux Arts, "in uniform and decorations," congratulated him in front of two hundred people at a gathering at the Ministry of State, where he had gone to seek support. When he learned that Lamartine had expressed admiration for the book, he called on him to thank him and ask his aid. It was promised, and the famous man treated him as a personage. "Modesty prevents me from repeating the ultra-flattering compliments that Lamartine made me," he told Achille. "He knows my book by heart, fully understands what I intended by it, and knows me to my very depths. He is going to give me a laudatory letter to submit to the court, and also certificates as to the morality of my book by the most prominent writers; this is important, Sénard says. My stock is going up: I have been asked to write a novel for the *Moniteur* at ten sous a line—which would make, for a book the length of *Bovary*, about ten thousand francs. That is where justice leads. Whether I am convicted or not, my reputation is made. And if *Bovary* is not suppressed, it will sell really well."

The thing dragged. There were rumours that both the Emperor and the Empress, influenced by society ladies of Max's acquaintance—"*Bovarystes enragées*," according to Flaubert—had ordered that proceedings be dropped; for a time they actually were dropped, and then they were resumed, with the Ministry of Justice now supporting the Ministry of the Interior; the closest inquiry seemed unable to locate the responsible officials in either ministry; an issue of a Belgian newspaper which spoke well of *Bovary* was banned from France; Flaubert described the whole thing as a "whirlpool of lies and infamies." "I expect no justice whatever," he told Achille. "I will serve my prison term. And of course I shall ask no clemency—that is the one thing that would dishonour me."

In general, however, he had no fears, for Sénard assured him that the whole thing was too stupid to be dangerous. One of the passages which the prosecution would particularly attack, it became known, was that in which Madame Bovary is given extreme unction, the description of which was considered sacrilegious; as it happened, Flaubert had merely translated the ceremony from the Latin of the Roman Catholic ritual, even omitting some of the strongest passages—there need be no fears on that score. The time drew nearer. "From minute to minute I expect the summons which will tell me the day when I must take my place on the bench of pickpockets and pederasts for the crime of having written in French. I expect a conviction because I do not merit it." He thanked Achille for his offer to have dinner with him on his first night in prison and promised to provide the proper trappings—a truss of damp straw and an assortment of strong chains. And when the summons finally arrived he wrote light-heartedly to the good doctor who had provided him with his adventure in Marseille when he was nineteen: "I hereby announce that tomorrow, the twenty-fourth of January, I shall honour with my presence the swindlers' bench of the sixth chamber of the criminal court, at ten o'clock in the morning. Ladies are admitted; decent and tasteful dress required." But as the thing stared him in the face he lost some of his frivolity: "I expect no justice whatever. I shall be convicted and perhaps even given the maximum sentence— sweet recompense for my labours, noble encouragement to literature!"

At the last minute the trial was postponed for a week, and when it took place everything was absurd except an excellent speech by Sénard. The court-room was full of literary people; when the prosecuting attorney solemnly declared that of the three defendants "Monsieur Pillet, the printer, is an honourable man against whom I have nothing to say," the entire assemblage burst into laughter. Even the presiding justice joined in; he was a man with literary pretensions, and welcomed the case as a change from the usual procession of thieves, pimps, and prostitutes which passed daily before his eyes in this same room. As a passage from *Madame Bovary* was read, his lips were even seen to form the word "Charming." The prosecutor read supposedly anti-religious passages from *Saint Antoine*, as they had recently appeared in *L'Artiste*, and his confusion of classical names caused more than one smile. Max, in the audience, exchanged winks with his friends in the dock. At the end of his final speech, the prosecutor urged the Court to be moderate toward Laurent-Pichat and the printer, but to use all possible severity toward Flaubert, the principal culprit.

The second half of the recommendation, however, the Court declined to follow. It was unable to resist a certain amount of literary comment, and expressed somewhat wistfully its preference for works which dealt less with life

as it is than with life as it should be, but in the end it stated
that "In the circumstances, be it known that it is not sufficiently proven that Pichat, Gustave Flaubert, and Pillet
are guilty of the misdemeanour with which they are
charged; the Court acquits them of the indictment brought
against them, and decrees a dismissal without costs."
Flaubert had saved the *Revue de Paris.*

He was so disgusted by everything that had happened to
him since he had undertaken to publish *Madame Bovary*
in the magazine that he was revolted by the idea of publishing it as a book. He thought of taking it home to
Croisset, putting it in a drawer with *Novembre* and the
others, and forgetting it as completely as he could. His
mother urged him to publish, however, since people like
Monsieur de Lamartine thought the novel so good, and
Bouilhet reminded him that by doing so he could restore
the text to its proper form. This decided him to accept the
offer of Michel Lévy. He sold all the rights to *Madame
Bovary* for five years for five hundred francs. It appeared
in two volumes, with a dedication to Louis Bouilhet and a
note of thanks to Maître Sénard, in April 1857, a year
after it had been completed, five and a half years after it
had been begun. Fifteen thousand copies were sold in two
months.

7.

Although most of the critics waited to write about *Madame Bovary* until they could read it between covers in
its authentic, unexpurgated form, an occasional review
appeared before book publication, based on the instalments
in the *Revue de Paris.* Among these was one by Duranty,
editor of the magazine *Réalisme,* the mouthpiece of the
new "Realists"; and although Flaubert was by this time
heartily sick of *Bovary,* and professed to have no interest
in what any critic might say about it, he read Duranty's
review with attention. He was curious to know what was
thought of his novel by a school which considered itself

realistic and whose chief productions he himself had found
so weak.

"*Madame Bovary*, the novel by Gustave Flaubert, represents the obstinacy of description. Details are counted one
by one, all are given equal value; every street, every house,
every room, every brook, every blade of grass, is described
in full; each character, as he enters the scene, makes preliminary remarks on extraneous and uninteresting subjects,
which serve merely to make known his degree of intelligence. There is neither emotion nor feeling nor life in this
novel. (I speak here for those who have been able to read
it.) The style is uneven, now imitative of other writers,
now lyrical, never personal. I repeat, always physical *description*, never *impression*. No purpose would be served
by a discussion of the point of view of a book in which,
owing to the above-mentioned defects, all interest is lacking. Excessive study is not a substitute for the spontaneity
which comes from *feeling*."

Such remarks as these touched some of the qualities of
the book which were most antipathetic to Flaubert himself—the lack of the spontaneity of the great geniuses, the
very obstinacy of description which he had found so tedious in the writing. And yet by some of Duranty's remarks
he could not help but feel complimented. To be accused of
excessive detail and lack of interest by the school of
Champfleury, to be blamed for impersonality of style
when that had been his aim: these were tributes in dis-
guise, and Flaubert carefully preserved the review from
Réalisme and often reread it in later years, always enjoying
the picture of himself as a man without feeling. This review was all the more piquant because Champfleury himself, considered by Duranty a true realist and a far greater
writer than Flaubert, was going about saying to everyone:
"Have you read *Madame Bovary?* It might be by me!"
and had written Flaubert a letter congratulating him on
his victory in court.

In May reviews began to appear in all the newspapers
and magazines, and Flaubert, who had returned to Croisset
for the summer, received the clippings from his Parisian
friends. Few of them were completely favourable. Some

were obviously disappointed at the lack of salaciousness in the passages that the *Revue* had omitted and the prosecutor denounced, and expressions of this same disappointment were heard from the general public, who were buying the book by the thousands. The realization that his success was in considerable part a *succès de scandale* filled Flaubert with his characteristic combination of delight and disgust. Other reviews, particularly in the Catholic publications, found the book utterly immoral and irreligious. Almost all professed to be shocked by its brutality, and all mentioned the influence of Balzac. None, however, dismissed it briefly; even those which pronounced it uninteresting filled several columns.

The most important critic in France, he whose judgment counted for most, was Sainte-Beuve, whose literary *feuilleton* had for many years appeared every Monday in the *Moniteur Universel,* the official government newspaper with a vast upper-bourgeois circulation throughout the country. Sainte-Beuve discussed only books which interested him—though frequently, as in the case of *Melænis,* he made brief and disparaging remarks about those which did not—and if he found no new book worthy of his attention he wrote about an old one. To a young writer, favourable mention by Sainte-Beuve was the opening of the door. Sainte-Beuve admired *Madame Bovary* as it appeared in the *Revue,* and, having met Flaubert at Gautier's, wrote and told him so, regretting that under the circumstances he felt unable to publish an article on the book: his newspaper was a government organ and, besides, he preferred never to become involved in any non-literary controversy. Shortly afterward, however, the *Moniteur* itself asked Sainte-Beuve to write on *Madame Bovary,* and he accordingly did so, on the fourth of May.

Now that the case was ended, he declared, *Madame Bovary* belonged solely to the realm of art, and was answerable only to literary criticism. It was a work which bore every evidence of having been carefully studied and wrought; it was entirely impersonal—a great proof of strength.

"One precious quality distinguishes Gustave Flaubert from the other more or less exact observers who in our time pride themselves on frankly reproducing the only reality and who occasionally succeed: he has *style*. He even has a trifle too much, and his pen delights in certain curiosities and minutiæ of continuous description which at times injure the total effect. The things or the persons who should be kept most prominently in view are a little dimmed or flattened by the excessive projection of surrounding subjects."

Many scenes, such as the wedding, the visit and ball at the château, and the agricultural show, he declared to be "pictures which, if they were painted with the brush as they are written, would be worthy of hanging in a gallery beside the best genre paintings." He considered that Flaubert had been too cruel to Emma, that the reader felt more indulgent toward her than did the author, and he thought that some of the more scabrous details should not have been included. Flaubert remained sharp and ironic even in these passages, he admitted, but even so it would have been better not to have written them at all, for one had to consider "the French reader, who is born malicious and injects his malice into anything within his reach." Then followed the chief reproach:

"There is no goodness in the book. Not a character represents it. In these provincial existences, which abound in bickerings, minor persecutions, mean ambitions, and pinpricks of all kinds, there are also to be found good and beautiful souls which have remained in a state of innocence, even more perfectly preserved and concentrated than elsewhere; modesty, resignation, devotion extending over long years—which of us has not seen examples of these in the provinces? I once knew, in the depths of a province in Central France, a woman still young, superior in intelligence, ardent of heart, and bored. Married but not a mother, having no child of her own to educate and love, what did she do to occupy the overflow of her mind and soul? She adopted the children about her. She made herself a benefactress, a bringer of civilization to the somewhat wild country in which fate had placed her. She taught children to read, instructed them in moral culture. Their villages were often far distant; at times she went a league and a half on foot; her pupil walked as far; and, meeting, they had their lesson beside a path, beneath a tree, on a heath. There are such souls as that in the provinces, in the country: why not indicate them, as well?

"Such are my objections to a book whose merits I none the less appraise very highly: observation, style (save a few blemishes), design, and composition. Son and brother of eminent doctors, M. Gustave Flaubert holds the pen as others hold the scalpel. Anatomists and physiologists, I find you on every page!"

This article had considerable effect. In the first place, Sainte-Beuve was known to be a man of such pure taste, personal respectability, and bourgeois habits (Gautier would not carry an umbrella because Sainte-Beuve did so), that the article was almost a certificate of moral character for *Madame Bovary* among the large mass of bourgeois readers—far more so than the acquittal in the court. And on the other hand, his praise caused a host of lesser critics, who were accustomed to await his verdict on a book and then appear with opposite opinions, to burst into violent attacks; and many a subsequent review, betraying itself in sarcastic references to Sainte-Beuve's pronouncements, declared that the character of Emma Bovary had been copied from that of Marguerite Gauthier in *La Dame aux Camélias,* or that the minor characters were manikins, or that Flaubert's language was affected or his style seldom distinguished. Thus the book was attacked by critics as a means of attacking Sainte-Beuve, as it had already been attacked by the government as a means of attacking the *Revue de Paris.* Sainte-Beuve was quite accustomed to having his opinions attacked— when they were not adopted—by lesser critics, and he wrote to a lady whom he knew: "When a talented book appears in France everyone begins by wanting to beat the author over the head. I do not share that impulse: where talent is, I bow, though always criticizing and making my reservations." And his private advice to the lady concerning *Madame Bovary* was: "Nevertheless, I do not advise you to read the book; it is too crude for most women, and would offend you. As I said, the fault of the author lies in being hard and a trifle cruel. That

does not keep him from being a great and truthful ob-
server—on the contrary; and he is a very great landscapist
besides. But once again: do not read it. You have preserved
too fine a soul."

There was a polite interchange of letters between
Flaubert and Sainte-Beuve following the appearance of
the review. The article was insufficiently penetrating
to arouse Flaubert to very enthusiastic thanks and, besides, he always remembered the critic's cruel advice to
Louis Bouilhet. But there was satisfaction of a sort to be
gained from the realization that the leading critic of the
day found him a good and serious writer, and the article—
in addition to selling more copies for Lévy—performed
the service of ending the inconvenient mutterings of the
Rouen bourgeois, who had followed the career of *Madame
Bovary* with intense interest and had lately been inclined
to apologize to non-Rouennais for the moral character of
the late Dr. Flaubert's second son. In many a bourgeois
home in Normandy, as in the other provinces of France,
the weekly article by Sainte-Beuve was the only dose of
literature, and it was comforting to have a native son
receive the official stamp of approval. And the appreciation of Sainte-Beuve, shallow though it was, made Flaubert
more contemptuous than ever of the general run of
reviews. He was amused to read that *Madame Bovary*
marked the transition of the French novel from the "bourgeois novel" to the "democratic novel," and he learned
with resignation that he had no concern for style at all,
that the impersonality of the book was the result of a lack
of personality in himself, that he was a bored country
gentleman who wrote casually, merely to occupy his
leisure time. The favourable reviews, which professed
to be astonished by the popular success of so good a
book, he found no more satisfactory. "I haven't yet
found a single one which scratches me in the sensitive
spot—that is, which praises me for the things I think
praiseworthy and blames me for those I know to be
faulty." And he was exultant that of all the reviewers who
had criticized his style and even accused him of writing
ungrammatically, not a single one had noticed a grave
grammatical fault—"a monstrosity"—in the letter of

thanks to Sénard, which had been written in haste as the book was going to press and placed in a prominent position following the title page.

One observation, however, repeated *ad nauseam* in the reviews, did annoy him. "As to Balzac, my ears are decidedly tingling," he wrote to a friend; he was irritated by the constant mention of his debt and resemblance to the great realist, and he resolved that his next work would be a "wild bellow" that would make any such comparison quite impossible.

The subject was chosen even before the publication of *Madame Bovary.* He had thought that the next book would be the revised *Saint Antoine,* or the tale about Saint Julian the Hospitaller; but the latter would be too short to publish by itself, and *Saint Antoine,* even in its new revised form, he reluctantly admitted, was not yet good enough. The extracts published in *L'Artiste* were satisfactory in themselves, and had been favourably received (though some notices described them as "imitations of Gautier"), but he recognized that the plan of the book and the character of the saint himself were still far from what they should be. Besides, he dared not publish it for fear of further prosecution. And so, instead, he determined now to write a version of the oriental tale which in one form or another had been vaguely in his head ever since 1845. He would give himself another bellyful of eastern colour and breathe once more the odour of antiquity; but this time he would not lose himself in eloquence; he would construct the book with care, with the same meticulous attention to detail which he had used in the thankless Norman scenes of *Madame Bovary.* *Anubis* having failed repeatedly to be born, he decided to construct his novel around the daughter of a Carthaginian general (physically she would probably resemble Kuchiouk Hanem) and to resurrect the Carthaginian world with all possible accuracy and all possible colour. It would be a book for those who, like himself, were "drunk with antiquity"; it would serve to banish the memory of the background and the scenes of *Madame Bovary;* it would be a book after his own heart, filled with exoticism, gore, and violence. Even Louis admitted that he now deserved to return to scenes which he adored: he had undoubtedly learned the lessons taught by the writing of *Bovary*. Louis was well satisfied with the fruits of his lecture after the reading of the first *Saint Antoine*.

Before leaving Paris for Croisset, therefore, Flaubert spent his days in the libraries making notes about Carthage, already seeking in antiquity relief from the troubles which had come his way since publication in the *Revue de Paris*. He rose every morning at eight and spent his evenings in study at home. "I am in the midst of devouring Aristotle's *Politics*, Procopius, and a Latin poem in six cantos on the Numidian war, by Corippus, which is boring me to death," he wrote to a friend. Between March and July he read about a hundred volumes on Carthage.

The reviews, however, were not the only comment on *Madame Bovary* which Flaubert received. There were dozens of letters, beginning with a hasty note from Bouilhet written as soon as he had read his copy of the printed book: "Impossible not to have a success with this!" There was a grandiose letter from Hugo, from whom Flaubert had not heard since the rupture with Louise; there was a letter from a friend in Grenoble, saying that all the Grenoble ladies were "Bovaryzing" and taking great pleasure in recognizing themselves in the book; there was the letter from Champfleury; and from Louise Colet there was a poem in a fashion magazine, entitled "*Amor nel Cor*" and declaring that *Madame Bovary* gave the impression of having been written by a travelling salesman.

Louise was considerably affected by the reading of *Bovary*. It was borne in upon her that she had supplied material not only for Emma Bovary's romantic girlhood dreams but for other aspects of the portrait as well. The cab in which Emma Bovary surrenders to her lover was for Louise less the curtained cab in which Flaubert had recently avoided her in Paris, than the cab which had borne them through the Bois de Boulogne on the July night in 1846, and when she discovered that Flaubert had made literary use of the bejewelled and inscribed cigar-holder she had given him, she was overwhelmed. "Imagine my indignation, you who have a righteous soul," she wrote to a friend, "when in reading *Madame Bovary* I came upon this passage: 'Besides the riding-whip with its silver-gilt handle, Rodolphe had received a seal bearing the motto *Amor nel Cor!*' I did my best to keep from laughing, and the next morning, when I told the story to Sainte-Beuve while he was shaving, he laid his razor on the edge of the mantelpiece to avoid cutting himself, he was laughing so." Actually, that little story was quite false: Sainte-Beuve had never admitted Louise into his house at the moment of shaving or at any other private moment, and it had been his secretary, Jules Troubat, who had told him the story about *Amor nel Cor* while he was wielding his razor, and who had thereafter told Louise of her critic's laughter. Sainte-Beuve was wary of Louise. One of her reasons for having chosen to live in the Rue de Sévres had been his proximity, but despite her most persistent efforts she had been no more successful in achieving the consecration of an article by him than she had been in her attempts at intimacy. "Allow me to admire you in silence," was his ingenious reply on one occasion when she said she longed to see her name in his columns.

In addition to the letters from friends, there were others. There was a long one from a neurasthenic provincial lady, in Angers, who wrote that she had identified herself with Madame Bovary and wept all day and stayed awake all night after reading the last instalment; she sent Flaubert three novels she herself had written, with many remarks on the sadness of life, and she struck a sympathetic chord: Flaubert replied at once, and although he had certain reservations about the lady's novels they maintained a correspondence for many years. There was a letter from an unknown gentleman, inquiring as to the original of the character of Emma Bovary, and to him Flaubert replied as follows:

"No, Monsieur; no model posed for me. Madame Bovary is a pure invention. All the characters in the book are completely imaginary. Yonville-l'Abbaye itself is a town which does not exist; the Rieulle is a non-existent stream, etc. That has not kept people here in Normandy, however, from choosing to discover that my novel is full of allusions. But if I had made them, my portraits would be less lifelike; for in that case I should have kept my eyes on individuals, whereas my desire was to portray types."

There was a letter from another gentleman, in Reims, who thanked Flaubert for having written the novel because it had avenged him for the infidelities of his wife. All the pharmacists of the Seine-Inférieure recognized themselves in Homais, and some of them discussed the advisability of calling on Flaubert and slapping his face. And several years later Flaubert discovered that in Africa there was a Frenchwoman named Madame Bovaries, who resembled Madame Bovary not only in being the wife of a doctor, but in other particulars as well. Flaubert was often asked who had been his model for Madame Bovary, but he invariably replied that he had invented her. "*Madame Bovary*," he always declared, "*c'est moi!*"

When Flaubert wrote that he had found none of the reviews satisfactory, he included even that by Sainte-Beuve. It was not until the book had been out for several months that he finally received a review which touched him deeply—a review written by a man who did not, so to speak, carry an umbrella.

At Gautier's he had by now frequently met Charles Baudelaire, the young poet about whom Maxime had made one of his infrequent social errors at the legation dinner in Constantinople, and whose articles on Poe Flaubert considered among the few good things published by the *Revue de Paris*. There was considerable sympathy between the two. Flaubert enjoyed the poet's grave, almost macabre, personal charm, and excused his affectations because of the strong and haunting beauty of his verses; each of them talked freely with the other about his work; and Baudelaire, who returned Flaubert's admiration, wrote soon after the publication of *Madame Bovary* that he esteemed it highly and was going to review it in *L'Artiste*.

The review was delayed, however. Baudelaire's *Les Fleurs du Mal* was in the process of being printed, and

the poet was watching over the proofs and the format
with nervous intensity, changing lines, rearranging typog-
raphy. The volume appeared early in July, and Flaubert
swiftly wrote Baudelaire to say that it "pleased and enchanted" him. "You have found the means of rejuvenating
romanticism," he said. "You are like no one else. . . .
You write of the flesh without loving it, in a melancholy,
detached manner which I find sympathetic. You are as
unyielding as marble, and as penetrating as an English
fog." To this Baudelaire made no reply, and the review
of *Bovary* still did not appear; Flaubert wondered about
the silence and the delay, when suddenly, in August, he
learned that Baudelaire was suffering the same fate as
himself: *Les Fleurs du Mal* was being prosecuted for immorality. He quickly wrote, asking for information; Baudelaire, who was in agony—for his character was less
stable than Flaubert's, and the prosecution was not political
this time but criminal, and there were things in *Les
Fleurs du Mal* which were impossible of explanation to
the non-literary—replied, giving him details; Flaubert
wrote again, suggesting certain moves. The prosecutor
and the judge were the same as in Flaubert's trial, but
despite the latter's love for literature and despite Flaubert's
suggestions Baudelaire lost his case. He was fined three
hundred francs, his publishers two hundred, and—far
more wounding even to a penniless poet—he was ordered to withdraw his volume until six of the poems it
contained should be removed. "I am writing you this short
and hasty note merely to express my contrition at not
having replied to your affectionate words of sympathy,"
he wrote to Flaubert, after his sentence. "But if you knew
into what an abyss of business I have been plunged! And
the article on *Madame Bovary* must still be postponed for
some time! What an interruption in life is an adventure as
ridiculous as this!"

Baudelaire's article on *Madame Bovary* finally appeared
in *L'Artiste* on the eighteenth of October.

Following the death of Balzac, it declared, interest in
the novel had disappeared; Flaubert had now revived it;
and Baudelaire proceeded to expound what he thought

must have been the workings of Flaubert's mind when he conceived *Madame Bovary:*

" 'We shall employ a style that is terse, vivid, subtle, and exact on a subject that is banal. We shall imprison the most burning and passionate feelings within the most commonplace intrigue. The most solemn utterances will come from the most imbecile mouths.

" 'What is the very home of imbecility, the most stupid society, most productive of absurdities, most abounding in intolerant fools?

" 'The provinces.

" 'Which of its inhabitants are the most insufferable?

" 'The common people, incessantly engaged in little employments, the very exercise of which distorts their ideas.

" 'What is the tritest possible human situation?

" 'Adultery.'

"To accomplish the *tour de force* in its entirety," Baudelaire continued, "it remained for the author only to divest himself (as much as possible) of his sex, and to become a woman. The result is a marvel; for despite all his zeal as an actor he was unable to keep from infusing his male blood into the veins of his creation, and Madame Bovary, in the most forceful and ambitious sides of her character, and also the most pensive, remained a man."

And in another paragraph he praised Flaubert for being the first to utilize hysteria, "that physiological mystery," as the "base and bedrock of a literary work," and he ended by saying:

"It would be easy for me to show that M. Gustave Flaubert has voluntarily concealed in *Madame Bovary* the lofty lyrical and ironic faculties manifested without reserve in the *Tentation de Saint Antoine,* and that this latter work, the secret chamber of his spirit, remains clearly the more interesting for poets and philosophers."

"I thank you, my dear friend," Flaubert wrote after reading this. "Your article has given me the greatest possible pleasure. You have entered into the secrets of the book as though my brain were yours. It is understood and felt to its deepest depths."

Of all the original critics of *Madame Bovary,* Baudelaire was the only one to understand and expound it with
a profundity and justice which satisfied the author. His
mention of *Saint Antoine* made Flaubert glow with pleasure, and it was considerably more subtle for Baudelaire
to have sensed that Flaubert *was* Madame Bovary, that
in his novel he himself had become a woman, than for
Sainte-Beuve to have perceived merely the anatomical turn
of the book. But then Sainte-Beuve, although he had
written poetry, was the very essence of a critic; whereas
Baudelaire had never been anything except the very essence of a poet—and for Flaubert one of those essences
was far more precious than the other. No one who knows
Louise Colet can read of Emma Bovary without having
Louise before his eyes; but no one who knows Flaubert
can read of her without a vision of the collegian who
longed to be a woman, of the youth who wrote to Louise:
"Whatever anyone may tell you, at bottom my nature is
that of the mountebank," of the man who, in his own
later words, had *"les deux sexes."* Of all the critics, only
Baudelaire saw this Flaubert; it was only he who sensed
the profoundest truth of *"Madame Bovary, c'est moi!"*

Most of the romanticism of which *Madame Bovary* is
so full was placed there very consciously indeed, to be
exploited deliberately and in cold blood as subject matter. But there are a few romantic touches which slipped
in for other reasons, and remained by accident. The
shying of Charles Bovary's horse at the first approach to
the Rouault farm, for example, and the singing entry of
the blind beggar as Emma lies dying—these stand out in
the otherwise realistic sequence of the book as romantic
blemishes, which escaped even the eyes of Bouilhet. But
these blemishes represent merely an excess of the very
elements which made it possible for Flaubert to write the
book at all: the years in the hospital, the bloody dramas
of the billiard-table theatre, the detestation of the bourgeois, the romantic longings poured out during the long
talks with Alfred and in the early letters to Louise, the
desperate boredom, the nervous collapse, the deaths, the
restlessness of his whole generation—all the thousand and
one details of his early life which the oriental journey,

itself made necessary by them, had in turn made fertile. And it was when Flaubert, composed of all these elements, turned himself into a woman, as it was also in his nature to do, and made this woman a romantic bourgeoise, and then examined her with pitiless eyes and described her with scrupulous pen, that there resulted a book which is still as Baudelaire described it: "essentially suggestive, and capable of inspiring a whole volume of commentary."

Afterword

s Flaubert grew older, and published other
books, he came to resent the fame of *Madame Bovary*. "I
should like to find some way of making a lot of money,"
he once said to Max, "so that I could buy up every copy of
Madame Bovary in existence, throw them all into the fire,
and never hear of the book again," and one of his favourite pastimes was to read aloud passages of the novel
to his friends and tear them jeeringly to pieces. He knew
that none of his subsequent books even remotely approached it in popularity, and that he was often spoken of
as a "one-book author," whereas he continued to regard
Bovary as an accident in his life, an uncongenial exercise.
But he was helpless before the fascination which the book
has always exerted on its readers. Its extraordinary illusion of life, achieved by his familiarity with the background and by his painful choice, inclusion, and presentation of detail, has never been equalled in any other novel,
though Flaubert's method quickly became a part of the
baggage of most of the world's novelists. He always suffered at hearing himself called "the head of the realistic
school," for the later realistic novels of Zola and the Goncourts contained too little beauty for his taste. Dramatists
frequently asked to be allowed to turn *Bovary* into a
play, but he always refused, considering the story unsuitable for dramatization. The first English translation was
made in 1886 by Eleanor Marx Aveling, a daughter of
Karl Marx, who later committed suicide in much the
same manner as Emma Bovary.

The phrase *"Madame Bovary, c'est moi!"* meant only
one thing to the inquirers to whom it was addressed. It
meant much more to Flaubert and to the critic in whom
he found such understanding, and as one looks over the
remainder of Flaubert's life one is tempted to make use

of the words to express still something else. For, just as in the glorious visions which had preceded his youthful attacks Flaubert subsisted magnificently for a few moments largely on golden dreams which he had already once had, so after *Madame Bovary* he subsisted chiefly on the ideas which had come to him during the turbulence of his youth. *Madame Bovary* was the first of his books to be published, but it was the last to be conceived. That is not to say that in 1855 Flaubert ceased to mature, or that the later version of the *Education Sentimentale*, for example, may not be a richer book than *Madame Bovary* or the definitive *Tentation de Saint Antoine* a more poetic one. But in 1856 he had already returned to the first *Saint Antoine*; in 1857 he began the oriental tale; in 1858 he composed for *L'Artiste* an article on Celtic archæology drawn from a chapter in the ten-year-old Breton book: and all his life he continued thus to return to his earlier environment and conceptions. "I have great respect for what I was in my youth (although I was thoroughly ridiculous)," he later said, "and if I am worth something now it may be because of that." "We were red romantics," he said again, "perfectly ridiculous, but of an efflorescence! The little value I still have dates from then."

For *Salammbô*, the Carthaginian story, he studied for six or eight months before beginning to write, but even in the rapture of his orgy of antique reading he realized that so archæological a book ran the risk of weakness on the human side. "I would give the demi-ream of notes that I have written during the past five months, and the ninety-eight volumes that I have read, to be really moved by the passion of my hero for just three seconds," he wrote to a friend. After writing the first chapter he felt he could not continue without visiting the site of Carthage, and he went to Tunis for two months. On the way, at Marseille, he revisited the house where in 1840 he had known Madame Foucaud. "Everything is changed!" he wrote to Bouilhet. "The ground floor, which used to be the parlour, is now a shop, and the upstairs is occupied by a barber. I went there twice to be shaved. I spare you all

Chateaubriandesque comments and reflections on the flight of time and the falling of leaves—and of my hair."

Salammbô was four years in the writing. It sold well, brought Flaubert ten thousand francs from Lévy instead of five hundred, and the humorous magazines of the day carried imaginary conversations between the Carthaginian girl and Emma Bovary. But despite Flaubert's best efforts, which included considerable "psycho-medical research on hysteria and insanity," and despite his own passion for the setting and the historical events, there is no indication that his longing to be moved by the passion of his hero for his heroine was ever fulfilled: he himself always admitted that "the pedestal was too big for the statue." The style and the archæology of the book were praised by most of the critics—Flaubert completely vanquished one professional archæologist who attacked his accuracy—but the public, after buying it in quantities, found it boring and excessively bloody, as the Academy had found his sacrifice scene in Louise's poem. So antique and obscure were many of its words that Sainte-Beuve declared he kept wishing he had a dictionary beside him as he read, and the same critic's comment on Chateaubriand's *Moïse*— "*O ennui, noble ennui!*"—has been applied to *Salammbô* as well, particularly since Flaubert was accustomed to say with pride: "*Salammbô, c'est du Chateaubriand!*" Flaubert was wounded by Sainte-Beuve's use of the word *sadique* to describe the flavour of the book. "*Salammbô, c'est un opéra!*" Sainte-Beuve also declared, and indeed the opera whose libretto was adapted from the book is still sung in Paris.

The next book was a different matter. *L'Education Sentimentale* which Flaubert published in 1869 bears the same title and contains the same themes as the *Education* with which he had read his father to sleep in 1845; but in the later version the friends whose diverging ways are described are not a shadowy romantic and an equally shadowy false romantic, but three clearly characterized young men who bear more than one resemblance to the young Flaubert, the young Bouilhet, and the young Du Camp. And the lady with whom the hero of the first

Education eloped to New York is replaced in the second by the heroine of *Mémoires d'un Fou*, the young mother at Trouville, with whom Flaubert continued always to correspond and who was a grandmother by the time the new *Education* appeared. Always cherished along with the rest of his early memories, his youthful passion for her assumed immense importance during the writing of the novel. The scene of the *Education Sentimentale* is chiefly Paris, and its period 1848; as Flaubert wrote he cursed himself for having followed the revolution with so little interest, and had to spend much time reading about the street-fighting in the newspapers of the period and consulting other persons who had watched the revolution more closely. The cast of characters and the scenes are more varied than in Flaubert's other books with modern settings; it is a *tour de force* as a picture of the late romantic generation —the generation coming to manhood between 1840 and 1848; and in it Flaubert's scrupulous art and his mastery of composition and narrative count for most. But the public found it cold, and was bewildered by the Flaubertian combination of detachment and lyricism, which is more apparent in the *Education Sentimentale* than anywhere else in Flaubert's writings except his letters. The book has never been popular or even well known; Flaubert always resented the lack of understanding with which it was received, and all his life was grateful to anyone who appreciated it.

Both *Salammbô* and the *Education Sentimentale* were written in constant consultation with Louis Bouilhet, whose literary verdicts were always law. Soon after the publication of *Madame Bovary* Bouilhet left Paris: he detested the city, and he felt that following his success with *Madame de Montarcy* he could write his plays elsewhere. Flaubert begged him not to return to the stifling atmosphere of Rouen, and he settled with his peasant companion in Mantes, a town through which in later years Flaubert "could not pass in the train without suppressing a sob." He lived there for ten years, continuing to have a *succès d'estime* with his poetry and having two or three more plays produced at the Odéon; Flaubert occasionally came down from Croisset for the day. But even with his theatrical earnings Bouilhet was always poor, and in 1867 he was glad to accept the post of chief librarian offered him by the city of Rouen. Almost immediately, however, his health failed, and a few weeks after helping Flaubert with the final corrections of the *Education* he died, leaving his friend in despair. "I have buried a part of myself," Flaubert wrote, and it was true. Especially during Bouilhet's last years his physical resemblance to Flaubert increased to an astonishing degree, and this and the devotion of the two friends gave birth to the story that Louis was an illegitimate son of Dr. Flaubert. That he was not, but the two were united even more surely than by blood. "*Non amici, fratres; non sanguine, corde*," Max justly quoted about them. Much of Flaubert's time during the rest of his life was spent in editing Bouilhet's posthumous poems and plays, trying, with occasional success, to get them published or produced. But the world in general has never shared Flaubert's high opinion of Louis's own compositions and has ignored his anonymous influence on Flaubert's.

Following the death of his friend, Flaubert turned once more, as though for consolation, to the *Tentation de Saint Antoine*, "the book of my entire life," and spent on its final revision more time than he had given to the writing of the whole of the original version. In its definitive form it is less than one-third of its length in 1849, and is "designed to be read swiftly, like a vision." In 1873 he wrote a play, *Le Candidat*, a political satire, but it was so roughly handled by the critics that he indignantly withdrew it on the fourth evening, though seats were selling well; and the next year he began *Bouvard et Pécuchet*, the story of two office clerks who discover the realm of ideas and stumble helplessly about within it. But even Flaubert found it almost unbearable to write an entire novel about the intellectual misconceptions of self-taught bourgeois—the character of Homais had been difficult and depressing enough—and *Bouvard et Pécuchet* was put aside for two years while he wrote *Trois Contes*, three short tales. He finished "*Saint Julien l'Hospitalier*," and wrote "*Hérodias*" and "*Un Cœur Simple*," combining in one volume the stained glass and the stone carvings of

the Rouen cathedral, and memories of an old family servant and of Kuchiouk Hanem—samples of all his literary
materials. The welcome given this jewel-like book gave
him the courage to resume *Bouvard et Pécuchet*, but he
did not live to complete it. He had always hoped to write
an account of the battle of Thermopylæ, and had planned
a novel on the modern Orient which would show the
mixture of the eastern and European worlds, and a novel
on French political life to be called *Monsieur le Préfet*.
But, like *Anubis*, none of these was even begun.

"I don't know how to dance, or waltz, or play a single
game of cards, or even make conversation in a salon,"
Flaubert wrote in one of his letters to the provincial lady
who had written him about *Madame Bovary*, but though
the rest of his life was almost empty of events, it was not
without social activities resulting from his recognition.
When he was in Paris he was in constant attendance at
the literary salon of Princess Mathilde Bonaparte in the
Rue de Berri, and in the summer he was often the guest
of the princess in her château at Saint-Gratien: it was she
who in 1866, when Flaubert was forty-five, finally obtained for him the decoration of the Legion of Honour
which Maxime had won almost twenty years before. As
her protégé he even attended imperial balls and recep-
tions at the Tuileries, always enjoying the splendour of
the scenes. He was never without a *pied-à-terre* in Paris,
where he usually spent the winter; Sunday afternoons he
was at home to his friends, and he moved about considerably in literary society, seeing particularly Sainte-
Beuve, Gautier, Turgeniev, the Goncourts, Zola, Taine,
Renan, Daudet, Maupassant, and George Sand. Madame
Sand, less romantic and less socialistic than in her youth,
became his dearest friend in the second half of his life,
and Maupassant, a nephew of Alfred Le Poittevin, was
his literary pupil and in some ways almost a reincarnated
Alfred. Never again did he have so prolonged a relationship with a woman as his relationship with Louise Colet,
although for a time Madame Flaubert encouraged his
intimacy with Caroline's second English governess—an
arrangement which suited the old lady's own convenience
by keeping her son at home.

He was, in fact, seldom separated from his mother. He continued to live with her at Croisset most of the year, and when he was in Paris she occupied an apartment under his. Madame Flaubert's health was weakened by the hardships and emotions of the war of 1870–1, when the house at Croisset was occupied by Prussian officers, and she died in 1872. Flaubert survived her for eight years, spending lonely and laborious months at Croisset (for Caroline had married and moved away) and dying there in 1880 from an attack of what would seem to have been apoplexy. His health was poor in later years; his youthful visits to prostitutes had not left him unscathed, during the distresses of 1870–1 he suffered, for the first and only time, a brief recurrence of his early nervous attacks, he was always hypochondriacal, and he habitually overate and took no exercise. Toward the end he lived in comparative poverty, having sacrificed a large part of his capital in a vain attempt to stave off the business collapse of Caroline's husband, a wholesale lumber merchant.

Flaubert's political and social views were as varied and conflicting as in the past, his humour was generally saturnine, and though in his last years he occasionally admitted that the bourgeois (i.e., the entire human race, which had become middle-class) might possess scattered virtues, few have held mankind in such fierce execration. The thought of the society of the future threw him into even greater disgust and gloom than the spectacle of his contemporaries, and the inhabitants of Rouen always remained particularly low in his esteem. "I took a walk in Rouen this afternoon," he wrote to Caroline in 1872, "and met three or four Rouennais. The sight of their vulgarity and of their very hats and overcoats, the things they said and the sound of their voices made me feel like vomiting and weeping all at once. Never since I have been in this world have I felt so suffocated by a disgust for mankind! I kept thinking of Gautier's love of art, and I felt that I was sinking into a swamp of filth—for Gautier died, I am convinced, of a prolonged suffocation caused by the stupidity of the modern age." And the Rouennais were never very proud of Flaubert. "Gustave Flaubert? Nothing but an eccentric," a respectable Rouen business man once replied when asked his opinion. "One day he's living quietly at Croisset, and the next day he packs his trunk and is off to Carthage! We don't like that sort of thing very much, in Rouen." Bourgeois boating parties on the Seine were frequently regaled by the sight of the large figure of Flaubert striding meditatively up and down on his terrace, clad in a dressing gown. He never thought of himself as an eccentric, and indeed, as he had indicated in one of the scathing letters to Max in 1852 and in the letter to Achille before the trial, he realized that in many respects he was himself a bourgeois. "Be regular and ordinary in your life, like a bourgeois," he once gave as a rule for artists, "so that you can be violent and original in your works."

He always declared that the discovery of a human turpitude gave him more pleasure than any possible gift, and perhaps the most intense pleasure of this kind in his later years was caused by the discovery that the prosecuting attorney who had tried to imprison him for the alleged indecencies of *Madame Bovary* was himself the author of a book of pornographic poems which was circulating secretly in Paris.

Maxime, Louise, and Caroline Hamard followed divergent paths.

Immediately following the appearance of *Madame Bovary*, just as after the presumptuous letters of 1851–2, Flaubert saw nothing of Max, and he shed no tears when the government soon found other means of suppressing the *Revue de Paris*. In subsequent years they were brought briefly together by events which affected them both—the deaths of friends and the miseries of war—but the deep intimacy was never resumed. Each always sent the other his books, and the change in the relationship did not prevent Max from pointing out two hundred and fifty-one phrases in *L'Education Sentimentale* which he thought Flaubert might have written better. Max continued to turn out journalistic volumes—on his travels, on the Commune, on the city of Paris, its water systems, transportation systems, etc.—and in 1880 he became—inevitably—a member of the French Academy. "A limitless reverie" was the mood into which Flaubert declared he was plunged on the receipt of this news. Immediately after Flaubert's death Max published his *Souvenirs Littéraires,* the first book to contain information—not all of it dependable—about Flaubert's early and private life.

It might almost be said that Alfred Le Poittevin played a larger part than Max in Flaubert's later life. Not only did Alfred live again in Guy de Maupassant, but Flaubert frequently wrote long letters of reminiscence to Guy's mother, Alfred's sister Laure. "There is not a day, I can almost say not an hour, when I do not think of him. . . . I think that I have never loved anyone (man or woman) as I loved him": that was his constant refrain.

Like Maxime's, Louise Colet's later activities were also largely journalistic, although following her ejection from Croisset she wrote two novels of revenge in which Flaubert, Bouilhet, Musset, and she herself played varying roles. Both her poetical celebrity and her poetical productions rapidly waned after the rupture, and in her latest years she was avoided by everyone. "Ugh! How ugly he is!" she exclaimed aloud when she and Henriette once met Flaubert face to face in the street. In 1869 she was sent by a newspaper to cover the opening of the Suez Canal, and while in Egypt made inquiries concerning the fate of Kuchiouk Hanem. In *Les Pays Lumineux,* her account of her journey, she declared that one hot night on the Nile she dreamed of "a person whom I loved in the blindness of my youth, and who had been buried in my heart for more than twenty years," and she said: "It suddenly occurred to me that he would be interested could he now see one of the seductive dancing girls who served his pleasure—and whom my heart found revolting when I read of her in his travel notes. She is still living—a living mummy." But when *Les Pays Lumineux* appeared, Louise herself was dead, and Flaubert was saddened by the flood of memories which the news unlocked for him. Maxime composed a cruel epitaph for the Muse: "Here lies the woman who compromised Victor Cousin, ridiculed Alfred de Musset, vilified Gustave Flaubert, and attempted to assassinate Alphonse Karr. R.I.P." It was Henriette Colet who later sold for publication the letters which Flaubert had written her mother.

On the death of Madame Flaubert the house at Croisset passed to Caroline, on the condition that Flaubert be allowed to inhabit it during the remainder of his life. Very shortly after his death it was sold, and a factory built on the site. Of the original buildings only the little summerhouse remains—the summerhouse with the wrought-iron balcony where Flaubert used to fish and of which he wrote so nostalgically from Egypt; it has been transformed into a Flaubert museum. Caroline inherited all her uncle's literary property—all his rights, his manuscripts and letters—and she quickly supervised the magazine publication of *Bouvard et Pécuchet,* with many more cuts than the *Revue de Paris* had ever wanted to make in *Madame Bovary.* After the death of her first husband, Monsieur Commanville, she married a Dr. Grout, and the Grout villa at Antibes, called the Villa Tanit after the name of the goddess in *Salammbô,* became a Flaubert shrine, to which scholars did not always gain admittance with ease. Madame Grout gradually superintended the publication of all Flaubert's unpublished youthful works, many of his letters, and some of the letters written him by friends. She destroyed all the letters from Louise because of the "horrors" which they contained; she was a very respectable woman, intelligent, imposing, religious, and cold. After her death in 1931 it was discovered that while she had left the most important of the manuscripts to various French libraries, she had ordered that a large amount of minor Flaubertiana be sold at auction. For several days the Villa Tanit was crowded as the public bid for the books which had been in Flaubert's library, the souvenirs he had brought back from Egypt, his lesser manuscripts, his pens, his inkwell, and even articles of his clothing. One of Flaubert's dressing gowns was knocked down to Sacha Guitry, the actor, for 2,950 francs.

Appendix

The following is a slightly clarified reproduction of the second scenario prepared by Flaubert.

MADAME BOVARY

1. Charles Bovary enters the fifth form during the one o'clock study hour—his country clothes—show him during the four o'clock recess—cuff-protectors, Neufchâtel cheese—supply of salt butter in his desk—wears his old clothes in class —wears the school uniform only for outings—his strange cap—remains at school three years—never has to be punished—punctual, quiet—his father a former army dentist, *chic empire*, retired to the country, a coarse drunkard—his mother a good woman, thin, intriguing, busybody, housewifely, proud of her family—during vacations he resumes all his country ways.

2. Medical student, lodges with a dyer —learns nothing—two or three shop-girls teach him what love is—his nature—gentle, sensitive, with youthful faults, a few café debts—he cannot concentrate on his work, and keeps dreaming of the country, where he lived till he was 15— knows how to groom horses and to make cider—fails one examination—passes the second—establishes himself as *officier de santé* at Tôtes. His mother settles him in his house—then marries him to a consumptive older woman who has 1,500 francs a year and who dies two years later.

Friend of the owner of the café, with whom he chats—once even helps him put wine in bottles.

At the time of the year when dissection classes begin and people eat chestnuts he thought of the smell of apples in the press, of the noise made by the screw, of the cider in bottles.

3. Describe the house at Tôtes—big barrack all on one floor—at 30 he marries Mlle Emma Lestiboudois Rouault—dresses more carefully—her father—downright type of Norman farmer—her mother died from cancer of the breast—Emma's education in the convent of Ernemont with the daughters of wealthy families—piano—drawing—embroidery—etc.—her native elegance, even though often affected and artificial—no real feel-

Following the death of the mother the farm deteriorated and the father, half through his own fault, half through bad luck, ruined himself more and more—he withdrew his daughter from the convent school at 16—she is glad to marry, to be rid of the country and the peasants.

ing for beauty, but dreams, etc.—draws badly, excels at dancing—allows herself to be married without repugnance or pleasure—she marries him in order not to have to marry a peasant; his hands are white, at least—has a certain affection for her husband, who developed physically very late and can pass for a good-looking fellow—even before her sensuality is developed she can no longer live with the husband—Bovary's mother comes from time to time to spend a week with her son.

4. Emma's solitary life—boredom. She keeps looking out her window onto the highway where the carriages and coaches pass on their way to Dieppe—she walks in the fields with her greyhound Djali, who keeps nibbling at the poppies—her husband never talks with her about anything, doesn't develop her; she feels a vague need for these things—behind the house, the curé's garden with cabbages and rose bushes—winter evenings, reading fashion magazines and novels—dreams of life in Paris—Charles often returns late from visits to patients, wet, dinner delayed.

> Silence—the cold autumn—red sunset behind a hill at a curve in the road—sandy earth, the young men who had gone hunting in the morning come back walking their horses.

5. A ball one autumn in a château in a valley between two streams; potted shrubbery on the staircase—she has this momentary vision of another, brilliant life—then returns to Tôtes in her husband's buggy.

6. Envy of luxury and wealth, mixed with love (after seduction) for a young beau she saw at this ball—and as time goes by it seems to her that her passion for him increases, whereas in reality it diminishes. But the thing with which she really fell in love, and which does not disappear, is the setting, the gilded life. She keeps waiting for a passion, an event, something new which does not come—the following year at the same season the ball is not given. Emma begins to abhor the life she leads—she detests the country—has vapours, crying spells; she shuts herself up in her house, and makes her husband leave Tôtes—they decide to establish themselves in Yonville, 7 leagues from Rouen—Charles believes that the air of Tôtes is bad for her, and leaves his practice.

> Little by little and without wishing to she spends more, forces her husband to buy a second horse and to harness them *à l'anglaise,* dreams of having a groom—is in despair over the servant in his blouse who does the heavy work in the morning, and over the maid with the noise of her sabots on the washed tiles of the floor.

II

Yonville-l'Abbaye—good-sized market town in a valley, a small stream—woods in the distance. Hôtel du Lion d'Or, run by "the widow LeFrançois, of the Lion d'Or." This is the starting point of the public carriage to Rouen, the *Hirondelle*, driven by Hivert, messenger who does everyone's errands in Rouen without knowing how to read—his good memory much admired by the local pharmacist. Mme Emma gives *chic anglais* to her garden—little stream at the bottom— beyond the stream a meadow—Mme Bovary's house is on the square—at one end of the square the market—beyond, the church, a new construction with a square, slate-covered steeple—new cemetery with only two or three graves; the old one is outside the town—opposite her house, the house of the pharmacist, which has a garden that is larger, better kept up, and with more flowers than Mme Bovary's—as gardener the pharmacist has a young relative of 14, Justin, who is at the same time his shop-assistant and his pupil. Justin helps Charles with bleedings and is sent for to hold patients' heads during tooth extractions. The pharmacist has a lodger, clerk to the lawyer Guillaumet, M. Léon Dupuis, character similar to Charles but superior to him both physically and mentally, particularly in education. A young man of good family—plays the piano—every day on his way to dinner at the Lion d'Or or to his office he passes Mme Bovary's windows, walking on the narrow cobbled sidewalk bordering the houses on the square—the leaders of the houses end three feet above the ground and splash water on the passers-by and wash the stones of the walk—he passes regularly at the emptiest moment of the day—Mme Bovary is alone at her window; it becomes a habit with her to watch his profile as he passes —first a few visits—then dinner once a week—then short visits every day, for no reason at all—she embroiders him a pair of slippers, a tobacco-pouch in needle-point—they read, talk—they have garden-ing, flowers in common—he brings her plants from Rouen when he goes there,

First show Yonville as a rather pleasant place (Emma enjoys it at the beginning), then as excruciatingly bor-ing when she comes to detest it.

or goes there expressly for them—they are in love without admitting it, finally Léon tells her—one winter evening beside the fire—just a kiss.

Emma is afraid—even the little love she has for her husband lets her see how dangerous it would be to let herself go—she resists—pretends to herself she is doing it for her daughter's sake. Léon plays with the child and loves it very much; she swears she will not yield, and does not do so—now that she is sure of herself, she takes pleasure in watching herself while in love—Léon tires little by little, his passion weakens—it comes to nothing because it has gone on too long without fulfilment—Emma continues to love Léon, but she sees that she is no longer sacrificing anything, that there is no longer anything for her to resist and that she need no longer struggle lest things go too far. Nonetheless, she resents her husband because for his sake she has sacrificed the love of a man who is superior to him—and the only result of her fidelity is hatred of her husband and a general state of passion without an object—adultery is all the stronger within her because she has not committed it—she becomes coquettish, spends hours at her dressing table. Homecomings of Charles at night—his cold feet in bed—Emma's feelings of repulsion, her mania for cleanliness—Charles's happiness in coming to bed, feeling himself beside his sweet little wife—the night-light burning beside the bed—Emma asleep—Charles awake thinking of his happiness—he is satisfied with his situation and with his work—the child in the cradle near them—or Emma, sleepless, pondering the past and the future.

To counteract Emma's apathies, distraction and exercise are prescribed—the distractions that are offered her.

She wastes away physically, suffers even more painfully than at Tôtes—thinks of herself at this period as very experienced, as having had recourse to everything, as very wise in the ways of the world; thinks she has nothing more to learn in life—inactive activity—she busies herself with her hands, but is con-

sumed with reveries—at Tôtes her trouble
was mere idleness.

Rodolphe Boulanger, 34—vigorous—
dark—a jolly fellow in all senses of the
term, man of wit and experience, self-
centred, pleasure-loving—a tanned hunter
in green velvet—a horse- and livestock-
dealer gradually ruining himself in horses
and in trips to Paris; keeps actresses in
Rouen—loves food—calls on Charles one
market-day—his gesture of surprise and
pleasure on seeing Mme Bovary—second
meeting at an agricultural show, followed
by dinner—two or three visits—impresses
Emma by his easy tongue and his wit—
he induces her to ride with him—in the
autumn woods—Emma's face, red from
the wind—her veil caught on the brush—
breathless from the gallop she dismounts
and has to lean against an oak—seduction.

Stupefaction resulting from first adultery—pride in her happiness—sabot-
maker's hut in the woods—for early-
morning rendezvous she runs through
the meadows wet with dew—if in the
evening, she returns home behind the
village and has to pass between the trees
and the river on a narrow and muddy
path at the risk of falling into the water—
snow—fear of being discovered—she
avenges herself in her heart for her life
hitherto—finally feels sexual pleasure—
her psychological desires result in her
having physical feeling—her physical feelings, in turn, increase her psychic feelings: result—"great love." Rodolphe
gradually becomes bored, and gradually
sees less and less of her—Rodolphe's château—large Norman château—beech-
grove—empty rooms—Emma comes there
two or three times—dull despair—she
thinks of suicide—illness—fear of death—
religious ideas; she becomes calmer—she
comes to have more kindly feelings for
Charles.

She is better again,
has never been more
beautiful.

Trip to Paris—by chance they meet
Léon in a theatre—he is now chief clerk
in Rouen.

Return to Yonville—Léon is three years
older—he has acquired a certain boldness
—he desires Mme Bovary, whom he previously lost and who is now in his grasp;
she excites him more than ever—Emma,

Neglects her daugh-
ter—Charles is obliged
to care for her and to
put her to bed when
her mother is not there
—he concentrates all
his expansiveness on
her—he is unhappy—
coughs from time to
time.

experienced as a result of Rodolphe's deceptions, and virtuously reconciled to life with her husband, resists a long time—however, she finally yields—one evening in her room, in the same armchair where they had exchanged their first and only kiss—it is exquisite, emotional, feverish; delight of Emma, who finally finds her dream completely realized—her husband comes in later; her indignation at seeing him sit on the chair Léon had sat on.

Charles's grief at his inability to make his wife happy; she never complains. He does not know what to do.

Trips to Rouen on the pretext of piano lessons or shopping—Hôtel des Empereurs on the river—balcony—small room, scratched mahogany bed with brass ornaments, blue curtains with white flowers—warm, close atmosphere of perspiration and food—blazing fire—with Rodolphe she was dominated, she was his mistress. Now it is rather Léon who is her mistress, she loves him more than he her, she is superior to him spiritually—joy of blazing love—her melancholy on the subject of Léon's future—"You will marry, you will have a wife," etc.—they have their miniatures painted (atrocious)— Emma in bed—the positions she assumes —when he is exhausted she revives him by countless tiny kisses on the eyes—interior of the public carriage, morning departure from Yonville while it is still dark, she gets up at six to dress—departure from Rouen, drunk with love and tears, with the thought of his hair, with champagne—she trembles and perspires in the carriage on the way back as she thinks of it all.

He attributes her headaches to her reading of novels, and forbids it; Emma's dull indignation at having to follow the judgment of her husband's contemptible intelligence —lending library in Rouen.

She dreams of having a small capital of her own, but . . .

He never suspects that Léon is his wife's lover—he is very fond of him.

Her new life makes her sensual—everything gives her sensual pleasure—perfumes—flowers, food, wine—she spends hours at her toilet—she trembles with voluptuousness at the feeling of her hair on her shoulders—she now wears only batiste—her despair at not having satisfied her need for comforts increases her poetic need for luxury—wild urge to spend—hidden extravagances—life of lies—increased psychological need to lie—in her passion with Rodolphe she insisted on sleeping in a separate bed from Charles—now she returns to his bed—she keeps the patients' fees for herself, pays tradesmen with them.

Depraved appetites of Mme Bovary, loves unripe fruit, likes her food undercooked, drinks vinegar, and eats pickles for breakfast.

Soon she forces her love, to get as intense feelings as possible—she digs more deeply into her heart, goads herself, finally she feels toward Léon as Rodolphe felt toward her, she does not love him, she has had her fill of him—she does not love him for himself, but for her own pleasure—she despises him, he is a coward—his fears of compromising himself—her lack of money—her financial ruin draws near—she is flooded with overdue bills—her perplexity—last expedients.

She is humiliated by the extent of her love for Léon, and sees with all her femininity the poverty of his nature—she sees the value of her husband in comparison with him—in her isolation, suffering from the lack of intelligence of all those who surround her, and increasingly devoured by sensuality, she thinks of returning to Rodolphe—the thought of seeing him again is intoxicating.

Desire to see Rodolphe—she goes to his house one day during a thaw—they become lovers again—intoxicating—she tries to return to Charles, whom she now finds more antipathetic than ever (to every unhappiness which comes her way she reacts with rage against her life, against her husband)—impossible to go on, madness, resolution.

Interview with Léon, hoping to feel again the same feelings she had had with him—but things do not come off—then, in sudden access of madness, idea of suicide—her calm returns when she is sure that she will die—suicide—she steals arsenic from the pharmacy. Death agony—precise medical details—"On such and such a day at three o'clock in the morning her vomiting returned," etc. Death.

The wake—rainy afternoon—open diligence that passes under the open window—burial—Charles's mother goes to Rouen to buy what is needed—funeral shopping—relatives come long distances for the occasion—sit silently together—all bored and careful to look sad—many unwilling to sleep at night, though they can be of no use whatever—pale faces in the morning; the pharmacist sits up with Charles and snores continually—funeral procession—Emma's father in black—blue marks

on his face from his new blue handkerchief with which he dries his tears—the
body is carried to the cemetery—description of landscape.

Farewells of Charles and his father-in-
law (who is stoical at the end, red-faced).

Emma's death is hidden from the little
girl—"Your mamma has gone on a trip"
—from time to time the child asks when
she will come back, then forgets her—
Emma's effects religiously preserved; it
is among these pathetic mementoes that
he discovers the proofs of his repeated
cuckoldry—elaborate monument erected
by Charles—a marble stone with a statue
and a fence tipped with brass balls—
Justin weeps constantly—Charles's empty
life with his little girl—takes pride in
dressing her well—plays with her evenings—discovery of appalling debts—
Léon's marriage, Charles attends—sudden death of Charles in his garden, sits
down to die under the arbor where
Emma and Rodolphe . . . —his daughter at charity school.

Selected Bibliography

BOOKS

Albalat, Antoine. *Comment on devient ecrivain.*
———. *Gustave Flaubert et ses amis.*
Bart, Benjamin F. *Flaubert.*
Bertrand, Louis. *Gustave Flaubert.*
———. *La Riviera que j'ai connue.*
Brombert, Victor. *The Novels of Flaubert.*
*Bruneau, Jean. *Les débuts littéraires de Gustave Flaubert.*
   Paris: Armand Colin, 1962. (See also Flaubert,
   Correspondance.)
Canat, René. *Une forme du mal du siècle, le sentiment de la
   solitude morale.*
Colum, Mary. *From These Roots.*
Degoumois, Léon. *Flaubert à l'école de Goethe.*
Descharmes, René (in collaboration with René Dumesnil).
   Autour de Flaubert.
Dumesnil, René. *Flaubert, son hérédité, son milieu, sa
   méthode.*
———. *La publication de "Madame Bovary".*
———. *Gustave Flaubert, l'homme et l'oeuvre.*
*Flaubert, Gustave. *Correspondance. Vol. 1, Janvier 1830 à
   Avril 1851.* Edited and annotated by Jean Bruneau. Paris:
   NRF, Gallimard, 1973. (Volume 2 forthcoming.)
———. *Intimate Notebook, 1840–1841.* Translated and edited
   by Francis Steegmuller. New York: Doubleday, 1967.
———. *Madame Bovary.* Translated by Francis Steegmuller.
   New York: Modern Library, 1957.
———. *November.* Translated by Frank Jellinek. New York:
Serendipity Press, 1967.

*Indicates a recommended recent work.

*Flaubert, Gustave (cont'd.)
———. *Selected Letters.* Translated and edited with an introduction by Francis Steegmuller. Freeport, N.Y.: Books for Libraries Press, 1971.
Frejlich, Hélène. *Les amants de Mantes.*
———. *Flaubert d'après sa correspondance.*
Frère. Etienne. *Louis Bouilhet.*
Gérard-Gailly. *Les véhémences de Louise Colet.*
———. *Flaubert et les fantômes de Trouville.*
———. *L'unique passion de Flaubert.*
Gaultier, Jules de. *Le Bovarysme.*
———. *Le génie de Flaubert.*
Gautier, Judith. *Le collier des jours, I et II.*
Gautier, Théophile. *L'histoire du romantisme.*
———. *Les Jeunes-France.*
———. *Mademoiselle de Maupin* (preface).
Goncourt, Jules et Edmond de. *Journal.*
Hunt, H.J. *Le romantisme et le socialisme en France.*
Jackson, Joseph F. *Louise Colet et ses amis littéraires.*
James, Henry. *Notes on Novelists.*
Lapierre, Charles. *Flaubert intime.*
Leleu, Gabrielle. *Madame Bovary: Ebauches et fragments inédits recueillis d'après les manuscrits.* (See also Pommier, Jean.)
LePoittevin, Alfred. *Une promenade de Bélial.*
*Levin, Harry. *The Gates of Horn.* New York: Oxford University Press, 1963.
Maigron, Louis. *Le romantisme et les moeurs.*
Maynial, Edouard. *Flaubert et son milieu.*
McKenzie, Aimee L. *The George Sand–Gustave Flaubert Letters* (translation).
Mestral Combremont. *La belle Madame Colet.*
Mirecourt, Eugène de. *Louise Colet.*
Pommier, Jean, and Leleu, Gabrielle. *Madame Bovary: Nouvelle version précédée des scénarios inédits. Textes établis sur les manuscrits de Rouen avec une introduction et des notes par Jean Pommier, Professeur au Collège de France, et Gabrielle Leleu, Bibliothécaire à Rouen.*
Praz, Mario. *The Romantic Agony.*
Reik, Theodore. *Flaubert und sein heiliger Antonius.*
Sartre, Jean-Paul. *L'Idiot de la famille: Gustave Flaubert de 1821 à 1857.* 2 vols.
Seillière, Ernest. *Le romantisme des réalistes.*

Shanks, Lewis Piaget. *Flaubert's Youth.*
*Starkie, Enid. *Flaubert: The Making of the Master.* New
    York: Atheneum, 1967.
————. *Flaubert the Master: A Critical and Biographical
    Study (1856–1880).* New York: Atheneum, 1971.
*Steegmuller, Francis. *Flaubert in Egypt: A Sensibility on
    Tour.* Boston: Atlantic–Little, Brown, 1973.
Thibaudet, Albert. *Gustave Flaubert.*
Wassermann, Julie. *Flaubert: ein Selbstporträt nach seinen
    Briefen.*

ARTICLES

Auriant. "Un Pylade littéraire: Maxime DuCamp." *Le
    manuscrit autographe,* nos. 18, 19, and 21 (1928–29).
————. "Histoire de Safia, dite Kutchouk-Hanem, Almée
    d'Esneh." *Les marges,* June 1926.
————. "Madame Bovary, née Colet." *Mercure de France,*
    1 June 1936.
Bonnerot, Jeanne. "Louise Colet et Sainte-Beuve." *Grande
    revue,* January 1934.
Chambon, Félix. "Deux amours d'un philosophe." *Les annales
    romantiques,* 1904.
Chevalley-Sabatier, Lucie. "Gustave Flaubert et sa soeur." *La
    revue hebdomadaire,* 12 December 1936.
Cigada, Sergio. "Genesi e struttura tematica di Emma
    Bovary." In *Pubblicazioni dell' Università Cattolica del
    Sacro Cuore,* n.s., vol. 72. Milan: Società editrice "Vita e
    Pensiero," 1959.
Commanville, Madame. "Souvenirs intimes." Conard Edition
    of Flaubert's correspondence, Vol. I.
Dumesnil, René. "La correspondance entre Victor Hugo et
    Louise Colet." *Les marges,* August and November 1926.
France, Anatole. "Une visite à Flaubert." *Les annales
    politiques et littéraires,* 1906.
H.L. "Petites notes vétilleuses sur *Madame Bovary.*" *Revue
    d'histoire de la France,* 1910.
Leleu, Gabrielle. "Une source inconnue de *Madame Bovary:*
    Le document Pradier." *Revue d'histoire littéraire de la
    France,* July–September 1947.
Lièvre, Pierre. "Pradier." *Revue de Paris,* August and
    September 1932.
————. "Flaubert et Pradier." *Les nouvelles littéraires,* 24 and
    31 December 1932, and 14 and 28 January 1933.

Pommier, Jean. "Critique préalable." *Revue d'histoire littéraire de la France*, July–September 1947.
Steckel, Henri. "La Villa Tanit, à Antibes." *Le monde illustré*, 13 June 1908.

The files of the *Journal de Rouen* abound in articles on Flaubert; among the most interesting are those by Georges Dubosc.

Index